CW00394466

PRAISE FOR THE AUTHOR

"This is a terrific book. With clarity and passion, Goldberg shows readers how the ideas of Wilhelm Reich, one of the most creative members of Freud's early inner circle, can be employed to promote organization improvement. It is a must-read for anyone seeking that outcome."

> —Harvey A. Hornstein, Professor Emeritus, Department of Social and Organizational Psychology, Columbia University, and author of *The Haves and the Have Nots*

"I fancy myself an able and informed consultant, operating from a base of long-considered principles and models. But Goldberg's work causes me to pause in my celebration of what I think I know. At the same time, he helps me see what I hold dear in a new light, deepening some of my own ideas and also offering me a finer appreciation of something I'd dealt with too casually. More largely, Goldberg's approach offers the promise of addressing the very heart of troubles and renewal in organizational life."

> —Geoff Bellman, author of *The Consultant's Calling* and *Extraordinary Groups*

"Anyone who has ever encountered organizations where employees appear passive, angry or stymied, must read Martin Goldberg's study of the energetic organization. Who does not want to be part of an exciting work group where, like the jazz ensemble playing at its best, spontaneity is valued, coordination is flawless and excitement drives performance? Connecting his erudite study of the psychiatrist and research scientist Wilhelm Reich's corpus of work to his decades of experience as a consultant, Goldberg shows how we can attend to the driving needs of the stuck organization and help it become what he terms the 'work democratic organization.' The master key, as Goldberg shows, is human energy at work in all its manifestations. Read this book!"

> —Larry Hirschhorn, Principal, The Center for Applied Research, Co-founder of the International Society for the Psychoanalytic Study of Organizations, and author of *The Workplace Within*

"*Out of The Workplace Trap* dares to examine the most intangible, but potent, dimension of any organization: its human energy flows. Energy for commerce is a critical concern today. But the human energy and emotional dynamics that propel organizations are quite often ignored, misunderstood, and suppressed. It is common to focus on the more machine-like aspects of organizations – the structures, strategy, processes, systems, and controls – often seeing money as the principal fuel and the investors providing it as the key stakeholders. The result: both organization and human energy blocks, creating systemic stasis and pathology. Goldberg, standing on the shoulders of Wilhelm Reich, and drawing on his own rich knowledge of and experience with organizations, helps us move past this in a bold, innovative theory of organization and consulting practice. He examines, with detailed case studies, the energetic origins and paths that lead to both healthy and productive workplaces and to neurotic, chronically 'armored' organizations. Goldberg makes clear that the ability to recognize energy and its flows and blockages, and to work with it, is the most important capability of any consultant or leader."

— Patricia McLagan, CEO, McLagan International, Inc., author
of *The Shadow Side of Power* and co-author of *The Age of Participation*

"It's rare one finds a fresh perspective on Organization Development (OD). Martin Goldberg provides just that. Goldberg's knowledge of and application of Reich's theory of energy is fascinating, as is his biography of Reich's life. In the process Goldberg makes practical application of Kurt Lewin's field theory and describes an approach that builds on Lewin in many ways. His critique of contemporary OD is also much needed. While Goldberg and I diverge at times on theory and practice, we are in agreement that effective OD changes and frees the energy flow in a system, both emotional and otherwise, leading to higher performance and morale. Goldberg illuminates that process in a new way. His writing is an important addition to organizational theory and practice."

— Gilmore Crosby, Social Scientist, author of *Planned Change* and
Diversity Without Dogma

"Provocative and engaging, this book enriches OD's depth psychology tradition by bringing forward a new lens for understanding systems—as patterns of emotional energy. Detailed illustrations of emotional dynamics and Goldberg's reflective deliberations on when and how to act—or, more importantly, not to—to intervene in them, are gems for any practitioner."

> —Karen Locke, Pat and Margaret Walsh Professor in Leadership and Ethics, Mason School of Business, College of William & Mary, author of *Grounded Theory in Management Research*

"In my 45-year career as a practitioner in the field of OD I have never met an individual more knowledgeable than Martin Goldberg about the deep conceptual foundations of the craft of intervention. Add to this his many years of consulting and managing other consultants, in many different environments and circumstances, and you have the perfect mentor/teacher. He has answered the 'what next?' question hundreds of times. He is a mature and practical person who deals with reality and does not retreat from challenging situations. Finally, Goldberg really cares about the craft and the people he works with. His work is beyond making a living for him. It is a vocation with deep meaning. He will both challenge you and support you—he's for real."

> —Tony Petrella (1935-2018), Co-founder and Managing Partner, Block Petrella Weisbord

Out of
THE
WORKPLACE
TRAP

A THEORY AND THERAPY OF ORGANIZATIONS BASED ON THE WORK OF WILHELM REICH

MARTIN GOLDBERG

nonlectures press

Out of The Workplace Trap:
A Theory and Therapy of Organizations Based on the Work of Wilhelm Reich

© 2023, Martin Goldberg. All rights reserved.
Published by nonlectures press, Easton, Maryland

ISBN 979-8-9874614-0-2 (hardcover)
ISBN 979-8-9874614-1-9 (paperback)
ISBN 979-8-9874614-2-6 (eBook)
Library of Congress Control Number: 2022924145

Author contact information: mdgdistantdrummer@gmail.com
Cover artwork by Stephanie Seymour: Instagram at stephanieseymourart

Without limiting the rights under copyright reserved above, no part of this publication may be reproduced, stored in or introduced into a retrieval system, or transmitted in any form or by any means (electronic, mechanical, photocopying, recording or otherwise whether now or hereafter known), without the prior written permission of both the copyright owner and the above publisher of this book, except by a reviewer who wishes to quote brief passages in connection with a review written for insertion in a magazine, newspaper, broadcast, website, blog or other outlet in conformity with United States and International Fair Use or comparable guidelines to such copyright exceptions.

This book is intended to provide accurate information with regard to its subject matter and reflects the opinion and perspective of the author. However, in times of rapid change, ensuring all information provided is entirely accurate and up-to-date at all times is not always possible. Therefore, the author and publisher accept no responsibility for inaccuracies or omissions and specifically disclaim any liability, loss or risk, personal, professional or otherwise, which may be incurred as a consequence, directly or indirectly, of the use and/or application of any of the contents of this book.

Publication managed by AuthorImprints.com

To the legacy of Wilhelm Reich

The basic problem of a genuine democracy, a work democracy, is more than just a problem of economy of labor. More than anything else it is a matter of changing the nature of work so that it ceases to be an onerous duty and becomes a gratifying fulfillment of a need... to harmonize the conditions and forms of work with the need to work and the pleasure of work, in short to eliminate the antithesis between pleasure and work. Here a vast new field is opened for human thought.... If man could again have a direct relationship to the product of his work, he would also be happy to bear the responsibility for his work, a responsibility that today he does not have or refuses to have.

— WILHELM REICH, *The Mass Psychology of Fascism*

CONTENTS

This book is the first to treat the classical field of Organization Development (OD), its theory and practice, in light of the far-reaching work of psychiatrist, social thinker and natural scientist, Wilhelm Reich (1897–1957).

Reich was among Freud's most brilliant students, who in addition to his clinical breakthroughs, went on to make stunning, experimental observations in biology and physics with revolutionary implications. While only in his twenties, he was widely considered the best clinical therapist of his generation because he was actually effecting cures for people in misery and advancing the theory of treatment. The mass scale of the neuroses he saw, and as it fueled the rise of fascism in his time, led him to explore neuroses' cultural dynamics in terms radically different than those of his teacher Freud, not much to his mentor's liking. Freud in the end saw repression as the price needed to maintain civilization, Reich just the opposite: Human beings, first and foremost, need free movement, thus social conditions and institutions ultimately need to change to satisfy their inherent longing. Nonetheless, Reich persisted. While Freud and his other followers moved increasingly into meta-psychological speculation, Reich grew increasingly curious about the tangible nature of the energy he saw driving human life. This led him to peer into its mysteries ever more closely, using state-of-the-art laboratory technique to see what he could find. His astonishing findings and their theoretical consequences stirred a furor, and Reich became one of the most contro-versial figures of his time—until today, he has largely been forgotten.

For foundational background and context in a special section before the first chapter, I will delve into the development of Reich's body of work and the controversies surrounding it. But for the moment, if one steps away from the sound and the fury, and just tries to see Reich's work on its merits, as there are signs afoot happening, a dif-ferent picture starts to emerge. It is a picture I believe with profound implications for our age and for the future—including the prospect of greater human fulfillment at work and in the workplace. This is the focus of this book.

THE PROBLEM OF HUMAN UNHAPPINESS AT WORK

Human unhappiness is so widespread at work today, and organiza-tions so broken in their functioning, that it is almost taken for grant-ed that life in the workplace is toxic. This reality is not exceptional but *average*, a common experience for people at all levels in orga-nizations: executives, mid-managers, and workers on the front line, young and old, across all types of enterprise, large and small, pub-lic and private, commercial and not-for-profit, traditional and often even new hybrid forms. This is so too, to a greater or lesser extent in many cultures across the globe. Yet people yearn for something more, based on moments when they have in fact experienced deep accomplishment and gratification at work, alone and together with co-workers, colleagues and customers. So, they know something more is possible, they sense it. We all do. But what? And how to get there?

When one considers Reich's clinical success with the human organ-ism emotionally in pain, coupled with his bold observations about the common energy dynamics of natural systems of any kind and scale, that alone suggests looking at the life of organizations in terms he has to offer. Given the widespread unhappiness people experience at work and in the workplace—misery, in fact for many—the stakes could not be higher. I believe applying Reich's work here offers a

heretofore unknown *clarity to help understand and practically allevi-*
ate this deep human unhappiness at work and the extensive way our
organizations are broken. *By and large, people have become ensnared*
in the ways of the workplace trap.

Reich's work first arose in the still young field of psychodynamic psychiatry in the 1920s and '30s, and later in the wider social and natural sciences in the '30s he worked in until the end of his life. The field
of OD emerged as a separate stream of work in the 1960s. Its overriding aim was to help restore the health of organizations, humanly and
in their capacity for productivity and innovation. OD, interestingly,
had its roots in earlier thinkers who were contemporaries of Reich's,
notably the pioneering social psychologist Kurt Lewin, another brilliant European refugee, who, like Reich, came to America in the
1930s to escape the plight of the Nazis. As it took shape, OD developed a small but growing body of practitioners to apply multifacet-
ed behavioral science to the issues of group and large-scale human
systems change. Although less disciplined, OD's development as a
profession with its growing number of specialists was reminiscent of
the rise of clinical psychotherapy as a professional field of study and
practice some forty years earlier.

OD had a "golden age" from the late '60s to the early '90s, when its
emphasis on the human side of enterprise began to be eclipsed by an
ever-increasing focus on performance, technology and keeping up
with the speed of change. Throughout OD's history, some important
principles and learnings arose to help organizations facilitate change
and become more self-directing. There were notable successes here
and there, but results from intervention efforts were uneven and in-
consistent. This is still true today.[1]

THE CONTINUING NEED FOR SOMETHING MORE IN OD

For the field of OD as a whole, a gap remains between theory and
practice, and the theory, such as it is, does not particularly go much
beyond "mid-range" models. Techniques are often splintered and
toolkit-like in application. And there still is very little *theory of prac-*

tice based on a deeper understanding of what an organization is at its roots. In the years since the '90s, although not gone, OD began to wane and be replaced with "change management," "human capital management" and the like. Technique began to "fractionate" even further, as a preeminent scholar-practitioner predicted.[2]

OD (and OD-like) specialists, whether as internal or external consultants, still tend to favor intervention from one side or another of an organization: *either* the behavioral (i.e., socially normative, attitudinal and educational) angle, *or* its structural side (formal strategy, policy, goals, design, roles, operating processes and systems). There are exceptions, such as socio-technical methodologies that have sought to combine each angle of vision, and they have done so with some eminent success.

Yet as a rule, there still is not a good understanding of the *whole* of an organization system's dynamics; a sharp understanding of why a practitioner should be fluent in a full spectrum of techniques; nor clarity about *the conditions under which specific techniques can knowledgably be used and joined for systemic effect.* As we will discuss, a handful of thinkers influenced by psychodynamic models have made interesting inroads, particularly in sharpening understanding of resistance at a social level. But their approaches tend to have a remote, heady quality about them and application remains problematic. Moreover, such approaches here often beg the question in practical terms—*resistance to what exactly and how at a whole systems level to unpack it?* Again, Lewin contributed mightily in understanding how driving and restraining forces operated in the "life space" of a social system, its "field." But even Lewin has tended to be forgotten insofar as his fundamental insights were not harnessed into a reliable framework to support large-scale change. That remains missing. Chapter 2 traces some of the history of this management thought, its leading figures, and state of the field today more fully, including its most recent trends.

When I first began over thirty years ago to connect Reich's learnings to OD, these were the gaps I found his work filled, where I found his work so apt and clarifying. As I studied and practiced, the natural affinity of his work with that of OD started to come into view. It changed how I saw organizations and what I have done with them ever since.

Put in its simplest terms: While the body of Reich's work is far-ranging in breadth and depth, throughout it, he relentlessly focused on the common functions of a system's free energy movement, blockage and on therapeutic interventions that unbound the energy to move freely again.

Applying these learnings to OD positions us to *understand organizations as natural, unitary energy systems operating in an energy field.* This is a new way of understanding organizations in particular and social systems in general—their governing dynamics and how to help better them in the face of great difficulties and need.

The concept of organization character and its intrinsic coupling with the movement of collective human energy at work is central to this book. Like Reich's understanding of how an individual's character structure gates his or her own expression of emotional energy, the basic formulation here is that the formation of an organizational-level character gates the underlying expression of the combined emotional energy in an enterprise—*the characteristic ways its work energy moves, streams together, concentrates, splits or otherwise blocks and finds expression in healthy or dysfunctional outlets.* Like its individual counterpart, this organizational character is *functionally adaptive* in service of the immediate homeostatic demands of the system's conditions—its inner energetic demands to those of the environment. *When conditions are such that the energy is chronically thwarted, the organization character becomes a predominant functional disorder, permeating how and how effectively the system works, observable in its patterns of strategy, operations, collective thinking, values and struc-*

ture. *It surfaces most palpably in the patterned emotional expressions of the system's members.*

The chronically blocked human organization in *its collective emotional structure—its organization character structure*—comes to function as a workplace trap. This trap will *always* compromise human happiness at work and the working life of the system. The open question is how badly? Sometimes, depending on circumstances, it will even extinguish them. This leads of course to the practical question, what is to be done about it?

Reich understood exactly that the same dynamics operated within individuals when conditions were such that *their own personal emotional structures, their individual character structures*, became traps. This too, he understood to be pervasive. In his unique clinical theory and therapy, Reich, along with his students such as Dr. Elsworth Baker, were devoted to helping individuals resolve the predicament of "man in the trap"—so they no longer had to run in circles, searching in vain for the exit and could lead more fulfilling lives.[3]

Out of The Workplace Trap is squarely in this tradition, but "kicked up" to the level of how an organization system, made up of many people, functions. As the *composite human energy* is persistently constrained, it piles up as excessive tension inside the workplace, and is thus less available for productive fulfillment. This affects those inside the organization and those in its surrounding field: customers, alliances and other stakeholders. The dysfunctional patterns of engagement manifest as an array of symptoms and, not infrequently, crises that leaders and others in the organization struggle with. This is usually what OD and other consultants, when sought, wrestle with piece by piece or with current conceptions of organization culture. More often than not, these are not enough.

This book describes this phenomenon and what can be done about it more fully by those in OD and other consultants called on to help. This functional disorder of the system becomes the primary target of diagnostic and intervention efforts on the part of the OD specialist trained in this method. It remains largely untreated in any other form of consultation because its existence is simply not recognized. This leaves it to the intuition, good contact and practiced experience of consulting specialists to make their way through it. That of course is possible—and there is no substitute for effective human instincts and presence on the part of the consultant. But even gifted consultants have been left alone to approach the task without this knowledge. That leaves them at a disadvantage. This is the void this book addresses.

I believe the theory and approach presented here provides a basis to resolve many of the longstanding conceptual and practical dilemmas in OD that have stymied results and, despite the field's other contributions, held it back from its greater potential: helping organization cultures be more fully productive, gratifying, and self-regulating—OD's long held dream.

Directed primarily at organization scholars, change practitioners, and those who otherwise consult to groups in facilitative roles, I hope others too—in the social sciences, psychology, business, and community health and wellness—will find this book meaningful and useful for their purposes. This book is meant as a discussion of the general principles, practices and ramifications of the approach, *not* as a how-to-manual. Guided training and practice are key.

LAYOUT OF THE BOOK

The book is divided into three parts, Fundamentals, Technical Dimensions, and Implications.

Chapter 1 will help the reader better grasp the centrality of work energy in human life—what it is and how it functions and develops, individually, in groups and in whole organizational systems. The most basic description of what an organization is in these terms, and thus essential *practically* in intervening to help, is laid out in Chapter 1. Chapters 2 and 3 speak to other fundamentals that distinguish the approach: conceptual gaps and practical dilemmas that have haunted OD throughout its history up to the present day, and which the application of Reich's work resolves; and central energic concepts of organizational health and pathology, whose knowledge of I believe greatly enhances effective support and intervention. Throughout the book, from the first pages of Chapter 1, I have used consulting cases of mine and other pertinent examples from business and the wider life of society to illustrate the major principles.

In Part II, Chapters 4 and 5 take a deeper, technical look at causal and structural factors at work in organizational systems, including the ways their top, middle and operating segments become disjointed and at odds with each other, yet systemically block the more natural, integrated streaming, concentration and expression of individual and collective energy. Chapters 6 and 7 present an organization character typology with six character types in all, including specific intervention strategies, major technique examples and consulting cases for each. One of the character types postulated in Chapter 6 is a healthy organizational form. Its discussion specifies criteria that make for the type's holistic movement of energy, movement leading to the system's resilience and capacity for sustained achievement, renewal and human fulfillment. This kind of rendering of organization health is a first, I believe, in the organizational literature. Chapter 7 in particular includes description of the enterprise consulting case in which the general formulation presented in the book originally crystallized; the case shows in full scale what the theory looks like in moment-to-moment practice and what results obtained. While the chapters in Part II are the most technical of the book, I hope even the more general reader will find them of interest.

In Part III, Chapter 8 discusses the ways the approach can help with the special issues and opportunities that present in the network enterprise era, moving closer to what Reich presciently called "work democratic" forms. The last chapter, Chapter 9, addresses the approach's wider implications for communities and society, providing a new way of thinking about social change, institutional reform and the rehumanization of the workplace.

Before turning to the main text, I want to share two other elements of context, because I think they lay the groundwork for better understanding of the material that follows and my own points of departure. The first element, next in this Preface, is how I came to OD, became aware of Reich's work in the first place and the origins and development of the book's main argument.

The second element is set off specially just before Chapter 1 as a Prolegomenon, a fancy word but the right one: It serves as an extended, foundational essay that gives a synopsis of Reich's life's work. I have written this to help the reader more clearly see the straight line from Reich's central findings and breakthroughs in theory to my application of them in the organizational realm. However, those who wish to go directly to the organizational material may prefer to simply start with Chapter 1, read through the rest of the chapters, then treat the Prolegomenon as Epilogue. As a piece, it gives my take on Reich's contributions, especially those germane in their underpinnings to this book's organizational themes. My intent is also to provide footing for those who may have previously heard of Reich's work and its controversy to better factually understand them, including the stirrings of a renewed climate for its reception. I hope this book is one of them.

HOW I CAME TO OD AND REICH AND HOW THIS BOOK CAME TO BE

This work began as a master's thesis in OD in 1988, and actually before that, at work and in what I had learned about Reich through my interests in history and social science when I was an undergraduate years before. Reich's *The Mass Psychology of Fascism* and *Character Analysis,* classics from the 1930s, made a strong impression on me in their originality and depth of understanding. I learned more about Reich's unique approach to therapy soon after college. When time had come to face some difficult feelings never resolved from my youth, I was drawn to seek out a therapist grounded in his teachings. I found a great one in Los Angeles where I lived, a physician trained by Reich, to help me. After two years of hard work, I could really breathe again and felt like I had gotten my life back. I mention this because reflecting on the course of my own therapy became a significant source of learning in the later development of my thinking about helping organizations, a reflection of the old OD wisdom, "self as instrument."

Fast forward to entering Pepperdine's celebrated MSOD program in 1986 as a mid-career professional in my early thirties. I wanted to learn more about OD's central concepts and the art of its practice, having recently begun OD work in an internal consulting role I had fashioned at a banking corporation. At Pepperdine, twenty-three of us from across the US, Canada, India and Venezuela came together as a cohort-based learning community, meeting ten days at a time, once a quarter over eighteen months. After the last cohort session, the program's remaining months were devoted to the completion of a thesis, often an action research project in which we were earlier absorbed and, with faculty approval, had settled on as a topic. We were fortunate that famous names in the field, from the academy and the world of practice, were our principal teachers as guest professors. We lived, worked, ate and off-hours played together, at entirely off-campus, in-residence retreat settings, alternating between Monterey and Palm Desert, California.

The whole approach was collaborative, the learning modes cognitive and experiential all at once. We read and heard about concepts in human dynamics and intervention as they pertain to individual, small group and wider organizational system levels. And while we studied, we lived and learned the process, with the cohort as a learning lab. We could see concepts vividly come to life as the community developed, and we could experiment with intervening over the course of the program to see how we could help improve the way we worked together as learners. The entire program experience was exhilarating, life-changing for some, unforgettable for all.

When it came time to consider a thesis topic, still early in the program, I first saw there might be a narrower application of one of Reich's early contributions to psychoanalytic technique, how resistance and countertransference arising between patient and therapist could be used as a diagnostic window into the very nature of the problem that tied up the patient in the first place. I was struck by this from what I saw in my early work at the bank, and from a passage I read from Warren Bennis pointing to a like-phenomenon in OD and "the fate of the change program."[4] Here were character dynamics at play at the organizational level. But as I continued to contemplate the similarities here and turned over ideas in my mind for a thesis that might have most value, I saw that a project could be pursued through a wider application of Reich's work. I was encouraged to go for it by a few close fellow students and the MSOD program director, Walt Ross, when they engaged with the ideas and heard my enthusiasm for the effort.

I applied to the main college of psychiatrists in Princeton, New Jersey, still actively practicing Reich's therapy, to study the clinical modality and was accepted as a social science type to apply its principles to organizational systems. Thus, side-by-side with the Pepperdine program, I flew across country monthly to attend the college's weekend introductory seminars, and later advanced ones, to learn the material. That thesis became *Work Energy and the Character of Organizations*, with Walt serving as my committee chair and the lead training psychiatrist, Peter Crist, as co-advisor. The effort was an ambitious one, but I had close attention and guidance from each, top people in their respective fields, who also worked in concert to support the development of the project. Lucky was I! The thesis earned me graduation with honors at Pepperdine and was published serially in the journal of the clinical school where I trained.[5]

While all this classroom education was going on, the California statewide business bank I was part of became the principal context I drew keen lessons from, seeing what I could make of what was happening in its dynamics, and how I could best be of supporting help. I was engaged in many projects, activities, and relationships at work, rich in learning, some still featured prominently as cases in this book.

For many of the years since the original development of the ideas presented here, I moved even more fully into the "organizational bush," becoming the managing partner in a change solutions group for a global consulting firm. I took the lead in building a practice of 150 people, focusing on as many as a dozen projects at a time. Many of the firms we consulted were Fortune 100 that ran the gamut across industry sectors; government organizations too, divisional and inter-agency. We worked extensively with high-tech firms, including early applications of human network organizational analysis. So, I was exposed to and learned a lot about organizational systems in change and their resistance to change, what worked to help move them in practical ways and seeing the extent to which they were really willing to work to get there.

We generally met with reasonable success in the limited sense our large consulting firm sought and contracted for, but we rarely got to the issues that held the organizations back more deeply. Thoroughgoing change was far from common, despite the many calls for "organization transformation." I remarked years later to master OD practitioner Tony Petrella, of boutique Block Petrella Weisbord fame, that as I looked back among the scores of client-systems our change solutions practice served, I thought there were maybe only five we made a fundamental difference with; that is, in helping them make qualitative, holistic shifts in their processes, performance, and quality of their products and human relationships. Tony looked at me from across the table where we were lunching and said, "Five? Wow, that's a lot." I realized here was a serious man and "co-conspirator" in OD, as Tony was fond of saying, and he became a close mentor and friend in the final years of his life.

Nonetheless, in the large firm, which I was with for more than a dozen years, I learned much about organizational life, reaching back to learnings from graduate school days and looking at things afresh. Too, the very experience of operating in a global knowledge organization served as a lab where I saw the pertinence of Reich's work—how sick an organization can become, its people literally too, when their natural energies at work, individually and combined, get turned back, frustrated and chronically stuck. I was witness to how the firm's own serious strategic and operating problems, recognized by many, went unaddressed because of overwhelming, charged emotional dynamics, and how that affected its fortune and fate. Indeed, the dynamics ultimately proved fatal to the firm as it filed Chapter 11, its remnants sold in pieces. This experience, as a case in itself, is discussed in this book's chapter on organization health and pathology, and it is touched on again in the later organization character typology as a specific type.

In 2010, I started my own little solo firm, to focus on doing more of the kind of work I loved, and with clients I found hungry for that kind of engagement. I found my way more fully back to my original work on the energy dynamics of organizations, building on it, reflecting on what worked and didn't, what I had gotten right and had missed in my earlier formulation. As a totality, as tough as many experiences of those consulting years were—and the big firm environment was especially tough—I grew from immersing myself in that world, enriching my work in organization theory and the theory of practice I had begun some thirty years before.

This book represents the culmination of those learnings, some features of my original thesis formulation strengthened or softened, added to or abandoned. That is the way forward—what Lewin called "action research" and Reich, more fully, "functional research"—true for the comprehension and resolution of cases, true for the development of ever-clearer theoretical understanding and knowing how to better put it to use.

A style note on the presentation of the book: Some of the more detailed discussion of Reich's ideas as they appeared in their original contexts, beyond the introductory foundational piece and selected passages in the chapters, will be found in the endnotes. My intent was to keep the book's main narrative as much focused on the organizational domain as possible. So, readers who wish to know more may additionally look there and to the section For Further Reading.

Easton, Maryland
2023

ACKNOWLEDGMENTS

I owe much to many in the development of this book.

First, to the late Dr. Walt Ross of Pepperdine University, for his openness, guidance, and support to me in doing a work of this kind when I first began it. He showed a genuine curiosity in the best tradition of the academy, the search to understand without prejudice. I also want to thank the Pepperdine business school, my fellow students in the Nu MSOD cohort, too, who I learned a great deal from.

Peter Crist, MD, President of the American College of Orgonomy (ACO) for many years, has been a remarkable teacher and mentor, colleague and friend from whom I learned so much about Reich's clinical modality and his approach more broadly to natural science. Peter fully engaged himself in the developing ideas during the thesis years and for years after. Thanks also for his facilitation of permission to draw substantially throughout this book from my previous papers in *The Journal of Orgonomy* and from a prior conference talk. To others at the College, its physician leaders, and students I originally trained with, I wish to say thanks as well.

In very recent years, my interactions with James Strick, PhD, of Franklin and Marshall College, and Renata Reich Moise, now President of the Wilhelm Reich Museum and Trust, were of valuable support. A paper I presented at a webinar sponsored by the Museum and Trust early in 2021, and as an article published that year through the Institute for Orgonomic Science, served as the basis for much of

Chapter 1; its *Annals* journal editor, Dr. Grier Sellers, gave me free use of that paper here.

I want to note the great importance of both the ACO and the Trust as institutions in preserving Reich's legacy true to his teachings: the College in its years of training psychiatrists and other clinical specialists to keep the modality alive; the Trust from its earliest years, seeing to the republication of all of Reich's books and correspondence, in concert with Farrar, Straus and Giroux.

Of course, the biggest debt is to Wilhelm Reich. The majesty of his legacy will still not be generally recognized, I think, for many years yet. But it is there on the record for all to see and come to in their own time, today and in future generations. I am humbled to apply to the organizational domain Reich's staggering contributions and add to their social science implications.

Elsworth Baker, MD, was a principal agent in carrying on Reich's legacy immediately after his death, seeing to the founding of the ACO, and the development of a regular curricula for psychiatrists in training. His classic book, *Man in the Trap*, serves as the model for how I present the organization character types in Chapters 6 and 7, and more generally, I have borrowed some of his language for its clarity of exposition. Baker's close friend and colleague, Dr. Albert Duvall, was the very gifted physician and therapist who helped me so personally in my early years. I also want to say thank you to my old friend Ken Levy, who first introduced me to Reich over fifty years ago.

Profound intellectual debt goes to Sigmund Freud, whose work was so basic to Reich's first discoveries. Despite their eventual estrangement and differences, both men suffered the loneliness of being pioneers whose work challenged the world.

From the world of OD and organization theory, the teachings of doctors Kurt Lewin, Eric Trist, Edgar Schein, Karl Weick, Barry Oshry, and Henry Mintzberg have been of the highest order. They offer pivotal contributions for OD scholars and specialists. The way many of their seminal concepts are joined, for theory and practice, can be found throughout this book and are especially noted in Chapter 2. Doctors Manfred Kets de Vries and Larry Hirschhorn have been significant innovators and sources of learning in the way they have brought psychodynamics into thinking about and consulting to organizational systems. My discussions with Larry these last years have been particularly significant to me in thinking more about the path from Freud to Reich in organizational terms.

In OD generally, Marv Weisbord, the late Tony Petrella, and Geoff Bellman have been important to me as mentors and friends; they each encouraged me to capture my observations and thinking into writing, and their candor was invaluable. My thanks also go to Dr. Harvey Hornstein for his willingness to engage the ideas presented here, our conversations, and his deep, firsthand understanding of the history of OD from its earliest days.

I thank, too, so many of my colleagues at work, my clients served, and the students I have had the pleasure to work with and learn from. Two executive clients and mentors, George Eltinge and Don Prell, each now gone, played important roles in my development; they were kindred spirits in the business world. I also want to note two teachers of mine, now deceased, Harold Wheatly and, of Reed College, Dr. John Tomsich for their lasting imprints.

I want to give special thanks to three colleagues and friends whom I hold dear, Stephen Pile, Rachel Mickelson, and Molly Brown Pickett. Alumni of the Pepperdine MSOD program spanning three different cohorts over twenty years, they encouraged my effort to write this book, and they offered insight and thoughtful comments on draft portions of the manuscript. My thanks also to Dr. Peter Erwin, Jim Hagy, Chris Lunney, Alfredo Lee, Karen Duggan, Matt Tabor, and Dr. Megan Hundley for their review of portions of the material. Thanks, too, to Gil Crosby for our earlier conversations on Kurt Lewin. I want to make clear that their support of my effort does not imply their agreement with the concepts and material presented. That goes equally for all the names cited here.

To my grown children, Tahasha Jenkins, Hannah Lucas Goldberg, Dr. Paul Goldberg, and Paul's wife Alexandra, thanks for your love and caring. I am thankful also to Cristi Lucas Goldberg for all the years. My stepmother, Patricia Goldberg, has been of abiding support. My dad, the late Dr. Richard J. Goldberg, was my first intellectual hero. A scientist of the highest rank, both in the development of theory and in applied research, he was a deep soul and force on this earth who touched many.

Finally, thanks to David Wogahn and his creative team at AuthorImprints for helping get this book to press; to Caryn Sobel for her meticulous proofing of the manuscript; to Mamta Jha for her creation of the Index; and to Stephanie Seymour of Perugia, Italy for permission to use her wonderful watercolor on the cover.

WILHELM REICH: CONTRIBUTIONS, CONTROVERSIES AND A COMING REAPPRAISAL?

The body of Reich's work is so far reaching, a basic understanding of it first is in order to see and appreciate its significance for human work, organizations and social systems. And not just as an interesting set of ideas, important as its application is for theory, but to grasp his work for its practical human consequences of helping to relieve peoples' suffering and reclaim fulfillment in their lives. This Prolegomenon sets this stage for the rest of the book. To help the reader, in addition to the background on Reich, it also builds a few initial bridges to the organizational theory and method to come.

B orn in Austria, Hungary, just before the end of the nineteenth century, Reich as noted earlier was an accomplished and hailed clinician. Freud called him the best *kopf* among the second-generation analysts. By the time he was twenty-seven, he was asked to head up the Psychoanalytic Association of Vienna's training seminar in technique. Reich led them by asking the analysts attending to focus on what was *not* working in their therapy with patients, the points where their case management broke down, in order to zero in on, through discussion and discovery, *why* that was happening. Always a head for the conceptual as well as the practical, Reich saw this also as the best way to advance psychoanalytic theory and its method of practice. Participating required analysts to set their egos and competitive ambitions aside, then be vulnerable to share such experiences openly with their peers. But the seminar soon proved popular for the lively discussion and learning it provoked, and as the therapy cases considered in the sessions better moved forward.

In his own work as a therapist, Reich kept looking at what made the difference between patients who got and stayed well and those who didn't. The desire of the patient and the good contact and skill of the therapist all mattered. But whether each of a patient's resistances were thoroughly handled, or the length of the treatment itself, did not seem to be decisive. He found that the most telling factor separating those cured from not was that the former had developed a satisfactory love life, the latter hadn't. *Felt gratification* in the sexual act with a beloved with full surrender, not its frequency, was defining. In fact, *Don Juanism* behavior typically indicated a *lack* of satisfaction, hence its "more and more" quality. The same may be said of habitual expressions of hysteria. Real mutual excitement, charge and complete discharge led to the feeling of tender gratification and relaxation for each of the partners. At the moment of peak excitement, they literally had the feeling of being one, each letting go, yielding one to the other. When that was not happening in a patient's life, the energy remained trapped internally, giving rise to marked buildup of unresolved tension and anxiety, fueling irrational ideas and behavior. The trapped energy was also accompanied by, and in turn refueled, certain latent oedipal identifications originating in early childhood that interfered with full intimacy, letting go, and release. In his clinical and social work, Reich saw that this was the average state of affairs for men and women as they presented and who remained unfulfilled. Neurotic symptoms were manifold in the forms they could take. On the other hand, in those who had come to establish and maintain a satisfying sexual life, he saw the symptoms abate. The symptoms were drained of their energy. What is more, beyond patients' ability to love more fully, their functioning improved as a matter of course across the board, in their ability to think more clearly and imaginatively, and to work in a way that felt truly productive and satisfying. A motto of Reich's reflecting this became an inscription at the beginning of all his later books: "Love, work and knowledge are the wellsprings of our lives. They should also govern it."

For Reich, this was startling confirmation of Freud's earlier postulation of the libido, pointing to how it must not simply be a metaphor but *an actual energy*. Trained in neurology, Freud originally held out hope that this driving source of energy, *this something*, would one day be understood in clear biological terms. Reich, virtually alone, took up this mantle.

I highlight this concentration on the sexual core of Reich's first findings for two reasons. One, it was the beginning of the controversy over his work, as we will come back to. Two, it is basic to his later investigations into the energy functioning of other natural systems and its importance to the present formulation for organization systems. I want to stress that although Reich's work originated in understanding the movement and blocking of sexual energy, this book will be looking at the underlying flow of its social movement as *work energy*. Reich came to see sexual and work energy as two aspects of the same underlying bioenergy, whose own primordial source and functions were directly at the root of any natural system, living or nonliving (such as atmospheric phenomena). We will return here too.

From the standpoint of the individual, even prior to Freud's recognition of the libidinal sources of neurosis, Freud with his colleague Joseph Breuer saw that dammed up emotional energy would attach itself to irrational ideas and present also as other psychological and physical symptoms—the *cathexis* of the emotions. The energy stasis in their terms was thus the *actual neurosis* that fueled and maintained the *psychoneurosis*, which Reich later came to clarify much more fully. It was the contemporary, quantitative factor in determining whether psychoneurotic marks, usually inescapable, were prominent and activated.

The energy source behind "ideas" and behaviors, what people experienced as emotions, now became pivotal. For Reich, this put a new emphasis on the here and now at every life stage, in the way people's deepest longings were either fulfilled or turned back by social strictures and structures—the family constellation in a person's earliest years, transmitting the values of the larger culture, but also as the imperatives of the energy kept playing out with new force in adolescence and adulthood. Past trauma of course directly impinged on this as Breuer and Freud clearly saw. But Reich further saw that it was *the energy functioning per se of the individual that got disturbed*, literally in his or her ability to freely pulsate and live. Therefore, for Reich, the movement and blocking of energy needed to remain central as the focus of treatment.

Conceptually, too, a moment's reflection shows the simple truth that the movement of such energy must be of primary significance. Otherwise, how could there be any human being alive who had not completed an analysis and resolved past psychic injury, still healthy enough to really love? But they exist—and have throughout human history, long before the invention of psychoanalysis. Thus, something deeper, some more natural force subject to being blocked, was at work. The trajectory psychoanalysis began to take, after its early years, focusing more and more on mental processes, conscious or unconscious, did not simply recognize this. Reich was the exception. This took him directly to better understand the natural biology of the drives. But it also led Reich to consider what in the wider world would profoundly affect and so routinely distort it. This led to his critique of the social order—an order especially harsh during the rise of authoritarianism in the world, and particularly fascist Europe.

Undaunted by the controversial dimensions of looking at sexuality frankly and fully—including what specifically made for deep gratification— Reich began his analysis of authoritarian traditions, in society and families, and how they were internalized in people's lives; he saw in this *the anchoring of culture and its typical suppression of gratification.* The implications of this went quite far, putting pressure on people to really look at themselves. Were they living in deeper, more spontaneous ways, including not becoming robotic in their work styles, caught up in mechanized work systems as Chaplin literally depicted in *Modern Times*? Or were they walling up internally against these emotional longings in the name of doing what is expected regardless, preserving the mores and morals of society—even "civilization" itself, as Freud argued was the necessary price to pay? Reich, again as he had seen in his patients, concluded that those who could sufficiently love and work in a way they truly felt gratifying would not build up a storehouse of distorted, reactive impulses in the first place, impulses which in turn would need to be contained, lest their wild fury—the "unleashed" *id* as Freud feared—break through.

Reich carried on. Committed to social reform, in Berlin in the early '30s, Reich began working as a physician opening up sexual counseling clinics for men and women and for adolescents bursting with unfulfilled longing and love. He advocated for relaxing divorce laws, free use of contraceptives, and the abolition of laws against abortion and homosexuality. Reich understood the price of such moralistic prohibitions, once internalized, inhibited natural development and compounded sexual stasis, deepening social and individual distress. All this proved too much for Freud and most of Reich's peers in the burgeoning psychoanalytic movement.

Freud was trying to assure the future of psychoanalysis, doing what he could to establish a kind of island for the movement and fly below the radar in the Nazi era. Then, here comes Reich going full throttle against the grain, including his 1933 *Die Massenpsychologie des Faschismus*, the first effort to integrate psychoanalytic insights with those of Marx. This was seen by some as all over the top. The Nazis in fact were the first to burn Reich's books. Reich was expelled from the International Psychoanalytic Association (IPA), amidst great gossip about him, and contracts on his books through the IPA were canceled. Freud's original discoveries had been truly radical, but he sought to button them up as to not cause further difficulties, whatever he may have thought of Reich's fiery temperament and willingness to go the limit.

Reich's focus so fully on the nature of satisfying sexuality as key to emotional health was at the origins of the controversy that marked him for the rest of his life. In this sense, he carried the mantle that saddled Freud more than twenty years before, when Freud published the first of his works on childhood sexuality. Freud received scorn and ridicule from the public and his professional peers. Now, temperamentally, Freud was rather cool and pessimistic. He did find ways to drive through his views despite their unpopularity.[1] But he increasingly bit down on them to protect what he had built, as the criticism and attacks of a reactionary political order mounted. Over time he began to deemphasize his early findings on sexuality, as he and his followers increasingly emphasized what became known as ego-psychology. Instead of the primacy of the libido, there was now a postulated "death instinct." Reich, forty years Freud's junior and of passionate mind, did not yield. He remained committed to understanding the more tangible basis of human life.

As he saw in his work with patients and through his social activism, Reich came to regard "work energy" and sexual energy as two sides of the same coin: the underlying bioenergy that suffuses the human organism and seeks free, fulfilling expression. The same life energy whose drive manifested in the deepest, intimate way sexually, also manifested in the social domain as a drive for fulfilling work, both productively and humanly. He understood how the dynamics functioned at work, individually and in groups as well. But he did not focus much attention on the functioning of organizations as systems per se. That is what the present volume does.

As discussed in the chapters describing organization-level character types, the blocking of the way work energy more naturally functions, both individually and collectively, has far-reaching consequence. For example, in what I term the "work aggressive" organization character type, it can result in those who thrill in the chase of one deal after another, with ever-more pressure to perform, but who often confess on closer examination how they are stuck in a downward spiral bigger than themselves and how they do not find their work satisfying. Players in such systems may be knocking the customer dead, but many recognize they are not fulfilling the customer's and other stakeholders' most important wants and needs—nor their own or those of their families when they come home from work at night. This characterizes many today with such exaggerated strivings: to sacrifice a rich life in the name of "being rich." Yet there never seems to be quite enough to fill up the hole inside. Is it really in the end a question of money? Or greed or fame? Greed or fame for what? What, at bottom, is the object of the desire?

Reich formulated the critical concept of *character* in his early years while he still considered himself a psychoanalyst. Understanding the function and formation of character had major diagnostic and treatment implications for therapy. His other major theoretical and practical advance just before he left the psychoanalytic fold was his *somatic* understanding of how individual character operated: the patient's whole body was intimately tied up in the suppressive process itself, typically through chronic muscular contraction that blocked freer and more fulfilling energy concentration, movement, and release.

Reich originated the concept of "character"—the individual's typical *configuration* of symptoms (and the suppressive energy functions it played in the person's life), not simply the symptoms themselves. Character literally represented the *characteristic* ways the person would act and react in the world as a way of warding off the expression of painful feelings and the spontaneous movement of energy that he found intolerable. This led Reich to the development of a character typology for individual treatment. As one type, he was the first to term stereotypical macho behavior as part of a "phallic, narcissistic character." The causation of individual character he saw in line with Freud's earlier elucidation of the psychosexual stages of development, and how they were frustrated in the patient's earliest social world at home. On the other hand, if a child could develop freely under favorable conditions, she would naturally grow into a more inherent, self-regulating way of living (assuming later conditions too were favorable to sustain it). Reich termed this individual type a "genital character." This represented a mode of integrated functioning where people were sufficiently able to express and satisfy themselves in life, including the capacity to be freely drawn to, merge with and yield to a beloved in full, mutually desired, gratifying union and release.

A woman and a man each with this kind of character Reich saw had the capacity to regularly build up, concentrate and feel their mutual charge—they *illuminated* in love—as they deeply drew to each other and thrilled in what Reich called "the genital embrace." Neurotic character was not in play to interfere with their natural energetic movement together. This primal energetic movement Reich concluded was basic for the organism to regulate its "energy household." When sexuality was like this, it served a *self-regulatory* function for each of the partners, individually and in their shared life. When it was not, a host of recurrent symptoms appeared in each person's own functioning and in their life together.

In this book, a functionally equivalent understanding of character at an organization system's level is substantially explored. *Organization character is understood to serve a work energetic self-regulating function for the system and those engaged with in its field. This book maintains that the natural self-regulation of the organization's composite pulsing work energy is either supported or constrained by its system's level character—the manner in which its energy is literally "normalized."* Full productive release of the system's energies and felt human fulfillment are either realized or seriously compromised by how its organization character has come to develop and work. When long term compromise of this order is in play, those in the system will often regard the ingrained dysfunction as "normal." Or else they will tend to regard the behavioral and structural symptoms that result as discreet entities that need to be handled as things in themselves. Regardless, many will inwardly feel something more basic is off and sense there is a more natural way of working, individually and collectively, to be attained.

Character in a *sociodynamic* respect is not unique to what is presented here. Edgar Schein, who for years directed MIT's Organization Studies Group, has long recognized a sense in which organization culture functions like character does in the individual realm.[2] But in Schein, the concept of culture is not coupled with an understanding of the actual, underlying collective energy dynamics it binds and expresses. It thus I think doesn't move much beyond being an interesting intellectual model, its value notwithstanding. The same may be said of others who have discussed organization culture to date. There is no basic understanding of the natural energy movement that suffuses and drives the system.

In Reich's psychotherapeutic work with individuals, this line of thinking became the basis of his classic text, *Character Analysis*, as a primary avenue for treatment.[3] He first came to this thinking because as a clinician he saw that symptom removal, the standard focus of treatment before him, wasn't enough. People in therapy weren't getting better in a way that would last and become self-sustaining until *the entire character* began to shift. This happened, he saw clinically, when the defensive functions a character served began to dissolve, through the use of specific character diagnoses and corresponding therapeutic intervention. And it happened as the patient was able to move to greater and greater natural self-regulation through a more truly gratifying love life. The aim of therapy, always, in Reich's method was to support the patient to better tolerate the natural, inherent forces driving to health on their own accord, to help the patient better breathe and move to the rhythm of life without shutting down.

Understanding how to get characterological roadblocks out of the way for this to occur was an indispensable part of therapy. When patients were able to tolerate the natural beat of life they made substantial progress.

This led Reich directly to an appreciation of how the whole body was involved in the process. "Learning" in this sense was hardly simply a cognitive process or a process of the central nervous system or even as it operated with the peripheral system. The emotional energy pulsated and streamed throughout the organism as a whole, radiating up and down the body fluidly from the heart and through the pelvis, mediated by neurophysiological processes, but not "dictated" by them. The "head" was not simply in charge, even as some brain science researchers, fascinated by the mechanisms of the mind, still contend today. I am emphasizing this just now because, as we shall see in the body of this book, this is equivalent to thinking the "head" of an organization is all that really matters in driving change, only really consulting with the top. This leads to the tendency to not see the whole of the organization, especially when it is working at its best: *as a fluid, pulsing unitary system moving in satisfying exchange with others in a dynamic, surrounding energy field.* Again, Lewin's field theory had somewhat anticipated this, but without the larger understanding of the deeper, core energy dynamics at work. And nothing I am aware of quite on a large scale has ever been done with the important force-field dynamics Lewin did describe. Lewin's prefigurement of the more particular energy dynamics that operate at the whole organizational level, as I describe in this book, is treated in Chapter 2.

For Reich, in working with individuals in therapy, excitement and charge were an emotional process, conscious or not, that had their own ways. He saw that it was not that a person's mind and body "interacted," but instead were a psychophysical unity in process, a process whereby the person's character in thought and habit was simultaneously reflected in their gait and way they chronically held their mouth, back and pelvis, for example—literally in the way they both moved and "stood still." And it was reflected in their ability to reach out to the world and make genuine contact—what they could literally see and touch—or in the manner that they would habitually withdraw. Chronic holding and contraction in certain muscular segments "contained" the character. He called this body armor.

This analytic breakthrough gave the therapist an entirely new realm in which to observe how and when patients "held back" and to work directly with them there. Therapy still had its verbal dimensions, of course, but now it also moved beyond this into the nonverbal realm to relieve the stasis, processes of the autonomic nervous system and the way they presented in the chronically contracted musculature of the body. Screams of rage, tears of heartbreak, grief, and joy, and the thrill of deep attraction, were now more immediately available than through the "talking cure." Here was the "unconscious" completely at work. Natural pulsation, the pulse of life, was profoundly affected. This could be seen regularly and in characteristically different ways in the inhibition of breathing, again autonomically regulated, as conditioned by the wider environment in which the patient had grown up and now lived.

In a comparable way, this book's readers will learn about the "*co-inspired* breathing" of a group and organization, what it looks like and how to intervene to handle it when it is blocked. Moreover, readers too will see, detailed in Chapter 5, how an organization's cross-cutting structural segments—essentially, its top, middle and operating core groupings—hold the emotional energy in work systems and literally represent the character of its movement. When the organizational character hardens and on balance inhibits the free movement of the composite energy, the character ossifies as bureaucracy and becomes "organization armor." I argue that understanding the presence of organization armor opens up new avenues of approach for consultants in their moment-to-moment assessments and interventions.

Clinically with individuals, as Reich saw how the whole body functioned as part of the neurotic process, this further convinced him that he was on the path to greater understanding of the biologically adaptive basis of human dynamics, as Freud originally hoped would one day come to pass. Along with Freud as his teacher at the University of Vienna medical school, Reich also trained with the neuropsychiatrist Julius von Wagner-Jauregg, who went on to become the first Nobel laureate in the field in 1927.

But what was the nature of this energy, Reich asked? Was it some kind of hormonal, other biochemical or bioelectric process? This led Reich into the lab. By now, it was 1934 and he had moved to Oslo to flee Eastern Europe. He continued to practice as a psychiatrist, teach and develop his clinical technique, while he began the first of many experiments that inquired into the existence of the energy.

Thinking at first it might be bioelectric because of the tension-charge-discharge-relaxation cycle observed in his patients, Reich conducted experiments in a set up that measured electrical potential at the surface of human subjects' skin, under conditions of both pleasure and anxiety. He confirmed there was a consistently stronger charge registered when the subject experienced pleasure, weaker when anxiety was felt. From this he reasoned that the movement of energy when pleasure was felt went outwards towards the periphery of the organism and moved inwards towards the center when anxiety was the case. He also saw in the readouts of the recorded results that the points of measurement moved in a smooth, wave-like manner, not a spiky motion that would have suggested the energy was bioelectrical. He thus inferred it must be something else. But what?[4]

Reich wondered whether more could be learned by looking at simpler forms of life. Using high-powered microscopes and time-lapse photography, he looked at the development of protozoa. He discovered under certain conditions, sterilized and unsterilized infusions of organic material began to disintegrate into pulsating vesicles that emitted a bluish color. Even after autoclaving the material, he also observed an internal motility to the vesicles, some of which emitted a radiation that had health giving properties, including the ability to kill bacteria and cancer cells when placed adjacently. But they also had other effects. Reich himself got conjunctivitis as he spent long hours peering into the microscope. Overall, what he observed did not obey known electromagnetic laws. It did not fit with "Brownian motion," and contamination by air germs was effectively contained. Professor Roger Du Teil of the French Academy of Science replicated Reich's experiments with the same results. But when Reich published his findings, the scientific and psychiatric communities responded with a year-long attack in the Norwegian press, claiming what Reich offered in fact was "junk science," though the term itself was not in use then. These were claims by those who had never repeated any of Reich's experiments, many with an axe to grind, and by those in the psychoanalytic movement who claimed he had incipient psychosis and *ipso facto* wrote off what he had to say.

For a fuller account of how Reich worked, what he saw and the experimental results that obtained, the reader is directed to Princeton-trained historian of science James Strick's 2015 *Wilhelm Reich: Biologist*. In his account, Strick, also a trained microbiologist, had worked carefully from recently unsealed laboratory notebooks of Reich's that had been archived at Harvard, whose university press also published Strick's book. Strick does not pass judgment on the validity of Reich's findings. But his inquiry certainly showed Reich's *bone fides* as a research scientist, the care Reich took in conducting his laboratory experiments, including the use of cutting-edge technique; that he was working within real if not dominant scientific traditions of the time; and that what he did could not at all be fairly dismissed with a wave of the hand.

Likewise, because Reich saw the effects of the radiation emitted, he conducted further experiments using a Faraday-like enclosure to study the phenomena now in physical, not just biological, terms. Reich began these experiments in 1939, after he finally emigrated to America with the help of scholars such as Theodore Wolfe, MD and Bronislaw Malinowski, assisting him to obtain his visa and a teaching assignment at the New School for Social Research in New

York. He constructed the enclosure of alternating layers of organic and metallic materials because in his earlier work in Oslo he had seen the radiation respectively charge and reflect back the charge of these materials. Thus, in the boxes he constructed, he sought to concentrate or *accumulate* the energy to observe its properties. He had meanwhile come to term this new form of energy, orgone energy, from its origins in his own work studying the function of the orgasm and as the energy moved throughout the organism. Through further studies, he concluded this energy existed in the atmosphere at large, as he observed its existence even in vacuum tubes after they were charged in the accumulators; after charging, the inside of the tubes now glowed blue and pulsed—unexpected properties he had also seen in his earlier laboratory research on biological materials under high-powered microscopes. These effects suggested the energy was a ubiquitous, dynamic, vibrant reality, hearkening back, though in a different and more specific way, to prior notions predominant in science of an ether. Perhaps space was not "empty" after all, but consisted of a physical energy that permeated all living things and existed even *prior* to matter?

In his physical experiments with the accumulator, one of the several other properties he observed was a temperature difference inside of it from that of a control box made of other materials. The regularly measured, higher heat inside the accumulator too was a shattering observation because it appeared to violate the Second Law of Thermodynamics, namely that energy at large ran downhill. In two long meetings with Einstein that were arranged at the physicist's home in Princeton, Einstein confirmed the thermal anomaly saying it would be a "bombshell" to science should the finding hold. Einstein asked if he might study the phenomenon further with a tabletop size accumulator Reich left with him; yet later, on the suggestion of an assistant who offered a simple conceptual explanation for the anomaly, Einstein pursued it no further. Reich's written reply to Einstein included new control experiments demonstrating that the *conceptual* objection was insufficient to account for the phenomenon they both saw. Einstein never responded. These controls have since been replicated using more sophisticated experimental methods than available then, as has been the case with Reich's earlier biological research in Oslo. Yet the claim that there was nothing to his findings still gets repeated today, as does the smear that he was somehow "running a sex-racket."

More than sixty years since Reich's death, there are those who continue to denigrate the man and his work. No matter again that they have not conducted any of the laboratory experiments under the protocols Reich laid out. More than a healthy dose of rational skepticism has been at play. These claims about his scientific research and Reich's lifelong focus on addressing widespread sexual misery roused the press and officials to continue to foment doubt. There were simultaneous claims Reich was a spy, a pornographer, a fascist and a communist, that he was a medical quack dangerous to the public, and to be shunned because he was mad.

Because of the radiation effects inside the accumulator, Reich's preliminary studies with cancer mice using small accumulators showed promise, with shrinkage of tumors compared to those in control groups, even though all of the animals eventually succumbed to the disease which Reich plainly reported. The studies showed enough initial possibility for Reich to begin modest experimental trials with terminally ill human volunteers who had run out of other treatment options, with their full consent, disclosure to them, no promise of a cure, and at no cost. But for some, all of this didn't matter, Reich simply needed to be stopped.

The IPA was proactive with the US FDA in the mid '50s in going after Reich. A federal injunction was issued to ban the interstate rentals of accumulators going to other doctors and patients interested in Reich's work. The rental fees covered the cost of the units' construction and helped fund continuing orgone research from Reich's lab in Rangeley, Maine. Here, too, patients who could not pay the rental fee were charged nothing. When an assistant of Reich's, without his knowledge, transferred some accumulators across state lines, Reich was arrested for violating the injunction, tried, and sent to prison for a two-year term. Before his sentencing in Federal court, Reich pleaded in vain with Judge Sweeney that he and his assistant, Dr. Silvert, were devoted to the promotion of new knowledge, not a cancer cure, and that they were "not crooks, not criminals, but courageous people."[5]

As part of the run up to the trial, in the most extreme example of censorship in US history, the FDA ordered all of Reich's books be burned in a New York City incinerator. The claim was that the mere mention in the books of the energy phenomena he termed orgone represented "labeling" for the "fraudulent" accumulator devices. This was the third time Reich had experienced official burning of his books. The first as noted earlier by the Nazi regime, the second by the Soviet Stalinists who claimed Reich's analysis of the mass psychology of fascism—in which they were not spared—was "counter-revolutionary." There too, the books, like Reich, just had to go. That Reich may have "gone mad," as some claimed, does not obviate the fact of the real, not imagined, destruction of his books and reputation, any merits of his laboratory work and prior acclaim in psychiatry be damned.

The cumulative experience of this must have been nearly unbearable for Reich, of Jewish heritage exiled from his homeland and isolated in his work, despite his repeated efforts to reach out to others of science for help. There were friends, yes, such as the Summerhill educator A.S. Neil, Sir Herbert Read and others in England who signed a letter of public protest over the destruction of Reich's materials in the US; but it was never published in any newspaper, nor was a press release issued by the ACLU in Reich's behalf. For Reich, "death by silence," as well as invective, was common.

In November 1957, after serving five months and up for parole in a week, Reich died in a Federal penitentiary, at night in his bed, of heart failure. As his biographer Myron Sharaf has said, he literally died of a broken heart. Just three years after his death, publisher Roger Straus of Farrar, Straus and Giroux, incensed at the book burning by the government, and on civil liberty grounds alone, saw to the first of the republication of all of Reich's books and letters, eventually in multiple languages. The initial entry of these was an introductory collection, *Wilhelm Reich, Selected Writings*.[6] Since then, twenty-three others of Reich's books and correspondence have been published, plus other journal material of his.

Today, much of Reich's work remains distorted, either by detractors or those who have idealized it. The internet today has greatly multiplied this distortion. Too few have seriously studied it. The efforts to write him out of the history of psychiatry and natural science and in the public mind, have largely succeeded, where today he is little known.

Yet Reich's work has still had powerful influence over the years. His later clinical work, for example, was predicate to Gestalt, body-mind and Janov's Primal Scream therapies, to name but three. And Reich's clinical conceptions, I contend, remain far more comprehensive and, in the right hands, therapeutically effective than those that followed. Similarly, Reich's and Baker's early innovations in understanding and mobilizing the ocular segment of the organism were forerunners to today's popular somatic EMDR techniques, though here too Reich's approach remains much more complete conceptually and clinically.[7] Moreover, Reich has had a pervasive influence across culture in the twentieth century among many leading figures, as listed by the Wilhelm Reich Museum and Trust.[8] So, despite the efforts to erase Reich from the history books, his contributions remained alive.

There are signs a fresh appraisal may be afoot. As referenced earlier, Harvard University Press's not long-ago published *Wilhelm Reich: Biologist* by Jim Strick, is one such sign. Increasing openness and interest in understanding natural energy functions, among researchers and the public, notably in health and wellness, are another. An increasing number of publications is evident addressing the healing properties of an energy at work in life—in Western and non-Western traditions alike, including their equivalence to what Chinese acupuncturists and others in the Far East have called *chi*, and in the Hindu tradition in India and elsewhere around the world, *prana*. What made Reich different was his elucidation of this energy in natural scientific terms through laboratory science and in tangible clinical observations of human dynamics.

This natural science inquiry took him quite far—to the understanding too of the energy at work in nonliving natural systems, as well as the living. His practical understanding of weather systems and atmospheric phenomena, including cloud formations, hurricanes, and the aurora borealis, are remarkable. Likewise, his views on common functioning principles at work in the spiraling arms of galactic systems as they stream together. He described this swirling motion of two energy streams—a process ubiquitous in nature—as "superimposition," from which greater form emerges. Astrophysicists today seem headed in a similar direction to Reich, as they seek to account for the buildup of scale and continuous creation teeming in the universe.[9]

Yet with all this, I am struck that as pioneering and radical as Reich's findings were in physics and biology, all of that will be easier for the world to accept than his views on human sexuality. *That* makes extraordinary demands on people in their ordinary lives and in the professions that seek to help them. As a result, my suspicion is that his understanding of natural human sexuality will be the last to find broad acceptance, even though people can inwardly feel its pull.

Given the functional identity of work energy and sexual energy, there will be challenges too to accord *felt gratification at work as the essential need* it is. We hear evidence of this disregard daily in our work organizations. Pleasure in the work process and joy in achievement are too commonly considered at best nice-to-haves or unnecessary altogether; the attitude is, "*We here are all about work.*" Accepting the natural, human need for gratifying work makes for difficult choices for us in what we do and how we live—and in the wider social order in which our organizations and other institutions are created, enacted and exist.

Change in the life of society is hard, as serous students and practitioners of OD recognize, and as this book underscores. Personally, even with some of the brightening notes above regarding the prospects for a reappraisal of Reich work, I was warned by some well-meaning people as I prepared this book to be careful about invoking his name. Might I want to change the nature of this book, de-emphasize his name or not mention it all to get a fuller readership? And so it goes. The pressure, consciously or not, to write Reich out of history remains. Yet the pleasure of writing something in its own terms meaningful to an author, and as he sees for others, remains too. That too is work.

There is a final irony. The success of efforts to expunge Reich from the record—leaving many unaware of who he was and what he found—may actually create a more objective environment for the evaluation of his work in the future, as more are less fettered by the prejudices and controversies of the past and can come to it with a more natural curiosity. Time will tell.

PART I:
FUNDAMENTALS

THE WORK ENERGY BASIS
OF ORGANIZATION LIFE

More than once have I been called in by an organization to salvage a consultation conducted by others that had gone off course. Not only had the expected "solution" bought and tried not worked, it commonly made matters worse. Whether the organizations were trying to develop new go-to-market strategies, make needed large-scale process changes, reorient roles and revamp organization structures, or implement new systemwide information technologies, their people often wouldn't agree on how to (or even if they should) go about it; they seemingly, in fact, often *couldn't* agree.

To manage the situation, leaders sometimes tried soft approaches when hard mandates wouldn't fly. Sometimes they switched back and forth. Change management techniques, high engagement strategies, additional structural changes, training, the introduction of new key replacement players, and alas exhortation (including consultants exhorting clients "to do more strategy") often made little difference in the end. The organizational system just ground on. Fear, expressed or just below the surface, was almost always in the picture.

Not only had the original situation failed to resolve, or the sought opportunity not materialized, but now the people in the organization—at all levels, top leaders too—were more stirred up and frustrated than before. Resistance to change largely hardened. Courage to try again was often shaken.

Some leaders and people still tried. By the time I arrived, often to the look of "what do I do now?" from the leaders, the efforts had typically stalled, sometimes dead in their tracks.

One such time was when I was called to reignite a stalled change initiative for a mid-cap investment brokerage firm.[1] Another top-name consulting firm had previously been engaged to study and propose solutions to extensive back-office operating problems. At the time, the company had been expanding rapidly during an economic boom in its markets, and it was posting aggressive profits. But the CEO was concerned about mounting transaction losses and overhead expense arising from poorly organized operating processes. Management accepted the consultants' report and recommendations for a significant reengineering effort, which had been generated in concert with a cross-functional employee team. However, the consultants' additional recommendation that they be retained to guide implementation of the effort was rebuffed. They were told that the firm would implement the proposed suggestions themselves and that their services would no longer be needed. Months passed and nothing happened. The employee team, which was charged with implementation, floundered with the sketchy implementation plan the consultants had left. I was called by the CEO, who had known me earlier, because he recognized the impasse and now had the added concern that the employees had been stirred up with no results to show. When I asked why he hadn't called back the original consultants, he responded that he wanted a fresh approach.

After an initial face-to-face with him, I had the immediate impression of a certain quality that ran throughout the company's change effort; a quality in the organization, its executives, the consulting firm, and in what I was now being asked to do. *The firm, repeatedly, it seemed "bit off more than it could chew."* My sense was that the resistance to following through on the project mirrored the very problems that had led to the engagement in the first place: The proposed solution was poorly planned and organized, unable to keep pace with the firm's appetite to book more and more business, and was thus simply more than the firm could handle. Furthermore, it was obvious that no one operating person was clearly in charge of the project, which, too, mirrored their day-to-day leadership ambiguity over their operations.

My intervention with the CEO was to quickly describe my impression of their characteristic overreach, then suggest we sharply scale back the project, appoint a project manager, and develop relatively tight project plans. I also suggested the two of us meet with the President to discuss the positioning of operations more generally. He agreed and said he would set up the meeting with the President the following week. He never did. After having put me off with the excuse of "scheduling problems," I phoned him again. The chief executive finally admitted that he didn't think the President, who seemed to overwhelmingly value sales, would be supportive of the process and was in fact frustrated with the whole endeavor, while struggling to keep silent. The President's struggle to keep quiet struck me too as overreach, as the way he played it out in the situation.

The CEO asked if he could meet with me alone to discuss the situation further. I did meet with him, then soon after with the senior middle levels of the employee team that had gotten squeezed in the effort. I then worked with the team to more sharply focus its efforts and get them moving. I also talked with the prior consulting group to get their take on what had happened. More on this case, its turn of events and outcomes, is discussed in Chapter 6. Suffice it here to say I was dealing from the start with the *character* of the organization, its persistent pattern of overreach, how it manifested at different levels, played out in its own ways, and locked up forward movement. The organization's energy had gotten stuck, its players increasingly frustrated, and desired results failed to take place.

Interestingly, I didn't have to work too hard to identify this characteristic pattern. It was all there in how the organization's situation immediately presented. But something had been missed—by the first consulting firm, and by the leaders and others in the organization. All sensed something was off, even from the beginning of their venture, and the players each had their particular explanations as to why. In fact, as I saw in my conversations with them, they all moved quickly to explanations, without lingering on their observations. This, again, was reflecting the character of the problem: They were rushing to solutions, without stepping back to really see the big picture—or the specific facts staring them in the face.

There was a patterned movement to their resistance, with evident qualities that interfered with forward movement. It was clear to me that people in the firm and the consultancy had wanted by and large to do their best. But something went sideways, which unfortunately too, is often the case. The organization and improvement efforts had run smack up against its culture—or more precisely, its organization character, as I define it, in the way it tied up its collective energy. In this way, the organization's character was operating a lot like the shark in the movie *Jaws*, devouring everything in its path, "a giant eating machine."

So, when this is the situation, it is sensible to ask, where do people start to get a handle on things? What is to be done first? Very often for many of the players the answer lies in one of two directions: either jump to solutions, as I saw in the case at hand, or in other cases the very opposite tendency, the tendency to study the problem—or talk the problem—to death. Consultants and others will frequently offer painstaking, detailed analysis of the situation, working jointly with client members, sometimes highly involved, in what seem like endless interviews, surveys and focus groups. Today, especially in vogue, is a new favorite of some in the field to bring forth something more generative: "dialogue."

I saw a very large US government agency get enmeshed in a whole series of structured dialogue sessions up and down the organization nationally. A consultancy its leaders were enamored with sold them on dialogue as a way for their people to take the wheel to establish a compelling vision of the organization's future. On the surface, it all sounded good. The problem, however, was people didn't end up really talking with each other. They weren't speaking their minds, much less getting to something effectively generative, and the project got shelved because the encounters felt ritualistic to the participants, irrelevant to their genuine concerns which they still experienced as *verboten* to express. *Emotional frustration inside the system remained locked up.* Resistance to the project went underground, the organization got stirred up, and funding for the effort stopped. A design flaw in the process or in how it was facilitated? Or was something bigger askew? Here, too, the underlying character of the system—and as it was operating in the here and now—was missed.

It's not that such interventions cannot be useful measures. They can. The problem is that they very often get *overdone*—and done in the wrong functional context. The interventions can become another means by which movement is stopped (jumping to solutions, paralysis by analysis or talking a problem to death), and in fact the big picture remains obscured. So, in an irony, the process both covers up observation and inhibits needed concerted action. Intentional or not, a collusion, an evasion with the client system, is at hand. The organization is further stilled.

What remains hidden is the structure to the resistance—and what it is resisting. But why not go right to the source of the problem to begin with—the energy dynamics of the organization? How does its energy characteristically move and how is its movement stopped?

Lest readers think that all organizations in distress exhibit the same characteristics as the investment brokerage firm in the first example, a closer reading shows this is not so. Some firms, for example, exhibit just the opposite tendency: They repeatedly shy away from any hint at overreach, including not trying even limited experiments; they gamble away chances when risk and innovation are called for and are, in fact, the prudent thing to do. Chapters 6 and 7 outline five varying types of organizational character disorders, with corresponding intervention strategies to address them. They also, in contrast, describe what a healthy organization character looks like, its structure and functional dynamics. I believe this healthy form is latent even in the disordered types, a form I see all organizations at least implicitly striving to realize. Such a healthy form, by definition, would be better in line with organizations' natural endeavors, free of many of the inhibitions that currently encumber them. However, for many firms, the chronically constrained organization character has become a trap.

Organizations, I believe, are functioning energy systems. They develop *system-level character structures*, consisting of social and formal structural features that express and block the movement of individual and collective work energy. In general, these organization character structures, in terms we will yet clarify:

- Run the gamut from healthy "work democratic" to various "armored" forms;
- Become *functional disorders* when in the organization's development and current situation it is significantly thwarted, that is, in its conditions, the hand it is dealt;
- Require different intervention strategies to restore better, fuller systems functioning when help is sought, even when the type of help needed is not completely recognized.

This chapter provides a general introduction here.

To start, we'll begin with what work energy is in human life, its nature and how it moves and functions. We'll then look at its root relationship with groups and organizations, how they form in the first place and come to represent new, constituted states of the energy at a social level. Their roots are "biosocial," as we'll describe, based on Reich's pioneering work, but as others have come to see aspects of as well. We'll look at how social constellations of work energy of any type are similar yet also different from biological systems per se, giving us a basis for better understanding the inherent possibilities and challenges of change in social systems, large and small.

OUR BIOSOCIAL NATURE, ENERGETIC ROOTS

As a psychiatrist, social thinker, and biologist, Reich understood that human life is essentially "interactional" in a "field." Human life is less "atomistic" than it is fundamentally relational between people, one-on-one, in families, groups, and the environment in which they live and work, the environment both physically and socially. The word "socially" here is used in broad terms, including sociologically, socioeconomically, social psychologically and culturally.

Here, the words are instructive: Culture, as in the lab, means the surrounding medium in which organisms reside, are nourished, thrive and grow, or lose their vitality. Human life is, by definition, *acculturated*.

On the subject of nature or nurture, in his 1952 interview in the book *Reich Speaks of Freud*, Reich has this to say: "It's not an either libido or society. The libido is the energy which is molded by society. There's no contradiction there.... The child brings with it a certain amount of energy. The world gets hold of it and shapes it. So, you have sociology and biology, both, in one organism."[2] Freud understood this too, as Reich stressed: The family is the crucible in which culture is transmitted and reproduced, and from which an individual's dynamics are primarily shaped.[3]

This leads to an even more fundamental point: *People are energetic creatures, interacting in a field that is itself energetic, part of the natural world.*

From Reich's initial understanding of the primacy of orgastic functioning—the deeply loving merger of two organisms in what he called "the genital embrace"—he came to understand sexual union as a special case of our larger biosocial nature. At the very core of human life was biological pulsation, energetic excitement and discharge in reciprocally desired sexual union. Energetic concentration and discharge also permeated all dimensions of a person's life: work, learning, other creative activities, and in all the ways the body naturally functioned. In the sexual act itself, this pulsation, excitement and discharge represented the spontaneous streaming of the energy culminating in the two partners coming together to form a single unit in gratifying emotional surrender and release. Both bodies interlocked, moving rhythmically, elliptically and irresistibly as one. This began with the early draw of attraction and felt stirrings between the two individuals, a physical not simply psychological phenomenon, one that was essentially *biosocial* in its mutuality.[4]

As Reich's clinical understanding became more and more somatic, he came to see that the pulsating energy streaming throughout the individual's entire body was processed by all the organs, concentrating and discharging most fully in those areas related to the natural function being performed and where contact with the outer world was immediately made. Thus, the physical, energetic working of the body was always in contact with the world around it and variably conditioned by the world. This affected the body's systemic and local functioning in health and disease states, including how the organism's various natural functions being carried out were either fulfilled or, to a greater or lesser extent, unsatisfactorily so. Reich also early understood specific ways in which neurophysiological mechanisms *intra*-mediated the energy's charge and movement within the body and intermediated its contact and discharge with the world.[5]

Fundamentally, Reich came to understand that the streaming bioenergy manifests, depending on life function, as sexual energy (when loving intimately, both creative and potentially procreative), and also as work energy (when securing the means of living, both productive and reproductive) more largely in the outside world. In the latter instance, this energy manifests as a "living, productive work power" that shapes, and is shaped by, a sustaining environment. This concept Reich derived from his studies of Marx, which Reich straight-forwardly lays out in his book, *People in Trouble*.[6]

That all human action occurs in an interactive "field" was also emphasized in the late 1930s and '40s by Kurt Lewin, founder of the modern field of group dynamics. I'm unaware if Reich knew of Lewin, but generally speaking such ideas were in the *zeitgeist*. Borrowing concepts from physics, Lewin saw the social field as the "life space" of dynamic forces at play surrounding individuals and groups.[7] Yet it was Reich's enormous contribution to see these organism-field interactions as *fundamentally biosocial natural phenomena*, and he saw them in quite distinct detail. Later yet, in his laboratory experiments in biology and physics, Reich came to see the wider field in which all life resides as a mass-free, luminating, energy continuum that can concentrate itself as energetic form.[8]

In his sociological thinking, Reich was clearly influenced by another Eastern European in the social sciences, the pioneering anthropologist Bronislaw Malinowski on the conditionability of our emotional drives—sexual and social, and their implications for civilizations and human fulfillment. Human life and culture were malleable and adaptive, but not at their limits without a price.[9]

Although highly simplified, in today's terms, we might say that this biological energy is reflected in the human animal in two types of complementary needs: ancient, harder-wired, primitive needs and more plastic needs of social construction and learning. The way the latter needs play out can affect the functioning of the former's, as in the powerful effects language, other symbolic creation, and technologies can have on physical and emotional functioning. Yet effective functioning of the needs for learning and social construction remain dependent on and influenced by the fulfillment of the ancient needs. People whose primal needs remain unfulfilled are typically affected in their capacity to see and think clearly, just as they are hampered in their ability to create constructively. Indeed, they are likely to be *destructive* in ways commensurate with the extent such basic needs are frustrated. Both types of needs are companion, *organismic* functions. They are mediated by processes in the central and peripheral nervous systems, and they are grounded in the oscillating functions of expansion and contraction of the autonomic nervous system, as Reich also very early grasped.

This active, biosocial nature is not unique to the human species. This social dimension exists across the animal world; for example, when ants work in colonies, birds fly in formation, wolves travel in packs, primates forage in troupes. Some years after Reich's death, the independent rise of "sociobiology" as a field, led by Harvard's Edward O. Wilson, recognized an evolutionary, biosocial reality in the animal world.[10]

It may fairly be said that our species' cognitive capabilities for adaptation, for good or ill, for health, well-being or neuroses, for social constructiveness or destructiveness, are more pronounced than other creatures', given our own evolutionary status.[11] I've come to think that understanding what sociality is for the human animal has less to do with sociology and even social psychology than that which has been more deeply identified with the intersection of biological and social anthropology.[12] Reich has much to teach us about understanding groups and organizations—their very nature—in basic energetic terms. This understanding is his work's distinguishing contribution related to organizational life, as he rudimentarily explored it in his writings and as can be more fully derived as I do in this book.

THE WORK ENERGETIC BASIS OF GROUPS AND SOCIAL LIFE

So, what is it that Reich's teachings tell us about the nature of social life? What exactly is meant when we say the "life of society" or the life of a social unit? Is it different and in what ways from individual life? And, how does it develop?

We've already established that individual life once formed is biosocial at its root. But what happens when a larger, social constellation forms? Is this a form of life with its own reality?

I found myself first interested in these questions in graduate school in the mid-1980s. I attended a week-long T-group with eleven participants. T-groups ("T" for training) are relatively unstructured, very lightly facilitated, learning laboratories developed by Lewin and others in the late 1940s. They were developed for experimental, experiential discovery about the nature of small group life, including how one, left to his or her own devices, tends to function in groups.

In my own T-group, after a while being together in the room where we met each day, sitting in a circle, people got to relax in the presence of each other. In a moment of prolonged silence, no talking, I experienced how participants were sitting back and just breathing together, in and out, in and out, in the same rhythm. *The group was palpably pulsating as one.* This grew more striking and exciting as the people in the room just let it be.

Here was life! More than the sum of the individuals, I experienced our collective or combined energies merging and working in a unitary way, literally, as a unit. Beyond the silence, such patterned movement was also evident in the cooperative action and joint rebellion against some expressions of others that spontaneously arose in the group.

Couples and mini sub-groups, sometimes cliques, also emerged, including the subjective experience of being "insiders" and "outsiders" of the group, as reported. The attraction of people was based on a spark, mutually expressed interests in what was happening, but also a felt excitement between them. The distancing between people was in contrast experienced as unpleasant, as a kind of repulsion. All this too was evident as the group settled into informal rituals or norms and in the way a group identity emerged and of which people spoke.

My observation that individuals' breathing is affected is not unique among those who have participated in T-groups. But I haven't heard others describe and draw attention to the *unitary breathing of the group itself.* That yet is a leading-edge observation today, according to Lewin scholar and T-group practitioner, Gil Crosby.[13] This is literally a process of "co-inspiration." Here, based on Reich's teachings and my T-group experience, I understand this "breathing together as one" in natural, spontaneous terms, autonomically mediated in a group's members, not in the intentional willful disobedient sense the term "conspire" has come to mean.

This breathing of the group as a single body immediately reminded me of those points at silence in my experience in Reich's therapy ten years earlier, when lying at rest on the therapy couch, I made simple contact with my own breathing moving up and down my whole body. *The T-group, itself as a body, had spontaneously formed its own energy and began to move as one.*

So, to summarize: Groups begin to form when there is a mutually excited charge. This represents the interlocking of emotional energies, from which collective movement, patterns and structure often form.

The banding together or formation and functioning of a group literally is *the association of the energies.* This seems the same functionally as Reich found in his early biological investigations in the lab and his later "cloudbusting" work in the atmosphere: an attraction or dissipation of energy, where form emerges with a vitality of its own.

This is consonant with the organizational thinker Karl Weick's notions about how organizations come to exist in the first place.[14] But it builds on Weick in that it accounts for the widely observed phenomena of *emotional charge and excitement almost always present at the founding of an enterprise.*

For example, the two individuals who came together to form Allied commercial bank, detailed in Chapter 7, had no preconceived, rational intent to start a bank when they first worked together. Instead, as independent import-export merchants, they simply had a certain mutuality of business interests, where they saw a new market opportunity for a different kind of bank existed. But, more basically, emotionally, they simply clicked. On its face, they had an energetic attraction to each other. When they struck on the idea of the bank, by all reports they were charged up and excited about it. This was literally the way the bank was "conceived."

I myself felt this energetic excitement in rock 'n roll bands that friends and I formed, played in and seemingly endlessly re-formed when we were teenagers. This thrill is evident in the performance of many musical ensembles, especially in the spontaneous inter-play of accomplished jazz musicians. The pure excitement of their interplay—their work—is predominant, not "anxiety" as tradition-al psychoanalytic models would have it. Understanding the work of great jazz ensembles —*what impels them to form, work together as they do, and perform*—seems important to me for understanding the high-trust, high collaborative relationships needed in the network organization era. In fact, this tells us a lot, I believe, about the nature of organization health itself. We'll explore the form of the jazz en-semble more fully as a model for health in Chapter 3, and as a form particularly suited for group functioning in organizational networks in Chapter 8.

So, to recap a bit more, "work energy" seems a distinct, active energy basic to the attraction and draw of people one to another at work as well as how they come to form groups and, indeed, whole organiza-tions.

However, can we say the T-group or a musical band—or all groups and organizations if we generalize—are purely living systems? *Are organisms*? They do form boundaries and identities, with character-istics and behaviors that are distinguishable one from another. And some groups certainly, over time, form more demarcated boundaries than others.

Tribalism is an example that reflects such a sharply drawn boundary, and in their negative charge, so do cliques and cults. Membership and belonging are jealously guarded, and outsiders are repelled and, to a greater or lesser degree, considered "repellent." Conceptually, what distinguishes an organization from a looser "crowd" or an "association" is its more defined, durable boundary in behalf of its participants' common function.

However, these boundaries cannot be considered membranes, a characteristic of living form, because they are yet more fluid. A group or organization's vitality is derived from the energies of the people who join to constitute the unit—or who leave it, drawing energy and its potential, positive or negative, out. Therefore, because groups and organizations lack a membrane per se, it is not strictly accurate to say they are living systems, while sharing some of their characteristics. Nonetheless, it is entirely fair to regard a group or organization as a special kind of *natural*, nonliving energy system predominantly made up of intermeshing living systems; they perform under certain bounded conditions and operate within a larger energy field. I've thus come to the conclusion that *groups and organizations represent a special class of unitary natural energy system.*[15]

Curiously, the greater natural elasticity of organizations makes them both harder to change yet easier too than in working with individuals in, say, coaching, counseling or psychotherapy. Social systems of all types, because they lack a membrane, are more fluid and pliable than individual organisms. This makes character formation a less bounded phenomenon than in individuals, though again, as we shall further see, they are capable of sharp rigidification. In general, the organization's inherently looser coupling than as in individuals alone can make it more slippery and harder to concentrate its form and effects. For example, turnover and some continuing formation and re-formation of different groups—people's comings and goings—are inherent to social process, even though those too of course are quite capable of distortion and dysfunctionality. So, the comparison between the individual and social realms only goes so far. Yes, the resemblance of certain character types and certain aspects of the two realms can be striking. Both realms are home to natural energy systems, yet there are differences important to appreciate.

That groups and social phenomena form special energetic realities of their own means their activities cannot simply be reduced to the sum of individual dynamics or even simply as "sets of relationships." This is where much of the field of OD leaves the matter today. Once formed, groups and organizations take on fundamental energy dynamics all their own, dynamics that are collective in nature and distinctive to the social domain. This may be the most important implication of Reich's work in the social realm; although I think as a phenomenon it is not widely understood, in OD and the management and social sciences generally, nor even by those trained in Reich's clinical modality and scientific research.

ORGANIZATION CHARACTER, ARMOR AND "WORK DEMOCRACY"

Certainly, some groups and organizations have more vitality and survival power than others. All work groups and organizations are charged with work energy, the interlocking energies that create work products and services and knowledge. These products and services are discharged into the world—into the market, socioeconomic, and ecological environments in which they interoperate.

Work energy is literally experienced as emotional energy at work: Our feeling of fulfillment when we complete a task or a job in a full way; or conversely, our feeling of frustration when we're inhibited, either by internal or external factors, in achieving our tasks. When we combine our work energies with others in a common endeavor, we have the beginnings of group formation. As a group's collective work energies continue to concentrate and expand, they begin to structuralize further, and we have the beginnings of an organization.

I have come to the view that after an organization is *conceived*, it *incubates* in a period of organization, then is *born* the moment it begins to operate. From here on out, the organization has a life of its own. It is a life certainly that continues to be influenced profoundly by its founders, who in addition to their external roles with their own interests, play inside roles without much exception. Nevertheless, the organization, now with its own core functions, dynamics and demands, has a life that is bigger than that of the individual members who found or constitute it. This is not always clearly understood, certainly by some entrepreneurs, but neither quite by some organizational scholars. The organization "psyche" cannot effectively be reduced to the personality dynamics of its founders or leaders. More is at play.

This life I see revolves around a central charge or core function directed outward towards the world. Thus, in the case of a bank, it is to provide certain financial services to facilitate the flow of commerce. In the case of a hospital, it is to provide community medical services; and so on. Now, in addition to a core energetic function, organizational life also encompasses certain historical and developmental processes; basic structural dimensions or segments; and characteristic social patterns, shared patterns of behaviors, values, and emotions. These start to take shape in what's been described for many years now as "organization culture," providing a specialized identity structure for the system.

I understand organization culture to be a mediating layer in the life of an enterprise, adaptive to outer and inner worlds, and which can promote the free and full expression of a system's core energy, alternatively constrict and suppress it, or frequently do both simultaneously. It seems to do so in each system in different proportions of health and dysfunction. I hold that this specialized layer mediates or *gates* the expression of the combined energy at work in a system. Organization culture, in this sense, seems more or less equivalent to character in the individual realm, as Reich has defined it.[16]

I am not alone in seeing organization culture as character in the psychodynamic sense of the term. Sociologist Philip Selznick recognized organization culture as character in the 1950s, referencing Reich's use of the term, [17] and thirty years later, Edgar Schein noted in his now classic *Organization Culture and Leadership*:

Culture solves problems for the group or organization, and even more important, it contains and reduces anxiety. The taken for granted assumptions that influenced the ways in which group members think, perceive and feel about the world, stabilize that world, give meaning to it and thereby reduce the anxiety that would result if we did not know how to categorize and respond to the environment. *In this sense, culture gives a group its character, and that character serves for the group, the function that character and defense mechanisms serve for the individual.*[18]

However, I want to emphasize that organizational character, in addition to serving a *defensive* function, serves an *expressive* function as well. To reiterate: *Organizational character serves to simultaneously express and bind the underlying emotional energy and excitement that represents the prime driving force of the organization. This is more than a defense against anxiety*, though that is there too, especially so when the energy is turned back upon itself. I believe this primary excitation and emotional energy at work represents the profound reservoir of health in an organization. Understanding its presence, I think is vital to the success of large-scale organizational consulting intervention.

Unfortunately, many organizations today block the effective concentration and expression of their energies. Instead of functioning in an expressly self-regulating manner, energy remains trapped inside the system, contained or circumscribed by the blocked organization characters. This results in what professors Manfred Kets de Vries and Danny Miller have elsewhere dubbed "the neurotic organization."[19] Like Schein, Kets de Vries and Miller do not recognize energy dynamics at the root of organization life, but much of what they describe in fact symptomatically seems correct. Regardless, these are organizations whose collective energies are not fully available for productive, gratifying work. They are tied up in fueling and sustaining the symptoms and the functioning character disorder.

This social character and structural entrapment of the energy produces the stagnation, the chronic immobility, and the high levels of frustration and anxiety so prominent in our institutions. These organizations siphon their vital energies into a regimen of bureaucratic policies, procedures, and characteristic attitudes with distinctive shapes. This regimen compounds their problems further. Rather than functioning in a rationally aligned and integrated manner to discharge their products and services outward in the world, these systems internally become disjointed and at odds with each other, and their markets ill-served. In fact, energy is often pulled up into the hierarchy of the systems themselves, stuck in overly charged, politicized, and rigid top-down operating arrangements, disempowering to their members and customers.

Instead of seeing these patterned problems clearly, organizational members typically rationalize and explain them away. Members become resigned to these conditions, sometimes numb to them, often believing they are universal, inevitable and even, as Peter Block has noted, just.[20] Some may explain their justifications as the need to "just survive," but is that universally the case? Might these members also be protecting themselves against feeling the full extent of their frustration? Or their intolerance of feeling and concentrating the excitement of the work itself? This in fact is a deadening process. The shared defense against seeing and attending to these problems in a direct manner becomes part and parcel of the organization's collective unconscious, part and parcel of a suppressive process per se. In a word, these organizations have become "armored."

Chapter 4 delves rather fully into the basis of how organizations develop such chronically blocked characters to begin with. The available evidence points to specific character structures arising as a result of how energies at primary group developmental stages are either frustrated or fulfilled in the way the youthful organization interacts with its founder and larger environment. Schein has termed these *socio-emotional* developmental stages. Sets of early developmental stages for organizations have also been noted by other scholars.[21] Yet they have not to date linked the developmental process to *the system's en-*

ergetic immobilization in and of itself—and thus not zeroed in on what must be a central requirement of any intervention: to relieve the stasis.

My contention is that if an organization can fully satisfy all its socio-emotional developmental stages, it will develop a healthy character, with a structure that is quite naturally aligned and in its behavior, open, resilient and productive. Fluid, rational and emotionally satisfying engagement in the work process is notable, as people experience when they find themselves in high-quality working situations. The work is spontaneously organized, concentrated and discharged by those responsible for its performance. Again, skilled jazz ensembles epitomize this. But we can also see this on a large scale. During World War II, the Manhattan Project functioned like this in the widely self-organizing, collaborative interaction of its knowledge specialists central to their common task.

In the social realm, this way of operating is approximately what Reich described in his sociological thought as a self-regulating, "work democratic" mode of functioning. As far back as the 1930s, Reich understood "work democracy" to be groups and social units of all kinds that are fluid and organically develop; cooperative endeavors driven principally by those responsible for doing the "vital necessary work," not managed top-down in bureaucratized hierarchies.[22]

The work democratic organization character, as it is delineated in Chapter 6, enlists the full participation of its members, doing what is necessary to reach towards its full potential, even when this means tackling difficult problems head-on, without rationalization or evasion. This kind of organization is not overwhelmed by its problems but motivated to directly address and move through them. It is not perfect, nor does it expect perfection; indeed, it comes across to its people and others as "real."[23]

I believe this formulation is unique in organization theory. Organizational health is not defined as a set of ideal behaviors, performance, or by the absence of disease, but by specific energetic dynamics with a specific hallmark of *productive, felt gratification.* Moreover, applying Reich's learnings in this way helps us understand that health for an organization is a natural dynamic. This generally implies there may be less need to "engineer" the remediation of poorly functioning organizations, as is widely thought, than to support their natural forces and help client-systems remove the blocks from their coming to the fore. Chapter 3 looks at this more closely.

In contrast, when an organization encounters significant frustration during its early developmental period in which it gets hung up, I believe it will develop a neurotic, armored character, corresponding to the chief developmental stages when blocking occurred. Without the right kind of help, internal or external to the system, these blocks often remain more or less fixed for the life of the organization, despite changes in membership and often even leadership.

There is evidence that these blocks become anchored in the basic structural segments of an organization, that is, in the way a system's "tops, middles and bottoms" (as Barry Oshry has boiled them down) each function and interact.[24] The current-day blocking of this energy keeps the historical conflicts current and continuously fueled. We take this up in detail in Chapter 5. This, too, follows Reich's pioneering insight into the way the musculature and other somatic features of the organism moor the neurotic, individual character.

I came to see the functional equivalent of the organism's somatic segments in an organization as these three main cross-cutting structural groupings. In somewhat less formal hierarchical terms than Oshry uses, Henry Mintzberg has called these the strategic apex, the middle line, and the operating core, each with natural functions: the strategic apex (or "head") that envisions, guides, and orients the work; the middle line that facilitates and inspires the flow of work; and the operating core that produces the chief task work.[25] When the natural movement of work energy is hindered, their operations and *interoperation* get disturbed and their functioning is impaired. Their natural functions get distorted, often over- or under-functioning.

Under adverse conditions, these structural segments rigidify and become the major sites of the organization armor, literally "containing" the emotional energy at work. In the armored state, organizations chronically stymie the *free flow, concentration and discharge of energy*. Entrenched patterns of armored holding or premature discharge form a defense against the energy's robust movement and expression, resulting in a less vital, more brittle state of affairs. When this happens, members individually and collectively experience walled-up frustration, unease and tension. The dammed-up energies, now mounting as a force, eventually leak or burst out as dysfunctional social and formal structural symptoms. The dysfunction is reproduced in the organization's daily grind and transmitted to new members who join.

Examples of such organizational symptoms are when needed communications go underground out of fear; conflicting goals are set leading to confusion; adequate environmental scanning mechanisms don't develop, obscuring insight from the market and customers; product development is inadequate, with new products released before they are ready or able to be processed; and turnover is unusually high, based on broad emotional, then actual, resignation. There are more. Such symptoms can proliferate, forming the basis for remedial OD (or OD-like) help, if it is sought. Unattended to, at the limit, organizations can start to hemorrhage from the inside, chronic mismanagement bleeding them of the resources—human and financial—needed to survive.

I have seen this firsthand, at close range, in large systems twice, multi-billion-dollar enterprises each profiled later. One, Allied Bank, nearing shut down, with help and many working together, reclaimed its spirit and continuing life. The other, the major global consulting firm of which I was a partner, dug in more and more as problems mounted, and then it died. The structural impact of the chronic dysfunction is palpable, as is what it means for people's lives and livelihoods. What was originally adaptive in the developing life of the system becomes a liability, the cost of its chronic armoring in its social character and body.

IMPLICATIONS FOR THE PRACTICE OF OD

The main object of OD intervention, grounded in Reich's principles, is to mobilize the work energy in the system as a whole, to relieve its stasis, and restore the way the energy more naturally functions when unimpeded. In this way, the ground is laid for the complicating symptoms, when the condition is not too far gone, to essentially abate on their own accord. The *symptoms* lose their energy. This is similar to what happens in the well-practiced form of Reich's individual therapy.

Akin to individual therapy, the specific aim of a *sociotherapy* here is to unlock the dammed-up organization segments, in effect restructuring the character, enabling the organization to charge and discharge its work energy in a more open and fulfilling manner. The three cross-cutting structural groupings, the organization's most essential subsystems, thus become especially important for the consultant to recognize and observe in their functioning, alone and with each other; they point the way to know when, where and how best to intervene—and in what sequence—to help loosen them up so the system becomes less immobilized.

This freeing up of the organization almost always needs to be done gradually. If done too suddenly and indiscriminately, flooding and reaction will occur, further locking up the system. This is the recipe for how organizations get worse with some interventions.

Because the organization as a whole is a system, holding and freeing up at any one segment necessarily affects (draws energy from or boosts the energy of) the other segments; thus, attention needs to be paid to all of them, even when immediately attending to one. I have found that as a consulting effort of this kind successfully proceeds, the organization moves more and more towards unitary functioning and alignment, from the inside-out.

What makes Reich's work of unique value for OD is that it helps practitioners clearly see, then attend to, what has thus far been largely unrecognized in organizational life: *the patterned movement of the energy itself.* This is to pay attention to the ways people come together and move as one—or not, as the case may be—in their common endeavors. Attention is paid to how their combined energy builds and flows, up, down, across, and outside the system; how and where the energy blocks, backs up, overflows or languishes; and the resulting effects and costs, in the system's viability and fulfillment people experience. Again, this is all there to be seen in the normative functioning of the organization and in its formal structure—and in much as it presents to the observing eye. This approach helps the practitioner maintain clear focus on this root phenomenon.

This does not imply that consulting practitioners can operate as if from a high horse, or from a traditional "doctor-patient" model in the sense Schein has critiqued.[26] They cannot, if they are to be effective, remain untouched by what they see, nor stand aside or astride the system trying to "manage" it with "expert prescriptions." If such change consultants are to be effective, they will not get lost intellectually in models, confuse models with knowledge, nor get preoccupied with sharing models with clients, as some in OD are bent on doing.

Consulting practitioners will instead see what is occurring on its own accord, not unduly swayed by an interpretive lens or the rhetoric of the system. They will describe what they see in real terms that will intuitively ring true to the client and feel relief in hearing and in finally being able to address. I have tried to illustrate how this happens in consulting cases throughout this book. Moreover, practitioners will remain grounded in the consulting endeavor not out of an ideal of dispassionate disinterest, but out of *full interest in the primary sense of care and concern.*[27] This sensibility lets them be of real service in the first place, working as partners with the client system, supporting its restoration of healthy functioning.

CHAPTER 2

CONCEPTUAL GAPS AND PRACTICAL DILEMMAS, PAST AND PRESENT

As a whole, OD has put forward many important principles and practices for understanding and improving organizational life. There have been distinguished contributions in the course of OD's development by scholars, practitioners and, perhaps in its most aspirational tradition, by scholar-practitioners; certainly at least by those who are "reflective practitioners," as one important figure noted looking across several of the helping professions.[1] As a field, OD first took shape in the 1960s. It was not meant to be an academic discipline, but a body of work standing between the academy and "real life," putting the learnings of behavioral science to use "to make a difference in the world—the organizational world, the individual world, and the community world to better the condition of things."[2]

Key understanding about group dynamics and insights about large-scale change have been gained. That organizations are both "technical" work systems and human social systems has been established. Important distinctions about different kinds of consulting roles have been described, and an array of intervention methods have been innovated. Groundbreaking insights in the psychodynamics of organization life and how culture functions have also been plowed. Pivotal names like Kurt Lewin, Eric Trist, Ed Schein and Karl Weick have laid down seminal concepts for understanding social systems and change. In this chapter, we will look at these thinkers, many of them high order scholar-practitioners—their contributions and those of others to both organization theory and change practice.

Yet, as in any field, especially those comparatively early in their development, there have been deficits too. There have been significant conceptual gaps and practical dilemmas, many which remain to this day confronting both scholars and consulting practitioners. This affects their ability to help an organization and the lives of its people as much as is desired. Some of these limitations have held OD's own development back, as scholars and practitioners retread old ground without ever quite getting to effective resolution of these persisting problems. Yes, there has been genuine innovation, but sometimes, when we look more closely, we see old wine in shiny, new bottles.

When I first began work linking Reich's work to organizations, I heard Ed Schein speak of several of these gaps and dilemmas:

- an overabundance of interventions and insufficient guiding or unifying theory, leading to an ever-increasing state of "fractionated technique";
- an inability to address the major change requirements of today's organizations;
- one-sided emphasis on performance, engineering and design over clinical insights;
- continuing concentration on refining hierarchical, bureaucratic systems rather than addressing the emerging reality of flatter, highly participative organization networks.[3]

Schein's remarks at the time struck a chord and helped me further think about what made me discontent with the prevailing state of the field—what I heard when I talked with others and what I saw in my own relatively new practice of it. There were countless frameworks, models and intervention techniques to draw from. But there was little theory, let alone sufficiently settled theory, I could turn to that was either robust or practical enough to guide which of the diverse techniques would be most useful—the when, where, and why of their application. Sometimes the approaches concentrated on the possibilities in organizational life, and sometimes they looked at organizations' severe limitations. But I almost never saw the possibilities and limitations understood together in a way that came to grips with the obvious fact that they co-existed as organizational realities, even of course within the same system.

As I entered and continued in the field, I was dizzy from the choices and efforts to apply what were mostly mid-range models to complex circumstances. The advice by some to just go with things as they are and to recognize the complexity in it all, didn't lead me much further either, however. So, at sea, interventions, when all was said and done, were often subject to proceed more or less seat of the pants. What colleague might I call, I imagined, who might have *something* they just did, *anywhere,* that might be used? I could see that many practitioners, even more advanced ones who worked elsewhere, were often in the same boat. It's not that I was looking for a cookbook, but for some fuller, orienting framework to better meet the system where it was at, including understanding its developmental potential and limitations.

If this weren't enough, tough emotional dynamics—almost always obviously present in the client situation—were hard *technically* to come to grips with in organizational settings; these emotional dynamics were also emotionally taxing for a consultant to deal with in and of themselves. They were thus easy to back away from and focus instead on something less charged. I was usually called to help the organization move towards something new or return to once better days, at least as they were seen. Sometimes there were calls for sweeping change. Often problems presented that were multi-faceted with significant, people-related issues. Regardless, in practice, improving organizational performance was almost always the narrow focus of consultative attention. Less so was there a focus on the human side of enterprise; true, improving the human element was not exactly one of lip service. But it was still a concern that was easy to feel the pressure to treat amorphously, peripherally, or in isolation without larger context. Or to altogether throw overboard.

I did not want this pressure to get the best of me. I was attracted to the field in the first place because I wanted to really help make something better for an organization and the lives of its people. I did not want to be one more who failed, when the moment was at hand, to home in on the essential dynamics at work, dynamics that seemed the source of the system's palpable distress and human unhappiness. I had already begun to see how such dynamics showed up widely in an organization's dysfunctional behaviors and structures, as well as its strategies and thinking. At the same time, I had a glimpse of what organizations could much more fully be when things just felt right. I had seen from my personal experience in Reich's therapy, and my later study of it, the power that a deeply grounded approach could make in very challenging human situations. I wondered might there be some approach akin to that which could help organizations address the distinct challenges of their own tough dynamics? I looked and looked but didn't find a sufficiently elaborated approach in the field.

But I did find fragments of what a fuller, grounded OD approach might be. As I got deeper into the field's classical literature, I learned of key principles and various approaches that were certainly important and useful. And there were references to some ideas drawn into the field that I recognized from my earlier schooling and experience, references I sometimes found quite solid or suggestive of ways they might be more fully developed and applied. However, I did not find the material sufficiently put together as a usable whole from which I hoped I might better, practically proceed. The ideas and practices that presented in the classical literature often remained discrete and disconnected.

I certainly recognized from my earlier studies, when I had done graduate work in the mid-'70s, the concept of organization culture. Culture had begun to be widely talked about some ten years later, in companies and business schools. I must say I felt in a way like I was at an advantage. I had already read a good deal of some of the best minds in what broadly is the Humanities—philosophy and literature, social and psychological theory. Hegel, Marx and Weber. Scheler and Buber, Wittgenstein and Kuhn. Malinowski and Lewin, Freud and others of their magnitude too. All of them seemed quite significant for OD as a field, though their names are sometimes not recognized in the literature. Many remain basic influences on OD's emerging concepts and trends. These thinkers' influence is strong, for example, on OD's emergent emphases on ethnography, "spirit," paradigms, epistemology and dialogue. OD's concept of "thinking in action" is in a like way derivative, as is the field's reference today to "the social construction of reality."

In this chapter, in addition to Reich, I bring some of these profound minds to the foreground because their original formulations add perspective and depth to ideas sometimes presented as new in OD. I believe understanding these ideas' lineage can help the field's use of them from becoming more than fashions, help better separate the wheat from the chaff. These thinkers' original formulations also help bear on the resolution of conceptual gaps in the field that practitioners wrestle with day-to-day. The consequences of these gaps and practical dilemmas remaining unresolved can leave people in organizations without effective help. And it can leave the problem of human unhappiness at work and toxic workplace cultures fundamentally unaddressed.

Among these thinkers all, Reich of course for me is pivotal. From Reich I had come to see we, first of all, were dealing with more than ideas. I had seen it in therapy in rather dramatic changes in my own way of functioning, body and mind, without "thinking my way into it." I had worked with a truly talented therapist armed with real knowledge and more than just an interesting set of ideas, interesting though they were. The therapy *moved* me.

Substantively, what I found most grounding about Reich's work was the way he conceived of a character structure that regulated the movement and flow of vital energy in human affairs. The sense in which I understood the interplay of energy and character when I first came to OD was visceral and, in a way, second nature to me. After therapy, I could see how they functioned in me in a much better way than before, and I came to see too how they functioned in others, sometimes well, sometimes not so well. I was struck of course when I saw references to energy and character appear in the literature and language of OD.

Energy is a concept that is by no means foreign to organizational theorists and change practitioners. Chris Argyris, Dick Beckhard, Robert R. Blake and Jane Mouton, Peter Block, David Nadler, Schein and others all make reference to the importance of energy in organizations. Yet their use of the term is scattered and largely metaphorical. And as we will discuss, the open systems conception of organizations, grounded in Bertalanffy's "General Systems Theory" writings and explicitly applied in the work of Katz and Kahn, is wholly founded on energy assumptions. Yet in these frameworks the energy is only seen as deriving from outside the system, not part of a structuralized, dynamic energetic core. Later, competing applications of "Chaos Theory" were brought to bear, but they seemed in the end more interesting aesthetically than practically of much use. Likewise, earlier in the few instances where energy was seen as a central reality endemic to the organization, the concept remained vague, not specifying how it functionally develops and behaves within particular systems. I couldn't get a handle on what this "energy" quite was and how to make use of it.

As with energy, the concept of character is not new to the field of OD. Certainly, its related concept of culture has become something of a cliché. Eric Berne, Manfred Kets de Vries and Danny Miller,

Schein and Philip Selznick are among those who use the term "organizational character" from a psychodynamic perspective. Unfortunately, while each of their references were suggestive, all were too briefly explored. Too, since none of their formulations were based on an energetic foundation, they remained primarily descriptive of dynamics, and then only partially so, rather than serving as dynamic frameworks for practical change.

Thus, while two of the twin themes of this book—energy and organizational character—are not new to OD, they each before now have been treated in fragmentary and partial ways. They have not been connected with each other in OD in fundamental terms.[4] From my standpoint, this is what leaves much current theory and practice in the field incomplete and less fertile than might otherwise be. Reich's monumental work is a bridge over this divide, giving us a way to help organizations—the people within them—work and function in fuller and more fulfilling, natural ways.

This chapter's survey of some of the leading contributions in the field includes certain of the most current trends. Important, classic OD literature is looked at first, then contributions from those in organization psychodynamics, and finally several threads that broadly can be described as "post-modern" are considered. All of these contributions are relevant as background and context for how the application of Reich's work I think fills the void; how it pulls many of these disparate contributions together; and how in a revolutionary and fruitful way it builds on them.

This review makes no pretense of comprehensiveness. There are many fine survey books and other literature that recount the development of OD as a field, and there are other very fine thinkers who have made important contributions and written powerfully about it.[5] I have necessarily been selective for purposes of focus. At times this chapter will dive into the somewhat deeper terrain of more abstract theory, as some of the OD thinkers referenced have gone there themselves as a basis for their claims. But I have tried not to lose sight of the concepts' practical consequences in the day-to-day. Nor lose sight of how "people in trouble" (to use a phrase of Reich's) are either seen or not seen, and what is to be done about it. I try to draw these real-world consequences out as they surface in actual consulting practice, and in the lives of people as they experience it in the realities of the workplace.

This chapter is bookended by the work of the two thinkers, I think, whose work is most consequential for the field. We begin with Kurt Lewin, with what he said that fed OD from the start, including his sober cautions; we conclude briefly with Reich and how he points us in a profound new direction.

KURT LEWIN: THE ROOTS OF THE FIELD

In a way, Lewin belongs in a class by himself. The great social psychologist's work is foundational to OD and in ways today that are sometimes not recognized. In some ways too, Lewin himself has become a neglected figure.[6]

Lewin's aim was not to found a field of OD, but, in the largest sense, to define that there is a social field of action in which we all exist. Indeed, he was preoccupied with what he called "field theory": the dynamic forces within the "life space" of who we are as "whole persons" and the specific environments in which we all move. Unlike Reich, Lewin did not use biological language or think in biological terms. He was principally concerned with interpersonal perceptions and action as they operated in the surrounding field. He did not especially ground perceptual phenomena in feelings or in the body, as was so central in Reich's work. In this way, Lewin was quite focused on mental processes and the products of the mind, distinct from impulses originating within the body. But he did think the whole person could only be understood as a function of an "organism-environment" relationship, including how perception got skewed when it did not fit or sit well with presenting circumstances. This, Lewin saw, could lead to destructive social ideologies and action in the field. Conversely, he also saw that when perception was more congruent with what was actually happening, it could promote constructive action. So, for Lewin, some ways of perceiving could be clearer than others and thus had normative value. And while he focused principally on social psychological processes, he made explicit use of the language of physics to explain his central points. These he often rendered in mathematical terms. While Lewin had his critics of course, I think it can easily be said that with the seriousness and care he took in his work he strove to be a true "social scientist."[7]

Theory for Lewin was a delicate thing—and a precise thing, not to be bandied about or invoked loosely. It had innate power, and as such, could not be divorced from things that were real. In fact, one of Lewin's many maxims is, "There is nothing quite so practical as a good theory." His definitive biography by Alfred Marrow is entitled *The Practical Theorist.*[8]

As such, the development of social theory for Lewin always needed to come about through a process he called "action research." Close observation and immersive practice in a stream of events would eventually yield larger comprehension—of the situation and of its more general implications. It was not as if a researcher didn't come to a social project without hunches. One of course could not but have them. But Lewin saw the importance of staying with the observed phenomena and the encounter, letting the ideas about it be *induced* by the situation. "Meaning" in this sense was imminent in the situation. The researcher just needed to let it be, and, as it were, be its instrument. This led him to another maxim: "The way to understand a system is to try to change it." Conjecture and ideation only took you so far; the limitations or boundaries of a system—its real complex of dynamic forces—would reveal themselves in that which would change and that which didn't over time. The limits or boundaries of the system—what defined it as a system—were there to be discovered through *action*, less than what those in the system claimed they were at any point in time. In most fundamental terms, the system was always in some state of development, "frozen" in time as it may be sometimes, as he described.

These dynamic forces at play in a system were made up of "driving" and "restraining" forces. Together, they formed a complex that always sought dynamic homeostasis, what he called "quasi-stationary equilibrium." Human systems—individuals, groups, organizations and communities—operating in a field of other systems surrounding it, were largely in motion, driving forces moving forward, restraining forces holding their movement back. Together, the forces drove to self-regulating states of balance between them. Driving and restraining forces Lewin recognized could both be internal or external to a system. They were all in play. They were not, however, simply random. Looking at any particular situation itself would reveal what the actual balance was. So, in any particular case, the nature of the balance was something empirical to discover—or put another way, to be "experienced" by the players themselves and by anyone conducting action research.[9]

Lewin didn't specify what the inner nature of the forces were, but they were effectively energetic in quality as he described them, impacting each other and the other objects of concern as they moved in the field of action. For this reason, *Lewin concluded as a rule that if one pushed the driving forces over and above the restraining forces, there would always be an immediate reaction that raised the power of the restraining forces.* Understanding the principles of self-regulation, meant that players within the system, and those intervening from outside of it, seeking to shift a status quo needed to focus most attention on what would lower the impact of the restraining forces; this would enable the driving forces *in their actuality* to drive forward, and then not substantially regress. That principle alone has huge implications for consulting and OD. I think many of the figures profiled in this chapter do not keep this at the center of their attention, and this is certainly the case I have found with very many consultants.

One simple example of this is in the use of large group methods.[10] Early on in these methods' development, scholar-practitioners saw that groups that focused too much on their discontent—or that had "a problem focus"—got increasingly depressed. So, they reasoned that a focus on the future, not the past, would be most helpful. In fact, some approaches would more or less begin with a "jump to the future" to inspire the group for collective movement. It's not that past and current conditions or constraints were wholly ignored in these approaches, but they were not dwelled on, lest the system, it was feared, get stuck. The problem with these large-group methods was they were too often reduced to one-shot affairs, even though follow-through measures were built into their processes. I myself have experienced large group events being reduced essentially to one-time events. The challenge of their follow through lay in the fact that they typically were introduced into powerful cultures that were deeply constraining. Yes, the approaches were often intended to help change the cultures and conventional ways of doing things. But this predilection to focus on the future ignored Lewin's basic teaching that pushing driving forces would necessarily marshal and heighten the restraining forces. So, their results are predictable. If such methods are used *intentionally* to surface such powerful resistance, then in turn unpack it, that would be one thing. But practitioners' use of the approach, as it is taught, tends *not* to treat the approach as a primary vehicle for bringing resistance to light. These methods tend to be seen as sufficient onto themselves to create collaboratively designed action plans, enabling the organization to push forward in alignment.

There was an infamous case of an extreme application of a jump-to-the-future approach.[11] The intervention, at the telephone utility PacBell in the late 1980s, was deployed by Charles Krone, a well-regarded OD consultant at the time. However bizarre one might regard what his consulting team prescribed, including "new thinking language," it seems clear that the continuity of resistance of the organizational system's old order was not adequately accounted for in the intervention design. To the contrary, the consulting team held the mistaken idea that de-regulation and the breakup of the parent AT&T implied a sudden, "discontinuous jump" to a new organizational reality, leaving a blank slate from which a new organizational mindset, a "new paradigm," could take hold. This led directly to the attempt to superimpose a new managerial lexicon and organizational processes atop the existing system and human dynamics. Disaster ensued, as employees rebelled, productivity suffered, management was fired, the consulting engagement terminated, and the situation was spotlighted throughout the national media. That the consulting endeavor here may have met a fitting end because of some strange notions and especially coercive ways is not the point. More mainstream change efforts—such as reengineering and mergers and acquisitions—frequently proceed with similar, if less explicit, disregard for the continuity and vitality of resistance. As a result, they often suffer from a similar, if less cataclysmic, fate.

As we will explore more fully in this chapter, "Appreciative Inquiry" methods suffer some of the same conceptual flaws and practical consequences. Yes, focusing on what is positive and intentional in an organization is helpful. But when there is a failure to appreciate the depths of the resistance, or that which is genuinely frustrating and causing unhappiness—that in fact is not being roundly appreciative. That is roughly equivalent to a parent telling a child who is truly upset and may be acting out, to not complain and just focus on what's good. There is a time and place of course for such a focus. But when the child faces heartbreak, there is nothing more that can really be done other than to provide a safe space and understanding heart to allow the child to go straight through to their deepest feelings—to let the thunderstorm come, then the bright sun come shining through after the rains stop and the clouds clear. How is it that people miss seeing this, including the most erudite scholars?

One sees this attitude of denial rather pervasively today in how the phrase "do not bring negative energy to work" is enthusiastically greeted. I saw this phrase posted to wide acclaim on LinkedIn recently. Indeed, on the social media site, a photograph of a sign with this phrase on it at the entrance to an office building got many hits of "like" and numerous comments of praise. The photograph was also accompanied by the caption, "Think about other employees."

But what's an upset employee supposed to do who sees chronic, consequential issues in an organization not get addressed, after she and others repeatedly try to bring this to management's attention? Sit on her feelings? That in fact is the message heard and what actually happens—until the consequences start to flow. Even then, widespread denial is in play. In the next chapter on organization health and pathology, we will see the fallout of this failure to come to grips with acknowledging and expressing powerful feelings of discontent in the case of the consulting firm that folded.

To be sure, measures that accent the positive can be useful. However, that is mostly only so when they are joined by a larger understanding of the systemic context in which they are tried—not as a means to skirt what is an underlying pattern of resistance and deeper, functional discontent.

Appreciating the structure of the resistance—the shape the restraining forces take—is the essence of where Reich's contributions meet Lewin's, although Reich's work yields a level of energy understanding of a whole different order. As we introduced in Chapter 1, the organization self-organizes a character to mediate its history and functions in its interaction with the outer world, its "field" as Lewin would say. When that character takes shape to thwart systemic expression of the underlying emotional energies, it will take center stage, and remain there until its force is effectively dissolved, its continuing function no longer in play.

But organization character, in its energetic sense, is not essentially recognized in OD, and therefore cannot be the object of attention of those in the field. Resistance is not seen as the core of the problem, but rather something more or less inconvenient or "irrational," something to be managed around, side-stepped or contained. In this way, Lewin's work anticipated the application of Reich in OD, though this has gone unrecognized until now, as far as I can see. The roots of the dynamics are there, if unclear in its specifics of what constitutes healthy systems functioning. However, even here, Lewin's commitment to democratic, non-authoritarian values in organizational life is consonant with Reich's teachings on "natural work democracy."

One last point from Lewin's work is worth emphasizing here: his understanding that social science methods must not be "prematurely formalized."[12] Conceptual understanding needs to patiently await the ripeness of what is fully seen in development. Elsewise, one is toying with concepts that may preempt deeper comprehension. The rush to find "solutions" has plagued many in OD and consulting, as we often see often in our client-systems, exemplified in the brokerage firm case at the top of Chapter 1. Zeal to formalize ideas without fuller comprehension necessarily results in shallow concepts and solutions that do not work.

OTHER SEMINAL THINKERS: TRIST, SCHEIN, WEICK AND OTHERS

If there is someone after Lewin who one could arguably make the case belongs in his own class, I think it would be Eric Trist. Unlike Lewin, who was an Eastern European transplant in the United States, Trist hailed from England. Lewin's work especially took root in America in the 1930s, first at MIT, then at the University of Michigan's Institute for Social Research, and finally in his later experimental work with T-groups in the 1940s at what became National Training Labs (NTL) in Bethel, Maine. Trist's work hearkened back to Europe, to the English psychoanalyst Wilfred Bion in the 1930s, who went on to found the Tavistock Institute for Human Relations in London at the same time NTL was born. Trist was keenly interested in the relationship between workers and work, especially as it was reflected in the social and psychological consequences of work in British coal mines, as he described in a major 1952 paper.[13] Both Lewin and Trist were absorbed with understanding group dynamics.

Associated with what grew out of Tavistock, Trist was among the early innovators of a "socio-technical" understanding of organizations. The workplace consisted both of "social" relationships and a "technical" subsystem of relationships. The technical dimension referred to the actual relationships of the system's flow of work tasks— the core work of the system and procedurally how it was performed. The social dimension, in distinction, referred to the quality of the human relationships between workers in their performance of the work. This social aspect dealt with the workers' openness to each other needed in doing the work. This included their communications, their attitudes to one another, and their approach to or avoidance of each other when problems in the work were seen —in other words, the dynamics of the group at work. This is where, for example, the group's characteristic patterns of "fight or flight"—among what Bion later called the "basic assumptions" of a group—were manifested.[14]

As socio-technical approaches to consulting emerged to help groups maximize their working effectiveness, Trist devised a method of bringing workers together to discuss their work, sort out the relevant obstacles to task effectiveness, then collectively decide on new ways to perform the work. This amounted to system work-redesign by the workers themselves. This sometimes led to considerable heat in the conversations, as people had strong sentiments about what was working or not and why. Here, the "social subsystem" emerged. There was a shape to the discourse and patterns of communications, conflict, problem solving and decision making. He saw the way to reshape the set of operating social relationships was through the redesign of the technical work. This made addressing conflict, when it existed, unavoidable. However, if norms present served to hold back conversation, that would show up in the quality of the dialogue about the work, inhibiting the group's ability to redesign the work process.[15]

Efforts to paper over a clash of ideas would be counterproductive to the redesign endeavor, just as it was to task performance in the wider workplace, when avoidance as a pattern was dominant. Trist understood that systematic, *unencumbered* pursuit of the dialogue would result in a restructured work situation—in the work itself and in the quality of the relationships—if those naturally involved in the work could honestly take their differences all the way through to resolution. (We will see later in this chapter how advocates of Dialogical

OD do not adequately see and address *the characterological realities that encumber dialogue* and therefore keep matters stalled.)

This required there be an openness from management and union leadership to the workers participating this way. So, here too, Trist saw that the management groupings formed an *administrative* sub-system. That subsystem too needed attention as part of the redesign process so it managed in a way where the redesign groups operated freely.

All of this was a serious advance in understanding what makes for effective change in organizational life. Important, general learnings arose from socio-technical interventions. There were successes, and there were those that failed. Moreover, not every group or organization was ready to undertake such a radical process—for the approach effectively challenged power relationships that existed up, down and across the system as a whole. Bill Passmore has identified some of these roadblocks through a careful review of socio-tech cases, some cases that were successful and sustained, and other cases that were troubled. The troubled cases faltered because they did not diffuse through the rest of the organization, reverted in their functioning or collapsed altogether.[16] Essentially, he found that unless conditions existed from the outset that were supportive of such change, including demand, leadership sponsorship and a history of relationships where people could effectively talk and collaborate with each other, the efforts were in peril. Passmore saw that political events within the organization would overtake the work restructuring initiatives.

Increasing pressure was felt by socio-technical practitioners to design their way out of the impasse, and there was a highly technical strain of variation analysis to lean on. Before long, this technical mode of analysis is by and large where the method went and what it became. When I was trained in the mode in the late '80s, I was struck by the mechanical quality of the approach, quite different from Trist's original group dynamics conception. Its human dimension had gotten reduced to checklists of participants and desired behaviors.

Other ways to mitigate the difficulties also developed in socio-tech. Some hoped fresh start-ups at certain plants, designed on its principles, might allow those at the front of change to handpick organization members as well as shield the new entity from the rest of the corporate dynamics. But even then, well-designed operations that were successfully stood up could collapse. This was the fate of the radical new Enfield plant within Digital Equipment Corporation in the 1990s, when the parent company shut it down despite its success. This was a prominent instance I was familiar with because Enfield's General Manager, key in the plant's original design several years earlier, was a classmate in the graduate OD program I attended at Pepperdine.

Looked at as a whole, these roadblocks represent aspects of the organization's character; in Lewinian terms, they represent the persistent shape the restraining forces take inside the system. If the preponderance of such a defensive structure militates against free expression, it will itself subsume efforts to restructure or sustain a restructured work process. Once again, we see the governing importance of the organization's energy dynamics and character, grounded in Reich's work. Thus, even in socio-technical approaches, despite their cogency when conditions are right, the underlying energy and character dynamics must be factored into any qualifying assessment and intervention design for the improvement to take hold. It appears that merely unfortunate political events do not randomly do the efforts in but follow a course of logic dictated by the encompassing reality of the organizational character.

In just this way, Ed Schein's understanding of the *defensive* aspects of an organization culture—its character, as he's likened it—comes into play. Part of this is his insight into how an organization develops a culture with inhibitory qualities in the first place. His analysis of the socioemotional stages of group development is extremely suggestive: A group's character is influenced by how it moves through its developmental stages, when facing critical "marker events" in its early life. What Schein implies is that the developing organization can get hung up in "unfinished business" (as the Gestaltists call it) at a particular stage, if the event overwhelms the emerging entity's ability to absorb and move through the dynamics. The dynamics can thus "create a kind of developmental arrest in [the organization's] subsequent growth and functioning, permeating its operations, the ground from which its particular culture can arise."[17]

As a practical way of addressing group dynamics in an organization's development, Schein, even before his inquiry into culture, formulated a method he named "Process Consultation."[18] Schein saw that "human process" could be directly accessed by witnessing in meetings how group members encountered each other in their course of working together. Intervention could be of varying depths. The first, most surface level was simple act of observation on the part of the consultant about what was happening. Next was asking questions to the group about *what they saw happening,* not through leading questions, but those directly asked out of real curiosity about what was occurring in the group. The next level of intensity of intervention was for the consultant to note what she saw happening, aloud to the group. Lastly, the deepest level was for the consultant to offer the group her interpretation (or hunch) about why what happened, did. All of these could have the effect of slowing the group down to look at its process. This is so even with the simple act of observing; the members' felt presence of another in the room at any given moment could have effect. As a rule, Schein maintained the consultant should try the least intrusive measures first, going to the deeper levels as needed by the situation. Regardless of how deep the consultant went, Schein saw the consultant as needing to stay quite neutral in role, remaining at the margins of the group and not usurping the group's responsibility for its own assessments, communications or decision making. Apart from the ethics of it all, Schein otherwise feared that an intervention would backfire, the group would not learn or grow in its capability, or else the group would turn on the consultant.

Process Consultation could be used with groups of all kinds, but it seemed that Schein in his own consulting did this as a general matter with top or near top-level management teams. Process Consultation, by virtue of its neutrality, was differentiated from traditional "expert" consulting, where the consultant served as a subject matter expert on content issues the group faced. Process Consultation was likewise differentiated from a special case of expert consulting—what Schein called a "doctor-patient model," where the consultant did expert diagnosis, then prescribed needed solutions or defined the range of solutions from which a client picked.

As a method, Process Consultation was not unlike Trist's understanding of how to work with groups to come to terms with their own dynamics. But it was a more generalized approach, outside or not limited to the context of work-redesign. Comparatively, a basic strength of Trist's approach is that a group's energy powerfully builds as it redesigns its "real work"; the energy is concentrated and activates basic emotional issues at play. Thus, the moment is ripe for a skilled consultant to help the group consider and work through the underlying dynamics that arise. Master OD craftsman Tony Petrella operated in just this way with his activist, interventionist style. He asked pointed human process questions to the teams as they did their redesign tasks, leading them to resolve basic problems in how they worked together. In this way, he helped Trist's and Schein's ideas vividly come alive.[19]

Notwithstanding its potential power, Process Consultation sometimes has its drawbacks. In the name of avoiding intrusion and a top-down, doctor-patient relationship, the approach's usual stance of keeping to a strict neutrality can end up leading the client astray. As far back as 1970, D. G. Bowers at Michigan's Institute for Social Research, wrote:

> A sick client system that is unwilling to provide necessary information [even] through anonymous instrumentation is scarcely likely to present it openly and voluntary simply because of "good process." Sick organizations, like sick human beings, often are unable to face their shortcomings, pains and problems, or at least are unable until a competent therapist has, using a competent

diagnosis, led them through to a point of some recovery. There is some likelihood—in fact some probability—that process consultation will often result in enthusiastic pursuit of the wrong treatment, a great-acting out of a rationalization. Evidence on this point is not likely to be forthcoming freely or soon. Client systems which are enjoying acting out a defense mechanism are likely to shower praise on the change agent who helped them do so, and the change agent is likely to mistake praise for a successful operation. In any event, neither is likely to want to devote much time or effort to probing for possible illusions in their joint undertaking. This suggests that a reevaluation of the comparative strengths and weaknesses of the process consultation and doctor-patient models may be in order. The latter is perhaps weak, but viable; the former may well suffer from a potentially fatal flaw.[20]

This has general implications for the practice of OD. As argued earlier, carrying out lengthy diagnostics or patiently working with the client system as the consultant goes from one presenting issue to another itself can backfire: The effort to keep to "good process" may set up a *verboten* where the consultant never quite gets to the issues' underlying connection, the underlying pattern of movement right in front of them. When this happens, the consultant gets caught up in following the lead of the client-system that is lost to begin with—and ends up going in circles. In psychotherapeutic treatment, this is akin to what Freud called "wild analysis," the therapist going in circles tracing every inch of one free association to another, but never quite getting the whole picture, never moving into deeper emotional territory, leading nowhere. Freud called this practice "wild" because there was plenty of motion and commotion, but not *movement towards* constructive therapeutic resolution. In this way, the analyst colluded with the defensive maneuvers of the patient. This is another risk it surely seems with Dialogic OD, where there is a strong anti-diagnostic bias.

Moreover, Bowers' insight uncovers a larger gap that has generally run through OD. The field by and large has not come to terms with the existence of organization pathology, nor known what to do with it when it is seen. Many practitioners, professors too, I find are squeamish on the subject. "Sick organizations" are often not amenable to educationally based strategies or ones focused on "mindset" shifts. Curiously, OD early came to stress its educational nature despite its roots in *group emotional dynamics* both from Lewinian and Tavistock traditions. As we shall see, some thinkers in their conceptions— all of the post--modern cast of mind—basically define sickness out of existence. Chapter 3 covers this subject in some depth, as it looks at very specific dimensions of organization health and sickness and why *both* are essential to understand. Reich's grasp of natural energy systems, lets us understand the full range of what is in play here: the rich sources of creatively constructive and emotionally fulfilling work *and* also the conditions under which the turned back energy becomes destructive.

The University of Michigan's Karl Weick very much saw dynamic movement as cardinal to organizational life. For Weick, organizations were entities inherently in action; in effect, more "verbs" than "nouns." This is literally reflected in the titling of his *The Social Psychology of Organizing*, which first appeared in 1969.[21] Organizations by nature are "loosely coupled" and "enacted," more elastic than engineered. They are in successive states of "being organized" from their conception on. For Weick, they form less out of rational, predetermined ends (or purposes, as theorists from Weber on down contend), than from a process where divergent interests first stream together then converge. Out of this, a larger interdependent function and collective structure emerges: "the organization." As referenced in Chapter 1, Weick recognizes that repetitive "interlocked behaviors" constitute the state of being organized. As the organization takes shape, he sees:

> . . .the [original] diverse ends remain, but they become subordinated to an emerging set of shared ends. This shift is one of the

most striking that occurs in group life and it is one of the most complex.[22]

Weick does not frame his conceptualization in energetic terms, but like Lewin's, his work has parsimony with Reich's. For Weick, his notions of the *structuralization* of an organization from divergent sources is consistent with Reich's conception of "superimposition" and self--organizing, streaming systems.

Yet Reich's understanding of a primary energy at work takes us further than Weick in fundamental ways. First, it accounts for the charge and excitement present and observable at the act of organizational creation. Secondly, Weick doesn't account for how culture, or character, itself represents a structuralized layer that is energetically derived and continually mediates the organization with the energetic field that surrounds it (as I theorized in Chapter 1). And because Weick does not see the energy at the root of dynamic social movement, he does not acknowledge the conditions under which such a structuralized layer becomes a functional disorder. This too becomes a limitation in seeing the reality of organizational sickness and a practical, regenerative path to health.

Like Weick, another theorist oriented to seeing organizational phenomena as organic and dynamic is McGill's Henry Mintzberg. For example, Mintzberg's 1994 *The Rise and Fall of Strategic Planning* concludes that the very term "strategic planning" is an oxymoron because strategy is a kind of spontaneous synthesis, while planning is a formal analytic process.[23] Overly structured departments and methods devoted to strategic planning can lead organizations to confined ways of operating when expansive and imaginative thinking are needed. The same sense of dynamism at work infuses Mintzberg's earlier *The Structuring of Organizations*, where he sees the organizing process as establishing "a system of regulated flows."[24] These flows of work, including their patterns of communication, action and decision making, are systemically regulated by a number of functional subsystems he sees as basic to all organizations. These subsystems constitute what he identifies as any organization's "deep structure": its *"strategic apex," "middle line" and "operating core."*[25] I came to call these subsystems, as a set, *the major cross--cutting segments of an organization, akin to Reich's somatic segments for individuals.*

Mintzberg recognizes that these major subsystems can themselves take variable shape. He sees their variation depends on the organization's age, the nature of its work and the complexity of the environment in which it functions. He also understands that these subsystems can become rigid in their functioning and very subject to political pressure in how they operate. However, Mintzberg does not see them informed by how the organization's *past* gets encoded into the structure based on the blocking of energy at early stages of the organization's development. In Chapters 4 and 5, I contend the organization develops normative and formal structure—*armor*—to defend against its early "unfinished, socioemotional business" and to contain the spontaneous movement of energy at work. This I see as the major source of the organization's difficulties. I see it as *an adaptive functional disorder* in the body of the firm, reflecting the character of the organization. In contrast, for Mintzberg, mischievous political behavior is the culprit when organization function and structures go badly awry.

Barry Oshry, who gave up an academic career at Boston University to instead immerse himself in group laboratory training workshops, saw these layers operating as a system's "tops, middles and bottoms." Oshry particularly emphasizes the dynamic interplay of these groupings, their cross--current behaviors and perceptions of each other, and in general terms, the characteristic ways they disempower themselves and affect the power of the others. In his 1994 book *Seeing Systems*, Oshry graphically depicts this interplay as a dance between the three subsystems.[26]

Oshry, like Mintzberg, sees "power" as the issue which is being mediated between the groupings. For Oshry, the ineffective use of power by tops, middles and bottoms to do their natural work, and the attitudes and emotional patterns they get stuck in, are the source of their own and the wider system's troubles. Oshry comes very close to Reich's understanding of work energy as "living, productive work power," the wellspring of social movement and social constellations. Another affinity with the organizational implications of Reich's work is Oshry's description of the characteristic ways tops, middles and bottoms poorly deploy their power and mutually get stuck in disempowering scenarios. True, Oshry doesn't recognize the resulting disempowerment in terms a more refined understanding of organization character type yields. Nor does he speak to different sequences of intervention needed to address and resolve the *particular way each character gets stuck*. But I have found his generic strategies and tactics that help mobilize tops, middles and bottoms to be very practical and valuable. I make use of his methods in my consulting work in light of the energy dynamics of character. I believe this more refined understanding of energy dynamics and character supports the fuller use of Oshry's methods in sustained, whole system intervention efforts. Chapters 6 and 7 describe my attention to the sequence of interventions in each of the character type consulting cases.[27]

One very influential, classical organization theory that speaks in expressly energetic terms is laid out in Katz and Kahn's *The Social Psychology of Organizations,* still a standard text in graduate organizational studies programs over fifty years from when it first appeared.[28] Derived from the biologist Ludwig von Bertalanffy's General Systems Theory, Katz and Kahn see organizations as a species of "energic input-output" social systems—"flagrantly open systems in that the input of energies and the conversion of output into further energic input consist of transactions between the organization and its environment."[29] The organization itself is reduced to a complex "throughput mechanism," in effect an elaborate machine. Because of the presumed universality of the Second Law of Thermodynamics, the view is that an organization must import and store more energy than it exports to counter the degenerative effects of entropy and thus maintain homeostasis. (Reich's laboratory research in physics, as noted in the Prolegomenon, challenges the universal entropy assumption.) Katz and Kahn do not see that the energy arises, once the organization is born, from a structuralized, dynamic energic core, a core that itself is spontaneously generative and regenerative, as Weick implies, and as the application of Reich's work to the organizational realm suggests.

Katz and Kahn's formulation leads to conceptual contradictions and practical difficulties in effecting organizational change. Without resorting to a "big bang" theory of an event that happened at the beginning of time, classical systems thinking has trouble coping with the logical question, "Where does the energy in the organization come from to begin with?" Its claim that it must be merely imported from other natural systems, of whatever kind, is illogical. The illogic arises because these systems too (even individual human systems) are assumed to derive their energy from outside from their conception. The interior or *endogenous* dimension of energy buildup, scaling and creation is missed in this formulation.

So, what actually is the nature of the energy being spoken of? And how exactly does it function in organizations? Yes, beyond physical resources, this energy must certainly be human labor. But human labor represents something more than inputs and outputs. People embody in organizations the streaming energy that Reich identified as the basic primary energy of life, an energy that functions differently than mechanical energy does as part of social units. So, once the energy concentrates into an organizational form, as I have contended, it begins to operate as a structuralized, dynamic core with creative, self-organizing properties of its own.

Without this understanding, the input-output conception becomes both mystical and mechanistic at the same time: mystical in that the system is seen as only endlessly "abstracting" energy from the outside; mechanistic in that it reduces organization life to a hollow, throughput mechanism. The synergistic and generative dynamics of the organization in this way are essentially neglected. Troubled intervention consequences naturally follow these two extremes of thinking: on the one hand, "starry eyed" transformation initiatives seeking to "infuse" change (as in the PacBell instance); and, on the other hand, highly rationalist approaches, as socio-tech increasingly became reduced, seeking to engineer or "design" systemic change on the other. In either case, the innate energy of the system is not fully accounted for. Nor is the structuralized character that contains and typically inhibits it. Thus, the interventions that come from such thinking are subject to failure and engender further troubles. The clinical, psychodynamic tradition in the field that we turn to next seeks to address the detrimental effects of an organization's character structure.

PSYCHODYNAMIC CONTRIBUTIONS: KETS DE VRIES AND HIRSCHHORN

It is curious that machine model images of organizations became so dominant in OD as a field, given the field's humanistic roots. Certainly, Frederick Taylor's early twentieth century application of Weber's principles in organizational improvement schema were mechanistic in quality. But Taylor's original industrial engineering school was soon followed by a more human relations brand of thinking, as reflected in the Hawthorne studies, Lewin's work and Bion's at Tavistock. This brand of thinking gave original impetus to OD and also ways of thinking about systems originally associated with Tavistock. Both traditions were heavily informed by psychodynamic approaches. For example, Bion, a physician trained in general psychotherapy and later psychoanalysis, was concerned throughout his career with the psychiatric casualties and group behavior effects of war. He held official British appointments attending to soldiers and others who suffered trauma in the First and Second World Wars. Likewise, group dynamics work associated with OD's NTL tradition was heavily influenced by depth psychology approaches over and above the influence of Lewin. Freud's work and those who followed, Jung, Adler, Perls and Rogers for example, clearly informed the work of more than a few OD scholars and practitioners.

There were a number of important organizational and management thinkers in the 1960s, '70s and '80s very influenced by Freud; Harry Levinson and Abraham Zaleznik two of prominence. Warren Bennis and Edgar Schein were also clearly influenced. However, the two I will focus on in this section have made particularly systemic contributions relevant to our study here, Manfred Kets de Vries and Larry Hirschhorn, both serious students of psychoanalysis. Together, they represent some of the strengths and limitations to date of the clinical approach to organizational life and change, to the phenomenon of "organizations on the couch," as Kets de Vries has termed it.[30]

Kets de Vries, with his associate Danny Miller, made a major contribution in the psychoanalytic tradition with 1984's *The Neurotic Organization: Diagnosing and Changing Counterproductive Styles of Management*.[31] This entry is essentially an organizational character typology, though a typology defined more loosely as a set of "styles" representing recurring, dysfunctional patterns of organizational behavior. Kets de Vries and Miller are quite explicit that they are dealing with organizational pathology and "sick" systems, and they recognize this sets them apart from many in the organizational change arena. The focus is on systems' collective, "neurotic" managing styles—distinguished by an organization's recurring, patterned interpersonal conflicts and shared fantasies, rationalizations and defensive routines. Kets de Vries and Miller make it clear they are not addressing anything as extreme as psychotic dysfunction at the organization level, but the average way many firms manage; that is, how such firms manage to make their way in the world as they compromise their work in the face of their psychopolitical realities. The authors make a point to say there is "no clear dividing line" between health and sickness in groups and organizations. This is in line with psychoanalytic therapy today; health is essentially seen as the relative absence of the disordered styles, less as something specific and definable unto itself. (Unlike this, Reich held to a specific, tangible, bioenergetic criterion of individual emotional health; this marked the beginning of his differentiation from the rest of psychoanalysis, which increasingly developed into ego-psychology.) A particular neurotic organizational style is meant to describe the way any individual organization may chiefly function, including the style's effects on a firm's *companywide* strategy, structure and performance. Nonetheless, the framework's primary intervention focus is on working with top leadership teams and other managers who set the tone for the rest of the system. This is also where Kets de Vries sees psychodynamically informed, one-on-one executive coaching can adjunctively be of help.

In all, five neurotic organizational styles are identified and impressively described, drawing on the authors' consulting experiences and psychoanalytic orientation: Paranoid, Compulsive, Dramatic, Depressive and Schizoid styles. There is no healthy type identified in the framework. The chief tenet is that organizations are managing basic conditions of uncertainty and therefore always handling relative degrees of anxiety; this is seen as inherent in people working together and in work itself. As is the case with individual psychoanalysis, the overarching, neurotic styles are essentially coping mechanisms to address core anxiety, activated in the organizational context by the system's encounters with the environment and especially by the personal and interpersonal dynamics of founders as well as executive team members. Clearly, while the authors recognize there are many "stakeholders of the organizational mind," to use a phrase of Ian Mitroff's, the dominant leadership team is seen as paramount.[32]

Multiple stakeholders or not, there is no recognition of natural energy dynamics at the very core of organizational life, dynamics that drive excitement—and provide a basis for chronic anxiety when frustrated in the first place—and which under supportive conditions drive towards health. The natural pulsatory cycle of expansion (excitement) and contraction (anxiety) is not recognized. Moreover, there *is no drive for health recognized*, no basic need for felt gratification at work suffusing all levels of the organization, top to bottom.

The implicit if unstated belief is that such a drive is a fantasy, a "utopian" wish, entirely an artifact of a neurotic individual or group style. This is vintage, late psychoanalysis, unlike the origins of the field in which the young Freud with Breuer recognized the *actual neurosis* and the primacy of the emotional energies, and to which Reich was heir. For Kets de Vries and Miller, it is all essentially psychological dysfunction at work, most importantly at the top of the organization—the organizational mind. It is a dysfunction assumed, at best, only something to mitigate.

But where is thrill and excitement of work in all this? Insuperable binds are created by this orientation. What is made of the genuine joy, fulfillment and relief people experience when a meaningful piece of work is accomplished—in vibrant concert with colleagues or in deep, satisfying solitude? How does one explain the systemic effects of an Oshry's work that helps free up and unleash the power of the middle of an organization? Or the amount of energy present in Mintzberg's continuous flows between subsystems and outer world? What is the source of the ever-present, creative self-organizing of groups and organizations a Weick recognizes? These phenomena are all ascribed to the avoidance of anxiety? Fantasy? If the "head" of the organization is simply in charge, then what is the "charge" felt in the entire body of the organization? And what can organizational leaders—or consultants—do to *help enable this natural excitement to flourish?* Is there no difference between a fantasy and a genuinely inspired organizational dream?

Surely, there are shared defenses operating that lead to destructive effects, including irrational organizational wishes, styles and behaviors. This includes of course those that are overly idealistic and without objective foundation as they present. This is the price of dysfunctional organizational character structures, sometimes, as already shown, entirely debilitating. Nonetheless, there is *a something* the character is defending against. To see it only as anxiety is terribly one-sided, whose net effect is to flatten out seeing and dealing with the full range of affect, including the core excitement of genuine achievement and fulfillment at work. In fact, I hold the view that it is this mutual core excitement that gets routinely frustrated in the first place, initially and primarily by frustrating external sources and events, then inwardly by the internalized group character that has arisen to cope with the frustration.

Larry Hirschhorn, an economist also learned in psychoanalysis, and who cofounded the International Society for the Psychoanalytic Study of Organizations, has come to recognize the fundamental problem of a singular focus on anxiety.

Hirschhorn's early thinking in *The Workplace Within* was largely grounded in the same assumptions as Kets de Vries and Miller's. For Hirschhorn, the inherent anxiety of work gives rise to "social defenses" within organizations to cope with it.[33] Hirschhorn provides rich descriptions of the moment-to-moment consulting process, the choices that confront those intervening to help "unpack" the defensive routines. And he uses a method that is largely based on Trist's original conception: engaging the organization in work-design and redesign efforts that bring the defenses to light in order then to lower them. Hirschhorn is a sophisticated practitioner who sees the social defenses operating deeply within the system, "the workplace within," less as a function of what is simply happening at the top. He moves close to seeing them as embodied phenomena. He doesn't drag up models in working with clients, but he strives to meet clients in terms they experience moment to moment.

Comparatively, as I see it, Hirschhorn goes to the root emotional dynamics that undergird the behavioral and cognitive patterns of systems more than it does seem Kets de Vries. For example, in a recent blog, where Kets de Vries applied his analytic insights to counter the broad social "addiction" to destructive charismatic leaders, he sees the needed remedies as heavy re-education and behavioral reinforcement, not an unwinding of the underlying dynamics, the ground of the addiction.[34] In contrast, Hirschhorn's instincts are to help organizations *unwind* their irrational strivings, step outside "the anxiety chain," and move towards work that is itself "reparative." More than simply offering up cognitive and behavioral remedies, this puts Hirschhorn, it seems, closer to addressing the primary energetic roots of a system's troubles.

Over the years, Hirschhorn has steadily moved in this direction. Without throwing away the dark forces that drive organizational life, as some in the post-modern vein do, he has come to see the presupposition of anxiety as the source of all the difficulties as not enough. In a 2021 paper, Hirschhorn writes:

> The Tavistock model of organisations is by far and away the most influential framework for considering how psychoanalytic thinking can inform our understanding of organisational functioning. In this article I suggest that, as powerful as it is, it is also limited because it *privileges the experience of anxiety as the master key* for unlocking why organisations succeed or fail. *In this regard, it omits a wider range of emotions that are salient to the understanding of the psychodynamics of organizations.*[35]

In his reworking of the Tavistock model, Hirschhorn sees the need to acknowledge other emotions as well, among them: "excitement," "happiness," "pleasure," "desire," "sadness" and "pain." He also sees Milhaly Cikzentmilalyi's concept of "work as flow" as vital to understand "work that is *intrinsically* satisfying and motivating." Hirschhorn notes this is quite evident in the work of craftspeople and artists, similar to how I describe the play and interplay of jazz musicians in Chapter 3.

There is more to Hirschhorn's complex rendering of the dynamics than I summarize here. But I wish to highlight two essential dimensions Hirschhorn brings forth. First, that core to what animates organizational life is "real work." This insight he particularly credits to Zaleznik's incisive thought. He sees the inherent risks and uncertainties in the performance of work—questions people ask themselves such as, "Can I count on others to do their part? What happens if. . .? Will I be up to the task?"—can of course be natural sources of anxiety. They can also lead, along with feelings of desire, as Hirschhorn stresses, to a sense of danger and even dread. All of these can give rise to the social defenses as functional hedges. And yet "real work," as Hirschhorn sees, is also the ground for excitement, joy and thrill experienced by those at work when conditions are right. Hirschhorn does not quite sight a vitalizing work energy at the bottom of it all, as Reich so clearly did and I contend, but this brings him close.

This starts to move us beyond the one-sidedness of the psychodynamic conception of work. Much clinical workplace theory and practice has essentially been trapped in a negative conception of organizational health. In this, it does not much differ from Katz and Kahn's view of the perpetual need to overcome entropy, to produce the effect of "negative entropy." A dark, empty universe is first in these conceptions. A more vibrant world at its roots, a world that is naturally self-organizing and generative, is something else entirely indeed. Groups and organizations that are reparative in nature require less engineering than they do support—"developmental cultures," as Hirschhorn says, that lower the need for social defenses to be enacted and let forces other than those compelled by avoidance to bloom. We are back to Lewin. And on more fundamental grounds, we are pointing to Reich's understanding of a bioenergy at work, the pulse of life.

POST-MODERN CONTRIBUTIONS—CHAOS, COMPLEXITY, APPRECIATIVE INQUIRY, DIALOGUE

There is a sense in which this is the aim of the organizational post-modernists: to rescue the world from some of the dark assumptions that have shrouded it. The scholar-practitioners I have described as post-modernists here have shed some interesting light, their work in this vein in OD all coming to the fore after the days of my thesis in the late '80s. I find their contributions significant in their own right and to consider in light of the energy and organizational character terms I've pursued understanding of over the years. I treat them as a group here, because I believe their approaches share certain common assumptions and strengths. But I also see them as sharing a fatal flaw. I believe in some ways, in trying to rescue the world from its dark hues and liberate organizations, they risk throwing the baby out with the bathwater, leading to building up the defensive routines of an organization unwittingly. To a greater or lesser degree, the post-modern strains in OD—Chaos and Complexity Theories, Appreciative Inquiry and Dialogical OD, the four treated here—I see still can perpetuate the darkness, despite their avowed intentions to do otherwise.

This was evident in the earlier example of the government agency in Chapter 1 whose large-scale use of a concerted dialogical method backfired. This is not a one-off. I will show how the common logic and assumptions of these approaches—current fashions in the field— *necessarily* must lead there, conceptually and practically, when powerful organizational character structures are operating and not at the center of consultative attention. These four strains also share a fundamental misunderstanding of energy dynamics in not seeing clearly when and how the dynamics can turn destructive in effect. These dynamics can prove detrimental to system performance and human fulfillment, and if not seen clearly can lead away from essential restorative pathways. Substantively, the existence of organization armor and character structure goes unrecognized in the post-modern conceptions, whatever terms are used. In the well-intentioned effort to recover wholeness and flow, I believe post-modern thinking generally overlooks what is prevalent and obvious in how organizations actually function—*organizations' frequent internalized blocking to the flow.* Moreover, post-modern thinking does not clearly see the functionally adaptive nature to the blocking. Thus, despite all the talk of deconstructing linear thinking, its proponents cannot focus intervention efforts on deconstructing chronically compromised structural dynamics: *dynamics that are functionally inhibitory when they come into play and while temporal in origin have become frozen in time.* The very emotional charge behind their structuralization means these dynamics cannot simply be re-educated, talked or thought out of existence. Nor can they be drummed out of life through behavior modification. An energetically effective *sociotherapy*, I maintain, is required.

Proponents of the application of Chaos Theory in OD, notably Meg Wheatley in her *Leadership and the New Science: Discovering Order in a Chaotic World*, see there is movement in nature that has flow at its source, building in swirls and other patterns observable throughout nature. She references Weick's striking organizational concepts and shows stunning photographs of recurrent patterns in nature.[36] This is all to the good. But there is no looking at how and where these swirls can ossify and become rigid, signature operating structures in organizations, embodying the character of the inhibited energy movement. They can become deeply anchored emotional patterns, where the energy turns over on itself in ever increasing concentration, given adverse conditions that then thwart its free, extended movement and discharge. The assertion is that order comes routinely out of chaos, in generative, mostly benign ways. But what happens when destructive, chaotic forces build and *become* ordered in organizations, characteristic patterns of dysfunction and human unhappiness at work? And how does this happen?

There is serious social science research in the application of Chaos Theory in human social process and organizations. The research recognizes the problem of self-organizing, hierarchically layered states of organizational dysfunction emerging from a wider social field. The emphasis is on understanding nature and the human world in the first place as consisting of unpredictable, nonlinear events. Some sympathetic to the social science application of Chaos models caution against their uncritical use and overuse because of the starting point of seeing human life as having greater unpredictability than other natural phenomena. Some advocates come close to saying human social systems lie outside nature—or at least claim that our ability to understand our roots in nature are inherently limited. They then proceed to throw nature out of organizational thinking categorically.[37] Reich's work is a direct challenge here, but so are others, as noted earlier, who have sought to integrate social and biological anthropology.

In the end, Chaos Theory seems locked in a Newtonian paradigm, despite its pretensions to break out of classical systems thinking. "Negative entropy"—grounded in the Second Law of Thermodynamics—is the theory's source of self-generative and regenerative phenomena, not an entirely free energy with properties and lawful, streaming movement of its own, an energy out of which mass and structure emerge. Again, the *something* that is spontaneously moving in the field, outwardly and inwardly in organized systems, living and nonliving, remains unexamined. This is what Reich came to call orgone energy, describing its rich properties. His understanding of it is still little appreciated or known, so in this the post-modernists are not alone.

Those working in the new Chaos paradigm remain unaware of Reich's anomalous experimental findings to the universality of entropy, even as Einstein had observed when he engaged with Reich in its laboratory inquiry and immediately saw its implications. And its proponents do not recognize a pulsating bioenergy central to human life, in sexuality or work life, with requirements for concentration and discharge. They are thus unable to bring to light the energy's inherent implications for social systems and human organizations. The energy itself remains in the dark and Chaos Theory literally remains in dark-matter physics. The consultant ends up not paying attention to the emergent character disorder; the central problem at the base of the organization's troubles once again it seems remains obscured, in the dark.

A close kin to Chaos Theory in its assumptions is Complexity Theory. Scholar-practitioner Patricia Shaw sees organizations as loosely coupled, nonlinear "webs of relationships" in generative flows, more than as bounded systems. However, unlike Wheatley's penchant to teach its general principles, this leads Shaw to focus on how an OD consultant enters and engages with a workplace's players day to day.

Her approach is not at all didactic, nor especially oriented to holding special workshops and events. As described in her 2002 account, *Changing Conversations in Organizations: A Complexity Approach to Change*, Shaw is very moment-to-moment and dialogically centered. The consulting role is that of a co-player in interchange with others, joining conversations where they stand, seeing where they go, with their meanings to be derived over time. She sees in fact the organization itself as a conversational process, made up of many conversations that are informal, improvised and emergent. As trust is gradually earned, the consultant is positioned to help knit the diverse conversations together, facilitating bringing others in for wider reach. Shaw seeks to effect socially constructive movement.[38]

It is an interesting, ethnographic approach, one of *living in* the system, not simply observing or doing something to it. She doesn't rule out the value of workshops, (e.g., large-scale events like Future Search), but sees these as simply moments in the much larger, real-time, "lived world" of the organization. I have experienced the value of being positioned as a consultant, both in external and internal OD roles, who helps in real time stitch together diverse activities for overall effect. In an organization I was in as an internal, I found its people especially appreciative of such a stitching-together role.

However, I was quite activist in my approach. As a "co-player," I was expected—and wanted—to do more than participate in conversations. I designed various events, initiated and participated in work-redesign sessions, helped people plan together, and even wrote speeches for top executives, sitting them down to think about what they wanted to say, then helping them say it—"conversations" with them certainly, and of a sort with the organization. These were activities without which these executives might otherwise have not shared their thoughts so fully on important matters with others in the enterprise. This was a very action-oriented culture, co-players didn't have a chance who were seen as passive, not taking initiative, and *doing something*. I had to find ways to embed conversations in action-taking roles, my own and those of others. I see this as one of several inherent limitations in Shaw's approach and in Complexity Theory more generally.

First, it presupposes the organizational environment is open to such a "conversational-only" role for the consultant—talking and more strictly listening, not doing. Organizations with a bias for action and "real work," much less ones that are toxically so, will almost out of hand reject consultants playing such a role from the start, making their facilitation of fuller organizational movement impossible. Such rejection in this kind of culture is the force and gating effect of organizational character, which is ignored in the approach. Gentler organizations might receive such an approach, but then they are the ones which may especially need a push, a kick-start, a designed event to help mobilize and *get them moving and "charged."* The energy at work in such a system as it presents could be so mild that it never sufficiently concentrates to develop the force of movement needed for effective flow and discharge; this inhibits the organization from getting its core or "real work" done. Conversational-only approaches do not seem suitable for an organization that is characteristically anemic. In fact, I have seen them collude with such a system, masking and creating further problems. Similarly, urgent organizational issues will not get addressed in time if characteristic sluggishness is at hand.

I was called to help a slow-moving business division at Hewlett Packard (HP) get moving on its efforts to speed up its product development life cycle. A sensitive, analytical and conversation-oriented organization, I found when I arrived its people had gotten stuck in endlessly talking about its culture; "the HP culture," as they described it. They analytically surfaced it in their conversations as a barrier that held them back. This *talking on and on about the culture* was a very example of the characteristic sluggishness operating. The sluggishness came in through the back door, as it were, by all the talk.

My help to start was by simply pointing this out—my impression that this was how the culture constrained them and slowed down their product cycle, and that they were enacting again as we spoke. There was indeed conversation about this, but what is notable is that it re-quired me to be *diagnostically proactive*. My comments rang true to them, quite immediately. It wasn't long from there, that what helped get them moving was a program of special work-redesign sessions *à la* Trist concentrating the division's charge, and where we could further unpack the sluggish behavioral patterns as they arose. At the bottom of it all seemed *fear of movement*. This took repeated efforts in different venues for them to tolerate seeing and get firmer traction on. But they did. *Movement, not talk, was key in helping them come to see.* We used words, yes, but visceral attitudes and observations operated more largely throughout the consultation to induce them to move. Sometimes, it was merely the right look into the eyes of anoth-er. Increasingly, this freed them up, and they felt some relief getting off the endless treadmill. Their need was *to feel* what was keeping them at bay, *to stop* constantly analyzing, "processing" and talking about it, and to feel the fulfillment in the flow and outcomes of what became its faster product cycle time.

Once again, we see the collision of energy and organizational char-acter at play and the need to mobilize movement. Ironically, the complex-conversational approach, especially when it is part of the characterological problem to begin with, ends up being overly sim-plistic, not meeting the system where it actually is—in action, not just its words. Processes *in action* reveal where and how a system is bounded, as Lewin reminds, in what changes and what stands still. This is organizational character at work. At HP, in this instance, it was essential to see and address the character inhibitions so the play-ers could collectively get off the dime.

Appreciative Inquiry (AI) has set off something of a stampede among OD people and others in recent years. The enthusiasm does not look like it will let up any time soon. What began as a variety of "positive psychology," as a strategy and method for change in organizations, has now become much bigger. Its practice has not just been seen as a set of tactics and techniques—if, important, empathic ones—for use especially in the right workplace circumstances. Nor has it simply

been seen as a general attitude and helpful state of mind for consultants, for people in organizations, or for people for that matter
at large. AI has become a self-described "philosophy of life."[39] AI's
chief architect and advocate, David Cooperrider has recently coedit-
ed a new volume claiming that AI is "the leadership revolution that
is changing *everything*" in the world.[40]

I have used appreciative methods to good effect, as I will describe.
But they have their limitations, in principle and practice.

AI's problems inhere in not recognizing that basic problems do exist,
that only possibilities do. This of course is self-contradictory and factually false. Are there not *possibilities* for problems to exist? And what
about finding possibilities in accepting some problems *as problems*,
not quickly dispatching them as "only really" possibilities? Certainly,
there are limitations of thinking everything is a problem—a tendency in classical organization analysis, with its emphasis on diagnostics
and interventions to "fix" problems. AI set itself early on against this
as a corrective. But is thinking all things to be only positive possibilities any truer? Are there not restraining forces as well as driving
forces? And what does one make of Lewin's insight that when there
is focus on pushing positive forces in a system's social field, whatever
restraining forces coexist will be heightened?

"The power of positive thinking," as Norman Vincent Peale made
popular in the 1950s, has its value, of course. But it is terribly
one-sided—as much as the psychodynamic theorists argued everything was simply a function of anxiety. Like Hirschhorn's critique of
the Tavistock model, there are other, even opposite variables at play,
a whole range of sentiments to consider.

I began this book with the stark observation that human unhappiness at work is widespread today. Human misery in the workplace
is a real thing. So is hope, disappointment, sadness, longing and
despair. Frustration, irritation, upset and anger. Just ask people, see
them and listen—to their words and body language. All this will not
be banished by saying these are solely a function of not looking on

the bright side nor seeing possibilities, yet *never facing the actuality of the problem at hand*. This is the collective problem of taking trips to Abilene, an organizational syndrome as Jerry Harvey has so well described: the failure to address conflict and disagreement in pursuit of specious agreement.[41] But this trap is what AI often falls into in its own diagnosis of interpersonal situations. In this way, AI, like Peale's thinking earlier, has its own dark side: When it comes down to it, it can be coercive, intolerant of admitting the existence of problems, much less work through them to get to the other side. This even has a native pessimism about it. The sun won't come out on its own if thunderstorms exist. We must force the sunshine and pretend there is no downpour.

AI gets trapped in its claims of universality, a limitless world that is all negotiated "social construction." However, people are not merely social beings. We are *embodied* beings, *biosocial* creatures as Reich made clear and as I contend is at root in organizational life. We pulsate, expand and contract, breathe in and out, hold our breath and rush breathlessly, inspire and expire, excite and bleed; we love, work and seek to know. This means we have *needs*, a full range of emotions that seek expression and satisfaction. All this cannot be seriously engaged by only admitting to the sweetness and light of life.

Of course, there is light. And even if darkness in the end is the absence of light, darkness still exists as reality—with real effects. Perceptions of the dark aspects of people's worlds may in part be socially construed and socially constructed, to be sure. But that also encompasses the social construction of their denial, their suppression, and the collective enactment of taboos, sometimes destructive of deeper drives. Taboos in the workplace cannot simply be talked out of existence, as seen in the case of the government agency whose dialogical effort failed. Taboos have emotional power that must be worked through, vicissitudes and all, if their disturbing aspects are to be dissolved. Constructive development, discovery and deed get sacrificed commonly at work by studied avoidance and evasion. What practiced OD person hasn't seen this and knows its truth? Needs and wants matter, and so does their internalized, social denial; they inevitably find their way into the picture. AI, I do not believe, is equipped to address them. I have suffered in work situations (and personally for that matter outside of work) from its misplaced use. Learning sometimes comes hard. And, yes, that can be appreciated, but it may not well come with a smile, at least not at first.

At the World Bank, in work with a thirty-person team, where I had been asked to help get better trust and morale jump-started, I saw the value and limitations of appreciative methods. The unit's two co-leaders who called me, told me that peoples' experience at work, with each other and those they served, was unpleasant, and the quality and quantity of the work getting done was compromised. They said that team members were stuck in a reactive, downward spiral. The co-leads also said this was true for their own experience with the team (and with each other as they came to admit). I worked with them to pull the team together in a two-day offsite so all the members could consider their way of working together, their relationships with each other (and with those outside the team in the wider system), and the unit's own operating model. In the planning for the offsite, the three of us held conversations, yes, but offline in between our talks, I did my own thinking and roughed out an initial design for the coming retreat. Not only did a fuller design for the event eventually emerge, which they and other team members came to shape and affirm, the two co-leads and I meeting together this way at first had the benefit of also giving them the opportunity to start facing and working through some of their own differences where it felt safe for them to do so. They were able to begin *naturally concentrating* on what some of these differences really were so they could openly and constructively address them. And they expressed their differences with an emotional quality. I did not rush them to find "common ground."

While the three of us made headway, I began holding preparatory one-on-one conversations with team members, to understand some of the background for the event, their concerns and frustrations, and to get a visceral impression of what they were willing and ready to deal with publicly. These conversations indeed proved generative. It dawned on me that what they were telling me would only have value if a way could be found for them to say their real thoughts to each other. I had listened of course appreciatively and was gauging how far they'd likely be ready to go public with their sentiments. I asked them about that—to get useful information to better help structure and pace the event, but to also soften the ground and build my own trusted relationships with them.

With the final design for the event now in hand, on day-one as the entire team gathered I put all of the members into fishbowl arrangements sequenced by organizational layer. I started with the top layer in the center of the circle, followed by section leaders, senior individual contributors, then support staff. Each group took their turns speaking to themselves in the center ring, with all those in the rest of the groups surrounding them, listening in.[42] From leaders to support staff, in response to prompts written on a flip chart, they discussed their hopes and wishes, their frustrations and disappointments, what they wanted and needed from others inside and outside the room. Many expressed strong feelings of being overwhelmed and powerless. These were not all happy, positive thoughts. These were feelings, positive and negative. Had they been held back in the name of seeing only positive possibilities, the moment would have been entirely missed. I did not encourage them to be prematurely positive; I rather helped set up the conditions where they felt safe to be real. The preliminary conversations ahead of the event let those sentiments concentrate, where they could begin to be better recognized and tolerated by each of the members themselves, then build for public expression with the group. This constituted a gradual energetic buildup—or charge—within the team.

For the collective, public expression—or discharge—then to work, the assembled team members had to do more of course than "call out" their unhappiness—and then bolt. This required a facilitative approach that helped them stay with the process to the best of their abilities and see it out as far as they could. The tendency often seen to drop a label on something, then quickly leave-the-scene is also a product of attitudes similar to those AI presents in excess: do what you need to do to get to the bright side quickly, even when there is gold to be mined by working through the difficulties. That would be equivalent of, again to use our earlier example and put it plainly, the child must not be allowed to cry, discomfort must be banished, not *moved through*.[43] Using labels and categories to dismiss things, represents an intellectualized dumping of the emotional energy at hand. Consultants in their work with clients have a higher duty I believe.

As it was, however, as the team members expressed and worked through their feelings more diligently, they all began to see each other as real and that the event was not "an exercise." Day-one was about understanding the totality of what was actually happening, and their discontent as a big part of the picture needed its day. The positivity could only come as a result of their hearing and accepting the present darkness of their worlds. They did not feel depressed by the experience. *They felt relief in its concentrated, collective expression.* That was evident in the group dinner that night, there was real lightness and buoyance in the air.

The event's day-two was about doing something about the difficulties—how to shift the operating model of the unit within the larger turbulent organizational environment. The team members came into the second day feeling much better understood and saw they did not need to water things down as much as they had thought going into the first day. With this, even greater sentiment was unleashed that proved to be difficult and *hard truth* in fashioning the best way forward in how to work together. People spoke up critically. Formal leaders asserted their authority. *De facto* leaders arose from the ranks. Possibilities for newer ways of organizing came, creative ones but only through the trespass into difficult emotions and concerns first. Again, there was palpable relief at the end of it all. People breathed together more freely. The event closed on appreciative insights and what they had come to learn and see they could build on in the future.

AI had functioned as a door opener at the beginning of the event and as a way to bring some closure at its end. But in between, there was largely storm, contained in a safe environment where people felt they did not have to pretend, gloss over the reality, or as an old expression says, "put lipstick on a pig." Or in the words of Herman Miller CEO Max Dupree, "put pink ice in the urinals."[44]

Knee jerk reframes that there are no problems, only possibilities would have squelched this. In fact, that was part of the problem going into the event—their presenting situation as a unit. Dare they speak the truth, their truths, and then work through them? The need to express what buoyed them as a group, but also their irritation, frustration and upset—not simply stay positive—about working together.

Using self as instrument, consultants can do the same, paying attention to the full range of their own feelings as they come up in the consulting encounter—clues to what is happening for the client—not denying them, trying to stay and appear all-affirming. True wholeness, as the great Martin Buber said in another context, can never come from that. Buber, a thinker of extraordinary depth and influence, is the father of dialogue in the West from the 1920s. As far as I can tell, he is nowhere credited in the literature of Dialogical OD, the last of the post-modern threads to which we now turn.

Dialogical OD too shares the basic assumptions of the other three post-modern strains.[45]

- Logical positivism and empiricism are rejected.
- Human reality is socially constructed and enacted, separate and apart from the natural world.
- Organizations are less structures than they are loosely coupled, self-organizing networks, emergent and generative.

- Possibilities, not problems, are what matter most. (Even what we call nature are merely sets of probabilities, so unpredictable in human social life they are not to be considered.)
- Changing mindsets is central.
- Dialogue is key.

Two of the leading figures in this OD movement are Gervase Bushe and Bob Marshak. They go so far in their conceptualization as to set up a polar opposition between Diagnostic OD and Dialogic OD, "old school versus new." Technically, the claim may be there is a continuum between the two. But the two schools are presented in a graphic where they stand in opposition to each other, and there is clearly a normative preference for the dialogic.[46]

The duality is odd as the declared intention is to move away from either-or thinking and normative claims of truth. Because "old school" diagnostics are explicitly rejected, there is no role to assess organizational character in Dialogic OD's work. Indeed, as with the other post-modern strains, organizational character is not recognized as a phenomenon. Nor is a pulsating bioenergy seen in humans, an energy that surfaces as emotional movement, supported or constrained by field conditions. There are no *natural* interior drives or forces, or if there are, not worth talking about. The question of what is inside people in the first place that makes for social reality—for social interaction, tradition and collective ideation—is not asked. There is no ground.[47]

As I have already discussed much of this in the other post-modern approaches, here I want to probe two aspects that especially stand out for me: Dialogic OD's very rootedness in dualism; and the limitations to observation, inquiry and action its rejection of empirical science imposes, including its implications for effective consultant engagement. Both these intellectual dimensions lead to a *de facto* rejection of the power of feelings in life, the power of the emotions in the human animal. This conclusion I think would surprise its proponents, who might argue they are very sympathetic to the emotional dimension. I will describe my contention here more fully, including dipping into some of the great thinkers of the past I referenced at the beginning of this chapter. But I believe this bias in Dialogic OD has serious, limiting consequences for practice in the field and its ability to serve people in organizations at any moment, especially when it may count most.

The post-modern concentration on discourse that organically develops of course has value, and so is the assertion that not all life is rational and planful. But the declared philosophical suppositions that Dialogic OD makes are tenuous and undermining here. Bushe and Marshak call out two important areas of philosophical inquiry as the basis for their claims: ontology and epistemology, the philosophy of being and philosophy of knowledge respectively.

Ontologically, Dialogic OD rests on a deep tradition from the sixteenth century in its modern incarnation in Western thought, Descartes' body-mind dualism. Body and mind are two separate things, Descartes asserts, and the Mind takes precedence. "I think therefore I am" is the maxim Descartes made famous. Mind, in the end, is what we can be confident about is the Cartesian claim. The products of the mind may not all be rational, but it is an understanding that things of human significance are a product of intention, will, thought and cognition in general.

There is much less understanding that human life is *sentient* and *embodied*. The Cartesian view ultimately lies in metaphysics, not physics; in fact, this curiously led Descartes to also be a rather radical empiricist, in what became the tradition of "scientism." The human and the natural remain two different spheres, hermetically sealed off from each other.[48] This dualism precludes seeing a psychophysical unity in the human condition—it literally sees life in parts, not in wholes. Again, the assumption is that what man thinks and can create is at the center of the universe in human affairs. This leads I think to the disastrous general view that man has dominion over nature and can be its master. Heart attacks due to reckless life styles and the human social impact on global warming are but two dreadful consequences associated with such thinking.

There is a long line of thinking in the West that challenges Cartesian thinking, thinking that cannot be simply dismissed as mechanistic or reductionist as the post-modernists do. Darwin, Scheler, Freud and Reich—all challenged what they saw as the conceit of man that he was simply in charge of his own nature, the product of his conscious will and mind, set apart from nature. Darwin's breakthrough understanding of human evolution as the unity of nature, including man, is in fact the opposite of mechanistic—or mystical, where everything is ascribed to an all-knowing God. Darwin saw human beings as a *species* of animal life, with far more shared among the animal world than those steeped in prior religious and philosophical traditions were prepared to accept. Darwin's field notes that grew into his book, *The Expression of the Emotions in Man and Animals*, clearly depict the continuity of life, emphasizing how human life is indeed sentient at its roots.[49]

A stunning, subtle work by the German philosopher and phenomenologist Max Scheler in 1928, *Man's Place in Nature*, emphasized the psychophysical unity and evolutionary line in plant, animal and man, and in the life of the human spirit.[50] In his other works too, Scheler saw sentiment and *ressentiment* as fundamental dimensions of human life—re-sentiment, literally, *resentment*, the continuous acting out of sentiment when it is frustrated and embittered.[51] Finally, these views informed Scheler's unique take on the sociology of knowledge—or "the social construction of reality" as those later in the tradition, Berger and Luckman and now Bushe and Marshak, call it. In Scheler's view, what we see and claim as true is much more complex than the simple cultural relativism of the post-modern school. Scheler's take was that each historical epoch has its own ways of apprehending and "knowing" the world, the universe. He called these ways of knowing the "sluice gates" of culture, regulating the perception of and flow of a universal, vital spirit—a spirit embodied in man in the emotions and the *ordo amoris*, the logic of the heart.[52]

Scheler's thought is not fully worked out, and it remains an abstract way of understanding energy dynamics. Yet he understands that all of human life cannot be purely relative (*a reductio ad absurdum*), that there are emotional truths operating in us as a species which are culturally conditionable, for good or ill. In this, his thinking has a strong affinity to Reich's. Reich, however unlike Scheler, derived his findings less from philosophical speculation but from clinical observation, social action research and laboratory inquiry.

This brings us to Dialogic OD's epistemological rejection of empiricism. Here too, there is a line of sophisticated and nuanced thinkers in the West which has wrestled with a much less one-sided view than where the post-modernists land. Before Scheler, the literary giant and naturalist Goethe's epistemology pointed here.[53] So does Edmund Husserl's phenomenology, including a new field of "somatology" he urged to investigate the interface of inner and outer worlds.[54] Others especially from the nineteenth century on also were not so quick to cut off empiricism, but to explore its depths. Reich was clearly in this tradition in his relentlessly pursued research, following where his findings took him.

Affiliated, if not completely in line with the Vienna Circle's school of logical positivism, the Austrian Ludwig Wittgenstein eventually came to a view that perceiving and knowing was an *embodied act*— not one of the mind divorced from a pre-existing, sensuous nature. Yet it was an act that still allowed us to observe and be "objective." In his notebooks from 1950, Wittgenstein writes:

> It is misleading then to talk of thinking as of a "mental activity." We may say that thinking is essentially the activity of operating with signs. This activity is performed by the hand, when we think by writing; by the mouth and larynx, when we think by speaking; and if we think by imagining signs or pictures, I can give you no agent that thinks. If then you say that in such cases the mind thinks, I would only draw your attention to the fact that you are using a metaphor.[55]

Yes, talking as in dialogue is an act, but there is more available to those in OD—much more, as people in organizations in motion indeed *know*. The social anthropologist David Sudnow goes further than Wittgenstein and much further than the post-modernists in his richly detailed account of how he learned to play improvisational jazz on the piano at the age of thirty, after only being trained in classical music. Sudnow was thus unusually positioned to do more than make philosophic pronouncements about the perceiving and learning process. His 2001 republished account, *Ways of the Hand*, notes how his hands were able to "grasp" something even before his mind, *a nonverbal, even non-visual function of the body as it moved; mentalized sense-making came afterwards.* Sudnow came to understand, like other jazz musicians, *a free, sensual, flow state was at work.*

> Sudnow is clear that it is not he but his hand that reaches for the jazz, as, in *The Odyssey*, Homer says of his heroes that, when they sat down to a banquet, "their hands went out to the food in front of them." ...Sudnow provides new insights into how the body takes over a domain and, most particularly, how it uses *various styles of pulsation* to coordinate the temporal unfolding of skilled activity, whether it be music or speech."[56]

Reich's understanding of the psychophysical unity of the human organism—and what the nature of perception is biologically—is the road to resolving the longstanding epistemological divide that those in the post-modern schools and so many others continue sharply to maintain. *Life is embodied.* Perception and seeing are anchored in the human animal *ocularly.* They are somatic energetic functions, originating in the streaming excitation throughout the whole organism. Where the pulsating energy functions free of inhibitions or internalized constraints, it naturally builds and is effectively discharged: Both inwardly directed "concentration" is effective and outwardly directed sight and perception is clearest. However, when blocked, the effect as it operates in mental activity is literally one of overconcentration ("overthinking") or insufficient concentration ("underthinking"). Under these conditions, the energy gets "stuck in the head"—staying stuck or prematurely discharged—in individuals or, as we shall see at the organizational level, *in the top* of the system. Vision is blurred, biased or otherwise distorted. Views are necessarily *partial.* This entire situation, individually or organizationally, can become chronic, that is, armored. But in life, there are parts *and* there are wholes, subsystems *and* systems, and fields *within* fields. In the presence of armor, these will not be clearly seen. One-sided views, often competing with each other, result.

Empirical scientists will not be able to fully see the objects of their inquiry in the presence of their own emotional armor, as it inevitably affects them ocularly. The armor means their sight will be compromised. The functional dynamics are the same for them individually and in how their professional social milieus operate and what they find acceptable.

Practically speaking, distinctions will not be clear or made at all. Complex things will be made too simple and simple things made too complex. This holds true for social scientists as well as those in the physical and life sciences. There is no fundamental or practical divide there, as the post-modernists contend, and others did before them.

These effects of not seeing clearly also hold true for consultants in their work with clients, as any seasoned one will tell you in a candid moment. And it is certainly so for people "in dialogue" in the workplace, when chronically dysfunctional social norms are deeply anchored, that is, when organizational armor is at work.

In this sense, when empirical science is "not so perfectly empirical," the post-modernists get it partly right. But what they don't see is that *empiricism* is not the problem, it is *that conception* of empiricism based on blocks within the investigator which is problematic. The post-modernists do not see the armor. Its perceptual effects are not understood, and instead are simply seen as "differences." All right, differences, if you like. But in an irony that is not seen either, *not all differences are the same.* The baby is thrown out with the bathwater.

There is as Reich and others famously in physics saw an energetic na-ture to the relationship of observer and observed, the demonstrable Heisenberg uncertainty effect. This energetic relationship is the basis for self as instrument: for scientists in the potential for insightful observation or for research bias, and for consultants either in the constructive or destructive potential in countertransference.

The consultant has her own sense-impressions that cannot be ignored. It is a fiction that she can stand "outside" the system, simply studying it, without having an effect or being affected. The post-modernists here too get this right. But when they claim that consultants are part of the system, they do not go far enough—or, more strictly speaking, deep enough. They think the consultant and other organizational players can stand outside their own feelings—and feeling itself—thinking and talking their way past them, especially when they are not positive. But is this how life actually works? Feelings in the end are central, you cannot stand outside of them either. That of course does not mean that feelings always need to be discharged. Some-times they need to be held. That is effectively concentrating them and tolerating their charge—*feeling* the feelings—until the moment and context is right for their appropriate expression.

Mind matters. But as we read in the novel *The Chosen,* "a mind with-out a heart is nothing," says a father to his grown son whose bril-liance as a boy led him to arrogance. With regret in his voice and tears in his eyes, that is why the father, a Chasidic *tzaddik*, tells the boy he chose to raise him in silence. "The wisdom and the pain of silence"—not talk—so the son's ceaseless chatter and *hubris* of the mind would yield.[57]

A powerful source of information is lost for consultants who distance themselves from the ground of their own feelings for the sake of oth-ers. This is a loss at odds with their work, given they are there to help. The times I have experienced something as "off" in client engage-ment, particularly as disturbing, have almost always been clues to what those in the system were inwardly experiencing and struggling with, sometimes the very core of their struggles. They have a very different quality than when I know I'm bringing my own baggage to a client situation. Naturally, I would check my sense-impressions out through questions and further observation. But I have paid close attention to them. My ability to accept and work with them has given me value to others. When I have not paid due attention to tolerating feeling them—not necessarily acting on them—I have gotten into trouble.

Civility and constructive dialogue of course count. But it is over-reach to take that as sacrificing, or even just suspending, your own sense-impressions—including your *feelings* about what others are feeling, whether they own up to them or not. Unexpressed resistances count too. Feeling is quickly abandoned in the post-modern equation. It is all Mind. And the commitment is to talk—and to listen to others talk and talk. Talk is fine if it can lead clients to the needed, liberating emotional shifts essential for meaningful change. But too often, there is no getting to the point, as we saw at first in the Hewlett Packard example. It is a tyranny of words.[58] Silence and solitude are sometimes far superior than dialogue. And monologue too will be important when properly focused and timed, when it reaches to the emotional depths. Should we consult Shakespeare on that? Each has its moments.

I find that post-modern thinking in the end devolves into conceptual contradictions and practical dead-ends. In its denial of what is there before our eyes, AI does not appreciate the *force* of the forces that have gone dark. Dialogue tries to talk its way past them. Complexity Theory ends up simplistic and one-dimensional. Chaos Theory denies the reality of the chaos; avalanches, floods and the ossification of structure into stone—*a petrified forest*—don't just happen "over there" in nature. They are palpable in organizations, natural energy systems, tightly or loosely bound. The flattening out of affect and distinctions *avoids* the complex. In this respect, they strike me as being unable to meet the smell test of a schoolgirl or schoolboy.

I said earlier that an irony of AI is that people where they are—*wherever* they are—may not be appreciated. People and workplaces in trouble may go unseen, just as the hurting child is often not really heard. There is a rush to make them happy, to make them whole. Life is more organic than that, more complex, and requires less rigidity and intolerance for what is allowed to come into view or simply be felt. The existence of work energy, character and armor—let alone their dynamics—are not seen. Reich was fond of quoting Goethe: "What is the hardest thing to see? That which lies before your eyes."

REICH: TOWARD A NEW WAY OF OBSERVING, INQUIRING AND ACTING IN OD

Reich points us to a whole new world. This is a world I think often unknown by those in classical OD but also by post-modern conceptions that remain trapped in Cartesian and Newtonian paradigms, the pretensions to move beyond to a "new science" notwithstanding. Through Reich's close observations of human dynamics as they actually operate and his inquiry into diverse other phenomena in nature, he points us to a fuller way of seeing, inquiring and thinking—and to restorative paths of action that make a practical difference in people's lives. It's not that Reich's thinking helps us see with "new eyes" but rather *open eyes*.

The accumulated weight of Reich's anomalous findings across the wide range of phenomena he dared look at makes the structure of much established thinking vulnerable—for those willing and able to see it. This is precisely what Kuhn has written about in *The Structure of Scientific Revolutions,* a text that some in OD also invoke. It is the *structure* of the thinking in an old paradigm—the shape of the bottle—that gets shattered, much like organization character structure itself must be deconstructed for the energy present and being held back to flow fruitfully and be illuminated. But as Kuhn recognizes, the holding on to the given order is less a matter of logic or evidence, much less one of "changing mindsets," than shifts in the *emotional investments* in and allegiances to the old traditions.[59]

This is as true for OD practitioners and scholars, old school or self-proclaimed new school, as much as it is for scientists. Without an emotional shift, acceptance of the discovered phenomena typically takes the arrival of a younger generation, not socialized and bogged down in the conventions and prejudices of the past. The OD grandmaster Bob Tannenbaum spoke to this directly, part of his caution to young people in the field, that the way to clarity and being truly helpful is less through acts of "mentalizing" than through the heart— "this path has a heart."[60]

Being able to observe and pay close attention to the movement of work energy *and* the constraints of organization character and armor are essential for those in OD—for helping people address shared troubles in the workplace, for better organizational flow and outcomes, and for fuller realization of their hopes and dreams. Reich's work and findings, I think, are key here.

We explore this territory in the rest of the book. We next look closely at the nature of organizational health and pathology: the existence of each; their relationship and dynamics; and what they imply for effective consultation that can fundamentally help people at work—and the working of organizations.

CHAPTER 3 ▬▬▬▬▬▬▬▬▬▬▬▬

ORGANIZATIONAL HEALTH AND PATHOLOGY

One of the stunning things when I first read the literature in OD was there was no obvious effort to define the existence of *both* organizational health and pathology. There was little effort to discuss what they are, their coexistence and relationship to each other in single organizations, or how they develop and function.

Plainly, there were normative efforts discussing organization effectiveness, many; Robert Blake's and Jane Mouton's famed "Managerial Grid" very prominent among them, one I found quite practically useful.[1] Yet such efforts, even going back to Lewin, tended to be regarded as normative sets of *values*—subjective realities, less what organizations' health and disorders are *in fact*. The latter felt like dangerous territory for OD scholars and practitioners to consider and tread. Then, foreshadowing Complexity Theory, competing views of "Contingency Theory" came about—an elaborate way of saying "it all depends."[2] There too, that organizations might have normative *and* contingent aspects at one and the same time I never saw wrestled with conceptually. There was a kind of strict duality operating, despite all the talk of pluralism.

Barry Johnson's "polarity thinking" seemed to help sidestep either-or views of organizational life—but even there, a dualism reentered the picture.[3] Those who did not hold to the holistic thinking he was driving at were implicitly wrong or at least "off." Pick the way you describe the poison. And then the approach still remained all about *thinking*, not the reality of the poison. There are, experientially and observationally in OD practice, obvious toxic and toxically felt sides of work life, frequently engulfing.

Yet explicit discussion of organizational pathology in the literature was infrequent. I found it limited mostly to the psychoanalysts, Kets de Vries, for example, as discussed earlier. But then, it was *all* pathology at work. No health, healthy type or criteria for health were identified to comparatively distinguish it. The post-modernists, as I see it, wanted to get at something positive—something on the bright side and spontaneously generative, but then left out, for all practical purposes, the dark aspects of organizational life, in effect waving them away.

I wondered, what was so hard for OD people to get? How is it that people can't see the coexistence of organizational health and pathology as *real* realities?

Health was there in organizations—joy when something great was achieved, individually or collaboratively, and also in the shared desire and drive in a system for something better. But obviously at play too were forces at work holding the organization back. And the two counterforces seemed very related to each other, as Lewin first described. The more you *pushed* the driving forces in a social field, the more restraining forces would gain charge.

But then after Lewin, I could see no work that explored what he described more deeply, inquired about the implications, or conceptually built on it for purposes of general practice. Surely, force field analysis that came out of Lewin's work was a valuable tool, whether performed behind-the-scenes or facilitated openly with a client group. But the tool basically remained a tactical exercise; no theory

or method of practice were developed to see what broader characteristic patterns the forces form, how and when restraining forces become structurally anchored, or its consequences for reparative organizational intervention that was systemic and conducted over time.

And there was more left unexplained: If a drive towards health and
generative wholeness in organizational life existed (latent even in
very troubled cases, as I had seen), how is it the reality of the system's
sickness comes about in the first place? Is it injected into the system
from the outside, like a virus, like some new toxic leader or some
crushing financial circumstance? Or does it arise from some more
complex internal process, triggered under certain circumstances by
outer conditions? People in toxic organizational environments not
infrequently get physically sick. I did at the big consulting firm I was
part of, so did others, as the toxicity could not be stomached. It did
not sit well with something inside of us. In the end, the toxicity in the
organizational system got to the point where the firm itself did not
survive. The organization's demise affected the lives of the thousands
of us there, our customers and their businesses.

So, what is at work here, individually and at a social systems level?
What is *systemic* organizational health *and* sickness? And what can
be done in the face of them "to better the condition of things" as OD
founder Dick Beckhard put it? I believe pursuing the answers here is
vital for OD, for those of us who practice it and the field itself. *For if
helping organizations move towards health is not explicitly the goal—a
goal requiring knowledge of what organizational health is and what it
is not—then why are we there in the first place?*

Specific understanding, criteria and definition of organizational
health and pathology are essential. Such understanding must also
recognize that organization health and illness operate as matters of
degree, as ratios one to another within an organization, and that they
exhibit fluidity in how they emerge and shift.

This chapter seeks to clarify the nature of organization health and pathology. Reich's understanding of a root bioenergy at work, I believe, is foundational.

A DEEPER LOOK AT THE BIOENERGY AT WORK

To understand how organizations function, it is important to take a closer look at how the basic bioenergy functions generally in an individual. Organizations, as defined in Chapter 1, are biosocial entities that have formed from the streaming together of the interests and energies of various individuals.

Reich understood at the core of human life is a natural, rhythmic pulsation of energy. What differentiates a live organism from one that just died, is that the latter no longer pulses. There is no breath, no inhalation and exhalation, no natural, oscillating expansion and contraction; the organism becomes all structure with no movement, *rigor mortis* sets in. Reich understood this primary rhythmic expansion and contraction of the organism as an *involuntary* biological process mediated by the autonomic nervous system, the parasympathetic and sympathetic functions, accompanied by the action of physiochemical mechanisms.[4]

Because these are naturally occurring functions does not mean they are not conditioned by the outer environment in which the person lives. Children and adults—and indeed whole groups of people—routinely hold their breath under conditions of threat or fear. It is an *autonomic* response—in distinction to "automatic" which is, strictly speaking, the operation of a machine. We are organisms with basic energetic functions and their mechanisms, not simply machines. That we have a sophisticated neurological apparatus does not change this. Yes, we can learn and with attention *unlearn* to hold out breath. But normally one doesn't think about breathing. One breathes. Breathing itself is a natural, continuous process of life.

Across all bodily functions, as energy is drawn in, it moves inward towards the center of the organism, and then as it builds charge, following a natural course, the energy reverses direction and moves outward to the periphery of the organism and through the skin (its outer membrane) as it is discharged, making contact with the world. The rhythmic inspiration and expiration oxygenate the body through the vascular system, with signals to and through the nervous system. We see this vividly in pulsation.

When we hold our breath out of fear, we literally contract, muscularly tighten up, and enter into an anxious state. When we are open enough, we *feel* the anxiety. It is possible of course for people to be shut down enough, or numb enough, to not feel the anxiety. But the anxiety is there regardless, stuck or continuing to move more and more to the center of the organism and pile up; the energy is less able to follow its natural course and rhythmically reverse direction, its natural outward movement and discharge in the world gets inhibited. The energy is overstimulated at the center, held back or prematurely discharged from timely, pleasurable expression.

Indeed, Reich demonstrated this process through his early bioelectric experiments. The studies showed that anxiety registered as movement of energy towards the center of the organism, and pleasure registered as energetic movement towards the organism's surface.[5] When the excited bioenergy is not inhibited, it streams inward and outward smoothly in its alternating movement, serving a natural charging and discharging function for the individual, psychically and somatically. Effective discharge is naturally accompanied by pleasurable feeling and relaxation.[6]

For individuals, Reich came to understand health as the natural rhythmic pulsation of the energy in the organism; sickness essentially as a disturbance of natural pulsation.

Such a disturbance in pulsation, can be fleeting in time, prolonged or even chronic, *frozen* in time. But as life functions carry on, this results in a disturbance in the pattern of the pulsation, depending on the circumstances as they affect the organism in question. The disturbance could typically be in the exaggeration of one of the two directions of the energy's movement: exaggerated states of expansion or contraction, exaggerated in their fullness and/or the speed of the two in alternation. Shallow or heavy breathing, hypo- or hyperventilation, are examples here. Emotionally they reflect anxiety, often fear, and sometimes panic.

Armoring is an example of the energy turning inward and freezing, where the tightened musculature forms a barrier to the outside disturbance from the world. In this sense, muscular armoring is neither "bad" nor "good"; *it is a natural capacity,* functional and adaptive. When it becomes frozen in time, the organism will be proportionately inhibited in its ability to experience streaming of the energy: the natural cycle of concentration, excited charge and discharge, and relaxation is no longer rhythmic. A chronic state of bodily contraction results, within which the continued living energy must pass, and is thereby distorted. Excess energetic buildup is followed by harsh or diminished charge and discharge. The organism's ability to tolerate energetic concentration goes haywire and is experienced as *unpleasant* tension by the individual and those in his immediate field—*the source of the anxiety to get rid of it.* For some individuals, and I would argue for our social culture at large today, this has become more or less chronic.

Clinically, Reich saw the inability to adequately concentrate energy and smoothly discharge it was largely variable depending on the nature and extent of the original, affecting inhibitions.[7] In just this way, Reich saw the adequacy of the environment with which the organism makes contact and interacts to be a critical variable. This adequacy is crucial in the person's early childhood years when he or she is most vulnerable and in most basic need, but also in the adequacy of the human environment in the individual's continuing and current life. This all attests to the basic fact that *we are biosocial creatures, not simply psychological "minds."*

Reich understood this oscillating movement of energy as basic to all life functions, thus he saw the real consequences of its constriction. He especially saw these consequences in armoring's effects on sexuality and the capacity for deep, loving surrender. But Reich also came to understand the biosocial disturbance of pulsation as *the pathogenic process per se* in the human animal, leading to an array of psychic and somatic illnesses.[8]

Reich saw these natural processes of life also operating in the human work function. We literally "make our living" in work. Our "living, productive, work-power," to use Reich's words, is the social manifestation of our bioenergy at work. In this way, he understood that work and sexuality are paired functions, each capable of anxiety and pleasurable excitement, and when blocked by social conditions can become antagonistic with each other. This he saw as the basis for the dualism Freud came to call "pleasure and reality principles." For the later Freud, these stood in timeless opposition to each other. But for Reich, these were not "principles" forever standing in conflict with each other. *Work and pleasure are living, natural processes; their antagonism is a historical product of chronically armored life operating in the human animal and in the social order.* Malinowski's ethnographic research with the Trobriand Islanders, which Reich studied, suggested such a split was not culturally universal or given in nature.[9] And there is a more immediate demonstration of this. All things being equal, a person directly engaged with her own work and where her productive power flourishes, is both productive *and* happy. When *unimpeded* by outer conditions or too much internalized earlier blocking, the functional identity of task fulfillment and human fulfillment is realized—*and real.*[10]

UNDERSTANDING ORGANIZATIONAL HEALTH AND SICKNESS

I believe organizations are more than sets of relationships among people. They are natural systems made up of interlocking energies of people bound by a common work function, in dynamic exchange with others in the fields in which they move. These interlocking human energies are temporary and intermittent, not naturally permanent. People go home from work at night, they sometimes hold more than one job, and they change companies and careers. Despite this, organizations remain natural human systems.

Of course, organizations are supported by mechanical technologies, like electronic information systems and operating processing equipment, but these too are designed, deployed and programmed at their source by human agency. The same may be said of capital that backs organizations as financial resources. Human labor and deliberate investment are at work. From first to last, organizations are natural systems of human energy at work—they are *biosocial* work systems. They inspire, they breathe, they expand and contract, charge and discharge, and, to one extent or another, merge with others in their fields. Sometimes they work well, sometimes they do not.

The Greek root of the word "organization" is *ergon*, which means work, energy and action. Organizations are *corporal* phenomena, embodied with members. They have core or central functions, and they have a periphery and boundary that differentiates them from the outer world and lets them internally function and buildup charge. At their outer periphery, organizations do not have skins, like animals do. There is no membrane *per se,* their *organization by nature* is looser. Organizations are not animals. They do however have a life of their own insofar they are animated by collective human energy moving in fulfillment of a common function in the world. In this respect, it is fair to speak about an organization's wellness or sickness as a system. *An organization's ability to mobilize its members for its common function defines its health or illness.* Let's take a closer look here.

As an organization operates in its field of action, its individual and collective energies move. Energy circulates among its members given their task interdependencies and inherent requirements for joint or concerted action. The better the energy circulates, the better the system works—as are its *works*, its finished goods or services in their own integrity and in the hands of the organization's customers. When functioning well, the circulatory, internal processes encompass the organization's refinement of products and services: its innovation of new ones altogether, or alternatively its actions to retire products and services from their portfolio of offerings. This movement forward and back occurs because the well-functioning organization understands the changing needs of those served in the outer world and is able to concentrate its energies for successful effect. This reflects the organization's natural capacity to expand *and* contract. The organization's members' interdependencies, specialty talents, and capacity for spontaneous creativity allow them to modify their work processes and products to fulfill the system's core function or set of functions as they operate over time.

There is of course a way we typically refer to an organization's growth as one of expansion, just as we refer to its curtailment of activity, such as consolidation of departments or the closing of branch, field offices, as contraction. But there is a more day-to-day sense of expansion and contraction at work in organizations. They have *a kind* of rhythmic pulsation—in some groups more than others, as in jazz ensembles. True, they do not pulse as regularly as an organism. Their inherent, looser coupling does not necessarily require the same level of integral regularity as an organism. But this very looseness seems to set organizations up, as it were, for rigidifying cultural structures and overly formalized processes and procedures. When ossified, organizations function as *bureaucracies*, characterologically and in their hierarchical formal structures. This inhibits the spontaneous, natural movement that is still required for the organization to function.

The organization's central functions do indeed require that dynamic movement. Despite more inherent looseness than an organism, organizations by their nature still exhibit deep properties of pulsing and energetic streaming. They consist of and are animated by human beings, living energy systems at work, that stream together, split in their movement, and also merge in their collective activity with the outer environment. And organizations have a deep structural core central to their functions—again, what Mintzberg called "the operating core"[11]—that must process and rhythmically "beat" in their activity and flows, in conjunction with the rest of the system, discharging its main works. An organization system reflects this kind of functioning when it regularly gets products and services out the door, as it also does in its ongoing efforts to adjust, renew and innovate its operations and goods. Such functioning flows systemically across what is classically called the organization's value chain. Human activity is continuously at work making things happen.

The operating core refers to a specialized complex in the developing system as it grows; this represents an instance of *structuralization* as Weick has generally described for organizations, and which Reich allows us to appreciate fully as energic formation. In addition to organizations forming a central core devoted to their primary function, they appear to always develop other basic subsystems, each with their own inherent functions serving the larger core function of the system. Like the larger organization, these subsystems are inherently energetic themselves, as they are peopled. They do not develop fully as internal organs surrounded by a somatic musculature as in a biological system. But they do take on distinct form and shapes, and they discharge their own functions in natural coordination with the other groupings and customers. As I touched on earlier, these subsystem groupings represent the "deep structure" of the organization. Mintzberg identified these and their rational, natural functions as:

- The "strategic apex" at the top of the organization that envisions, guides and orients the work, when it functions well. This top grouping is commonly called the "head" of the organization.
- The "middle line" that facilitates and inspires the daily flow of work, when it operates effectively.
- The "operating core" that directly processes and discharges the chief work function of the enterprise (and, again, that does so effectively when its functioning is supported).

As organizations grow in scale, two other structural subsystems seem to develop as specializations of the middle line, in service of the strategic apex and operating core:

- The "technostructure" that provides special content and systems work. These, for example, include R&D, SME and IT functions.
- The "support staff" that provides instrumental administrative work, such as finance, human resources, audit functions, and the like.

For Mintzberg, all of these subsystems' shapes are malleable depending on the nature of the organization's work, size and processing complexity; their formal shape, population, and functioning also depend on where the system is in its life cycle. For example, a simple group or smaller entrepreneurial organization may dictate the work of these subsystems be performed largely by the same people in roles they move in and out of, often doing so on the fly. Such smaller organizations are comparatively loosely coupled in composition and function. In this way too a more general principle obtains: the natural functions of each of the subsystems do not necessarily correspond to formal layers of a hierarchy. They rather represent *natural orders of functioning all organizations must perform regardless of formal structure*. As the organization grows in size, the division and splitting apart of these groupings seems essential as specialization to support the system's continued movement and scale. The degree to which divisionalization, formalization and hierarchical layers occur is variable. These are discussed in greater depth in Chapter 5.

Briefly, these subsystem groups run laterally across the system. I refer to them as "organizational segments" constituted by particular, cross-cutting functional units. Hence, as they specialize in form, the strategic apex is made up of the top executives, from both line and staff, usually constituting or directly serving the general policy making committee of an enterprise; the middle line is represented by senior and middle managers who lead the operating and supporting units; and the operating core consists of those principally called "the line" who specialize in developing, processing and getting the main work of the organization out the door.

Because these cross-cutting segments do not have membranes as organs do in the human body, they have a certain inherent openness—people come and go and may indeed occupy functional positions in one or more of the other segments, even in complex organizations, of course. However, under adverse conditions, these segments become the sites of what I've called organization armor, where energy is more or less stuck inside the subsystem and whose specialized work is therefore not effectively discharged. This energetic hang-up is one and the same as the gating effect of the organizational character, manifesting at the level of the segments. In fact, the segments' root openness it seems leaves them especially susceptible to two distinct possibilities of unhealthy, systemic functioning when they incur blocking—*overconcentration* or *underconcentration* of their energies. Either of these directly impact the fulfillment of the segments' natural functions and flows with each other and the world.

Such underconcentration is represented, for example, when a group or whole organization never sits still enough to substantially develop its thinking and capabilities for new offerings, but sends them out into the market impulsively, and with fanfare to boot. I saw this recently in a high-tech client organization whose *modus operandi* was to *only* be on the move, there was little *rhythm* to the movement; what came out as a result was spotty and weak; its products didn't always work.

In comparison, overconcentration of energy has other distorting effects. If, for example, energy is sucked up in the head of the organization and becomes compacted, the top will likely be unclear in seeing and articulating priorities for the organization. This will in effect leave the middle line on hold—its managers literally holding their breath as a group, waiting endlessly for clarity, guidance and support (and sometimes "for the other shoe to drop"). The middle line will become immobilized and often characteristically depressed. This results in one of two reverberating effects from the middle line: first, concentrating even more of its energy towards the top as mid-line members seek guidance and assurance; and secondly, the mid-line will not have the available energy to sufficiently inspire and support the operating core so it can effectively discharge its own tasks. Oshry has described such dynamics as power conflicts and the disempowering interplay of "tops, middles and bottoms." The Allied Bank case in Chapter 7 describes this very situation in detail as it affected the energy functioning of each of the segments and the system as a whole. Throughout the Allied consultation, the aim was to effectively reverse the characteristic pattern of blocking and help the company more fully function. I have found that different types of organization characters block energy movement at the segments in distinctive ways, requiring different kinds and sequencing of interventions to successfully mobilize the system (without creating demobilizing side-effects).

These kinds of dynamics have general implications for identifying the markers of organizational health and illness. In a fundamentally healthy organization, the energy freely circulates, concentrates and is discharged *in a mutually fulfilling way for the broad range of its stakeholders, internal and external.* Organization health is a whole systems matter operating in a dynamic field, recognizable in objective and subjective ways.

Objectively, a healthy organization at work can be recognized in the extent of its *complete product or service fulfillment*—its work is fully discharged. Subjectively, it can be recognized by its *peoples' felt fulfillment* in their work, independently and interdependently—as in "this was a pleasure to work on," "it's a pleasure to work with you," or "it's a pleasure to do business with you." *Both product and process, fully valued, fully work.* In chronically compromised systems, *some* energy is discharged, but product and service delivery are *partial.* In this case, process and satisfaction are notably uneven, or worse, and there are a host of accompanying symptoms which present behaviorally and structurally. The major cross-cutting segments become disjointed and misaligned, and as the energy backs up in or is withheld from each, the discharge of their work diminishes. This inevitably leads to customers and markets being underserved; there too, customer losses can be measured objectively in retention and in satisfaction ratings. In contrast, when an organization functions in a fluid, healthy way, the segments function integrally. I define that state as a "work democratic" character, following Reich's use of the term, but in language as others like Emery and Trist used too.[12]

Productive, felt gratification is the hallmark of organizational health. It follows then that the central OD task in the restoration or renewal of a system is this: helping the people within an organization work and develop in ways, individually and in concert, that are *both demonstrably productive and feel gratifying* in discharging the system's core work functions in the world. This seems evident whether the organization is comparatively tightly bound as in a traditional hierarchy, or whether it is more loosely configured as a network, as we will discuss in Chapter 8.

The presence or absence of productive, felt gratification can often be ascertained by the experienced consultant by looking at just a handful of presenting phenomena. This requires first being ready to see the severity of the deprivation present. In a basic way, premature efforts to "fix" the deprivation before understanding how it systemically functions will always be counterproductive to the task of organization renewal. Such premature efforts however are unfortunately common; I think this is so regardless if the attempted fix is in "explaining," "appreciating," "talking" or "futuring" the existing deprivation away. The deprivation has the upper hand until the blocking present is sufficiently dissolved and the system's energetic stasis is actually relieved. Such intervention fixes on their own may have a relatively good chance as long as little chronic functional disorder and organizational armoring are present. However, that seems rarely the case in the contemporary world. The majority of organizations it appears are chronically blocked to one extent or another. The impact of an organization's chronic disorder will have decisive impact on large-scale systemic change efforts. This blocking and the extent of its dysfunctional extent are variable depending on the organization character—and the depth of its anchoring in the system.

As it happens, not all organizations will have it in them—in fact, most won't I believe—to *restructure their organizational characters* through thoroughgoing consultation suited to the task. But I think even some poorly functioning ones that find their way to get help can be "cleaned up" to some degree with appropriate intervention. Greater charge and discharge can result in such systems, with their symptoms less present, when enough readiness exists and conditions are not yet too late. Stasis can be lessened and human satisfaction enhanced. This is discussed more fully in Chapters 6 and 7 on the organization character types and their consulting case examples.

To extend and further flesh out our understanding of organization health and pathology, I turn now to two concrete cases in point.

The first is that of jazz ensembles, as they provide a model of healthy group functioning. They model ways of operating especially apt in the network organizational age. And they also show us how even healthy organizational forms can become impaired and break down. Famous examples in the history of jazz are illustrative.

The second case in point is that of the major consulting firm I was a partner in and referenced earlier: how its strategic and operating functioning collapsed; how the positive sources of renewal present turned sour and were overwhelmed, leading to the firm's filing Chapter 11 and being sold; and how the nature of its sale as a merger with another entity became subject to significant "post-merger drift," common in mergers that are successful and in those that fail.

THE ORGANIZATIONAL HEALTH AND DYSFUNCTION OF JAZZ ENSEMBLES

Jazz ensembles, when they are at their best in their work together, almost purely exhibit the signs of organizational health in the terms described above. They represent the spontaneous interplay of musicians streaming together, culminating in peak performance as evident in the quality and the beauty of their work. And, subjectively, they display how group members *as a group* experience and express the motivating excitement and joy—and a whole range of emotions—in the process of play. The happiness generated is electrifying—"sexy," as is said. And, of course, such ensembles do not shy away from but rather embrace the blues. Appreciation of the quality of the play and its emotional depth is completely evoked in the audience in what are often intimate club settings just beyond the periphery of the stage. The audience in its receptivity and expression of joy in turn inspires the ensemble. The energetic excitement and experience of ensemble and audience is mutual. Audience and ensemble are drawn together, their energies build, and in moments of peak excitement, they become one.

In the last installment of his excellent documentary series *Jazz*, Ken Burns highlights a mid-1960s career phase of Miles Davis—"the great, perpetually restless trumpet player"—when he changed musical direction once again and introduced lyricism into the most avant-garde trends in jazz. Davis, despite his outer shell of toughness and his earlier "birth of the cool" style, at this time assembled a new group of virtuosos to play alongside him in a new quintet—Herbie Hancock on piano, Ron Carter on bass, Tony Williams on drums, Wayne Shorter on tenor sax, and Freddie Hubbard sometimes sitting in for Miles. They made history, as the documentary describes, "creating some of the most intricate and imaginative jazz ever played." What follows are excerpts from the episode that speak to the work of the group and its inner workings.[13]

> *Herbie Hancock*: We weren't playing chords anymore, it's really hard to describe what we were doing. We didn't talk in detail about what we were doing, things would just kind of happen and everybody was constantly working on one thing or another. *You just had to keep your ears open, your eyes open, and keep your heart open.*

> *Joshua Redmond*: I don't know if there's ever been a group of five musicians who *communicated spontaneously* with each other as well

as those five musicians did. They could do anything, with any form, with any tune, because *they knew each other so well as musicians*.

Michael Cuscana: What Ron Carter and Tony William and Herbie Hancock did was that *they created an elasticity. . . they could stretch sections, they could stretch or contract the tempo, and there was an empathy among those five people where they could think as one. They were never inhibited by structure*, they were never inhibited by predictability, they were never inhibited by musical signposts. . . they were free to go anywhere they wanted to, and they knew everyone else would follow. That's a luxury that few of us ever experience. . . in marriage, or in music, or in any kind of art form, or any kind of teamwork.

I share this, not because every group, or even most groups in an organization, will ever be called on to work just like this; many times, of course, repetitive operational tasks must be performed. Yet the underpinnings here I think are more than luxuries. Creative work in organizations, certainly those of R&D groups or even whole organizations, as the Manhattan Project mentioned earlier, working under the most severe, mission-critical constraints and deadlines— to invent and build an atomic bomb before Hitler's scientists did— sometimes need to function as if they were an interconnected series of jazz ensembles.[14] Today's agile software development teams and inventive skunkworks efforts often operate like jazz ensembles too.

Jazz history is filled with examples of special clubs that provided protected space for musicians to come and play late at night to their hearts' content, beyond the constraining standardized fare they felt commercially forced to take in their "day" jobs. *More fundamentally, the wellspring of energy, momentum and spontaneous movement exists in people even undertaking ordinary tasks in everyday jobs; these are needs that seek satisfaction and productive outlet.* Organizational norms that support real-time problem recognition and continuous improvement on assembly lines exemplify this and point the way to what I believe is coming in the future. Future organizations that rely heavily on human talent will surely require more and more skilled and unscripted interplay—and cultures that nourish and support this. The currents running through great jazz ensembles are markers of organizational health. They show what extraordinary possibilities *are possible.*

Jazz groups can also exhibit properties where they cease to function well and break down altogether. There are lessons for us here too. Sometimes these are related to what have been described as the "inner demons" of jazz greats. Miles Davis himself is an example. With Davis, it never reached the point where his work broke down, though relationships with others he played with, and those in his life, were sharply affected.

Not so with Charlie Parker, one of the most brilliant to ever play and influence the field, but whose inner torments also proved personally and professionally self-destructive, doing great damage to others too, individually and in some of the music they played together.[15] In the passages below, we consider Parker in the context of his group play and age as well as in the implications for understanding health and pathology in individual and workgroup life. The functions of bio-energy, character and armoring gone haywire—in their individual, professional milieu and wider social forms—are in clear display in the story of Parker and his times.

Sometimes an individual gets so far out ahead of the traditions of the field that the sources of his work that proved so inspiring doubles back on him—and on others too. This happens when the combination of the inherent excitement, especially when it is strong, runs up against previously internalized blocks, and the emotional needs present of others in the group. In Parker's case, his instincts for brilliance and innovation crashed up against these inner walls and the emotional longings of others, co-musicians and audience. This left some of the work in his hands "unreliable," as his mentor and friend Dizzy Gillespie said. Putting forth the original impulse takes courage and risk, yes, qualities needed in group and organizational life. But when the force of the energy meets blocks and is overpowering, it turns over on itself and can tear a group apart.

Parker first came into prominence just after World War II, as big band swing music was fading and a new, more provocative music was being born. In jazz, that music gestated earlier in the small, private clubs where "musicians' musicians" came to play in the wee hours of the morning. Parker's and Gillespie's "Salted Peanuts" blew a wide audience away when they first heard the recording in 1946. It was like nothing else they ever heard, and even progressive jazz musicians thought this themselves. The music as Burns describes was "frenetic and exciting and fast and furious—and brilliant."

The work in itself was different, and so were the roles and structured movement of the groups that played it. Parker and Gillespie, each quite cerebral who seriously studied and endlessly practiced, were at the leading edge of what became known soon after it arrived as "bebop." In the new form, as the documentary tells, "The old steady rhythm of the dance band broke up in new ways of drumming, rhythm sections were freer now to interact with the horns, and musicians used unexpected intervals that created dissonant sound." Parker's play especially at first shocked audiences with his "speed, fire, and ferocious concentration, ideas pouring out of him as if his life depended on it." It apparently did.

The music suited the era. It was an antidote and expression of the pent-up frustration to the balm of the post-year years, a rebellion against mass convention, suburban white flight, and inner-city ghettos left to fester. The threat of nuclear annihilation too loomed ever-present in the background. In the '50s, the emergence of rock 'n roll growing out of rhythm and blues reflected a popular and commercial version of this appeal. Bebop was ahead of the curve—and more pointed and darker.

Parker, whose nickname was "Bird," epitomized this. In his play and person, he became increasingly frenetic and turned to heroin. He was certainly not the first in jazz to fall prey to this, or the last, a refuge of musicians of all colors. But it was deadening to the life of play, and life itself, and ever consuming to feed the habit. Gillespie turned away from Parker, leaving him in the early '50s on the road, when Parker stranded the group wandering off to find a fix. Addictive behavior is like that. I believe it comes out of an unsatisfied life-force in people, so vivid in Parker's instance. Parker was even thrown out of his own group at the New York club Birdland, named in his honor, when he got seriously out of hand with his band members. Right afterwards, he drank iodine in an effort to kill himself, was rushed to the hospital and committed to a mental sanitarium.

Within a year, after a brief recovery where he could be seen playing motionless, except for the movement of his eyes and hands, Parker was dead. He was worn out, his internal organs shot, gone at the age of thirty-four. His music continued to live on and take root, but a younger generation described the following period for its lost potential, "the unlived future."

Both the fire and the frenzy of Parker's play was the pure excitement of his enormous energy backing up, then crashing through his own somatic armor. As with any man or woman, the armor is what prevents the satisfaction and creates the trouble, not the excitement of the energy itself. *That*, I believe, was Parker's health and genius. Gillespie himself chose a different path that let him take his gifts in another direction. His path allowed him to stay with the play of music he deeply loved *and* live in a hearty way. From Parker, Gillespie withdrew, like a bad habit he had to kick. But he didn't withdraw from the world, he invited others in—reaching out to a wider, less niched audience for bebop and to other musicians he was so consistently giving to. Gillespie moved on, but he was forever saddened that Parker's troubles put an end to their creative collaboration—and to their close friendship. Twenty-five years after Parker's death, in 1980 in Montreal, Gillespie organized and led "The Concert of the Century: A Tribute to Charlie Parker." Other jazz greats who played with and were influenced by Parker played that day.

We see three layers of armoring at work as they affected Parker: first, his own armoring, deeply anchored in his body; next, the tight commercial conventions in the music world—the social armoring of his professional milieu—that he and others managed to break through but not without real, making-a-living and other life-style costs; and finally, the armoring of the larger social order with its conformity, bigotry, and its runaway and displaced fear.

A word about institutional, color segregation and prejudice as they continued to affect the jazz movement in mid-century America. This helps us begin to understand the function of wider social armor operating in work life and in an organization's "field." Indeed, today American businesses especially still wrestle with issues of diversity, equity and inclusion (DEI).

From its beginnings, jazz found cracks in existing social walls to increase communications and better contact between blacks and whites. But in Parker's day, the same era where Jackie Robinson broke the color line, racism continued to haunt the play of teams and groups of all kinds. The integration of jazz groups in America was rare until a few brave souls, black, white and brown band leaders and players, challenged it; they bucked rigid social norms of color in band membership and where they could eat and stay on the road together. This took on greater urgency in the post-war years when Parker, Gillespie and others began to rise.

But, of course, all was not well. In 1959 despite his worldwide fame, Miles Davis was met outside Birdland, where he was playing and taking a break, by a police officer who ordered him to move. When Davis said, "For what?", the officer ended up arresting him, and in an ensuing scuffle, beat him badly. Davis was acquitted on all charges. Around the same time, radical "free jazz" innovator Ornette Coleman yet took heat from black musicians for hiring the white bassist Charlie Haden as a full-time member of his quartet. As for women, they were not seen as instrumentalists or musical arrangers side-by-side men until later in the century; a handful of notable exceptions earlier were all women of color, hired by black band leaders. These are all examples of social armoring operating in the workplace: *ingrained, widely shared cultural patterns that restrict social movement natural to the work at hand.*

Interestingly, this kind of social armoring as it impacted the reception of black jazz musicians was less evident in mid-century France, the same as it was years before with the dancer Josephine Baker and the way she freely moved. When Parker went to Europe in 1949, he played some of his most lyrical and accessible music ever. This was heard on his recording of "April in Paris" and other songs from the album *Charlie Parker Plays Strings*, backed with lush orchestral arrangements. Miles Davis, after his first of many visits in Paris, remarked how wonderful it felt being in a country where he was "treated as a man." The nature of experience from social encounter runs deep.

How deep color prejudice runs in American culture and history! How deeply anchored it becomes in each generation who learns its ways, even though it is obviously foreign to any child of five who has kept an open heart. As a very general matter, young children are apt to look past skin color with barely a second thought. It is a plain thing to see such children excitedly run up and throw their arms around each other. They have to be *taught* to not ask their natural question to their mom or dad, when the moment arrives: "Why can't Billy swim in the neighborhood pool with me?" The power of socialization—at work or in play—is huge.[16] Culture can support or run counter to natural human expression and movement, and it anchors deeply inside of people in this respect, as Reich so well understood

As America's most original contribution to the arts, jazz was deeply informed from its inception by institutional racism, and jazz was among the forces leading the way to challenge it throughout the twentieth century. Parker's life and work reflects both sides of this. It's been said as "Bird," Parker found jazz a sanctuary from the impoverished realities of the inner city, where he could "fly into his head, with passion and imagination, and soar." Clearly, Parker had his own private demons in the way he grew up and how his energy functioned, both in gifted and highly disordered ways.

Parker's head provided the first place all that soaring energy could go, and it provided protection against the world, public and private, but at a price: the prison of his brain. In playing jazz, he found a way to release it—*partially*. His energy powerfully charged and moved in his music, but there was no full, natural release in his life the way Reich has described. His body and mind were at odds, not one in their functioning. Heroin was a substitute, an induced high he would inject into his body to feel again, but that wrecked his relationships, his work, and cost him his life and the world his gift. Ashamed of his habit, able to kick it from time to time but always where he returned, he said to his last wife Chan, "You can get it out of your body, but you can't get it out of your brain."[17]

Parker did become a phenomenon. But this was not only for the brilliance of his play. He also fell prey and came to resent the adulation and worshipful idolatry of many who identified with him, musicians and mesmerized fans. Some were influenced by his example and by the social norms of groups to which they belonged to do hard drugs (jazz groups but a notorious example). The idol worship were their needs, not his, but it did not help him.

This kind of celebrity and idol worship is a general dynamic at work that Reich has described in *The Mass Psychology of Fascism*, where people, hungry emotionally, and where conditions are otherwise ripe, can come to need and create the soil for a *führer*.[18]

Group and organizational life are not immune from this kind of leadership and followership dynamic in various shades. The clamor for strong leadership is different than a natural desire for clear and sound leaders. But this distinction can get lost in the shuffle when people awash in deprivation cannot readily see the difference. They enact the need for a strongman and give their power away. They literally substitute their own energies and transfer them to others, others with whom they then identify and seek, under the safety of cover, to draw it back from. Oshry, in his empowerment labs and writings, has focused persistently on the effects of people giving away their power in organizational life.[19]

One last, vivid lesson that jazz gives us regarding organizational health and illness: When a Parker or a Gillespie tap into the streaming energy at work that gives them genuine excitement and pleasure in what they do, individually or together, they are for that moment very much alive. They feel it. This is consequential in people's willingness to sustain difficulties to do the work they love.

As a general matter, it seems that when healthy social streaming is available at work, a fuller, further feeling of life and healthy functioning can be breathed into the individual. The stasis for that moment is relieved. In this case, if people's personal armoring is not tightly wound, and the work system's character is amply supportive, they will indeed do better—in their individual, organizational and community worlds. There appears to be healthy spill-over effects throughout their individual lives. However, because even healthy groups have natural comings and goings, this health-giving effect on an individual is susceptible not to last, certainly for people who in their own person are heavily armored. Moreover, when the effects of blocking are predominant in a group and its members' individual lives, the *work of the group as a group* is in jeopardy. Its members can drift even into even greater personal distress and illness.[20]

I believe the excursion we've taken to understand jazz ensembles in their group health and illness, and in the context of their individual member and larger social dynamics, has import. It reminds us that in the end, groups and organizations are mini *biosocial* systems—*biosocial energy systems*, at that—as they operate in a wider energy field. This ground of being for groups and organizations, and for all those inside them, affects the vitality of each, for good or ill.

THE PATHOGENIC DEMISE OF A MAJOR CONSULTING FIRM

Just as work groups exhibit healthy and unhealthy expressions of energy in their dynamics, organizations exhibit a drive for health and the potential for serious dysfunction in how their collective energies move and block. We now turn to a large-scale organization case, where the health present proved too weak in the face of its systemic character disorder and armor that had developed over time. The firm found itself in a death spiral. As its ingrained functional disorder gained strength, soaking up the available energy in the system, the health of the organization grew fainter and fainter, proving fatal to the enterprise. As a member and later partner in the firm, I saw this at close range.

I first joined KPMG Consulting, a privately held partnership in 1995, one of the Big Six firms of the time. The firm went public in 1999, taking on a formal corporate structure, and two years later changed its name to BearingPoint. In the US, the firm became regulated by the SEC. In the wake of the fresh Arthur Andersen Enron scandal, the firm's corporatization and name change came about to create distance from its original parent accounting firm, KPMG. Separate corporate structures for the consulting entities within KPMG globally were also set up under each country's regulatory arrangements.

KPMG Consulting's reputation at the time I joined was as one of the loosest, least bureaucratized consultancies of the Big Six. Compared to the others, the firm was considered more "blue color," more rough-and-tumble—in its groups' daily interactions, the autonomy of its divisions and practice groups, and its thin coordinating infrastructure. The firm was a loosely federated set of fiefdoms of individualized partnerships. There was a certain spirit of the enterprise, a get-it-done, go-do-deals atmosphere. This spirit existed of course in the rest of the Big Six's consulting divisions. But others like Deloitte, Ernst & Young and PriceWaterhouse had a reputation as being more elite, more deliberate and more formalized in their operations to discipline the energies of the firm. With these others, this may have been part show, part *façade* (Andersen is a good example of this, as Enron revealed). But at KPMG Consulting, an elite image and reputation for being highly formalized in process were of less concern. While there were exceptions within the firm, KPMG generally wore its directness and unsubtle, "just go get business" manner on its sleeve.

When I began there in 1995, I actually was part of a smaller boutique division, Nolan Norton and Company, an acquisition of a renowned IT business strategy firm some years earlier. That division had originally been founded by Dick Nolan of Harvard and by David Norton who was famous for his innovation of the "Balanced Scorecard." I was relatively newly hired when I saw Nolan Norton, with its own elite pedigree, get crushed by KPMG that would not let it function. Those of us who survived were merged into another division within the larger consultancy, and the contrast in the quality of the leadership and deep competence was striking. I remember just before the collapse of Nolan Norton, seeing one of the leaders from the umbrella firm speak at a conference, following a presentation by Dick Nolan. How sophomoric I thought the content of the concepts presented were compared to Nolan's, who still held a chair at Harvard. I thought to myself about the young executive from the larger firm, "Gee, mayor on Boys' Day," as if in an old Mickey Rooney film. Nolan's presentation had depth and was of the first order, the other one, well, comparatively glib.

That was not incidental. I later saw in different ways how at KPMG Consulting (BearingPoint after the name change) deeper reflection did not seem to be the firm's strong suit. The firm had a strong drive and was not caught up in especially looking pretty or excessive structure. To the contrary, the firm rather prided itself in its freedom to go make things happen. That I liked. But concerted thinking and deliberation in how things were done generally seemed limited. Day-to-day street-smarts, as I saw it, seemed not enough. Greater forethought was needed. The very looseness of the firm often meant lack of concentration of effort.

For example, when after the fall of Andersen in 2002, and we acquired their many suddenly available consulting partners, they joined us at KPMG without top-to-bottom due-diligence interviews. That was a night and day difference to how Deloitte handled the acquisition of our large Public Services business unit, of which I was member, after our firm's demise seven years later. Even after our unit's later sale to Deloitte was inked, each of our hundred partners had to go through multiple interviews with Deloitte partners (some very senior, like Deloitte's Chairman) to see if they would take us in as direct entry principals. Deloitte was more deliberate in manner with us than we had been earlier with the Andersen partners. Some number of our partners didn't make it through Deloitte's screening; they were demoted or not brought in at all. On the same theme of BearingPoint's want of thoughtful practice, I remember once rolling my eyes when a co-partner announced during a major new business proposal, "Never write a sentence with more than sixteen words in it." There was disproportionate concern with form (and poorly conceived form at that!) over substance. No matter, given the character of the firm, "winning" was all.

This lack of reflection, this "let's just win" attitude, showed up routinely in the firm. It showed up in the difficulty itself of bringing different specialty units together to respond to large, complex proposals. And it often showed up in difficulty effectively delivering the work when won. There was frequent bickering on which units would take the lead in driving proposals; on who would lead and staff the work; and how revenue would flow to the different practice groups. Few standard protocols existed to guide us. The default focus was almost always sales, not the quality needed to perform the work. This led the firm, hungry for big revenue engagements, into selling work not properly structured or resourced to effectively discharge it, operationally or financially. In all, the firm displayed a "work aggressive" organization character, as I delineate the character type more generally in Chapter 6.

Given the firm's character, only belatedly did top leaders acknowledge that better, less patchwork IT systems than we had were needed. Even then, the recognition seemed forced by regulators in their corporate oversight duties. The slapdash way the new technology was installed ended up costing the firm hundreds of thousands of hours and millions of dollars for outsiders to come in and fix. We didn't have the internal resources available to do the remedial work. By that time, our people were entirely consumed with pumping out revenue. All the remedial expense came at a time we were experiencing other six- and seven-figure hits to the bottom line: write-offs from inadequately thought-through deals that should have never been booked. This led to more and more borrowing from banks to keep the firm afloat. All this came to a head in 2009, as a reckoning with crushing debt eventually arrived.

But for a number of years before the end came, efforts had been made to try to right the ship. Much of what was sound came from the health of the firm's best managed business division, Public Services. Yet the firm as a whole struggled, and some of the aggressive character of its ways showed—first in the firm's efforts at growth, then in the manner it managed efforts to turn things around.

Historically, as a loose federation of partnerships and business units, the North American firm never had developed a robust central executive function. When the consulting entity corporatized in 2001, two prominent younger partners took command. But as talented as they were, neither had practiced, public-firm executive experience to personally draw on Some of us down the chain in the managerial hierarchy, started to see early signs of inadequate decision making in systems and operations; in the careless acquisition of the Andersen partners; and in premature global expansion plans that were impulsively announced and then suddenly withdrawn. Again, I thought to myself "mayor on Boys' Day" about one of the leaders. New operating demands as a corporate entity required an even greater level of coordination and well-conceived strategy than had been the firm's typical way. Our operational performance was now public, not private. Problems could not as easily be swept under the rug.

The newly chartered Board replaced the top leaders after a couple of years with a very intelligent, outsider CEO. Rather charismatic, he came from a different industry and with a financial transaction background, without hands-on experience of the core work. He would need to learn on the job what now had to happen operationally and organizationally. Even if the Board's reasoning for his selection was to get the business cleaned up for eventual sale, it seemed he would not know enough to steer the best decisions related to the actual work of the business to maximize the firm's value. He did help for a short time rebuild morale and hope. But the firm's problems deepened, and a third CEO came in the space of three years. We were running out of time and money to get things right. Worried about staff retention, the third CEO tried to put a good face on things so people wouldn't jump ship. Yet it wasn't long before he disclosed he was working on finding a buyer for the firm. Many in the firm and on the street had naturally speculated anyway that had been afoot. How could there not have been heavy off-the-record buzz about it, especially in an organization dominated by looseness and informality? As speculation about the firm's future viability rapidly spread, worry intensified over staff retention needed to keep the business running and revenue flowing before the whole thing came crashing down.

The character of the organization I've been describing ran through the Board's decision making and that of the top executive team; their literal "charge" of the situation struck me and other practice leaders as weak. Energetic concentration was limited and what was there was often aggressively discharged in premature action. By the time the third CEO arrived, real anxiety, distraction and unhappiness loomed wide in the workforce. Tensions swelled in the system. Given the state of the firm's pathology, AI or purely dialogic intervention methods would have been irrelevant to try. The firm in its characteristic haste would have blown by any suggestion of them. Different remedial efforts in the organization were needed. Some of us tried.

As practice group leaders, we were not immune from the feelings the rest of the workforce had. We had been called "managing directors" since the partnership legally dissolved and the firm went public. New EVP, SVP and VP titles were also formally established. But the new titles did little to alter the organization's actual power dynamics or to effectively steer. The firm's operating character and the way its composite energy moved remained the same, even with all the top leadership replacement and other changes.

With the real support of the top of the Public Services division I was a part of, some of us began to take matters into our own hands as much as we could. That we did so I think reflected the health of the organization still present—the positive wellspring of the get-it-done attitude, not unduly held back by formal structures.

Indeed, the strategy partner I reported to had devised a new, excellent operating model for the division—a model that proposed much clearer interoperating protocols between the division's vertical and horizontal service delivery units than had been in place in the past. As a technical organization design matter, such a redesign was essential for the kind of complex, more networked-like organization that BearingPoint in some ways aspired to be. Its future growth would require this to be able to effectively interoperate and scale, just as Dick Nolan had taught (and was indeed one of the first in the world to recognize).[21] Those of us working in the change solutions client-service space had the background to help with this. *But in empowering ourselves to help, we also took advantage of the culture's freedom and action-orientation as we conceived, pushed for and enacted this new set of organizational arrangements.* There were receptive ears at the top of our division to move on this.

Alas, this was not the case for the wider company to affect the firm's overall operations. The total organization remained too diffuse to get any attention on such a more broadly proposed change. The state of the firm's overall financial health, in any case, was perhaps too far gone for such an intervention to have had effect across the board.

The corporate chiefs remained distracted by the ever-greater urgency to find a buyer for the firm, and they kept up their public happy talk. So, while some of us came forward, *the energy was not available at the top.* The strategic apex function was characterologically disabled, drawn away from being able to consider, digest and deploy better arrangements. Culturally and economically, such suggestions by then, like others, would have been easy to dismiss.

Across the firm as a whole, many in the middle retreated to their splintered and individualized ways, keeping their heads down in the face of all the troubles. There was an "every man for himself" dynamic at play, middle line managing directors now preoccupied with career concerns, not wanting to be seen as rebels. Energy in the middle thus never really had a chance to congeal to even try to better pull in the top for improved operational focus and attention.

The rational, organizational redesign solution that proved effective within Public Services was not all that complicated to figure out for those schooled in the disciplines. However, what is of note here is not simply the rationality of the solution's design, but something else: The solution was able to be activated in the division because the unit remained sufficiently financially healthy and was culturally open to it. Public Services was characteristically not beset with the same amount of chronic armor and blocking elsewhere in the firm. The division apart from the rest of the company in this respect. Public Services was more flexible, less extreme in its work aggressive character. And its leadership reflected this.

As I look back, Public Services it seems retained its regenerative capacity for health even at the end. This was evident in the division's continued effective leadership, even given its own transitions, and in the concerted action and spirit many within the division continued to express. That unitary energy even seemed to grow during the many months, years even, of crisis. However, across the firm, the same I believe was not the case.

The wider company remained a disconnected set of divisions and ensembles, aggressively pushing ahead, but not seeing their way out of difficulties very clearly or thoroughly. Yes, despite the prevalent splintering and isolation, some of the practice areas across the firm performed well enough. However, as problems mounted, adequate performance proved less reliably the case. Groups' performance and their people's happiness, suffered as their energies inadequately concentrated, streamed together and deployed for more solid effect. And more than this, only on occasion did the wider company's divisions and groups seem to really *play well together*. In the end, the business simply fell apart.[22]

Ultimately, the operating results for the firm were all telling. So was the unhappiness on people's faces and as so many of us felt it in our hearts. Productive gratification, individually and collectively, was gone. Shortly after filing Chapter 11, the business was sold in pieces to different corporate buyers, highly undervalued for the contracts on the books.

The large and comparatively healthy Public Services division was sold to Deloitte, sold in a deal that the top of the unit maneuvered on its own to do. Public Services, its basic health remaining, operated with a freer spirit than BearingPoint's other divisions. The healthy actions of the unit's leaders operated outside corporate's attempts to curb a deal of our own being struck. Public Services was sold with the far highest valuation of any of the other divisions.

The separate sale of the Public Services to Deloitte, announced as a merger, was a good and noble effort. It gave the unit's people continuity in their jobs and our customers continued service. To all affected, it gave a bridge to the future, where we could make our own decisions to stay or leave, without sudden loss of personal income.

Nonetheless, as an operating committee member of the newly combined Deloitte Federal Services entity, I could see some important structural challenges the integration of the two firms posed. And it seemed, as I witnessed in the new entity, important challenges were not going to be addressed. It's not that Deloitte's legacy leaders did not hold effective power to make that happen. Indeed, while Deloitte was characterized by a softer collaborative *façade* than BearingPoint, its culture was highly competitive, much fiercer and sharper in how it actually functioned I was struck by than was that of our old Public Services group. The merger conditions only sharpened the competitive character at work, as the original Deloitte players and those from BearingPoint vied for power. In that competition, Deloitte's leadership seemed more commanding, both in position status and in style. The character of BearingPoint's old Public Services group seemed actually more collaborative, less harsh.

Once the two firms merged, I remember seeing this strong internal competition and the comparative characters of the two firms vividly at work in my first few months there. I experienced the familiar fight over who would take the lead on accounts. But now that fight was between Deloitte's legacy service delivery leaders and those from BearingPoint. Sometimes the BearingPointers were just cut out without any advance notice, and though we fought, we showed a tendency also to retreat. Not unusual in corporate mergers, there were winners and losers. On paper, at least, there were efforts to have equity between the two firms. Co-lead roles, one from each of the legacy firm, were established for each of the functional units of the combined entity. And the chief executive role of the new entity overall even went to a former BearingPoint leader.

The twenty-five-member operating committee, which met weekly, reflected the power dynamics, both formally and informally. The committee was formally designed to be a collaborative forum of equals, with all of us sitting around an open table set-up when we met. But as I saw during more than one meeting, all eyes were fixed upon one particular Deloitte partner. The image of an emperor struck me, as I had just returned from a needed vacation in Rome after the long tumult of BearingPoint. Visiting the ruins of the Coliseum, I had seen the concrete chair in the round where the Caesar sat.

A suggestion I made in one of the committee meetings, respectful in tone, fell on deaf ears. I addressed the merger's need for better interoperating protocols, as we had earlier introduced at Bearing-Point. They seemed needed now more than ever, at the beginning of the new entity, given the internal competition, the complexity of the integration and to make the merger work. I was alone in publicly making that suggestion. Some of my old fellow BearingPoint partners on committee were rather shocked when I made it. Privately, they told me how much they agreed with the point but said they wouldn't dare speak it openly. Now they were the ones keeping their heads down, part of "entry behavior" into the new system, jockeying for acceptance and positioning. I was not so inclined. Having been through the experience of BearingPoint, I wanted better. I did first take the time to work on the proposed idea with others behind the scenes, but when there was opportunity to be public about it in committee, I spoke up.

I made the suggestion for two reasons. First, I'd say, on grounds of its merit. I thought the proposition important, to consider at least, on how to best meet the operating needs of the new entity's work; and to also meet the merger's announced, highest purpose—to capture the value of both firms for synergistic effect. Secondly, I made the suggestion to test and see how open the system actually was for real public discourse on strategic organizational matters. As it was early in the game, I was still pondering if I would stay or leave (once I saw the people in my own practice settled). Beholding the reception to the proposal would help me make up my mind. My "intervention" with the suggestion essentially followed a Lewinian principle: "The way to understand a system is to try to change it." I thought I had made the suggestion in a way well enough to see what the future held there —and if that would be enough for me now, given all I had experienced at BearingPoint.

My experience at the new firm of not being heard was not unique, and I ended up being the first of the original hundred BearingPoint principals to leave. The kind of disappointment I felt, and my conclusion that things would not work as advertised, is also not uncommon in mergers. It reflects some the dysfunctional fallout from what is called "post-merger drift," where noble sounding unity goals give way to the actual interests in fusing two firms.[23]

The marriage, as it were, was one of convenience and expedience, not love. The real motivations and preoccupations were ones of survival for those of us from BearingPoint, ones of financial gain and market share for Deloitte. That is a *kind* of match of course. But it is one where the natural value of the firm's real work (in this case, consulting services) is compromised and not the primary drive. *Despite what was proclaimed, real concentration on the work itself or the synergy of the companies were not the merger's primary aims.*

Soon, other of the BearingPoint legacy partners began to leave. While some left because they were not able to sustain their individual performance and there was some natural turnover in retirements, it seems at least curious that only a small minority of the original BearingPoint leaders over time remained.

In this respect, the fusion of the two organizations turned out to be *an acquisition—an acquisition of business—not a merger of the human enterprises*, despite what was at least half-believed and certainly mutually declared at the outset. This net result is actually commonplace in corporate mergers. In this instance, the combination of the firms was an expedient transaction whose core drive was *marketplace dominance*—a remnant of BearingPoint's overall character and a sure sign of Deloitte's. Using Reich's language, the merger was not borne out the need to perform "vitally necessary work," work, that is, which is central to the combined entity's natural work function. As a member of the new, combined organization, something felt off to me right after it was born.

Once this came into focus for me, I knew it was time to leave the big bands and form my own private ensemble—in this case, becoming a soloist in concert with others to play a more fulfilling type of music. To be sure, inconvenience and challenges existed to set out on my own. But I was struck that the challenges would at least be *real* ones to face, not symptomatic challenges of an overriding organizational character I had found so draining—and from the old business's standpoint so debilitating. Besides, I concluded, starting out anew on my own represented the opportunity to contribute something more directly of value, work that was in line with what I now felt I needed to do to live a gratifying work life.

Work is best when it has a natural quality I believe. For work in an organization, that basically happens when the work directly expresses the system's natural, core function. To the extent it does not, the work function will be disordered—for the firm and for its members.

A major, perhaps surprising and controversial implication coming out of this I think is this: *The natural work function of a group or organization can never primarily be one of commercial purposes.* Even in market-oriented contexts, it seems this implication holds. Yes, making money of course matters, tremendously so in private enterprise organizations. But what is determinative of health is the answer to the question, *"making money doing what?"* That points us to *what the actual nature of the work to be performed is in the organization.* It also points us to *the quality with which the work must be performed, technically and humanly,* if the organization's natural function is to be fulfilled. Overt behaviors alone don't mark the human score. It is what is *felt*, or not felt as the case may be, that often counts most.

This implication seems to hold even if the specific, natural work of the system is to make cash available to others (inherent, for example, as part of a bank's core work). Nor does this implication seem to contradict the general need for organizations to accumulate capital to support and sustain their natural work functions. Firms regularly die because they are cash starved. BearingPoint did. But the accumulation of capital for its own sake, divorced from the natural function of the business itself, is something else indeed. That I believe is a characterological distortion at the organization systems-level and reflects certain imperatives at a wider social level. I take up this discussion of such wider social implications in the book's final chapter.

Jazz musicians and their bands are at their best when they play from the heart, not simply in rote fashion for the cash, inimical to the purposes of jazz. Time and again in jazz history, when playing became too much that way, the spontaneous movement of musicians' inherent energies broke through convention, yielding up creative new sounds that thrilled them and audiences alike. To achieve this of course, musicians' long hours of concentrated practice, individually and together, were almost always required. But such practice is done out of the love of the work itself and the natural rhythm of its learning.

Likewise, I think a major consulting firm's natural work can never genuinely be one of financial gain or scoring deals for their own sake. Inherently, its core work necessarily flows out of its natural function to provide advisory services that help other organizations flourish in their own endeavors, hopes and dreams. I believe when the interests of money overtake the primary natural function of an enterprise, the outcomes will always be colored—sometimes where the work gets twisted and is never fully discharged. Or worse: where twisting and turning reach the point where the firm ceases to exist. This kind of experience and record of failure in mergers too is common.

The health of organizations is inherently tied to their ability to do their natural work and for their people, individually and together, to work naturally at it. They will draw in their energies to concentrate charge then discharge what is vital in the first place. Excitement, genuine achievement and felt human happiness are its hallmarks.

SOME SUMMARY DIFFERENCES BETWEEN HEALTHY AND CHRONICALLY ARMORED ORGANIZATIONS

Looked at overall, there are qualitative differences separating healthy functioning organizations—those that operate as "natural work democracies" as Reich described—from those that are neurotic, chronically armored and compromised. Table I summarizes and contrasts these differences. The table is presented as is from its original publication in 1990.[24] The general attributes described here are still applicable as far as I can see. I believe they are even more relevant today, with the coming of the network organization, a kind of organization that BearingPoint labored in its own way to become, but was characterologically, in the end, unable to live.

TABLE I
General Comparison of Work Democratic and Armored, Neurotic Organizations

Effective/Self-Regulating Organizations (Work Democratic)		*Ineffective/Chronically Blocked Organizations (Armored, Neurotic)*
Work/pleasure unity (Work experienced as pleasurable)	⟷	Work/pleasure antithesis (Work as a duty and a "burden")
Immersion in the work process	⟷	Compulsive fixation on task or inability to work or concentrate
Confrontive of problems at root	⟷	Evades problems; "blames" symptoms
Clear sense of direction/ flexible in action	⟷	Rigid direction or aimlessness
Attitudes of empowerment	⟷	Attitudes of powerlessness or compensatory attitudes of grandeur
Work experienced as "meaningful"	⟷	Robotic/mechanistic work styles
Sociostructural unity, harmony	⟷	Sociostructural contradictions, tension
System and subsystems move smoothly as a unit	⟷	Poor integration/ coordination between sub-systems
Flexible task assignment and roles	⟷	Structural rigidity in task and role assignment
Use of well-defined temporary systems	⟷	Fixed or insufficient systems
Open internal and external feedback systems	⟷	Weak or closed feedback systems
Integration of strategic reflection *and* action	⟷	Disjointed or one-sided emphasis on strategy and action
Mutually satisfying customer relations	⟷	Dissatisfying customer relationships

PART II:
TECHNICAL DIMENSIONS

CHAPTER 4

CONSTITUTIONAL AND SOCIOEMOTIONAL DEVELOPMENT

I t is generally well established that groups with work to do, once assembled, go through stages of development, each stage with its own work and shared emotional functions. Perhaps the most famous model of group development stages is Bruce Tuckman's, going back to the very early days of OD and in his follow-up work with Mary Jensen. Tuckman described stages of "forming, storming, norming, and performing" (and later adding a terminal stage, "adjourning"). Based on close observation of new groups' dynamics, these stages have been understood to operate in workplace groups, learning groups, therapy groups, T-groups—groups of all kinds. Each group exists to perform certain work, be they standing groups or formed for temporary purposes.[1]

Like Tuckman, other scholars have observed and described various stages too, many of these converging with Tuckman's, some of them in part differing. Tuckman, in his original formulation, reviews the various contributions here, including those from Warren Bennis and Herb Shepard, pioneers in OD who had seen many T-groups. Many years since the developmental dynamics of small groups were first looked at, they have remained a continuing area of study with open questions, though there is less empirical inquiry of a broad nature than one might imagine.[2] This chapter continues the exploration of stage development theory. This chapter is perhaps the most speculative and complex of the book, though it includes descriptive cases to help advance and sharpen general understanding—and the questions themselves.

As originally asked, such questions have included: What time frames do such developmental stages take? How may the stages overlap? And how strictly sequential are they? Beyond these, further questions that Ed Schein's work opened the door to are: How, at an organization's founding, do small group dynamics get translated into larger patterns of organizational behavior and culture? What happens to the dynamics of development when a founder is an active participant in the process? What happens when blocking or frustration occurs at each stage? And how might the actual nature of the group's work affect its developmental stage process?[3]

I believe Wilhelm Reich's clinical and natural scientific work fundamentally deepens and extends our understanding here. His unswerving focus on energy dynamics at the root of human development, growth and functioning suggests further elaboration of the stages of group development—and that, even before these stages, an organization first develops and *constitutes a nature, the very nature of the work it will drive to fulfill.*

Reich, as a student of Freud's, understood that much of individual human character was shaped by the time a child was five or so— through early, inner stages of psychosexual development. These stages Reich understood, like Freud, were conditioned by outer factors, most immediately those of the family constellation in which the child was greeted in the world after birth. In this chapter, we will look at the organization-level analogues of the psychosexual stages: the primary *socioemotional* stages of group life and organization character development, after the group is born. This discussion culminates in a new, modified set of socioemotional development stages that I propose; stages that start to kick in immediately after a group is born.

I also see two other fundamental developmental considerations operating. First, the early set of socioemotional stages I see are preceded by *an even earlier period of development: when the group's nature is constituted from conception through an incubating period of organization.* Secondly, I see *the stages iterating, in whole or part, at later major life-cycle junctions as the organization matures.* I believe these considerations, taken together with the socioemotional stages, yield a more unified picture of how groups and organizations fully develop. It is an overall picture, too, that is new, heavily informed by the application of Reich's work to the organizational domain. But before we dive into the material at the organizational level, let's further consider Reich's understanding of energy development in an individual's life, in the womb and in early childhood, adolescent and adult years.

REICH'S UNDERSTANDING OF INDIVIDUAL DEVELOPMENT

As Reich increasingly recognized the presence of a tangible, primordial energy in life, he saw how the origins of an individual's character could begin to emerge even earlier than through the psychosexual stages. He was among the first, for example, to understand that character could be predisposed in the child's intrauterine environment in cases where deprivation and chronic contraction existed. Furthermore, Reich came to see even after the profound shaping of individual character in early childhood development, it continued to be influenced in later ages of life, too, during puberty, later adolescence and adulthood. The work of one of the first life-stage psychosocial theorists, Erik Erickson, was explicitly indebted to Reich's work in this regard.[4] Reich remained focused on a tangible life energy moving through every age of a person's life. Reich did not simply reduce life to a series of probabilistic, molecular collisions—the unfortunate view that came to dominate modern biological science, including psychiatry's prevailing understanding and pharmacological character of treatment now too.

Understanding that an individual's life is first and foremost energetic does not preclude an appreciation of constitutional, genetic factors or physiochemistry. It's not that these are not at play; but that much of their salience lies in *the innate intensity and threshold they signify for charge and discharge—for natural pulsation*—which each organism in a variable way possesses.[5] Each organism is also adaptive to outer conditions in the way it pulsates. We are *biosocial* creatures from conception.

That some individuals have higher energy charge and thresholds than others seems evident in everyday speech, as when we sometimes admire and remark upon how much energy a person seems to naturally possess. Reich saw that when individuals' natural capacity for charge and discharge was high, they seemed able to better move through challenging situations that faced them in the world. They tended not to easily give up when they encountered difficulties. The implication of this understanding for thinking about individual stage development is this: The innate strength of the person's energy charge may predispose them to handle the vicissitudes of early childhood development relatively well, even sometimes under quite difficult circumstances.[6] Of course, such adaptive resilience is not unlimited. Comparatively harsh circumstances in early childhood, prevalent in the world, typically leave their marks in character. They are scars. And as we discussed in Chapter 3, Reich was among the very first to specifically describe how the adaptive response of the organism to very tough conditions can misfire in deep cellular and metabolic disturbance. He detailed how it did so in a number of somatic disease states he called "biopathies" that can strike people at various ages.

Reich did understand that the nature of the energy, *as long as it remains viable*, keeps pulsing and moving throughout the life-ages of the individual, often stunningly so. Reich's emphasis, for example, on understanding and accepting adolescent sexuality and the push of energy at puberty reflects this. Adolescence is a period when the natural force of the energy is acute, when excitement and anxiety naturally run high. Teenagers of course regularly experience challenges—severe and rather common challenges at that, given the simple tasks of living and family and cultural dynamics at hand. Nonetheless, the natural strength of the energy that streams inside of teenagers carries most of them forward. Their longing for life is real.[7]

Any number of examples show the power of the teen period's energetic force. It shows in how some teens, disaffected in their upbringing, will find ways to move out of unappreciative family homes and get on their own feet early in life. It shows in how some youth seek out work opportunities just for the pleasure of it. It shows in how some teens find new bursts of energy (or renewed bursts carrying over from their childhood) in playing organized sports or in creative endeavors like the arts. And it shows in how many will seek early sexual intimacy and relationships. They will be open to experiment in life to see for themselves what gives them genuine pleasure and that what does not. The trials of romance, frowning social convention and outright prohibition will not often stop motivated teens to pursue intimate friendships and union.

Yet the force of the energy at adolescence also makes teens especially susceptible to difficulties when internalized individual blocking exists. Teens may be especially vulnerable to get *sucked into* damaging experiments with drugs, gangs, cults, and into neurotic relationships and routines, substitutes, as it were, for what they themselves experience as "the real thing." Still, adolescents' natural gravitation to seek genuine satisfaction can mean many will be able to spontaneously leave damaging situations behind, seeking more fulfilling work situations, personal relationships and habits.

As adolescents grow into adulthood many will come to seek healthier friendships, marriages and work than they earlier enjoyed or felt trapped in. The charge of energy streaming in life continues. Adulthood is especially a period where the charge of energy takes on special force in work and in a person's work life. Work energy and sexual energy for Reich were two sides of the same bioenergetic coin. Thus, adolescence and adulthood are periods where energy continues to drive forward for expression and satisfaction.

The energy's impact is not simply derivative of the way it is affected in primary early childhood stages of development, though the first years of life are profoundly powerful. Because the energy is a *living* force, individuals' healthy functioning will be affected *at any time of life* when the energy's natural rhythms are seriously compromised. When that occurs, people will need to find constructive ways to unlock the pent-up energy so it moves freely and vigorously once again—effectively concentrating, flowing and being productively discharged. People will always experience this as relief, individually, and as I contend below, in group and organizational contexts. This restoration of natural movement, in effect, means meeting life anew ("letting go and moving on")—the essence of growth and renewal.

APPLYING REICH'S UNDERSTANDING OF INDIVIDUAL DEVELOPMENT TO GROUP DEVELOPMENT

Reich's comprehension of an innate bioenergy continuously at play in individuals translates well I think into understanding the developmental life of organizations, *as organizations are collectively peopled in their drives* (as Chapter 1 describes).

Specifically, Reich's understanding lets us consider *what it is that is moving* through the stages of group development when organizations are born. I believe Reich's work helps us uniquely see:

- what a group's *natural work* is that is going through the stages in the first place;
- what the natural work of a *particular* group developmental stage is;
- what the function of *a staging of work development* is at all; and
- what happens when a group's emotional energy gets frustrated, turns back on itself, and does not effectively fulfill the work of a stage.

Crucially, this helps us grasp how the larger, core work function of the group or organization never gets completely performed. When blocked from free, natural movement, some of the entity's energy gets consumed at the stage, then structuralizes into a character dynamic, inhibiting further flow. *As a system, the entity can thus get energetically stuck in one or more stages of work.* The frustrated energies of the stages, I argue, are the historic origins of an organization's character and are the current-day fuel that sustains the character's troubling symptoms. Subsequent frustrations retrigger the force of the system's original dammed-up energies too, reinforcing the difficulties. The system's character structure becomes a trap.

Applying Reich's understanding to the development of organizations leads us to the vital distinction referenced earlier. It elucidates how a natural, core work function arises in a founding group or emergent organization even before it begins to operate. This process seems distinct from the primary socioemotional developmental stage period which happens *after* the organization is born. *Thus, there appears to be an earlier gestation period, after conception but before birth, that establishes the core function of the group—its nature. The subsequent socioemotional developmental stages then condition and bring that organizational nature to fuller fruition.* The dividing line between gestation and birth in an organization is not as discrete as in a biological system, but a differentiation between an "organizing period" and launch seems real. The socioemotional stages thus seem to be the primary means by which the expression of the organization's nature and continued growth is *acculturated* early in its life through enacted norms and culture (or more specifically character as I have used the term). *A group or organization's nature is different from its culture or character.* I believe this distinction is new for the field of organizational science and for OD.

With this by way of introduction, we turn now to more specific considerations of the gestation period during which the organization's basic nature emerges. This is followed by discussion of the socioemotional stages through which this primary nature passes and matures as it moves. Observations from consulting cases, a T-group experience, and a famous example from the history of corporate life are used to help clarify the picture.

THE CONSTITUTION OF A WORK GROUP'S NATURE

The time it takes for a new group to gestate can be long or short. Sometimes it can be fleeting. The formal creation of a corporation, before it launches, is described as its "organizing period." But whether long or swift, certain essential elements it seems are always at play.

This gestation period is the time the embryonic organization's nature crystallizes and obtains its status as an organization; it becomes a bounded system that undergoes continuing development the rest of its days. The elements that come together to constitute the organization address what the organization is founded to do, by whom and with whom to start. In a kind of sheltered space, founders and a few key starting members meet to provisionally consider what primary constituency will be served, with what work products, via what organizational means before it launches. These first provisional sessions are in fact largely *improvisational*. As the energies of the founding players converge around these elements, the nature of the group emerges, becomes demarcated, and takes a starting shape. I contend its core work function gels during gestation, subject to further development. After this, and depending on particular circumstances and other needed preparation, the organization is ready to commence the work natural to it. Notably, this founding period is typically one of felt excitement and high anticipation; *the atmosphere is charged.*

Said another way, during gestation the group's or organization's basic energetic nature is *constituted*. What seems to define it literally, or *constitutionally*, are *the constituents* to be served. The organization's external constituents are those in its field that the work will be principally for, those the organization will engage with in dynamic exchange. Internal constituents of course also exist—employees, for example. But whether internal or external, as a bounded system, the organization's most basic nature seems to be distinguished by those its work will primarily serve. In market-oriented contexts, these *primary* constituents will invariably be customers. But other, non-commercial enterprises (like government agency services organizations) will principally serve those outside themselves too.[8]

We've already discussed in earlier chapters how, for example, the nature of a bank is to provide financial services to facilitate the flow of commerce; and a hospital's natural work is to serve a community's medical needs. But in the real world, specific banks and hospitals are conceived to do something even more particular than these general descriptions suggest. Their natures are more concrete. At Allied Bank, for instance, the driving conception was to meet the needs of an underserved, mid-market customer base; Allied was founded to be a "merchant bank." In a hospital instance, a new Children's Heart Institute, as part of a major university teaching hospital, was conceived to serve the needs of the most difficult pediatric cardiology cases in the world, regardless of a family's means. These were the specific, core work functions each of these enterprises set out to fulfill.

The core work functions necessarily imply natural subsidiary functions. They naturally define the requirements of those who will perform the operating work (their needed knowledge, skills, abilities and temperaments), just as the core work also defines the basic organizational operating requirements that its starting form must satisfy. Finally, the nature of the work defines the potential for pleasure and risks inherent in its performance. For example, a loan decision for a merchant customer carries different risks (and complex judgements and assessments) than does lending money to a consumer or Fortune 50 customer base; loans to merchant bank customers are generally more difficult decisions to make and "get right." Yet if soundly made, they can yield enormous pleasure and value to both customer and lender. Special personnel and operating structures and processes—such as the distinct way a merchant bank's loan committee must work—are also implied by the constituency served. And almost any new organization will need initial staff, information systems, communication networks and channels, at whatever level deemed sufficient, to operate successfully from day one.

Once up and running, satisfying the core and subsidiary work functions—*satisfying the inherent functions natural to the organization*—defines the basis for its success or failure. In the energetic terms we have used, the extent of this satisfaction defines the endeavor's health, defining the extent its product, process and felt human fulfillment are even possible.

The starting form coming out of gestation must be whatever is at least minimally necessary for the entity to be *viable*. It must be sufficiently constituted so *the structural basis of future performance* is established. If successful after launch, the organization will continue to develop and grow in its features and functions, its qualities and size, its learnings and capabilities. Its membership, elaboration of its subsystems and networks, and presence in the field will expand. Indeed, the successful organization's surrounding field will widen. However, if the gestation period is unduly rushed, a *premature* organization is born that may not prove viable. Key people may abruptly leave, work product may fail, and the group may fall apart or never quite get off the ground. If an organization is born prematurely (e.g., it starts to have to work too early as it still needs to gestate), its continued development and growth will be in question.

In fact, a *generic fragility* seems to exist for any new organization. This has significant implications, I believe, for organization theory. Beyond the gestation period, any new organization, as soon as it opens its doors, will continue to be vulnerable. It will be especially vulnerable to critical events that occur in its environment as it begins to operate. And, more than this, the entity is hardly done growing. Indeed, it is just getting started. Therefore, *a layer of adaptive capability* seems inherent in any organization beyond its core, constituted nature. A malleable layer of norms and culture emerges as a basic function *to mediate* the organization's energetic movement out into the world and its internal development and adaptability. This mediated layer between core and world provides the basis for the organization to maintain dynamic equilibrium in Lewin's sense, as the entity grows. I contend this is the root function of organization culture (or character), giving the organization means to self-regulate its inner and outward oscillating energies and movement throughout its life. The development of this mediating layer gives the organization *ordered flexibility for its natural energy regulation, survival, adaptability and future growth.*

It seems just after the organization's birth, the system organically develops through graduated stages of work—internal development work that the organization still needs to undergo for growth and to make its way in the world. I hold that these graduated stages are the organization's *primary socioemotional developmental stages*, running from the system's first days after launch through the early days of its actual operating performance. I believe fulfilling the work each stage represents solidifies the basis for the core, energetic nature of the enterprise to flourish in the world.

But the system's energy can also become *functionally disordered*, I contend, if it meets with overwhelming (or near-overwhelming) conditions at any of its socioemotional stages. Under these conditions, the organization can become seriously compromised as it typically starts to function. A disordered organization character emerges. The array of disordered organizational functioning is widely evident in the real world. We will take a close look at the socioemotional stages shortly. Our discussion includes the way *character formation and arrest occur when the natural work of a stage (or stages) gets compromised,* even as the organization strives forward. This of course is not unusual when the firm's environment and inner conditions are such that quickly making money and proving itself are strong. This too is part of an organization's generic fragility and continued viability.

Returning to our discussion of the gestation period: A starting structure first emerges in behalf of the newly congealed, core work function. This structure can run from being very simple to more complex. If the intention is for the new entity to simply remain a small group, or begin its life this way, its size and players may well be limited to the founding tribe, with a few others added just before or soon after the group begins its work. During the gestating period, a few basic roles and their most elementary functions will likely have been identified, as well as those who will perform, share or rotate through them. This period where the nascent organization is constituted will also likely include first efforts to define the most basic goals, work products, ways to initially communicate and make decisions. Sometimes how decisions will be made and who will make them are explicit, sometimes they are implicit and somehow just made. Regardless, the *manner* in which they are made, even before the doors of the entity are open, already begins to structuralize the group. This *structuralization* occurs even if decisions made are incoherent, recognized or not as such. In that instance, an incoherent way of how its people work together has already begun to be established. Its consequences inhibit the organization *constitutionally*, laying the ground, I argue, for *misshapen* top-middle-bottom segments that are starting or will soon start to form.

As already touched on, this can happen if gestation is rushed. In this instance, there *is too little concentration of initial energies brought to the table around the inherent work to be performed. This can lead to the emerging entity's nature to never quite gel.* (This can also happen, sometimes radically so, if enough founding members get spooked and give up the effort in the organizing period, the nascent entity dying *in utero.*) If founders are impatient and anxious to get started, or other circumstances are overly pressing, gestation will be rushed. *Significantly, rushed gestation may set the scene for rushed development after birth during the early socioemotional stage*s, as we shall see. In a related way, if excitement never fully builds around its core function while in gestation because actual interests lie elsewhere, the core identify of the entity can get *constitutionally* compromised. I have seen this.

This occurs, notably, when founders' principal interest is in the money-making function of an enterprise, not *the inherent value of the work* provided for those served and who stand to benefit from it. The organization's work in that case is instrumental of serving other and others' needs (in whole or part); its primary function gets "mixed up," as it were. This has enormous implications. For the group or organization, its native identity may remain confused, not only in the marketplace, but within the enterprise itself. Such confusion became a chronic problem at Allied Bank, as we shall further see, anchored in the way the top of the organization forever afterwards wrestled with. More generally, such subordination of work's natural value to a primary interest of financial gain poses, I believe, major problems for the wider social order: for capital enterprise itself and for the possibilities of work that can be fulfilling. We take this up again in the last chapter.

On the other hand, it seems *when the natural work of the emergent organization is clear and the strength of its core charge is vibrant, the organization can withstand many challenges that may come its way, early on and throughout its life.* A legendary example of this is the Walt Disney Company.

From the very start, Walt ventured to bring pleasure to the world through entertainment media—to a natural constituency of children and adults "who keep the feeling of childhood alive inside themselves." This was so from Walt's earliest little company's efforts creating animated shorts. He was only twenty at the time. Having returned home from World War I and after briefly serving as a cartoonist-apprentice at another company, Disney began dreaming up an idea for his own business. He conferred with a few fellow cartoonists, found an investor for a little seed money, and the doors of Laugh-O-Gram soon opened in a storefront studio in his hometown, Kansas City.

Walt Disney as a company founder experienced many challenges and setbacks, just as his own father had in his own business life. These setbacks showed up even as Walt was trying to get his first little business and its successor off the ground. But he never gave up. He kept his eye and drive on his original, native dream relatively purely throughout his life—and in the various incarnations of the enterprise over its many years.[9]

Walt clearly learned from his experiences in business early on. He learned enough to recognize he needed to bring his older brother Roy in as his partner to oversee finance and administration before he relaunched the failed Laugh-O-Gram as another new, little business in Los Angeles in 1923. (In fact, Walt likely rushed gestation of Laugh-O-Gram without adequate capitalization, when he started selling product with no margin.) Walt recognized that Roy was more talented in finance and administration than him, and he also recognized how necessary that was to allow him to stay focused on the company's creative thrust. So, with Roy in place with the basic structure he insisted on, *the new business was launched on much firmer footing*. But Walt also always remembered that finance and administration were never the name of the game, even in much later years. Walt had monetary ambitions, sure, but his *primary* drive in the founding and the running of the business was never to make a lot of money. His dream remained the same as when he started Laugh-O-Gram. Financial fortune came for Walt, but as a result of his genius in continuously figuring out right new ways to keep meeting the aspirations of his natural constituency in accord with the business's deep natural drive. *Essentially, the nature of the work was all.* This meant too, as with Roy, Walt from the start was unafraid to bring in people who were better than him in certain essential functions and crafts—like the cartoonist Ub Iwerks, with Disney for a lifetime—so that the venture's nature could be fulfilled. Walt did not need to vainly compete with others on his team. The organization's needs and those of its natural constituency served superseded that.

This core, natural drive of the organization continued to play out during successive difficult transitions later in the life of the business—transitions into full length animation, special television series,

and development of its theme parks. These were all pioneering efforts where Walt also had to work through difficult strategic conflicts
with Roy and bankers, and move his way past public opinion-makers
who criticized his efforts. He did not always get things right. There
were mistakes and misjudgments along the way. Pettiness, some vin-
dictiveness, blind spots, and real emotional difficulties were part of
the picture. But Disney's early drive and commitment to the enterprise, even though it bore his name, came to stand for something
much bigger than that. This led to an *organization culture characterized by work that flourished in gratifying achievement.* I believe a
"work democratic organization character," as I designate the type
in Chapter 6, had essentially emerged. The quality of the company's
character endured challenges throughout its later life. Some of these
challenges, as we shall see, like its labor difficulties in the 1940s, were
successfully resolved by the system at large, even in the face of Walt's
own later autocratic response. The healthy dynamics of the system,
imprinted in the organization's nature *and* character, appears to have
trumped the current-day dysfunctional behaviors even of its famed
founder-leader.

The main point I want to stress here is *the vitality inherent in the
Disney company at its founding and early years appeared again and
again in its later life.* This vitality remains today nearly sixty years
after Walt's death. Its staying power is reflected through its successive generations of CEOs, both faltering and successful; through the
company's various market transitions and eras; and throughout the
emergence of the firm's many business units, subsidiaries and acquisitions. "Adjournment" of the Disney journey, it seems, is not in
sight.

As a general matter, I contend that a firm's original vital drive is
conditioned and shaped, for good or ill, through the developmental
stages during the early life of an enterprise following birth. Organizations with strong drives to begin with may do better than others in
moving through the stages. I strongly suspect Disney was one such
company. I argue that a system's core, constituted natural drive is ei-

ther nurtured, thwarted or compromised during its next pivotal early years, giving rise to healthy or disordered organizational character structures that stay with them.

THE SOCIOEMOTIONAL STAGES OF GROUP DEVELOPMENT

After a group or organization starts to operate, it seems to immediately begin passing through a set of socioemotional development stages. Quite generally, the classic group dynamics literature looks at groups once they have assembled to start work, as in T-groups.

Even in T-groups, however, there are preliminaries that *conceive, incubate and constitute* the group before it first meets. First, the group is one whose core work, whose *nature*, is conceived to be one of joint self-learning of participants (about self and group dynamics). The decision of conveners to hold such a particular group at a particular moment in time represents its actual *conception*. The T-group's core conception creates boundary conditions for the group, as does the fact that the group's constituency is entirely internal to it.[10] Following conception, the T-group then incubates before it first meets and goes to work: The group *gestates* in a period in which it begins to structurally form and be constituted. This seems little discussed in the classic literature.

In constituting the T-group, prospective members are informed about the general nature of the group being conducted. People then apply to the group, then are selected. *Some* screening criteria are almost always applied by conveners to make the applicant selection, as was the case in the T-group I participated in at Pepperdine. Convening faculty screened out candidates in advance of program acceptance if faculty saw enough evidence in an applicant's background that seemed would be disruptive to the genuine learning of the group. The T-group thus had certain "natural" defining requirements for membership. I see that such considerations during incubation are, in effect, concerns about energy functioning in constituting the group—how energy could be severely sucked out of the group once on its way if membership did not match the work's natural requirements. Before commencing, participants are also of course told where and when the group will take place, its ending point, and general schedule of sessions. Only then, does the group assemble and begin its actual work of self-learning. This means there is a bigger context for development than the sociodynamic stages that T-groups first revealed.

Even so, once in assembly, the T-group doesn't just perform its work of self-learning automatically. The assembled group *must now grow into its work* of self-learning. Its self-learning seems *naturally staged.* A bit more on how T-groups classically function after they launch can help us better grasp the socioemotional developmental stages as we discuss in this chapter.

Once convened, the T-group often begins by the facilitator addressing how the work of self-learning will principally be done by the learners themselves; what they learn will be through their own efforts of encountering each other and exploring the possibilities of the group, not through the active intervention of the facilitator.[11] The facilitator explains her role as one who is not directive about the group's content or process, but as one who remains just outside the margins of the group, helping only to "hold space" for the group to perform its work. Beyond this, the facilitator's brief remarks about her role will center around her remaining present to help the group in an "emergency"; that is, if people get so stuck in the process that the group's continuance is jeopardized. In all other traditional respects, the group is "leaderless." The cord is now cut.

Leadership for the group must now emerge from within the group. If it doesn't come or comes very slowly (it will often be too slow for some people), the group will likely thrash about. This itself becomes grist for the group's self-learning. From here, further group development occurs, and leadership resources from within the group almost always arise (be they effective or not). The classic literature, as in Tuckman's research, describes a common sequence of group development dynamics.

The facilitator's opening remarks are first of a high-level *orienting* nature, but, classically, she offers little more to orient the group throughout the rest of the learning forum. The rest of the learning will need to come from the T-group members themselves. It is a group whose core nature is one of self-learning.

Without concrete direction, amidst initial silence, members of the group now start to make short statements, sometimes expressing surprise, sometimes nervous efforts at humor to see and gauge the reactions of others. They begin to open their eyes to the T-group task in front of them. They may ask questions of each other, and there may be an effort or two to draw the facilitator back in with questions to seek more clarity. While facilitator styles will vary, she will likely say little in response (some may say nothing at all), leaving the group to its own devices.

The first exchanges in the room have a tentative quality. Members are feeling their way through the early exchanges. But it is not quite accurate to say the movements are random. There appears to be a natural pattern to them. Members will first be inwardly concerned about their own manner of "being in the group." Very shortly, the questions and utterances start to converge around coming to some kind of understanding of *what the group's fuller orientation will be—what it will do with its given opportunity, its work, its highly open nature.* "What are we going to do here on this journey? What am I going to do here on it? What will come out of me? How will I and others be?" These are the common questions asked as the group seeks to orient itself and the members themselves individually too within the group. It is up to the members, individually and as a group, to explore and come to terms with what they will make of the opportunity at hand; this becomes the group's earliest *vision.* This first, emergent dynamic is almost universally found in all small group development research. Researchers' resulting schematic renderings of the stages almost always starts with a group first coming to understand what it is about, an *orientation* function.

The natural work of any emergent group, I believe, T-group or not, will be for its energies to largely be devoted to the work of the stages. The group's overall work is not yet discharged in full swing. For a T-group at its beginning, that full work yet remains unknown. This means, however, that if the emergent group is a not a T-group but a young organization with products or services, its first work will not all be entirely (or even mostly) devoted to serving its core constituents in its field. The organization still needs to spend substantial energy on its internal development. This includes envisioning its further fuller size, shape, and development of its capabilities for some short and longer terms, *as far as can be seen just then*. That is natural work to be performed too, not just immediate sales, product or service delivery. This first development work will include further definition of the organization's product and service offerings and its further elaboration of structure.

After having its vision come better into focus, the new organization then seems confronted with having to work through subsequent development stages natural for its fuller functioning. From what I have experienced and studied, I have come to understand these subsequent stages are those that successively work through how its members will: be supported; establish independent and interdependent capabilities; then productively get work out the door (first in the entity's ability to routinely perform the work and then in ways more wholly effective and fulfilling). These may not be strictly sequential stages, and their own emergence may overlap and blur. Yet the organization during this early developmental period seems to grow in its capabilities to concentrate and discharge its working energies more completely, assuming conditions are supportive of that growth. That growth seems to follow a natural sequence of stages. Experiences during the socioemotional stages very much seem formative and gradual in emergence.

One more general note about T-groups because of their experimental, research nature: "Pure" T-groups represent an extreme, test-tube-like look at the origins and development of group and organizational life. A pure T-group represents a group under controlled conditions, where effort is made for nothing other than the participants to enter the room that could affect the group's internal development. The impinging action of an outside field on the group is held in abeyance. The T-group's members are, with the few exceptions of researchers who may observe from a distance, the sole constituency.[12]

In the real world of organizational life, the emergent system is less radically and immediately on its own than in a T-group, and it is much less exempt from external contingencies. A real-world organization is more fluid in its operations, and the action of its field can be strong. Founders, for example, usually remain present, often pressing in on the need to get going. Also, very strong can be immediate customer demands and the need for investors to see cash generated—let alone the business's own vital demands for revenue. In the real world, a principal founder generally continues on as an internal group member, very frequently assuming a permanent role as its formal leader. *A founder in this way is both parent and player.* The ambiguity in this can make for both *overweening and underweening effects* in the new group's development. Underweening occurs when the founder's presence is too much, when she presses in too much or too quickly given the total situation. Overweening can occur when she does not assert herself forcefully or soon enough for the developing needs.

All of this of course is multiplied in effect, since every organization member brings and inwardly refers to their prior group experiences and sense of their own competence to the task at hand. These experiences draw from their earlier worlds of work, learning, social experiences and family of origin, the last of which prevalently evoke issues of authority and counter-authority. Tavistock workshops make a good deal of authority and exercise-of-power concerns as they transfer to present-day organizational tasks. All of these conditions are in play during the primary socioemotional development period. This makes the early development period in the life of an organization complex, rich in potential and possibilities, but also vulnerable to challenges, risk and danger.

In fact, such conditions seem inherent in the actual timing of when primary socioemotional development takes place. In the real world of organizations, systems may likely be compelled to perform some level of core work almost immediately after launch (a few even before). It is common for some to line up and prepare for that work before the new entity opens its doors. Organizational systems we know are socio-technical in nature with energies directed at work activity from the start. This has important theoretical implications for stage theory: *The primary socioemotional stages may always play out in the context of the immediate task demands of the system. The stages likely will not wait to play out.* This doesn't contravene the stages' essential building-block nature that they play out early in an organization's life, or that *they need to play out.* Rather, this understanding points to *the likely condition that the primary stages will kick in and will need to be worked through when real work is at hand.* This seems a critical difference between the individual human organism and an organization, between psychosexual development in a child and primary socioemotional development in a new organization. This complicates matters in the origins of character development at the organizational level. Conditions are set up for socioemotional development to likely be rushed. Yet, as I will argue below, the socioemotional dynamics of the young organization are *still* being played out, performance of its "real work" begun or not.

Stage-level frustration leads to *characteristic constellations of symptoms* as I will describe. And it is these presenting constellations that consultants can then work back from in the approaches they use to help mobilize the system. *Consultants' understanding of the frustrated developmental stage in which the organization got stuck will tell them "the what" that needs attention in their sociotherapeutic work. Thus, as conceived here, stage theory points to the underlying issues to address and remedy the systemic disorder at hand.* Understanding this has practical consequences for the consultant; he will better recognize the deeper issues at play in the current life of the organization, issues needing appropriate treatment. These deeper issues, I submit, are manifested in the persistent organization character that arises. The implications here are discussed in the origins and the sociotherapy of each organization character type described in Chapters 6 and 7.

As I first began to learn about group development dynamics through my graduate studies and reflections on my experiences, I found Ed Schein's schema for the developmental stages of groups particularly striking—for the descriptive language that he used and for how he ties it into the origins and development of an organization's culture.[13]

Building on Tuckman's pioneering work, Schein clearly described the staged interpersonal learning going on as *socioemotional work*. He spoke to the existence of a "formation stage" (what Tuckman called "forming"), where, among other things, basic orientation and leadership dependency issues are worked through. Schein next spoke of a stage concerned with group building and cohesion (roughly equivalent to Tuckman's "norming"); this stage culminated in an emotional state that Schein termed "fusion." The fusion stage, as Schein describes it, is when the group comes into its own, is focused on harmony, and where members begin to "idealize the group as an object." However, moments eventually come when movement towards group oneness turn into pressures for compliance and conformity. These pressures sooner or later prove limiting to getting actual work done, so members start to push against the limitations and push against each other; conflict and means of trying to contend with conflict emerge ("storming"). If the differences that surface during the fusion stage are sufficiently worked through, the group, Schein says, passes into a productive "group work stage" focused on achievement ("performing"). Finally, Schein concludes his own schema with a "maturity" stage, one of integration but one also that risks self-satisfaction. The entity is then susceptible to rigidification, its continuance threatened as it becomes less flexible to respond to future events (a prelude to a potential terminal state similar to what Tuckman called "adjourning").

In Schein's work on culture formation, he stresses the important role of founders and critical external pressures the organization faces. Schein recognizes the powerful influence each exert, but he is less specific about *how* founders in particular affect development during the socioemotional stages. This is in part due to Schein's focus on laboratory groups in his discussion of the stages; again, the stages are less affected in that context because founders and external events are essentially absent in the test-tube-like T-group situation.

Yet Schein's work implies how founders could influence socioemotional development in the real world in which most groups and organizations function. In the transition to each stage, Schein recognizes how decisive "marker" and "critical incident" occurrences emerge and must be worked through. He describes *how a group could get stuck in a stage if the emotional functions of the stage remain unfulfilled.* He sees in the development stages the original means by which organizational culture emerges, implying the specific means whereby *a particular, historically derived organization culture originates.*

In this way, powerful external pressures and founders playing internal leader roles affect the work at each of the stages. If founders' actions are nurturing, for example, they will have a positive effect on the group being able to satisfy the work of the stage; if frustrating, the group could be left with unresolved, "unfinished business" of the stage's work. The interaction of the outer world and influence of the founder, now from the inside, intersect with the group's natural development needs to shape its emerging norms and organizational character.

However, because Schein does not see the ground of a driving work energy at play, he does not see how the unfinished work of the stage *sustains and continues to feed* the organization character. *Logically, the dynamics of a culture must be an energetically present phenomenon, not simply a historical artifact. The constraining effect of the organization character remains because energy continues to be expended trying to fulfill the natural work of the stage in question; thus, as I will describe, only a partial amount of the system's energy is available to reach a final, full work stage of gratifying achievement. This, as I see it, is how the organization develops a character that compromises the full discharge of its work.*

Regardless, all this is very reminiscent of how parents and outer world events shape internal developmental stages of early childhood—Freud's psychosexual stages of development[14]—and the way certain resulting attitudes and traits can stay with a person in their continuing growth and adulthood. Psychodynamically, this is discussed as a "fixation" on the original frustrated impulses, the basis for neuroses. The great vulnerability of early childhood life means that children are entirely *impressionable* by parent and world. The impressions are stimulated by how parents transmit the values of the world and of course by how parents through word and deed nourish or frustrate the fulfillment of the stage in the child's developing life.

The socioemotional stages of group development seem to serve similar functions in an organization's early years. Moreover, the socioemotional stages appear to follow a sequence resembling the natural order of the psychosexual stages: *from orientation, dependency, independence, performance, and full self-regulation.*[15] Some investigators of group dynamics, such as Warren Bennis, have called out this functional resemblance.[16]

Although Schein does not speak of the members' collective *energies* being so conditioned, his approach to the stages seems to provide an avenue to incorporate this, despite its other details. Nor does Schein speak about a group *nature* being formed in a gestational period, before conditioning developmental stages occur. Schein indeed does see a formation stage, sheltered at its start, with aspects of its primary functions determined by founders. However, his conceptualization of the formation stage is blurred with other orientation functions once the group is live. There is no distinct gestation period recognized. Others who have studied group dynamics have not made this distinction either.

So, we'll make a fresh start of formulating the socioemotional stages that includes their differentiation from a group's basic work drive. The new framework I propose below is rendered in light of our earlier discussion of a natural work energy in motion—and the development of functioning organizational character structures, be they healthy or chronically blocked, that grow out of it. In addition to the observable organization dynamics, Reich's description of an individual's staged development in light of the movement of bioenergy is suggestive for understanding what goes on in group life. Let's return for a moment to Reich's understanding of developmental dynamics in the individual realm.

Clinically, Reich rooted his understanding of how *individual* character types first evolve during the psychosexual developmental stages as Freud originally articulated. But Reich modified his understanding of the stages—seeing their blended flow and differentiating and enriching them further—as he increasingly appreciated the bioenergetic nature of the human animal, the organism's streaming energy charging and discharging over its entire life, shaped powerfully in early childhood but appearing forcefully too in adolescence and adulthood.

As Reich's clinical understanding and practice moved in this direction, the patient's history and the therapeutic aim of awaking unconscious *past memory* became less important to completely uncover as it had remained in psychoanalysis. Reich now had additional, direct *present-day means* to access the movement of the energy and the potent emotions the neurotic defenses held at bay: *by working directly with the body. Reich could now work somatically on the armor, right in the moment,* in addition to working through the rigid character attitudes the somatic armor contained. Restoring the individual's capacity for charge and discharge could be approached in therapy now through attention to the individual's breathing, muscular contractions, and the way deep feelings were liberated for expression. This gradually built the person's capacity in how he functioned day to day. This supported self-reinforcing change. A patient's memories and reflective insight of course accompanied this more open access to feelings too, so the mental and cognitive side of things were not ignored in Reich's therapy. Overall, if a child's development was allowed to take its natural course under supportive conditions, the basis was laid for functioning that was healthy and satisfying, not disabling as in neurosis. Adolescence and adulthood provided further periods for the energy to be concentrated and released. The adolescent period, where the urge for sexual expression and union emerged, gave people in effect a "second chance" at life. And in adulthood, the energy appeared especially strongly again in the functions of love, work and knowledge.

Applying this understanding to the organizational domain—keeping the similarities and differences in mind we've already discussed between individual and social system realms—yields a modified set of socioemotional stages. I believe these are basic in the development of an organization's life.

Before laying out my modified group stage formulation, I want to call attention to three items that have distinctive implications for the formulation because of their bioenergetic roots. Each are firsts in the organizational literature.

First, clinically, Reich and his students (especially Elsworth Baker) increasingly came to emphasize the eyes as an erogenous zone in psychosexual development. This was evident they found, for example, in the ability for healthy flirting with the eyes and also evident neurotically in voyeurism. This distinction of the eyes Freud did *not* make in delineating what was his first orientation and dependency stage, the oral stage. Baker came to term this new, earliest stage of psychosexual development the "ocular" stage; this differentiation is well laid out in *Man in The Trap*.[17] This distinction has resonance for the differentiation you will see below in the formulation of a new, separate *vision stage* for group development. The organization literature is riddled with references to vision and visioning within organizations. The status I give to a vision stage of development here, I believe, grounds the understanding of vision more fully in the core development of an organization—including what gets in the way developmentally to obscure its vision so widely.

Secondly, there is another major way a bioenergetically grounded understanding of individual stage theory informs socioemotional stage thinking: It helps us understand how *waste*, both naturally and in potentially disordered ways, builds up in an organization and is discharged throughout the system's life. This is reflected in scrap work, rework, unsuccessful R&D trials, but also in how people end up getting "wasted" in the beat of organizational life when it is disordered. As described below, I contend the process of waste regulation is highly conditioned during the group-level *fusion stage* (roughly equivalent in function to the psychosexual *anal* stage of development). This linking I am making to emergent group attitudes about waste at work—and to how waste is effectively processed and disposed of—is new in the literature of group dynamics too.[18]

Thirdly, you will see in the modified stages a differentiation in the group-work stage: an initial *work-aggressive stage* of development is defined, then followed by a *work-democratic stage*. This new distinction is suggested by three factors: by the enriched way Reich described equivalent stages of childhood psychosexual development; by empirical observation of organization dynamics; and by the logic of how a healthy organizational character type could come to develop at all. I argue that the delineation of a work-democratic stage allows us to appreciate systems that develop the capacity for work quite *fulfilling in its achievements and human satisfaction. Developmentally, such a stage seems to distinguish a fully functioning organization from one that seems stuck in simply aggressively performing work, one characterized by its prideful pushing of work out.*

Summarizing what we've said to date: Overall, the socioemotional development stages first come into play immediately after the birth of the new organization, itself coming out of gestation when the firm's nature is constituted. What transpires during the stages then condition that nature from which a specific organization character emerges. *The stages represent the natural, successive staging of the work native to the enterprise.* Building on each other, *the extent of the satisfaction within each stage affects whether and how the organization's work will be fulfilled and experienced as fulfilling—or the extent its work will be discharged in a way that is only partial and unfulfilling.* Each stage has its own natural work functions and socioemotional concerns to work out. And I believe each organization's own complex set of circumstances will affect the timing and emergence of the stages.

With this said, following in Table II is the new group development framework I propose. The table is followed by discussion of each of the stages. This chapter concludes with a fuller description of how the stages do not seem to be one-time events, but ones that iterate at subsystem levels and at various critical junctures of an enterprise's life cycle.

The Vision Stage[19]

The vision stage that I propose emerges immediately out of the gestation period. This stage marks the beginning of the primary socioemotional development period. The vision stage may emerge more than once in the organization's life, as can the subsequent socioemotional stages. They can iterate during critical life cycle points and in various subsystems, which we will address shortly. But as the vision stage first appears in the primary period, it immediately affects the entire organization as assembled at launch.

The vision stage serves to *orient* inaugural members of the organization as to what the nature of their work will *look like*. The stage also provides a period for group members to work through their self-understanding of *who they will be* in the organization, providing a first picture of how they will belong in the group and roles they may play. These orienting work functions have powerful accompanying socioemotional concerns, as noted in Table II: *"How much will we be able to look at and see what is actually happening? How clearly?*

How confidently? How much will we need to turn away from what we see?" The set of questions listed in the table are not comprehensive, there are undoubtedly more. But the experiences and satisfaction encountered during the stage inform the organization's future ability to focus, to have perspective and be collectively introspective, to see things imaginatively *and* to also see what is really happening even when it is difficult to bear.

Lack of satisfaction at the stage sets up the basis for disorientation, confusion, lack of focus, the need to turn away from seeing certain crucial truths, and more. Blocks encountered at any of the early stages lay the foundations for the organization's emerging character, leading to stereotypical patterns of acting and reacting in the organization's life. This further inhibits freer, natural movement because the energy is tied up in the unfinished work and unfulfilled socio-emotional needs of the affected stage. In the instance of the vision stage, an organization's needed, natural visioning capabilities going forward become compromised.

For example, we can see how organizations at their start may go through initial planning exercises too quickly or mechanically ("going through the motions"), because founders are pushing to get going in the marketplace before there is sufficient clarity. Or the opposite could be the case. Too much time is spent gazing in visioning exercises before there are sufficient facts or experience to work with or the new firm is looking away from important critical tasks to perform right away—all leading to perceptual distortions that do not accord with reality. In that case, it's as if a group is *staring at questions of "being and becoming," intellectualizing about them, rather than letting a wider view emerge in its own time.* The essential point is that discordant events in the work of the stage can become inhibitory and create frustration—and character arrest (or inhibition). A founder may think she is getting the group to move faster. But in this way, she is holding the group back because its energies remain stuck. Yes, the organization is born *to move.* But that does not mean to anxiously rush about and hurry things—or again for that matter, in its opposite

TABLE II

Reformulated Socioemotional Development Stages

DEVELOPMENTAL STAGE & WORK OF STAGE	SOCIOEMOTIONAL CONCERNS & FUNCTION	EFFECTS & BEGINNING CAPABILITIES WHEN FULFILLED	EFFECTS WHEN UNFULFILLED
VISION STAGE - Orientating period - Group's first understanding of the nature of its work - Members' initial self-understanding of who they will be in the group	*"How much will we be able to look at and see what is actually happening? How clearly? How confidently? How much will we need to turn away from what we see?"*	- Clarity and focus - Perceptiveness and perspective - Reflection, insight and foresight - Able to see imaginative possibilities - Able to see difficult realities - Breadth/depth of views, near and far - Able to distinguish the essential - Group life seen in full spectrum color	- Disorientation, confusion - Blurred sight of present and future direction and possibilities - Myopic sight and thinking - Not paying attention to what's right in front of group or members - Fleeting attention span - Flying blind - Things seen in only black and white or only shades of gray
DEPENDENCY STAGE - Nurturance period - Group receives and reaches out for support from leader in behalf of task and member development needs	*"How much will we be able to trust others' presence? Seek and receive help and support? Be able to stand on our own?"*	- Members' trust in leader's managerial and interpersonal competence and presence - Members' felt support from leader to help them fulfill their task and developmental needs - Leaders' ability to count on members - Expression of wants and need - People willing to speak their minds - Group's ability to effectively operate with the needed independence to act	- Over-reliance on the leader - Felt abandonment by the leader, undernourishment - Chronically felt disappointment, depression - Leaders chronic second-guessing and checking - People reticent to "open their mouths" - Norms to hush up in the group - Especially harsh rebellion to leader, early or late

(Continued)

TABLE II (continued)

DEVELOPMENTAL STAGE & WORK OF STAGE	SOCIOEMOTIONAL CONCERNS & FUNCTION	EFFECTS & BEGINNING CAPABILITIES WHEN FULFILLED	EFFECTS WHEN UNFULFILLED
FUSION STAGE - Group independence and interdependence period - Drive for "groupness," group harmony - Group becomes idealized object - Differences and conflicts emerge for resolution	*"How much will we feel we are a group? Be able to be ourselves in the group without fear of rejection? Differ among ourselves? Work through conflicts?"*	- Belief in the group, pride - Effective, flexible teaming - Broad range of emotional expression supported by the group - Knowing things at times will not work - Appreciation of differences - Tolerance for mistakes - Effective group conflict resolution - People treated well, even those involuntarily terminated	- Immobilization - Group stuck on itself - Pressures to conform - Compulsive, overcontrolling - Demands for obedience, perfectionism - Emotional differences suppressed, flat affect or gushiness - Fears of messing things up and falling apart—be they latent or expressed - Over-analysis, caution and doubt - Robotic or "dreamy" work styles
WORK-AGGRESSIVE STAGE - Performance period - Group members mobilized to discharge its "real work" in the world - Push, promote and provide goods to the world	*"How much will we be able to just get it done? Move ahead? How strong will we be? What happens if we fail?"*	- Product and service delivery accomplishment - Members take pride in their key work accomplishments - Healthy growth and expansion - Attitude of let's go to it - Growing appreciation of "human side of enterprise"	- Narrow production focus - Aggressive and self-aggrandizing work styles - Insufficient attention to group process and human fulfillment - Fixation on "more and more" and "bigger and better" - Fear of failure, weakness, challenge - Desire to "knock the customer dead" and "blow the competition away"

(Continued)

TABLE II *(continued)*

DEVELOPMENTAL STAGE & WORK OF STAGE	SOCIOEMOTIONAL CONCERNS & FUNCTION	EFFECTS & BEGINNING CAPABILITIES WHEN FULFILLED	EFFECTS WHEN UNFULFILLED
- Deal with loss, internal group weaknesses in way of working			- Felt need to bear up and cover up signs of weakness
WORK-DEMOCRATIC STAGE - Wide self-regulation attained - Full concentration, flow and discharge of work energies in behalf of core group function - Full integration of earlier socio-emotional capabilities - Integrity of pleasure and work	*"How much will we be able to do our vital work in a fully productive and fulfilling way? How do we assure we sustain ourselves? Sustain this way of working?"*	- Productive gratification - Full product/service and human fulfillment, for all stakeholders - Regular excitement in the work process a felt reality - Effective movement of people in, up, down, across, and out - Innovation and invention to satisfy changing needs - Effective, flexible use of people, processes and supporting systems - Spontaneity, self-regulated as needed - Absence of chronic armoring	- Temporary stasis or chronic flightiness in discharging work energies - Simple, supportive interventions may be enough in the absence of chronic armoring - Dissatisfaction may be more plainly expressed and addressed

manifestation, to anxiously hold still gazing for fear of spontaneous movement.

I contend that disturbances encountered during the vision stage can get anchored in the shape and structure the early top-level subsystem segment takes (the "strategic apex" or "head"). This can start to lock in the disturbance energetically in an organization. The ongoing, deep anchoring of a vision block in the head of an organization may mean the top never develops the needed strategic apparatus to scan the environment, neither seeing or foreseeing the opportunities and threats posed. The organization's "field" is not adequately seen. Comparable anchoring happens in the other stages too with respect to the "deep structure" cross-cutting subsystem segments.

A severe example of the effects of blocking during the vision stage happened in the history at Allied Bank. In fact, the socioemotional block was built on initial discordance between the two co-founders during the earlier organizing period before the bank was launched. In this way, I strongly suspect, the bank moved into the vision stage with an *inherent* lack of clarity. *During the vision stage, it seems this distortion was then iterated and socially reinforced*; lack of strategic clarity remained an issue throughout the organization's forty-year life.[20]

To briefly describe: Allied Bank seemed split in what its two founders conceived the organization to be. One was primarily oriented to its "dream"—its core merchant bank function; the other primarily saw the organization as a vehicle "to make things happen," perhaps reflecting greater focus on the entity's money-making function. While not immediately debilitating, this may have set up a *constitutional disposition* for confused vision that came to characterize the organization. This it seems was the genetic origin of the firm's character, what I have called an "aggressive vision blocked" type, more fully described in Chapter 7. On top of the constitutional disorder, there appeared to be rushed development in the early vision period of the organization; planning, for example, did not sufficiently occur in the organization's early life. It rushed its way to the market. The organization confused the need to spend more time on planning with the part of its merchant bank mission dedicated to go make things happen. The need for that quality of planning was not easily seen. An attitude of "TNT"—literally one of its mottos, "Today Not Tomorrow"—developed. This attitude, I think, essentially got habituated during the vision stage. It betrayed a dark side of rushing to action, not backing up long enough to see and consider things first more clearly before moving. The humorous saying, "If you see something moving in the bush, shoot it," captures this attitude. This character trait contributed to a major later organizational crisis, though the bank successfully managed through it, given the enterprise's remaining capability to marshal its other inner resources of health.

As a little coda to the story, it is interesting to note that when the more visionary founder died thirty-five years after the organization was launched, the other more get-it-done founder took complete charge—and senior talent which had been politically aligned with the now gone visionary founder were rapidly purged. Within a few short years, although a variety of factors were in play, the organization was sold as a vehicle for cash accumulation, its legacy not living on in the hands of its natural heirs. The novel dream of the organization—and its life—was gone.

A final point on the vision stage: Not all organizations even if frustrated here will get *hung up* at this stage. There appear to be a number of factors at play. One of these, as already suggested, is the extent of the frustration and integrity of the organization's nature as it is conceived and develops during its organizing period. Another consideration is this: Because of the systemic nature of the organization generally and the relationship of the stages to each other, *blocks in later stages will necessarily impact the ability of the organization in discharging its vision-related functions.* If energy is stuck at later stages or elsewhere in the body of the enterprise, it seems it will necessarily affect how all other things are seen and *able to be seen.* *This leads to limitations in perspective and line of sight in all of the disordered character types and how they go about their work.* This is evident in how so many organizations have difficulty with strategic thinking and effective strategic planning. Whether severely blocked at the vision stage or not, the inhibitions elsewhere in the organizations' development appear to affect their current day visioning function and apparatus. The organization's ability to concentrate and expend its energies here gets constricted. The whole system is affected.

The Dependency Stage[21]

As the youthful organization moves through the vision stage, fully satisfied or not, it continues its growth and enters a dependency stage. Now what becomes primary is this: *for its leaders to provide—and other members to receive—enough support, information, communications, other resources and emotional backing to grow and develop.* This builds on the clarity and confidence obtained during the vision stage around where the organization is headed and how it will get there. During the dependency stage, members' dominant socioemotional concerns are *to* develop *trust in the presence of leaders, confidence the leader will be there for them, and not simply have their human concerns skipped over for organization task concerns. Leaders during this stage too will be concerned and want to see that members can be counted on.* "Will employees show up, make good contact, and take the initiative? Can I count on them?" A leader after all is dependent on the good faith actions of others. Many leaders of course have ineffective management styles that pull them in too near or far away from the organization's other members and field of action. But there is little question too this can be a two-way affair. Leaders can be pulled into the affairs of the organization too much because of the undependable actions of others. Either way, such behaviors are seen in organizations where there are special shared hang-ups in dependency needs.[22]

The basic *nurturance* of the stage prepares organization members, and the organization itself, *to stand on their own,* without undue reliance on the leader—operationally and socioemotionally. When the stage is satisfied, this shows up as people starting to operate and act independently from the leader, and also in their willingness to speak their own minds. When frustrated, communications and norms will develop with just the opposite effect—members will remain dependent, be reticent to speak up, and keep looking for approval from the leader before taking what would otherwise be natural action.

The energy stuck there, will eventually result in a buildup of inner organizational tension that can peak in a particularly *sharp* rebellion against the leader. When thwarted, delayed independence can lead to highly charged *anti-authority* impulses, issues and lack of member trust in the leader. This phenomenon is found regularly in T-groups and is well documented. Likewise, leaders can develop too little trust in members to properly function; they may keep interrupting the work with their own interests, their redundant presence ("hovering"), and their efforts to remain on top of everything, needed or not (overly controlling). In any case, the need for the organization to develop real functional independence is crucial in order to do its work. This is the final work of the dependency stage.

Based on my OD experience and understanding of how the cross-cutting segments embody blocks in the system, blocks at this dependency stage seem to particularly get lodged in the head of the organization (like its emergent chief operating officer function); they can also get housed elsewhere in the organization among those in roles performing related support work to the top. One manifestation of the blockage in executive function is *the hampered ability to communicate (literally "feed") vital information to members. Leaders can remain mum themselves, not only not knowing what to say, but how to effectively communicate that they don't know something fully yet. They lack the confidence to speak up. Or they may simply be afraid to speak up. Or they may spout off all too much or inappropriately.* Such symptoms may all be triggered from objective difficulties encountered during the primary years of speaking up. The *vocal* function of the executives gets disturbed. Upward communications from the body of the organization also gets disturbed. Table II lays out some of the main features and effects of the stage.

The Fusion Stage[23]

As the organization begins to develop its needed independence, including abilities to begin to act interdependently, the object of attention in the stages now turns to a drive for "groupness," a greater sense of members being "one team," together in a common endeavor. They start to see and *feel* themselves part of a larger whole. Maintaining the harmony of the organization becomes uppermost in mind, and the organization becomes an "idealized object" in the eyes of its members.

Yet here differences and conflicts among the members will start to emerge. They will require, in light of the need for harmony, constructive ways for members to see the challenges clearly—and to see them through. Socioemotionally, initial concerns in the fusion stage center around members' acceptance of others as part of a unified team. This is followed by questions of whether that acceptance will extend *to tolerating divergence and dissent*, accommodating them without sweeping them away or abandoning ship. This has special salience especially when substantive differences are expressed that are meritorious given the matter at hand. And more: Will needed difference and dissent be richly *drawn into* the team and *drawn on* for its work? Will dissenters be *extruded* from the system, as sociodynamic thinker Barbara Bunker has asked? Will people step up to discuss the differences as the work requires, but also when it draws energy away from their emotionally conditioned need to idealize the group?

When such questions are not effectively worked through, the need for group harmony can turn into demand for "perfection" and "compliance"—traits that when distorted are characteristically *compulsive*—excessively controlling, ritualistic, analytic, with flat or, alternately, "gushy" affect. When gushy, members' overall affect presents as a dreamy-like love for the group or organization. When flat, affect is absent. This leads to exaggerated attitudes of "we're all about work here." Feelings and expressions of pleasure and joy in work are driven out and considered off limits. Excitement becomes intolerable. Characteristic attitudes of extreme caution, skepticism and doubt can arise, showing up behaviorally as endless questioning and nit-picking. Gushy affect typically mutes expressions of conflict and frustration; they are not tolerated. The function here is to keep movement in the organization at bay, clamping down on it, lest spontaneity and feelings surface. This dampens creativity and innovation.

I saw one organization demand that proposed innovation efforts meet rigorous ROI tests and projections before any such projections were even possible; those would have needed some exploratory, initial action to derive. R&D efforts, anywhere along the line, require *some* trial and error. (As Thomas Edison famously said about inventing the light bulb: "I will not say I failed a thousand times. I will say that I discovered there are a thousand ways that can cause failure.") In this organization, the innovation efforts were dead before they even started, killed off. The need for disciplined investment in new ideas is of course generally wise. But in this instance there was an overly analytic and ritualistic quality to the call for rigor that seemed foreign to the natural task.

Fusion inhibited traits it seems can especially result in issues of how people come to feel disposable, wasted, and bad about their work in an organization. How will those who don't fit or are no longer needed be treated? Will there be frequent distortions in how people, or for that matter processes and products, are retired, turned over or otherwise disposed? There are a host of other fusion-related indicators as well: Is there excessive employee turnover at the C-suite or in the body of the organization? Will bureaucratic, "it's-our-policy" regimen be retained when it no longer serves a purpose? Will it be acceptable corporately for people to feel (and in fact *be*) wasted? When people are terminated, will the company only speak in euphemisms, formally and informally out of exaggerated fears of liability (in the end, fear itself)? Or keep quiet about it when almost anyone leaves, catching those remaining by surprise, even when there is need to know?

When the fusion stage is unfulfilled these are the distortions, I submit, that can readily occur. They are all based on fear that things will fall apart, get messed up, "the center will not hold," to borrow a phrase of Joan Didion's. This unresolved fear is powerful. Failure to confront futile efforts in the name of group harmony—*spurious*, superficial consensus—is the essence of the organizational syndrome known as the "Abilene Paradox."[24] These distortions and outlook are likely to play out at any level of the organization—tops, middles and bottoms.

The alternative, when the fusion stage is adequately worked through, is that certain amounts of *natural* turnover, portfolio changes, R&D waste, and performance termination will of course happen and be tolerated in the organization's life. The same is so with failed ventures the organization may have tried. But a predisposition will exist that these be handled rather openly, as a matter of course and with human understanding and even grace. That seems a hallmark that the fusion socioemotional stage has been fulfilled.

The Work-Aggressive Stage[25]

The organization's people now feeling good about themselves as a group, able to handle differences and separation with integrity, and unafraid it will fall apart are now better prepared to enter the first rung of its work stage. This developmental period I have termed the "work-aggressive stage," because its first preoccupation is with simply being able to get its goods, products and services routinely out the door. As noted earlier, there may be special pressure soon after the organization is born for such work to be performed; this means the work will not have the fulfillment of the earlier socioemotional needs behind it. The work then will likely have a pushed, breathless and anxious quality to it. I have seen this and felt this. The work-aggressive stage is the first of all the socioemotional stages where the organization makes contact with its constituents in behalf of the core work drive. Production, promotion and provisioning of its goods are dominant concerns as the organization works through this stage. If fulfilled, organizational members feel resulting pride in the demonstration of the company's wares and the strength of their showing. The human factor is not ignored here, but it is basically seen—and talked about—as instrumental to getting product out. Besides feelings of pride and powerfulness, excitement is experienced in the process, leading to celebration of real and felt "wins." As the stage is worked through, people's anxiety, irritation at others and events seen as getting in the way of work are also experienced and expressed; these sentiments are less likely to be simply stuffed down.

However, if the organization meets significant roadblocks during this stage, characteristic exaggerations in functioning start to appear. Production and performance start to become *all*. *Felt* power becomes a strong motivator, often an object unto itself; the actual work becomes subordinate to the *feeling* of powerfulness. There is *great push* to get things done. People being and feeling highly pushed—like having to work long, exhausting hours that do not bring pleasure—can become the norm. More than a natural drive for growth, there is an ever-increasing appetite for *more and more*. "Bigger is better, no matter what" is the underlying attitude. Aggravation may be habitually expressed or go underground passive-aggressively. All organization segments are in play and chronically push in the way they function when the work-aggressive stage has been blocked; the top, middle and the operating core, all heavily pushing product out the door. Those higher up in the organization when this happens will be characteristically pushing *for* product to get out the door. Organization policy, process and tempo will come to reflect this.

The group or organization in this state can of course falter as it rushes and pushes its way through its development. Such faltering will stimulate its people's desire to push through those problems too, often not working effectively to examine or attend to the real issues. The point to stress is that for all the organization's emphasis on power and performance, under these circumstances its weaknesses are exposed. Developmentally, *the organization still needs to build ca-pacity to confront and deal with these weaknesses straightforwardly.* It will need to do so in two principal ways: first, in reflecting on the genuine strength of how its operating strategies and processes actu-ally work; and secondly, in its people's ability to more fully collab-orate, including understanding and satisfying customer needs. The capacity for collaborative partnering, both inside the organization and among other external stakeholders, needs to further develop for the system's fuller functioning. That fuller functioning signals the fulfillment of the final stage of socioemotional development, the "work-democratic stage." That stage comes, I contend, *if* the orga-nization does not get hung up in the work-aggressive stage, stuck without effective resolution.

The Work-Democratic Stage[26]

The work-democratic stage I propose as a new stage in sociodynamic development theory. A generalized work stage in the classic litera-ture—Tuckman's "performing" or Schein's "group work" stage—does not differentiate a work-aggressive period from one focused on de-veloping capacity to perform work in more fully productive, human-ly fulfilling ways. Again, Reich's own treatment of individual stage development growing out of psychoanalytic theory suggests this. So does the inner logic of how development must occur in group socio-emotional dynamics for there to be such a capacity in the first place. Finally, such a stage is suggested by observation of corresponding, current-day group and organizational phenomena, then working backwards to conceptually infer the stage. By and large, the man-agement literature treats these capabilities as values, rather than un-derstanding them, as I do here, as effects of natural developmental dynamics, where energy builds and moves quite freely.

This stage signals the arrival and development of a capability where full organizational functioning becomes possible. There still is work of the stage that must be effectively fulfilled. But if so, the result is an organization which is strong, flexible and resilient, an organization able to perform the natural work of the system in a fulfilling, self-regulating way. If the work-democratic stage is effectively satisfied, its effects seem quite *secure*; organizations of this type, such as I have seen them, seem able to sustain a quality of functioning even when later, difficult circumstances are encountered. This seems so because of the consistent integration and flow of their work-energy concentration and discharge. A work democratic organization character structure I believe emerges from the fulfillment of the stage. It is embodied in the well-defined and fluid interplay between the organization segments and between the organization as a whole and its surrounding stakeholders. The general features of this stage when it is worked through can be found in Table II as well as earlier in Table I. Chapter 6 provides a fuller portrait of the work democratic character type and a descriptive case example.

When this developmental stage is fulfilled, no need for chronic organizational armoring seems to result. The organization will certainly take protective measures and "pull in" as needed, but it will tend not to develop formal structures or attitudes among its membership that *chronically* block its natural movement. Under later challenging unfavorable conditions, the work democratic organization type may develop a work stasis, but its attainment of well-developed, self-regulating capabilities will tend to lead it to resolve the conditions, on its own or to seek help to effectively do so. In the latter instance, simple supportive consulting interventions—more purely cognitive, behavioral or design oriented—may be sufficient because there is no chronic armor to contend with. Organizational members will more rationally respond—and be more open to rationally respond in the face of facts.

When the work-democratic stage is substantially frustrated during primary development, the basis is laid for a more *work dramatic organization character* to emerge. This conclusion is based on the theory already presented. The work-democratic *stage* is reached but with anxiety due to marked situational disturbances that occur during its period; these in turn are internalized by the organization's members in the way they interdependently function. In this case, work energy piles up and is dysfunctionally discharged in restless, flighty, approach-avoidance patterns of behavior, much less in productive, gratifying work. Members may speak of that state as an ideal but attaining that state it seems remains an unattainable goal. The work energy stirs and floods the system in an excited way, but remains trapped without productive, gratifying release. In the case of the work dramatic character, organizational armor seems light and shifting. When this occurs and is recognized, more thorough sociotherapeutic attention is in order. Chapter 6 describes how I have worked to resolve issues with this type.

ORGANIZATION LIFE CYCLES, SUBSYSTEMS AND CONTEMPORARY IMPLICATIONS

This chapter's final section briefly considers the implications of constitutional and socioemotional factors for:

- an organization's wider "age of life" or life cycle;
- its subsystems that develop; and
- how, despite the fact that these original factors are *historically* derived, they appear to also emerge *contemporarily* and need to be addressed as they emerge.

As powerfully shaping as the socioemotional stages seem to be in the primary development years of an organization's life, they can reoccur in some way, in whole or part, at later organization life cycle junctures. The stages reoccur, too, as new subsystems—divisions, subsidiaries, company spinoffs—originate and develop. Lastly, the stages always also appear to have present-day implications, as their effects representing the character of their bound energy manifest in the moment. This presents opportunities for consultants to work with their effects locally with systemic consequence.

Organization life cycle—the major junctures of aging over the entire arc of the enterprise's life—is a different thing than its basic nature or its conditioning socioemotional stages. Classic group stage theory does not clearly differentiate the concept of life cycle from socioemotional development (neither does it differentiate a group's nature).

As earlier noted, Tuckman recognizes a "forming" stage as does Schein in group development, but these are blurred with orienting and leadership dependency functions. Moreover, there is no distinct gestation period after conception, the first life cycle period, as I contend. Likewise, Schein recognizes a "maturity" stage. This too seems fundamentally a life cycle phase but blurred with socioemotional development as a class of phenomena. I think clearer understanding of what is happening, as I've argued, comes by seeing that groups and emergent organizations *first* develop natures, *then* pass through socioemotional development stages that shape their characters, *then* continue to evolve over the course of the organization's life, especially at major juncture points. *Organization nature, socioemotional development, and life cycle are three different phenomena that come together in an organization's development. This formulation offers a panoramic view of how an organization develops—and what that development naturally consists of—over its life.*

As interest in more naturalistic models of organizations has waned, coinciding with the rise of post-modern conceptions, it appears there is less literature on organization life cycles than one could find some years ago. But organization life cycle studies generally point to the following major periods in the life of an enterprise: *startup, growth, maturity, renewal or decline, and termination.*[27] Such a sequence of ages is also suggested in S-curve, capability maturity models as they have been applied to understanding organizations.[28]

We will not look at each of these junctures here, but instead highlight a more general implication: *Organization character formation and inhibition at any of the socioemotional stages will necessarily affect how the organization moves through its major periods of aging.*

At the growth phase after startup, for example, there will be natural concentrated charge, giving the organization additional push to drive forward. Logically, the conditions could trigger the organization to look at wherever might exist that slows growth, which could then trigger the reoccurrence of one or more of the stages. This would seem especially the case if earlier, significant blocking and "holding" of the energy inhibited needed new action at the beginning of the growth phase. Yet in the presence of blocks or not, the onset of the growth phase itself may trigger the organization to take a strategic relook at its entire way of operating. In this case, many of the stages, fully or in part, could still need to be reworked through. Circumstances, it seems, will dictate the chain of events.

Major organizational anniversary milestones may create opportunity for some stage development to reoccur. Allied Bank, for example, took a serious, strategic relook at itself as its twenty-fifth anniversary arrived; it did not simply treat the occasion as cause for celebration. In fact, this was a time when some of the deeper visioning block—and the aggressive way the firm tried to blow past it—seemed to slow down and open up in a qualitatively new way. A new level of maturity resulted—its character was softened, and earlier patterns of holding freed. A good deal of its former bound-up, built up energy was finally discharged, as we will discuss in Chapter 7. The point here is that at a mature age, Allied did not exhibit the characteristics that Schein outlines in his "maturity" socioemotional stage. It did not shrivel up, as it were, get-self-satisfied and set the stage for it to die. Rather, its character renewed and in some ways "gave." This occurred right after the firm had successfully handled a major crisis just prior to its twenty-fifth anniversary. This gave Allied the impetus, it seems, to go through reinforcing healthy, vision stage redevelopment as its major anniversary year approached.

Schein's description of "maturity" as a socioemotional stage, rather than as part of a life cycle phenomenon, leads him I think to conflate one type of character response (and a dysfunctional one at that) with other forks in the road possible for organizations that reach maturity. We know from S-curve maturity models that pivotal opportunities for renewal and even transformation present themselves as mature organizations reach the top of their first curve. Their products and services now fully harvested, their continued natural viability is now in question. They are thus confronted, not with the inevitability of decline, but with a choice: either "reinvent" themselves in a way in tune with their natures— new, but not entirely discontinuous from their first curve capabilities—or follow a downward slope until the organizations are no more. The death of an organization can happen it surely seems in more natural ways, as when the organization's inherent function no longer serves its field; the firm decelerates gradually, time permitting, as its core charge dims and finally fades away. Or it can happen in characterologically blocked and armored ways, as Schein's maturity stage example, I believe, represents. This hastens the path to demise. This was certainly the case with BearingPoint as a whole. Its characterological pathology brought the organization, literally, down. The inference for character is that organizations that have reached a work-democratic stage of functioning would logically seem better able to handle decline than systems that are severely blocked. The company's phase-out would more likely be handled planfully, with due regard for its people and customers. New bridges to organizations to serve would likely be thoughtfully created, along with continuing career pathways.

It is important to remember that organizations by nature are more loosely coupled than biological systems and have no bounding membrane. This has several implications in our discussion here. First, it implies in some ways organizations inherently may be "ageless." There are organizations on earth that have existed for centuries. Secondly, this loose coupling means, as with the life cycle periods, that the timing, number and sequence of the socioemotional stages' recurrence are variable too. This has relevance in the way the emergence of new functions, markets, products and services, divisionalization and formalization of work will naturally trigger the stages recurrence. This is certainly evident in the emergence of new subsidiaries, but also in an organization's new departments and major business units. Indeed, subsidiaries provide occasion for the "parent" to highly shape the character of the subsidiary, that is, in how it engages with the youthful organization's socioemotional development, and earlier of course, at its conception and gestation. The new entity would certainly seem to move through a new full sequence of primary socioemotional stage development. Regardless of the level or autonomy of new functions and units, issues and opportunities related to organizational work energy movement and blockage, character and armor, will come into play, demanding attention.

Our example in Chapter 3 of the Public Services business unit of BearingPoint is telling here. This division reflected both the nature and the character of BearingPoint more largely. But the business unit, as a system unto itself, yet demonstrated some of its own freer character dynamics. That was evident in its own ability to innovate and embrace major divisionwide improvements and in how it freely broke away from BearingPoint, finding a new home for the unit's people and customers as the larger firm rapidly deteriorated. One can infer Public Services must have had a freer, better set of conditions and supporting environment under which it originally developed. That conclusion is supported by the record of the solid business unit leadership that brought the division to life in the first place and how the succeeding generation of its leaders performed. The Public Services unit was at least one independent fiefdom in the original mix of the firm's partnerships that generally played well together and managed itself with integrity.

The socioemotional stages' historic effects on how an organization carries out its natural function have important implications that present in entirely contemporary ways—in how they are in the moment. The effects of organization character and armor play out moment-to-moment, and in this way are a *re-presentation* of an organization's history in the here and now. This is significant for consulting intervention: *This history can be tapped, and unfrozen, by working backwards, as it were, from the presenting situation.* The more deeply charged issues, often with their still lived memory, can emerge (the remembered or passed-on stories people tell themselves). In fact, more novice practitioners can often run into difficulties—unleashing more energy than they bargained for—in attempted interventions that go too deep, too fast. The energy unleashed is what is at issue when consultants "choose the depth of an organizational intervention."[29]

Yet our understanding of collective energy being bound allows us to worry less about a thorough working through of the history. Rather, consultants can more clearly focus on mobilizing and supporting the bound-up energy for effective discharge—discharged in ways that are productive and with a human touch and care. This is comparable to how Reich's clinical therapy came to concentrate on here-and-now character and somatic manifestations that did not *necessarily* need a complete resolution of historic conflicts. As organizations are able to invest their energies into more healthy ways of working, their stasis is broken, and fuller ways of functioning seem to emerge. This is not a matter of behavior and mechanical repetition. It is about opening the gate for the energy to more fully flow.

For example, consultants' attention to freeing up energy in blocked visioning-related organization segments—by way of top-level strategic retreats—will draw or feed needed energy for circulation elsewhere in the system. If supported by related intervention elsewhere in the system, the retreat can be an effective means for freeing up energy in the other segments. The same is true for leadership development interventions that help dissolve dependency hang-ups and engender greater trust. The same systemic energy draw and diffusion throughout the system will better happen—and more, if its charge is effectively concentrated by the right consultative attention. If the groundwork is attended to in the right order and with an eye on the whole, interventions can be designed in ways to better connect the operating core with the middle line, with those at the top and with customers. The energy throughout the system better flows, concentrates and discharges. In all of this, past development issues are likely to surface—some holding significant energy in members' memory. As such memories arise, consultants can see them as source material relevant to their consulting tasks: the when, where and how to intervene; provide facilitative support; and make simple contact with those in the system. Consultants' knowledge of the underlying energy dynamics at play will make a difference in the sequence, timing and interlacing of their interventions.

The organization's natural work energy, conditioned by its socio-emotional stages, is relevant to understand as it shows up *moment to moment*; this is how the energy actually shows up over the arc of an enterprise's life. The work energy inherent in the system can move freely or it can get stuck, sometimes stuck only for a short time, sometimes characteristically and over the long haul. I believe the present formulation represents a start at understanding *how* organizations get stuck—and what can be done about it—better than other approaches to date.

The way an organization's nature, socioemotional stages and life cycle come together to affect the development of its basic cross-cutting segments kick off our next chapter. The chapter then focuses on the segments' essential functions and how they become the sites of organization armor.

CHAPTER 5

ORGANIZATION STRUCTURAL SEGMENTS AND ARMOR

A s a unique kind of unitary, natural energy system, organizations stand somewhere between living and nonliving natural systems in their make-up. They lack a membrane as living systems all possess, but they have self-regulating features in the way their innate, human membership streams together and functions. These give organizations life and make them more than what is classically recognized as "information processing machines."[1] The living systems inherent to an organization *animate* it. The animated quality of organizations includes the way they incorporate mechanical systems. Human-machine interfaces in IT and processing equipment are features, but wholly serve human work energy functions in how an enterprise operates.

Organization character serves vital self-regulating functions in how these enterprises marshal their collective energies in going out to the world—the surrounding field of other energy systems among which they move and otherwise engage in dynamic exchange. Organizations also develop *formal structures* to congeal and process work energy functioning, helping to stabilize and give some regularity to organizational life in line with their constituted natural functions. After all, organizations are more than a loose assemblage of people not bound by a common function or discharging a common endeavor. Crowds are more like that, and, as crowds, they often do not develop such persistent, formal structures to concentrate and bind energy before its discharge.[2]

Organizations, during their gestation and after birth, do commonly develop such structures—subsystems of human work energy. These subsystems are literally *elaborated* in the developing life of the organization; that is, they are *peopled* with common subsystem functions and features in service of the larger enterprise system. These formal subsystem functions are thus work energetic too in nature. They come to specialize, divisionalize and develop structural arrangements usually staffed with the same people who come to work each day—until they move elsewhere in the system through promotion, transfer or move out of the system altogether, as in voluntary or involuntary turnover. Organizational members may also of course serve in more than one subsystem at a time in an organization. And they may serve in two or more different companies or community service organizations where they play different roles. And even those on late shifts regularly go home to rest and recharge and pursue other dimensions of their lives.

Since people move in and out of these structures in a given organization, these subsystems do not develop membranes nor are they completely integrated organs as animals have in service of their larger organism. But these subsystems do operate in a locale with a regularity and integrity in their functioning and interplay with each other when they effectively work. *Organizational structures are special configurations of human energy to facilitate and process the pulsing movement of the system's overall work energy in conducting its business in the world.*

Some of these functional structures are more tightly wound or bound than others, given their natural work. Some are embedded nearer the center of the organization, with deep internal processing functions; some are located closer to the surface and periphery of the organizations; and some extend directly into its surrounding field, where they serve as means for building relationships, transacting business and recruiting new members. This chapter's discussion understanding organizational substructures in terms of their centralized interior or their more perimeter, surface locations and functions is something else new I believe in organization studies literature.

Depending on their positioning and functions, the various structures will require different natural degrees of regularity and freedom of movement. They all, however, charge, concentrate and discharge work energy, both themselves and in concert with the whole organization. When they have developed and function effectively, these structures are tied together by a series of *energetically driven network flows*—information, communication, decision-making and coordinative action flows—some are unidirectional, others multi-directional and radiating out. Sometimes these networks are elaborated as *channels* for more robust concentration, flow and discharge of their energetic functions.

An organization's subsystems, networks and channels, because they operate in a larger system themselves, are also subject to the characteristic ways the organization has adopted to act and react in the world. As touched on in Chapter 4, subsystem functions indeed appear to develop their own norms and characteristic ways of operating. However, by definition, they inherit and operate in service of the larger organization character that envelops them. Thus, when the organization character serves healthy organizational ends, the structures will tend to perform in healthy ways themselves; their inherent energies will have conditions favorable to their effective functioning. When the organization character has become functionally disordered, this too will be reflected in how the subsystems operate. They will function in armored, disjointed ways, where the energy turns inward, becomes unduly frozen, then is weakly or harshly discharged, as the energy pushes through the armor to keep going. The subsystem structures thus I believe become the sites of the organization's armor that contain the character of the system. When this happens, the circulation and discharge of the energy, within and out of the system, becomes structurally inhibited and compromised. The networks and channels that facilitate circulation and flow become jammed. All these structures themselves become subject to damage and breakdown if their energy isn't sufficiently discharged and gets stuck to the point where it keeps backing up inside of them without release.

This chapter looks more closely at all these considerations, including use of illustrative instances. We'll touch on, too, the role and principles of an energetic based sociotherapy to help free up accumulated blockages in the segments, structures and coordinating networks that constrict the natural movement of the energy, so the whole system may better function. These overall principles are a prelude to what we will address more specifically in Chapters 6 and 7 as sociotherapeutic strategies for organization character types and for characteranalytic consulting technique.

CROSS-CUTTING STRUCTURAL SEGMENTS: THEIR NATURAL FUNCTIONS, PERIMETER AND INTERNAL STRUCTURES, AND ARMORING

All organizations, whatever their scale, appear to have common, basic structures that operate and interoperate in natural ways and that, under unfavorable conditions, are also subject to distortion in their shape and functioning. Two seminal contributors in understanding these universal, structural components in classical organization theory and OD are Henry Mintzberg and Barry Oshry.[3] Mintzberg, in effect, has defined these components *as structural building blocks for any organization*, and he has delineated them in their structural details. (Readers who want more detail on the structural features than provided in this chapter are referred to his work.) Oshry has mainly addressed the three major components' power *dynamics*, their interplay with each other and the outer world, and with customers and other stakeholders. The application of Wilhelm Reich's theoretical and practical work—clinically and in understanding living and nonliving natural energy systems—gives a more encompassing and dimensional understanding of organizational form and function yet.[4]

As earlier chapters generally discussed, these main structural components follow *a naturally ordered hierarchy of functions*—what Oshry called "tops, middles and bottoms," and Mintzberg, more precisely, the "strategic apex," "middle line" and "operating core." Oshry also understands the customers in the surrounding field as another major formal force, and Mintzberg recognizes two specialized internal formal structures in adjunctive middle line roles, the "technostructure" and "support staff." While these naturally ordered functions do not necessarily correspond to *formal* hierarchies, for the most part they do. Even contemporary, flatter network and other platform-based organizations exhibit these ordered functions, as we will say more on in this chapter and give special attention to in Chapter 8.

Over the years, I have come to see these universal components as an organization's *cross-cutting structural segments*. They are roughly equivalent in overall function to the somatic segments that Reich identified in the human body. By cross-cutting, I mean they run *across* the organization's head to toe operations, they are *horizontal subsystems linking people in laterally related functional units*, even though the specifics of their functions may vary.

Some elementary examples of this: at the top, senior level executives, each directing their own business units, but also making up a cross-organization peer group, working together in general policy making or management committee functions. Or in the middle of an organization: mid-managers leading various operating units, each having peer level interests in understanding overall organizational priorities and policies that give them more or less direction and freedom of movement to operate. "Middles," as Oshry has termed them, may meet together in various problem solving and work design forums; their very overlapping interests and certain interdependencies will also give them lateral connection, with shared ends and means of working. Or, below that, operating workers: they may form peer-level working groups under supportive work conditions that value their interactive contribution. They may connect commonly in union efforts, work improvement, and training and development venues that support their collective efforts developing, producing, and delivering goods and services.

When effectively functioning, the cross-cutting segments serve *integrative and facilitative* functions in the organization to promote work energy concentration, flow and discharge. The segments do so up, down, across and out of the organization and in dynamic interaction with the surrounding field. To the extent the segments become blocked (either temporarily or in more chronic, armored ways), they become *congested* in their functioning and *constrict* the natural buildup, movement and release of energy natural to the organization's work. Internalized structural blocking appears to correspond to the socioemotional development stage or stages the organization has gotten hung up with when the natural work of the stage was insufficiently fulfilled.

The three main cross-cutting segments are each discussed below. This includes brief treatment of their structures and specialized functions located near the organization's perimeter (and surface) to those more deeply interior, situated centrally. The descriptions here do not go beyond what is presently understood about them energetically. How each of the three cross-cutting segments form armor, too, is addressed. Technostructure and support staff structures, while essentially middle line specializations, may be situationally housed in the top or operating core segments, with close affinities in their functions and identifications there; the technostructure and support functions are thus discussed as part of the three main lateral segments, depending on the primary segment they immediately support.

Strategic Apex or "Head" Segment[5]
The strategic apex structures are responsible largely for:

- formulating and executing the organization's *general capabilities* in visioning, governance, investment in and intake of resources, and formal alliances developed in the field;
- formulating and articulating policy; and
- establishing basic conditions conducive to work achievement, human support and satisfaction.

These capabilities can commonly be seen as corporately distributed CEO and COO-related functions. Well-functioning Boards also commonly share in pivotal governance and investment decisions.

Executive and management committee functions are deep central subsystems, whereas those that operate nearer the perimeter and surface of the system include those that scan the organization's immediate and wider environments to understand and anticipate changes, challenges and opportunities; such scanning capabilities are important for regulating market products and portfolios, priority and policy changes, and major new organizational arrangements. Support staff, technical specialists and technologies directly supporting such scanning are closely tied to the head, especially those related to general visioning and governing policy functions. Some support staff functions are located near the surface where they make contact with the outside world, some lie deeper within the segment, performing analytical, strategic and internal processing tasks.

General direction on the quality and quantity of human resources the organization should consume typically reside near COO functions. They serve perimeter-related functions for resource intake from the world, routinely carried out by middle line planning, recruitment and placement support staff. But once the resources are taken in, they are channeled more fully inside the system for orientation, development and deployment. Top executives too make direct contact with the world to ingest certain vitally deemed human resources. These resources seem to represent basic "packets" (or *quanta*) of energy that stream as part of the system's general work energy.

CEO and COO-related structures may also be directly engaged with discharging resources through policy-based layoff decisions or one-on-one "firings" with resources deemed no longer fit. These are interesting I think to consider as energic, emotional phenomena. Terminations are sometimes handled sensitively and with human concern; and sometimes, under more armored organizational conditions, they are very anxiously delayed or otherwise handled coldly and bureaucratically. Often, terminations evoke strong emotions—anxiety, frustration, anger, then relief in resolution. In such cases, my experience is that little is vocalized to the organization about them, sometimes nothing at all, even when it is important for people to otherwise be in the know. Contact with those who are discharged or those remaining in the organization is characteristically minimal and "tasky" in feel. People who are discharged often leave feeling worse than they might otherwise had things been handled with a more human touch. These are functions of disposal and waste, associated with the fusion stage of development, I believe, as argued in Chapter 4.

Typically, the terminal discharge of people is at least partially dispatched to HR departments to execute (a support staff function). This further creates emotional distance in the process. Sometimes, the human touch is literally "outsourced" to special outplacement firms to handle. While such outsourcing may create some efficiency and positive concentration of effort, I have seen this have the net effect of distancing people emotionally from each other who remain in the firm. They can reflect a characteristic lack of affect when blocking at the fusion stage has occurred. When the system is chronically blocked, the people executing the terminations also may not experience substantial relief afterwards either. This "chilling" effect is immediately recognizable to most people in organizations. I believe this generally indicates some larger intolerance in the system for its natural pulsing functions—*and for its emotional expression*—in discharging work, reflected in some level of human disregard. A consultant's understanding of how terminations are routinely handled and communicated in an organization is valuable diagnostic data to gauge the system's energetic levels of tolerance in addition to its character dynamics.

Armoring in general at the strategic apex is always a result of too much energy being trapped inside its functions. Energy overly concentrates in the head often out of fear of what the consequences of effective contact and discharge of its work will bring. There is emotional distortion that occurs in this case, blurring what is seen and how it is handled. Tension then builds that is not satisfactorily resolved. This can manifest in executives at the top not confronting each other with hard truths, or working through hard decisions, or generally just backing down and "going out of it" (literally going out of contact). As Chapter 4 argued, such characteristic blocking may well happen during the organization's primary socioemotional development stages when frustration that is incurred is not adequately worked through. While frustration or satisfaction at each of the socioemotional stages will condition the functioning of the top, in the case of chronic blocks at the head of the system, these seem to be most associated with the vision and dependency stages. These two stages seem directly tied to CEO and COO-related current-day functions, respectively. Some of the distorting effects of armoring stemming from blocking at these stages are summarized in Table II and are also discussed in the chapter on organization character types.

The main point to emphasize with respect to chronic blocking at the strategic apex—or at any of the major cross-cutting segments, for that matter—is this: *The subsystem structure anchors the block, keeping its energy dammed up and curtailing productive discharge of the segment's current, natural work.* The subsystem becomes a site of organization armor. To this extent, the productive work contribution of the segment's overall function is withheld and less available to the enterprise more widely. Sometimes, it simply becomes unavailable. However, what the segment still does convey when it is blocked is the emotional dissatisfaction present; sometimes it is strongly felt in an underground way, but generally *verboten* to bring up anywhere except to peers (and sometimes to subordinates), guardedly, at the water cooler. *I believe it is this functional, structural withdrawal of energy at the top segment which is the underlying basis for widespread lack of leadership seen in organizations in our time.* Inside organizations today, people widely, if quietly, whisper about this too at the water cooler. This is a whole system effect when the top is blocked.

I have found in my consulting experience that organizations whose people whisper, who don't speak up, who choke on difficult matters before them will have blockages at or near the COO-related functions. This is the primary area that gives voice to overall enterprise concerns, typically with the help of support communications or PR staff.

Emotional unmentionables in organizations will stem from overwhelming energy generated in the system. In this instance, the most salient blocks to movement will be located in the COO-related functions that cannot rise to their expression or find ways to talk about them more straightforwardly. Thus, the top segment goes on hold regarding their more complete expression or sends out confusing, mixed signals. This distorts the top's natural work functions. The effects of this will spill over on others in the system below. Emotionally, people down the line will inwardly fear being forcibly ejected by management if they speak up on issues they see, so they will keep their own voices low. This is *the energic basis for the reenactment of the norm* the COO models. In point of fact, the weak vocalization *is the character of the system anchored structurally.* I believe this represents a phenomenon bigger than the personality or style of incumbents in the role. Again, the major block seems resident at or just below the head segment played out by executive support staff who will ghost or craft messages for general broadcast about such difficult concerns. Often, they are crafted with euphemisms that will ring hollow—and that some of the messaging staff know will ring hollow even as they write the words. The emotional truth begs to be screamed out, but it is zipped up, muzzled. The primal fear: "Make trouble, and tell it like it really is, and someone will reach down and throw you out. You will not be stomached."

In the face of persistent, structural armoring, when executive resources fail, management development programs, turnaround coaching, and even replacement of the players are commonly not enough. We saw this at the head segment in the BearingPoint case where a succession of CEOs could not adequately handle the problems in front of them. Indeed, the character of the system was anchored too in the functioning of the Board, as I described. At the company, most in the middle line kept quiet, embodying too the character of the system. Fear, as we described, was dominant and in the end kept revival of the system at bay.

In such severe cases, proper organization character diagnosis and corresponding interventions that are even well-aimed and sequenced may not be enough either. If the organization is bent on self-destruction or its breakdown is so severe that a point of no-return has been reached, little may be able to be done. The organization's inherent capacity and potential for healthy energetic charge and discharge has been depleted. Heroic rescue expectations, too often pursued in OD, are not in order. As Baker has said of the efficacy of Reich's individual therapeutic mode: "The approach is no panacea; not every case can be helped, and cases are at best difficult and require courage and hard work. But the energic concept strikes at the very roots of disease and mobilizes many who could not otherwise be touched."[6]

Middle Line Segment[7]

The middle line consists most obviously of mid-management functions running across the enterprise that supervise line and staff units, serving as a halfway house between the top of the organization and the operating core. But the middle line also consists of deeper interior processing structures, like central operations functions, literally at the heart of the enterprise. When well-functioning, I see the middle line functions serving to regulate the organization's day-to-day circulation of energy and to provide the system its daily tempo and beat. Consultants can easily see when mid-line managers are *disheartened* and *dispirited;* dominant effects at the middle, as I've seen it, when significant organization dysfunction is at work. Most others in the system, top to bottom, can also usually sense the discouragement of middles when that is the case.

Mintzberg depicts technostructure and support staff functions as flanking the middle line in his organization structure graphics. Technostructure functions include IT, R&D, Treasury functions, SME and other technical professionals with deep expertise performing specialized, non-line roles critical for the organization to function. Support staff functions include Finance, HR, Audit, real estate and facilities, other administrative support and the like.

Oshry's contribution clarifying the functions of "the middles" especially grasps their crucial integrating role between tops and bottoms. Because they are in the middle, the ever-present risk they experience is that they will be "torn apart"—*dis-integrate*. As Oshry describes, being in the middle when the system is clogged can make its members feel like "a sewer pit"; their routine efforts at transmitting information and decisions from top to bottom, and bottom to top, are jammed. Unfortunately, in very common scenarios, middles are commonly seen as inept to tops, powerless to bottoms, and irrelevant to themselves. Oshry has a variety of supporting interventions to get the middle line moving to more fully function, to help its members better take matters into their own hands. Middles' very integrative nature means their empowerment is vital to organizational effectiveness. Oshry has largely devoted his life's work to the empowerment of middle line players.

In this middle role, the middle line's chief function is to *facilitate the flow of actual work*, the "real work" of the system making goods that go to market. These goods flow through the organization as they are prepared for effective discharge. The middle line has major roles to regulate the expansion and contraction of the flow—to inspire and breathe out energies to keep the system moving. Middle line players do not do this alone. They are connected by networks and channels of communications, influence and decision making. These networks and channels run from head and operating core as well as from specialized middle line functions that review, analyze, package and otherwise process transmissions along the way.

Two examples of middle line regulation of expansion and contraction flows can be seen in Finance and HR functions, especially as they shape, interpret and apply administrative policies throughout an organization. A finance department's fashioning of budget policies (under the direction of a CFO, a COO-allied function) can give more or less freedom to line and staff units up, down and across the organization. It can *expand or constrict freedom of movement*, at the behest of the top, to the rest of the organization. This, for example, can show up as policy that offers line units the ability to spend certain earned or allocated monies at their discretion—or not at all. Under tough economic conditions, such constriction seems self-regulatory for the system. However, if decisions are predominantly driven by the dysfunctional organizational character, such constriction will be exaggerated and will interfere with effective concentration, flow and discharge of work. And under different conditions, over-expansive exaggerated reactions can occur. Similarly, HR policies that give greater or lesser discretion in promotion, hiring, and certain compensation decisions can have the same effect in their area of focus. When such policies are *too narrowly* fashioned and applied, these will be experienced by organizational members as *bottlenecks*, disjunctures in natural work flow. Members will feel squeezed. In fact, they are. The organization's people and processes are now subservient to the functional disorder of the organization character. The circulating *bound-up* energy continues to power the force of the disordered character.

Hardened structures like these are all mini examples of organizational armoring in the middle segment. Unlike the head, armoring in the middle seems to occur not in one-to-one correspondence with socioemotional stage blocking. This I believe is because the middle line's nature is mostly interior, with little surface contact with the world. Even interviewing outside candidates for hire, for instance, serves an internal filtering function. In contrast, the head and operating core both directly touch the world, and they seem primarily subject to conditioning by the socioemotional stage when such blocking was incurred. (The head seems particularly affected by blocking at the vision stage, the operating core by blocking during the work stage.) By this logic, armoring in the middle line, just because it is in the middle of the system, will be a result of the way the system *integrally* handles the blocks of the stages, functionally adopting to and facilitating functioning in light of them, whether effective or not.[8]

When the middle line works well, its major natural functions of inspiration also give emotional heart to the organization—to those at the bottom, top and others in the middle. The organization will swell with a naturally felt pride. In the middle line, notably, its members will feel and will operate expansively as they draw in and express their power. The mid-line's movement will have a rhythmic quality in tempo. But when habitually frustrated, its systemic and local effects will be the opposite, as Oshry describes.

Where there is significant dysfunction present, the middle line, especially, will look and act depressed in functioning, drawing in and discharging little power. This is evident in the looks on their people's faces, their murmurs and the courage they fail to show when important to the effective discharge of their work. This is important for consultants to attend to, helping those in the middle better get in touch with their feelings about their work situation and the fact *that* they are avoiding them. All systems, I contend, with functionally disordered characters will show these signs and symptoms in the middle line. Oshry's understanding of the malaise of middles is generally existential—"a possibility" as he describes it in the nature of all systems—not something driven by a specific disordered character.[9]

In contrast, *a character-based analysis helps us understand how symptoms represent chronically shut down responses to specific conditions embedded in the system.* It helps us understand *the adaptive nature of their disorder. In this case, the armoring of the middle line serves to functionally cage the system's energy because the organization cannot tolerate natural movement.* This shows up in the character of mid-line members' collective attitudes and where their energies go, resist going and do not go in taking action. There is much "holding still" in the middle. Many in the middle will present with a hard, cynical shell—a "what's the point in trying?" attitude, an attitude of giving up and emotional resignation. I have seen and heard this expressed many times. At the bottom of it all is chronic energetic holding in the system—the opposite of energetic buildup, flow and discharge.

This cynical attitude was pervasive in the middle line of one client, one of the largest public transit authorities in the US. Over the course of a major enterprisewide initiative, I attended to this attitude continually as it resurfaced. I pointed out over and over again middles' cynical expressions of resignation. Gradually, I found the system's middles would acknowledge the attitude, then alternately respond more openly to what was actually happening before them. This did not always at first lead to bliss. Middles, when they drop the cynicism, sometimes awake to the depth of the problems they face and that they are not happy about it. Frustration and sadness may result for a time as it did in this system. Yet such recognition is needed if they are to address it. That too is emotional acceptance. Organizational life is not all one of happy thoughts and moments. (Thus, the limitation, as I have argued, of much of how AI is practically applied in change efforts.) This public transit authority in any case did get better in its general functioning as it moved through its presenting difficulties and sentiments aroused.

In another case, I saw this cynicism and depression present across many of the organization's different mid-line functional units. Allied Bank bristled with the hard shell and haplessness of the middle. One major grouping within its middle line, a senior group of operations managers occupying corporate and field office positions, had important charge for key operating activities. Their work itself served key instrumental functions in supporting and booking primary lending and core deposit activities of the bank (activities considered "the main line" of the business). The senior managers' operations function, corporately and even in the branches, was largely an *interior* one within the firm.

But the operations managers did not feel valued for this. They were often treated—and *felt treated*—as "second class." This they felt coming from the top and mostly from their regional lending management peers. They felt squeezed, "in the middle." It is not incidental I think that the operations managers were all mostly women amidst the main tribe of male hunters originating the loans and deposits in the market. The operations managers mind you were *not* poorly compensated, without title or without some recognition that they appreciated. Yet they were left alone, as it were, to tend the hearth, stuck in administrative details they regarded as neither exciting nor effective in impact. They longed for impact.

When I first got a call to work with two of these ops managers as part of a larger renewal effort, they presented with a cynical shell. They were plaintive about their lack of power in correcting widespread practices (both technical and human) that begged attention from their lending peers and top management. The managers complained about their own lack of muscle and clout in the organization. My own efforts to help them were the target of some disparagement (transference) when I discussed possibilities of working with them, leaving me feeling somewhat bad and powerless myself (a countertransference). I recognized these were a mirror of their feelings about themselves, and I saw enough deeper recognition from them that what we were discussing might actually offer real help through their troubles. Despite their plaintiveness, they did not seem like they would be difficult to work with. Were they testing me, I wondered, to see if I would leave at the drop of a hat? I did not.

I should note there was a lack of muscle *in the very manner* in which they articulated the problems to me. The problems they referenced were serious and I could decipher them, but they were not delivered to me with punch. Their plaintiveness had an air of weakness about it. I realized I would need to address that quality in helping them get moving. I felt if they could *concentrate* their feelings of dissatisfaction (and not weakly leak them out through chronic complaining) the managers could likely draw new strength for change. I reasoned this would help create *charge* for them, which they could then *discharge* in their work for impact.

I went to work in a series of meetings with them. A well-respected subgroup of six of the ops managers, each with the same functions for different regions, running across the enterprise, was formed. I convened them to discuss their work, their feelings about it, and what to do about it. In facilitated sessions, the group openly exchanged views on the bigger work issues in front of them, both what they were and their importance. As I asked questions, this led them to discuss *their feelings about themselves for having done nothing substantially about the work issues.* Harsher feelings about others, then themselves, emerged, but we worked through them in our sessions. There was dialogue, but there were concentrated expressions of individual feelings—mini-*monologues* in fact. Some of them went on but with genuine affect, while others listened supportively. Meanwhile, various work- and role-redesign themes emerged for the needed work to be performed. The subgroup members continued these conversations outside of the facilitated sessions in their offline talk with each other.

As a result of our efforts together, they were starting to function differently on their own. One topic the managers chose to really go after together was how they could pack the company's sprawling but thinly spread operations policies and procedures with more punch—clustering the voluminous number of policies around more clearly focused general thrusts and impacts. This action they anticipated would have weighty implications, and they foresaw others in the system would see it that way too. They stopped complaining about it and *seized* what was waiting for them to simply go after. There were other topics too that emerged that they tackled, a number becoming new project initiatives the group successfully launched, drove forward and secured rounds of funding for when needed.

In all, they started to act more boldly and to take charge on their own. They brought their energies forward to pull more senior corporate leaders in on their efforts for change. This gave those players in turn more courage in pushing the energy further up the chain —and out to the rest of the organization. The managers now brought their hard won, self-secured efforts to their own operating staffs and to their regional lending peers. As the managers' self-confidence solidified in facing their feelings and putting their held back energies into their work, their hard-shell cynicism basically evaporated, without special attention from me. (They did not need behavioral training nor continued reinforcement to "not be cynical.") The lingering gender issues they had also previously perceived as important were largely rendered moot. Their concerns about this largely abated, and they came to serve as role models for other women in the organization who they also now actively mentored. They were now seen by themselves and others in the organization, including those at the very top of the house, as important players in the enterprise.

Moreover, their efforts systemically added to the net effect of mobilizing the entire middle of the organization, where I concurrently was working with other functions, for collective punch. A major one of these other mid-line functions as it so happened was the male dominated central loan administration unit, which provided critical dotted-line oversight of lending officers throughout the system. Those in this interior Loan Administration function also had originally presented as feeling too little heard and not sufficiently powerful. This had little to do with gender. The concurrent work with this group of middles, too, largely changed their functioning. This larger systems effect of mobilizing the middle line at Allied Bank is discussed in the full-scale case presented in Chapter 7.

At Allied and elsewhere, when I have seen significant blocking like this, I have focused much of my energy in helping get the middle line mobilized. The aim was always to help open up movement in the organization, to help reanimate the middle to better draw in then discharge its energies. I would not do this with the middles in isolation from other work at the top or operating core segments. Nor was the work with the middle a one-shot affair. I found myself coming at it repeatedly, and from different angles, across the course of an enterprisewide effort.

The moral of the story? *The middle line, chronically stuck or not, serves a natural integrative function for an organization system.* When it is stuck, a consultant's work to mobilize it—as Reich's clinical somatic method amply demonstrates in mobilizing a patient's chest in better breathing and heart to feelings— takes advantage of the segment's natural work and radiating effect on the entire system.

Operating Core Segment[10]

The operating core consists essentially of those units, players and processes doing the "real work" of the organization: tailoring, preparing, packaging and delivering the chief goods and services of the organization to market. The products may be wholesale or retail—deliverables and consumables that customers receive, make use of and otherwise engage with. Services principally include human deliverable activities, including knowledge and advice, sometimes packaged as "offerings." Products and human services are almost universally supported by extensive electronic information technologies in addition to other mechanical equipment. The operating core can consist of any single or combination of hourly workers, salaried staff, help desk personnel, professionals, managers, executives—anyone whose work directly or indirectly touches customers in their routine sphere of work. Union employees covered under labor agreements as well as non-union employees are part of this segment.

The word "union" is, in a sense larger than formal collective bargaining, the relevant term in discussing the operating core. *The effective work of the operating core is typically performed by workers in concert with each other—how they operate in union.* In the shift to an industrial economy at the beginning of the twentieth century, the work of the operating core became associated with mass-production processes such as assembly lines. But in the post-industrial and information-age eras, the operating core has come to be distinguished by less linear, more collaborative, interdependent ways key work is organized and performed. The operating core can take shape as standing organizations or forms that are more temporary in nature. Its work and workers can be highly centralized or distributed. The operating core is usually large. But operating core substructures can also be small—more intimate team ensembles, for example, that form for unique, one-time development or delivery purposes (skunkworks for example).

Depending on specialized function, operating core subsystems can be deeply interior to an organization, or closer to its surface and perimeter; they also often extend as field operations that routinely meet with prospective and current customers (e.g., sales and service functions or the line unit work of branch operations). The range of productive activities that operating core members perform are those associated with classical functions of the supply chain as they operate at very detailed levels: plan, source, make, deliver and return. When well-functioning, some of the planning activities will be carried out jointly or in joint communications with administrative support planning units operating in the middle and in association with the head—strategic demand planning, for example. But they may well involve specialized scanning and forecasting roles seated within the operating core itself, providing intelligence from both internal inventory turnover and data-driven demand projections. Field salespeople have routinely been charged with gathering such information, if not always reliable in documenting it. Technology systems are often programmed to do much of this in real time today, getting the information to the right people at the right time to enable the flow. Such planning has sped up incredibly in recent times with real-time ordering and on-demand manufacturing for tailored "batch of one" goods, delivered virtually or in days door-to-door (Amazon home delivery for example).

These all represent recurrent energy flows—sources of data, analyses, communications, decision points, and mechanisms to mobilize and regulate human and technological levels of effort. Processes in the operating core are frequently transactional and to a greater or less extent routine, but they all are founded on motivated and mobilized human energy streaming together to sustain them. Their steady flow of activity in fact makes sustaining *relationships* in the core all the more essential. However, sharp inhibitions on the development and healthy functioning of relationships seem an inherent risk in the frequent character of work and organizations in the network-organization age. Chapter 8 is devoted to some of the inherent challenges of the era, including what seems required for the difficulties' needed prevention or remediation.

Organizations seem quite subject to becoming armored in the operating core. A sign of the core's armoring is when work is only pushed out mechanically at the core, accompanied by little human gratification. When this is the case, human engagement even with customers will be minimized in the name of efficiency and economy. For example, automated product and service delivery fulfillment *without human fulfillment* will become the norm: The pleasure of those in the system and those they serve will be sacrificed. This is a common experience today.[11] The mounting frustration *manufactured* as a by-product in the process, sooner or later, can make these work functions fail. Chronic blocking in the operating core shows up in rigid processes with poor regard for human satisfaction.

Blocks within the operating core, based on our present understanding of group dynamics, are thought to originate in frustrations during the fusion and work stages of the organization's primary socioemotional development. As I have argued, exaggerated intolerance of risk or excessive waste (including people "wasted" in the process) will surface as symptoms of fusion stage dysfunctions. So will the mechanical quality of the work. Work-aggressive stage frustration can result in goods brought to market prematurely, underinvestment in R&D, and overambitious production schedules. Some other symptoms when the natural work of the fusion and work stages goes unfulfilled are summarized in Table II. The "work dramatic," "work aggressive," and "fusion blocked" organization types, described in the character typology, epitomize these systemwide disorders characterologically.

Structurally anchored blocking in the head and middle line segments will also greatly affect the present-day functioning of the operating core. The energy is less available for productive and satisfying fulfillment. Such upper level blocking is also reinforced and continually refueled by the energy blocks in the operating core. *The three segments ultimately function as a unit—even when disjointed. They will feed each other's dysfunctional ways. The principle of armor removal, akin to that in the individual clinical modality, is generally to proceed sequentially from the head of the system down.* There will be some exceptions here, depending on the character type and circumstances present. Some systems will require consultations that begin by addressing blocks in the middle line; this, in order to mobilize and draw energy down from the head and up from the operating core as may be needed to get started. As a general rule of thumb, the consultant should first take cognizance of where the armoring in the system seems greatest, then time and prepare to address the armoring in the most highly blocked locales as the organization can tolerate without shutting down, also attending to the systemic effects the local unblocking then brings. A strong caveat to this guidance is the operating core when it is heavily blocked. Because it contains so much energy, one must always start by working with the top then middle line of the system or subsystem in question, not only contracting the consultation, but clearing the way forward to safely mobilize the operating core.

The operating core represents the greatest concentration of potential energy in a system as it is the culmination of where the natural flow of work energy as a whole is fully discharged. For this reason, freeing up the operating core prematurely will predictably result in "internal flooding" and shutting the rest of the system down. This is the major source of difficulty I believe in socio-technical system interventions that bypass organization character considerations and their armoring, as discussed in Chapter 2. These interventions can themselves get caught up in overreach by trying to refashion the core work of the system without recognizing that character and armoring are in play. Recognizing those dynamics can of course slow the organization and consultants down in their joint endeavor. Neither the organization nor the consultant may be able to tolerate that slow-down.[12]

Unleashing too much energy in a system too fast will almost always lead to poor results. I have seen this in consultations that too quickly tried to mobilize a critical mass of the employee population in a disordered system. This is particularly a risk in interventions with the operating core. On the surface, large scale, "whole system in the room" interventions such as Future Search can seem to make sense. Their proposition is attractive: Get a large mass of the organization in a single place to self-assess its core issues and opportunities in light of its "big dream," then make plans and take strides to attain it. But when characteristic organizational blocking and structural armoring is present, releasing the energy of the operating core too early will predictably lead to collapse of the effort and a more stirred up, dissatisfied system.

At a French-based telecom, I was invited at the last minute to join a consulting effort in Nice to assist facilitating an imminent Future Search conference. Company unit leaders, many managers and staff from around the world (some 75 in all) would convene over four days to sketch out and recommend a new set of global product offerings. The agenda was well structured by the event's consultant-client planning team. Funding of it had been secured. But as I came to see once I'd arrived, besides the sponsoring senior marketing executive and CIO, there had been far too little attention paid to top management; they had only casually been made aware of the process in advance. The client staff, two Europeans and an American from the mid-line who served the top, feared "making too much" of the event with the top executives up front might lead to its cancellation. That fear, too quickly swallowed by the staff, proved telling.

The very top leaders thus had little idea what they were really walking into when it came time to attend a plenary session on the event's last day. In real-time, as the "whole system in the room" listened intently, the *Président-Directeur General* abruptly shot down the assembly's recommendations. Three other top executives now present also piled on. You could literally see the energy go out of the room. The event's mid-line planning staff were speechless, as were the event's two senior sponsors. They just shrank; *they contracted.* And the attendees from around the world were shocked; they left for the airport to get on their planes and go home, now cynical with stories to tell. For all their work and hopes, people were crestfallen. Frustration and further resistance to change at all levels, including the executives now, were manufactured on the spot. This was a complete consulting misread of the organizational dynamics at play and the attention needed to be paid to the system's character and structure, *segment by segment.* New problems now needed to be addressed, but the opportunity for a continuing consulting contract vanished.

Planners' fears in approaching certain subjects should not be simply worked around. Nor should managements' common fears of getting large numbers of employees in a room to consider issues be underestimated or pooh-poohed. Those fears, consultatively, should be surfaced and worked through first with the right players, then, generally speaking, fold in ever-widening inclusion of the membership as the human facts in the case warrant. Otherwise, too much energy may be released in the system all at once, which no one is prepared to deal with. I have seen this and committed this error myself in my work with organizations more than once. In this sense, the actual change problem and opportunity is missed. The operating core represents the full power and potential of the organization at work, so it must be addressed in a way that is commensurate with the actual character of the system. Approaching this in the appropriate way, in fact, is the central opportunity I believe for change.

In contrast to the telecom company effort, I led an OD consultation for a US intelligence agency where the positive effect of large-scale intervention was realized. *Mobilization of the operating core happened gradually using a series of large-scale meetings, but they were first preceded by a stream of other events, out of which the larger meetings organically grew.* The whole process took into account the agency's current work situation, conditions and character dynamics, and then the moment ripened to consider incorporating large conference methods in the mix.

Advance work was done with a senior staff group to address general circumstances for intervening in the agency; in this instance, to look at overall organizational strategy, structure, job design, and policies and processes that would lead a makeover for a "workforce of the future." New, asymmetric warfare conditions, in the aftermath of the Cold War, made for transformative needs in the way the organization now needed to operate and *inter*operate. The agency's character of the old era was still reflected in its highly stovepiped, compartmentalized, "every man for himself" ways of operating. By design, roles in the past had been narrow, much was underground, and heroic individual action, not open teamplay, was widely acclaimed.

Part of what presented as a difficulty in the consultation, in fact reflected the agency's typically splintered ways of structuring its work: A separate, competitive consultancy's effort was jointly launched to look at the intersection of general business needs and organizational strategy as it would affect the workforce. Our consultancy, on the other hand, was charged with more on-the-ground organization redesign. The agency's decision to compartmentalize the consultancies boded a disconnect between grandly conceived strategy and actual OD driven work-design aimed at the operating core. Notwithstanding the client's avowed intention to link up the two consultancies' work, the character of the workforce transformation effort re-enacted that of the organization: Its "head" and "body" were split. All of us involved would need to try and overcome this for our work to best succeed. This became an effort unto itself.

My OD consulting team carried on, seeking to make the best of things as the situation presented. Our initial work with the senior staff group was not to plan "an event" or structure an effort that would get the whole organization immediately engaged. It was rather to discuss how a wider initiative might be shaped that would affect and *ultimately* enlist the efforts of enterprise staff for wide and deep change throughout the operating ranks. This led first to extensive one-on-one and small group conversations with the agency's top leadership: its Executive Director, Deputy Director, Chief Administrative and senior executive staff. We also worked to build bridges with the other consultancy, not always easy given our competitive enrollment in the initiative. But such efforts from the outset were critical given the looming, recapitulating disconnect with general strategy. Each of the agency's executives held genuine power in the organization despite their overall diffusion. And our consultancy's work in the body of the system needed to be synchronized with (and very much affect) the concepts being generated at the top.

Working with the head-segment, a wide frame for thinking about organization strategy was jointly pondered, as was a wider way of thinking about the need to engage the workforce. A concrete approach emerged. Senior managers supervising the half dozen, autonomous operating lines of business were next engaged to further shape the approach; I met with these mid-line managers to consider ways they best engage their own units' people in the initiative. This included how to find out more what their own people wanted and how to keep top executives involved. Central and field operating personnel were then selectively engaged in small focus groups for workforce needs assessment. More such personnel soon became further engaged too but using survey data-collection to pull in needed information. These relatively modest means of engaging the operating core first were used *just because* they were light in touch—they elicited less emotion than trying to quickly bring large numbers of people together all at once. The ground for that first needed to be softened if something deeper and wider were to take hold and grow. Many experienced OD practitioners have had to learn this the hard way.

Thus, before our OD team did too much work with the operating core, we recognized *sufficient charge and tolerance in the system needed to be built for its collective energy to cohere.* Eventually, all the advance work with the top and the middle did lead to the development of six large conferences, including wide numbers from the operating core (sixty people in each conference). People from the core were convened to be briefed and share their thinking together, along with top level leaders and mid-managers in attendance to present, listen and engage. The series of conferences considered workforce-need findings to date, then openly pondered future courses of action. The conference series represented a first that this many people in the agency were ever convened for collective discourse and action. The series itself had the effect of gradually building-up energy in the system, energy which the entire organization could tolerate and sustain without shutting down. Indeed, the conferences were very well received, and people up and down the system were actually excited. News of the events spread, and their follow-on activities had the energy, motivation and structure to move forward and take root.

The consultation lasted over two years, helping to further support and mobilize the collective energy in the system to take its fuller, natural course. Imaginative cross-functional work- and organization redesign activities arose with genuine support top to bottom. Whole new operating roles, technologies, and policies, processes and structures emerged. Our consulting team in this case did not lead with the idea of large group intervention. That would have been a fruitless effort to make the tail wag the dog. Instead, the consulting team helped foster conditions to let tops, middles and bottoms better align as they naturally saw the need. We let the dog wag the tail. The way we thought about our broad intent to engage the totality of the workforce, given the conditions of the organization's character and armoring, pointed the way.

A final note: Even though the nature of the system's work as an intel agency was literally clandestine and "compartmentalized," the system's internal operations through the consulting process quite fully opened up, suited to the new field conditions the agency faced. The agency's *knee-jerk* armored walls began to come down, and a start was made to function more work democratically. The agency still of course needed to operate with structural confidentiality and appropriate security classifications, but the "new workforce of tomorrow" was being enacted.

LINKING NETWORKS AND CHANNELS FOR ENERGETIC CIRCULATION AND PULSATION

We have already touched on these, but they are called out briefly here for closing emphasis given their crucial nature.

The major lateral cross-cutting segments are themselves linked together by vertical and horizontal network and specialized channel flows. These too can function in healthy and dysfunctional ways. In highly disordered systems, the links and flows may be quite broken; in some systems, they may have never properly developed constitutionally to begin with.

In healthy systems, I believe these flows function in behalf of system self-regulation and collective pulsing movement. They help the system function flexibly and with resilience to changing inner and outer conditions. In chronically blocked systems, the networks and channels themselves armor, so the work energy in transit does not sufficiently flow. Concentration, circulation and discharge of the energy gets acutely constricted.

The networks and channels do indeed process "information," as the classic organizational literature contends, but the flows at play are more fundamental than this. They are *energy* flows. Information is but one kind of flow—and a general description of it at that. There are point-to-point and general communications to relay, receive and broadcast; problems to be pondered and resolved; junctures of conflict handled; decision points to cross; actions to be coordinated and mobilized; and lessons to reflect and further act on. And there is more than cognitive processing at work. There are *emotions* that are streaming and that drive work. More than "feedback" occurs. Energy flow is multi-directional, rhythmic and pulsing.

The concept of "Information" flowing does of course imply a cognitive dimension, and in this sense it accords a rationality and a kind of neural equivalent at work in a social system. The strategic apex structures are connected up, down, across and out the organization by a systemic range of information networks transmitting intelligence from one point to another. These extend from perimeter, surface situated subsystems, including those in the wider field, to subsystems that are more deeply interior. This is energy being activated for concentration, flow and discharge in their functions—energy within and between local subsystem units, the cross-cutting segments, and throughout the system as a whole for integrative functioning.

In a like manner, an empowered middle line pumps *courage and encouragement*—the natural actions of the heart, *le coeur*—through channels and as its work otherwise inspires and radiates throughout the body of the organization. This middle line function at the center of organization life is more immediately sentient than the informational, cognitive networks tied to the head segment. Of course, in a well-functioning system, in line with the organization's nature, *the networks and channels work naturally in concert* for full, holistic and organic effect. They too are tied together.

In armored organizations—average in today's world—the cognitive and affective dimensions of work are split apart, an "all knowing" head denying the emotional root at work. This distortion goes quite far. As discussed in Chapter 2, there are whole schools of OD thought (Dialogical OD for example today) that explicitly claim "mindset" and the sanctity of one's "perspective" are essentially everything, unknowingly recapitulating this duality. *Perception and sensation are conceived as disconnected in these approaches.* In contrast, the approach here, through an application of Reich's understanding of natural systems functioning, differs fundamentally.[13]

When networks thicken because of the density of their transmissions they begin to resemble subsystems themselves; they become, in effect, *channels* with permeable boundaries. They too are not membraned. Common organization language reflects the use of networks and channel as terms. Communications within organizations are deemed to occur through networks, increasingly through formal "channels" as they become more heavily structured and official. Those that are more lightly structured may remain networks; these may often emerge and operate as more spontaneous, *de facto* networks of how people confer with each other to get work done outside of formal chains of command. These too are functionally adaptive and improvisational in nature, and they may prove to be early forms of healthy, budding structure in an organization. These "shadow networks" sometimes are the seeds of new organizational form.

I saw this consulting to AT&T's Network Computing Support Division, a 1,000-person nationwide organization with shadow networks among its field-unit people. The networks operated underground, outside the bounds of official corporate policy. One shadow network emerged to help the field units carry out their provisioning work; it arose when official channels to obtain computer parts from the corporate center proved unreliable and bureaucratic. People in the units across the country began improvising ways with each other to directly swap hard-to-access parts. A rather sophisticated underground trading network arose. While it contravened policy, it proved efficient and effective. This went on for a while, until the division's executive leader recognized its value. He called us in as consultants to develop better understanding within the division of how the network worked. As consultants we had to contend with fear in the system that exposing what was underground—and that people found satisfaction in its effectiveness and in their own freedom of movement—

could be jeopardized. But we worked with people top, middle and bottom in one-on-ones, groups and through the careful use of organization network analysis that people grew comfortable with. Soon, as the shadow network's significance, value and further potential were widely grasped, what was at first an improvised work-around process became the authorized new standard: regional hubs with official sanctioned channels were established and displaced the old structure. As a side effect of the effort's results and means, people also became more open and trusting in working with each other.

Sanctioned or not, such emergent, *de facto* networks are all responding to the force—or power—of the energy to move forward to get things done. All organizational emergence appears to operate this way, as described in Chapter 1. Social groupings represent a streaming and convergence of energies together. But even networks and channels are subject to becoming armored. The channels can ossify, as the original central provisioning channel did at AT&T; it had become bureaucratic, thus *the workarounds spontaneously arose*. Armored organization cultures may try to police them out of existence when they arise. Healthier organizations systems with more work democratic energies at their disposal will typically be more lenient and flexible in tolerating their emergence and flow. This proved to be the case at AT&T. Yet even so-called enlightened management approaches, insisting that everyone "play by the rules" regardless of circumstance, can unfortunately play into intolerance of spontaneous movement and lack of acceptance of the new.

HR units can be notorious for such intolerance and their *policing* of corporate policies. This often creates unhappy, forced compliance, where people become silent; they may cease operating in informal ways, and their own initiative and work begin to atrophy. If taken to an extreme, this can represent a micro-dying of the organization. Attention by consultants can be effective if caught early enough to help reverse the process. Often remedies lie not in replacing personnel or "changing mindsets" (through training or other means, as is common). Often there are bigger systemic issues at play, ones of energy, flow and group character at work. What is experienced and felt emotionally by the players are in the thick of things.

The questions always to be asked by consultants are: *"What, in sum, is the picture of things inhibiting flow? What feelings are being stirred and what does that tell us? What conditions need to be (or put) in play to restore effective flow?"* Organizational character dysfunction at work cannot be ignored if the system retains capacity for spontaneous movement and improvement.

A future task of scholar-practitioners seeking to build out an energic understanding of organizational flows through networks and channels would be to map these out more fully. Here they are only primitively treated. Their more complete identification and descriptions—as well as those especially of the deep interior functioning subsystems they connect—must await another day. For now, I hope it sufficient we have distinguished the centrality of their energetic nature, a nature in service of localized and systemic charge, concentration, flow and discharge in the life of an organization.

A TYPOLOGY OF ORGANIZATION CHARACTER FORMS (I)

This chapter introduces a typology of organization character forms. These range from a general healthy type to five neurotic, armored forms. The first three types are presented in this chapter, the remaining three in the next. Before we begin discussion of each of the types, first a few general considerations.

GENERAL CONSIDERATIONS

A *typology* is presented because, as Reich first discovered with patients struggling with persistent emotional disorders, understanding a broad range of common individual character types made a significant difference in the efficacy of therapy. The intent of Reich's classic text *Character Analysis* was not to delineate the types as an interesting intellectual exercise, but to give therapists knowledge and tools where to look, then when and how to intervene to best help the patient move towards health.[1] These were later codified further by Reich's student and colleague Dr. Elsworth Baker in his own now classic *Man in the Trap*.[2] Similarly, I believe recognizing common organizational character structures is instrumental to effective, systemic OD consulting.

Organization character describes the stereotypical ways the system acts and reacts in the world, the way its combined work energies *characteristically* move. More specific than the concept of organization culture and its use to date, the system's character delimits the way the energy typically flows, concentrates, blocks and is discharged as the organization carries out its work in the world. It shows up systemically. First and foremost, it shows up in *the system's characteristic emotional expressions and in the quality of its expressed attitudes—*including what stands out as *unexpressed* when there is apparent longing to convey something important. Character also presents in the organization's habitual patterns of thinking, assumptions, values, beliefs and behaviors, as well as goals, roles, strategies, structures, policies and processes an organization's members enact—that is, in the way organization members customarily *move* and are *stilled. The focus on movement and patterns of emotional expression and characteristic attitudes is a major distinguishing mark that separates the concept of organization character from that of culture, including its practical consulting use. This distinction becomes key in assessment and intervention with systems in trouble or those otherwise seeking significant change.*

Each organization character type represents a distinct, recognizable configuration of energy movement. It serves both expressive and defensive functions with respect to the system's driving, collective emotional energies at work—*its root work energy.* Organization character gates the system's flow of the work energy, serving a self-regulating function; this is so, even when the energy is chronically inhibited, creating stasis and character-specific symptoms. When this happens, as described in Part I of this book, the organization character becomes *a functional disorder.*

Such systemic functional disorders are common in organizational life today. In fact, in my experience, they are more or less average in occurrence, looking at organizations across the board. Many scholars and change practitioners recognize the ubiquity of tenacious organization problems, and it is common to hear organizational members complain about aspects of the persistent disorders without using any formal terms.

Sometimes these functional disorders can be extreme, other times they can be milder in their effects. But they all result to a greater or lesser degree in system stasis, always giving rise to organizational symptoms (including chronic but unsatisfied complaining). These symptoms show up humanly and in formal structures, and the energy stasis always manifests as compromise in productive fulfillment of the organization's work. *The greater the hold of the character disorder on an organization, the greater that human unhappiness is present and is reproduced in the system.* I have seen this to be true in every organization I have ever consulted with. The BearingPoint case discussed in Chapter 3 is a glaring example. Those engaged within the system's surrounding field—customers and other stakeholders, including employees' family members—are also affected.

The organization types described here are derived from what I have seen in my consulting experience across a wide range of enterprises, large and small, public and private, industry sectors and cultures around the world. The first version of this typology appeared in my master's thesis, published in *The Journal of Orgonomy* in 1990.[3] But they are described more richly here using a fuller range of illustrative examples; there is greater emphasis now on the systemic energy stasis they each create and what must be done in intervening to relieve the stasis. The types here also draw on specific culture types described by other organizational change thinkers, including those of Kets de Vries and Miller who describe in behavioral terms counterproductive styles of managing in a typology of their own.[4] Finally, they derive from some roughly equivalent individual types first identified by Reich in his own pioneering characteranalytic method and by those who closely followed and built on it.

Organization character is the central target of change in the consulting method, or the *sociotherapy,* this book presents. The way character expresses and binds the core energy of the system is not recognized elsewhere in OD or in other forms of management consulting or theory, as discussed in Chapter 2. Yet the concept answers I believe many of the theoretical gaps and practical dilemmas that have stymied results with clients and held the development of OD as a field back. *The diagnostic framework provides the basis for strategic intervention to restructure the character to enable fuller types of organizational functioning to emerge, in line with the system's inherent natural forces driving to health.* This is unique to this method. In its orientation and approach, this method also helps position less ambitious change efforts, where only incremental improvement is sought, to generally go better.

Understanding organization character builds on all of what we have previously discussed—biosocial energy, organizational health and illness, the socioemotional developmental stages, and the embodiment of character in a system's cross-cutting structural segments in how the segments operate and become armored.

This typology is not meant to be exhaustive or final. The character forms described are what I have principally seen. Others I have little doubt exist, as do various subtypes of character forms. In any case, a typology only represents *a heuristic understanding* of the phenomena it describes—in this case, the free movement and blocking of the energy flow at work in an organization. Over the years, I have seen the types here conform closely to what can be observed, but the types described themselves remain concepts. The attention of consultants must always be, first and last, on the unfolding reality and dynamics presenting in front of them. The theory here and character types give us, I have found, effective clues as to where to look and ways to proceed in intervening. I think this has special importance given the real variability of organizational life on the ground. Grasping the reality of the variability can elude us without some orienting map.

In real life, organization character broadly defined is an admixture of types of blocks. Blocks may be temporary and situational or chronic. Moreover, practically speaking, *all organizations are admixtures of health and characterological limitations*—there are driving forces inherent in the nature of the organization's work and there are restraining characterological forces when its natural free movement is markedly inhibited.

The format of the presentation in this chapter and the next describes each character type's:

- characteristics—and in the chronically blocked forms, also their symptoms;
- socioemotional genesis;
- strategic *pathways* for consulting intervention; and
- organization consulting case study.

In addition to strategic intervention pathways, specific techniques, touched on earlier, are woven in here to illustrate concrete ways of working with the character types and to highlight certain intervention principles in the method. These principles and some main techniques (or tactics) are described especially in the sections on sociotherapy and in the case studies. The tactics detailed are not comprehensive but are presented to bring out certain ways of helping each character that may also, depending on circumstances, be used with others. Each of the tactics described are distinct and generally only mentioned once in the typology, and as they pertain to a particular character, so the reader is not sidetracked with needless repetition. Again, I want to stress this book is *not* a how-to-manual but meant to illustrate the theory and method for general understanding. Training and supervision in their application are essential for their effective use and practice, just because we are dealing with powerful emotional realities in organizations.

I want to emphasize that *diagnosing organizational character is the responsibility of the consultant, and in fact his or hers alone. This is their work.* It is entirely fair for the client to expect the consultant to be competent in this work as the two come together in their joint endeavor. The types are not "models" to share with the client for intellectual purposes or to validate the construct because of consultant anxiety. This sharing does of course happen with change practitioners under developmental and training supervision for purposes of their craft. But more widely, this sharing has no value or meaning for the average client, and as such would get in the way and in fact be an imposition. It is one thing of course to share the general manner of working with clients as part of contracting, quite another to try to go into technical details and descriptions of a method. That would indeed be a distraction from simply engaging the client—and the consultant's avoidance of simply doing his part in their work together.

We are dealing here with the underlying structure of the organization's members' shared *emotional* dynamics at work—both that which is spontaneous and naturally feels right to them and that which is functionally disordered, where something is and feels off (even if they can't fully name it, which is usually the case). *The underlying structure to these dynamics only surfaces in a way that is meaningful for client-members through their lived and experienced realities. That actual, lived experience is what matters, as they strive to grow into fuller, more satisfying ways of working.* Organizations may double-down on their characteristic patterns of behavior when first and later probed. "Well," as Reich might have said, "it can't be helped." The system will seek to hold on to its customary ways of acting and reacting as it begins to move. Some intolerance of movement and fear will naturally present. Persistence, patience and care are incumbent on the part of the consultant to help the system in its greater fight for life.

In the method's use, the organizational types and the typology itself remain a "black box" to clients, as my original OD advisor Walt Ross recognized and termed. *Nonetheless, clients remain in charge, as it were, as they validate what is almost always the consultant's emergent understanding of the character through the client-consultant, action-research partnership. This is a partnership that inquires and intervenes into the realities of those in the system as they are actually experienced and present.*

Each party brings something to the table. You as consultant bring hunches based on what you are seeing moment to moment, described in behavioral terms with plain language. This is done if and when appropriate, and it includes bringing the client's attention to certain character attitudes and formal structural features that appear over the course of the consultation to consider and work through. This is the foreground of your work. Your earlier experiences, study and knowledge of this method are the background to help you in your questions, observations and hunches. So is your own personal therapeutic work in having worked through conflicts and accepted your own deeper feelings in order to remain present and minimize distorting projections. Clients through word and deed will let you know if you have understood the terrain well enough to serve—and continue to serve—as trusted guide and partner. And they continue to live the organizational dynamics every day.

If you remain alert, you'll know soon enough whether or not you are on the mark. Your understanding will become ever clearer as you engage. *Clients' understanding too of the character, in ways meaningful to them as they open up, will gradually dawn. Then the understanding is entirely theirs. You have not given it to them—nor tried to. They have actually experienced how the system's character has held them back.* Sharing some models may sometimes be of value, but they remain mentalistic when it is the emotional predicament of the system that is the hurdle. And since character dynamics in chronically blocked organizations represent *stuck defenses against feelings*, describing them *intellectually* to clients almost invariably heightens resistance. I know. I tried that earlier in my career and it added to the problems. The sociotherapeutic path, in contrast, *works through them.* Describing what you see as it presents in terms the client will readily recognize—holding up a mirror to the patterns of movement when the time is ripe—is fine. The manner and moment of engagement is everything; in Shakespeare's words, "readiness is all." This is true for clients of course, but it is equally true for consultants.

This take on the reciprocal roles inherent in the client-consultant partnership is completely in keeping with Lewin's grand insight about how understanding social systems change really comes about through joint *action*. The way each party actually engages the other is the heart of the dialogue—"true meeting" in Buber's sense—in the client-consultant encounter.

Our presentation of the types in this chapter begins with the healthy form, what I have called the work democratic organization character, followed by discussion of two chronically blocked, disordered types: the work dramatic and work aggressive organization characters. The three of them are bundled together in this chapter because all have reached *the work stage* of socioemotional development, as defined in Chapter 4, without major blocks at earlier pre-work stages. However, only the first of them, the work democratic type, represents a fully functioning form; the other two have developed chronic inhibitions based on distinctive blocking that occurs during the work stage of development, as will be described below when we get to each of them. The discussion on the work democratic type represents a newly postulated healthy organization form. The detail in its case example (when outside consulting support was still required) is presented to illustrate the actuality of the type and what can be different about intervention, when called on, into a basically healthy system.

THE WORK DEMOCRATIC ORGANIZATION CHARACTER[5]

The work democratic character represents a robust, healthy organization form in its quite fully realized capacity for productive achievement and human fulfillment. It is an organization type whose individual and collective human energies are able to freely concentrate, flow and discharge work in a way that is roundly generative and gratifying, both in product and process for a broad mass of its stakeholders. The organization's capacity for this is systemwide, experienced up, down, and across the enterprise and by those served and engaged in its surrounding field. The organization with a work democratic character finds ways to engage the talents and voices of nearly all its people, in concert and as individuals. It does not shut out differences, dissent or innovation but draws on them for strength. Wide and deep participation is the norm. The firm operates as a *company*—companions, as it were, each can count on in their common endeavor.

The work democratic organization is not perfect. It will make mistakes, take missteps and at times falter. Conflicts will occur. Members will experience frustration and upset, as well as excitement and joy in their joint efforts. But as a type, the character is distinctive because its members will be able to tolerate frank expression of such feelings in the interests of bettering the work. They will not easily give up in the face of conflict and challenges when evidence suggests a situation is resolvable. In contrast, members of armored forms of organization frequently shrink and keep quiet in the face of strong emotions and tough realities. Not easily overwhelmed by its problems, the work democratic enterprise is characteristically resilient and self-regenerating. It is flexible but operates with integrity and a good sense of direction. The type is distinguishable in its normative, forthright capacity to step up to problems, recognize in timely ways when it is off course, and seek and find ways to right the ship.

Although all organizations seek some *kind* of satisfaction in the way they function, work democratic systems are able to more fully realize and live it. While it is common for organizations to talk about the value of such a way of operating—it is a wish inside very many organizations, latent I think in most—the work democratic form seems relatively rare on the organization landscape. Its existence is not a matter of an organization's rhetoric, declared values, meticulous plans or even good intentions, but how it *actually* operates day to day. The characteristic strength and quality of its performance is an outcome of this way of functioning.

There is much in the classic organizational change literature that discusses effective workplaces with the characteristics described here: "systems that are open, inquiring, productive, and fully actualizing of their human potential."[6] Names like Mayo, McGregor, Likert, Tannenbaum, Beckhard, Bennis, Blake and Mouton, Oshry, Senge and others all describe systems that strongly tend in this direction. Similar themes are evoked in Peter Block's distinction between "entrepreneurial and bureaucratic cycles" in an organization's empowerment of its members.[7]

In the main, however, the classic literature discusses the *health* of an enterprise only in terms of desirable values, behaviors, or, for those of a "no nonsense" business mind, a matter that is basically to be reduced to impressive numbers. Whether values, behaviors or numbers, the classic literature often *idealizes* them, and OD and other consulting practice often treat them as prescriptive targets *to push* for change. *The way an organization's collective emotional energy spontaneously moves is ignored.*

Sometimes when organization health is discussed, it is framed in essentially negative terms, as the absence of dysfunction. Kets de Vries and Miller, in their psychoanalytic organizational typology, do not even recognize a healthy type. They, like those in the Tavistock tradition as Hirschhorn has come to critique, see coping with anxiety as the mainspring of organization behavior, something to mitigate, sublimate or otherwise tamp down through insight, behavioral or cognitive reinforcement.[8] They do not see the root of organizational life: *the organization's fundamental movement to fulfill the work that is natural to it.*

That an organization is inherently animated by a driving energy to fulfill is unique to the theory and method presented in this book. The work democratic type supports full concentration and expression of this vibrant energy in the first place; thus, runaway anxiety, unpalatable values and detrimental behaviors tend not to become entrenched and chronically hold the organization back. The natural excitement of work is not stripped away by a fixation on outcomes or numbers alone. Said in Lewinian terms, work democratic organizations do not siphon their energies into becoming institutionalized forces of restraint; instead, they concentrate and discharge energy and attention to support the inherent, spontaneously moving driving forces natural to its health. Their people *feel* the vibrant energy that exists and are part of its swim.

By the late 1930s, Reich was writing about the nature and emergence of natural work democratic forms of social functioning. In addition to its macro social dimensions, he understood work democracy to include the self-administration of firms by those who performed their "vital necessary work." This is broadly consistent, as noted earlier, with how Emery, Trist and others have used the language of industrial work democracy.[9]

The inscription at the beginning of this book, drawn from Reich's 1945 edition of his *Mass Psychology*, underscores the aptness of the term "work democratic" to describe the healthy organization type: it is a system that seeks *"to harmonize the conditions and forms of work with the need to work and the pleasure of work, in short to eliminate the antithesis between pleasure and work."*[10]

Characteristics

Revisiting Table I at the end of Chapter 3 will give the reader a summary of the general features of the work democratic organization and as they contrast with those of neurotic, armored forms. The work democratic organization's functions and structures are harmonious. Its subsystems are well aligned and work smoothly in the system as a whole to discharge its primary and other work in the world. The enterprise itself and its peopled components operate with rhythm in the organization's natural, everyday pulsing cycles of expansion and contraction: drawing energy in, letting the energy suffuse the needed internal operating structures for productive processing, then facilitating its movement outward past the perimeter of the system to engage its constituents in its field. The system's stakeholders, internal and external, move in concert, dynamically coming together to enjoy the fruits of the labor. In work democratic systems there is little unproductive discord between customers and the organization. Customers and others in alliances are widely regarded as *partners in en-*

terprise; they are often more than those to simply build relationships with, and much more than those with whom to do transactions.

Accomplished jazz ensembles, as we discussed in Chapter 3, function essentially as work democratic units. The ensemble moves rhythmically in its play, and its audience is equally "jazzed" in the performance. A major feature is the fluidity of the *interplay* between the group's sections (horns, keyboards, bass, and drums, for example). Since the big band era, and hearkening back to jazz's original days, each section moves spontaneously, often improvisationally, making its own special contribution, while working together as a whole, using recurring themes for overall effect. There is play as soloists, accompanists and as a whole combo. Members move in and out of roles freely but at the same time in structured ways too. For example, as each player plays, they transmit signals to the others in the group—sometimes in structured motifs and tempos, sometimes a nod of the head—to pick up the action. The structured motifs used this way are essentially *channels* that facilitate the musical flow. Communication is exquisite. Technical competence (if not mastery) with one's own instrument *and* person-to-person trust are high. There usually is a "head" to the group, most often as founder and band leader, who sets out the nature and direction of the group. But top, middle line and operating core functions are also generally shared, as the instrumentalists move in and out of lead, hand off and supporting roles during any point of play. Productive gratification is very much its hallmark. When things really work, the music *both sounds and feels good*—to the players and audience. Symphonious or dissonant, the music of the accomplished ensemble generates excitement. These attributes I contend are all indicative of work democratic functioning for any kind of group or system.

Jazz ensembles—and the concept itself of ensembles—are discussed again in Chapter 8 as work forms especially suited for the long-anticipated network organization era now well underway. Work democratic organizations are naturally suited for the age and demonstrate many properties consistent with organizations described as networks: human systems that are relatively flat and loose in structure, retain an entrepreneurial spirit, are scalable, flexible and collaborative, and tend to spread out in their fields like a web. They tend to be more driven by strategic function than form, value open and reinventive cultures, and interoperate cooperatively within ecologies of organizations.[11] However, even as networks, organizations are quite capable of chronic inhibition in their development and functioning. When this is the case, they will essentially operate as one of the disordered character types described later in this chapter and the next. Chapter 8 will describe the special vulnerabilities, signs and symptoms of disordered organization network enterprises.

The work democratic type displays distinctive features in its major cross-cutting organizational subsystems (or segments, as I have called them). Let's look at these major horizontal segments one by one as they function in the work democratic character form.

At the strategic apex, or head of the organization, work democratic systems exhibit robust qualities of vision, imaginative thinking, penetrating insights and strategic reflection, and clarity of perspective. The top executives as a group do not shut their eyes to genuine issues or use pretense to cover them up or lessen their seriousness. At the same time, they do not show the penchant to exaggerate issues or their effects. There is little fear in their eyes to perceive threats that are not there, externally or internally, and thus reflexively clamp down on them. Priorities and goals in such systems are typically clear. Structurally, in organizations of size, environmental scanning mechanisms, strategic planning processes, and the governance apparatus are well developed and deployed. These are all used in a facilitative way to support the organization. They help provide direction, but do not have a dictatorial or imperious quality. Members of the top do not confuse being respected for the effective discharge of their executive functions with being catered to by staff and others. They recognize there are other people and vital functions in the system that they at best can support, not drive as their master. The top players do not have an exaggerated sense of their own importance. The contrast with neurotic, armored organizations is striking. Outrageous executive compensation (for example, seen in ratios of pay of top to bottom) is an earmark of distorted functions at the top, representing an overconcentration of energy locked up in what has become the system's big brain. Rather than serving as effective incentives and rewards for steering the business, such structured comp packages further insulate the top from the rest of the organization—a "head" more or less disconnected from the "body" of the enterprise.[12] Work democratic systems function in just the opposite way: more rationally and with systemic, self-regulating integrity.

In addition to the top's clear-eyed visual functioning, the work democratic character will also be able to articulate important matters about the system to its employees and the world. Executives will seek genuine feedback from customers where they actually hear a customer's voice, not confine customer feedback to aggregated Likert scale reports that remove the emotional quality of the experience. Live communication, not simply management by memo or email, is the rule. Similarly, the executive team will encourage others within the system to speak up, and more generally will support and nourish the growth of the organization and development of its members. Hang-ups associated with "unfinished business" at the vision and dependency stages of socioemotional development (seen in Table II) are relatively absent in the system and the functioning of the top.

The middle line of the work democratic character is inspirational and facilitative in function. Its members serve to hold the center of the organization together, providing key processing capabilities that help make the total system's energy circulate and be available to the whole of the system. In management and supervisorial roles, mid-line members too will tend to be oriented as coaches, more than arbitrarily preoccupied with compliance to rule-sets. They are supportive and *facilitative* of spontaneous movement of human energy. They too, like the top of the system, will provide guidance and support and nourishment to the organization, top and bottom and with each other. In work democratic systems, those in the middle segment will function like Oshry's ideal: They will tend to act like tops when they can, bring people together when that is needed, and get out of the way when their presence is not needed.[13] Indeed, in Richard Nolan's schema of future well-functioning organizations, an overcontrolling middle line is necessarily thinned out, having largely served historically as thicketed sublayers of authority without adding value. Nolan saw that IT networks, if properly established, can serve information transmission requirements that render all, if not most, of *that* middle management function unnecessary.[14] So overall in work democratic systems, the middle's coaching, convening and genuine integrative functions will be performed robustly, but needless oversight roles will be especially dispensed with.

In general, work democratic organizations tend to be self-directing in function and structure. This is a striking feature of its operating core. There is strong, cross-functional participation in process improvement and system implementation projects. Increasingly so, as organizations become more and more project-centric in their core functions. Participation tends to be self-directing, without administrative managers who serve no practical, working purpose. Robust engagement in actual problem solving on the line in daily work and in special projects is the norm. As is the behavior that people speak up. They are typically not afraid to surface important process or product problems, and they are encouraged to do so—be they real-time problems they see in the production process on assembly lines, or issues they identify in nonlinear agile system and process development teams. Nor are they afraid to speak about their personal needs and concerns. Interestingly, a hyper-focus on career is generally absent as people's energy is on work that captures their imagination and interest—work, that is, they *feel* they really want to do and find sufficiently absorbing.

Operating core members exhibit strong interest in quality of work life issues *and* in work quality. Pride in craft is obvious. And their opinions, given their intimate knowledge of the work itself, count. This was the basis for the original work-redesign method undertaken by the workers themselves in Trist's coal mine studies, built on in follow up socio-tech efforts; widespread later too in the Quality initiative era. Participation in special work improvement projects is high and seriously engaged with. There is little persistent skepticism and groans about corporate's latest "project of the month" initiative or employee attitude surveys that so often have yielded little over the years. "We-they" language tends to be gone. This is not a result of tutored corporate rhetoric, or the latest "culture change" or "employee engagement" programs that management or HR, sometimes with the help of consultants, trot out. Operating core members become genuinely engaged because they are part of the daily life of the enterprise; their vital contributions to the company's achievements are truly seen and its problems are not hidden from their view. *Members feel valued because they are.*

Genesis

As hypothesized in Chapter 4, this healthy organization character type emerges out of satisfaction of the work-democratic stage of development in its primary years. Satisfaction of the preceding socio-emotional stages has been attained or sufficiently worked through too; this allows the young organization to reach the work-democratic stage of development and the opportunity to fulfill the natural work of the system, given the contingencies of its continuing years. The function of the work-democratic stage answers the basic questions: *"How much will we be able to do our vital work in a fully productive and fulfilling way? How do we assure we sustain ourselves? Sustain this way of working?"* The work democratic character, or shades of it, may also emerge in certain armored organizations. This appears to happen when later life-cycle ages, crises or other events trigger the reoccurrence of the developmental stages and whose current-day circumstances, external and internal, call for effective resolution of the earlier chronic blocks. We saw some of this in the case references to Allied Bank and the intel agency in Chapters 4 and 5 respectively.

Sociotherapy

Because there is no chronic armoring in the functioning and structure of the work democratic type, consultative help when called on may generally be of a straightforward educational, behavioral or structural design nature. If the particular help sought is that of an OD nature, a classical action research approach would likely be sufficient. The system at all levels, depending on where any temporary or current problem or opportunity presents, will generally be able to hear and rationally respond to data-collection and feedback, while engaging appropriate stakeholders in assessment, planning and taking action solutions. They also seek out sound advice when truly value-added. Consultants have no characterological interference to have to contend with in how they specially position and make use of interventions. Under these conditions, simple appreciative inquiry, dialogic, and even more complex socio-tech interventions could be quite apropos.

If special contemporary conditions are such, however, where a work democratic organization cannot satisfactorily perform its work for some extended period, a stasis may occur. Its work energy may get pooled up and not circulate effectively, when its discharge is temporarily stopped. Work stoppages and labor strikes may be examples here, though they may not easily reach a point where they are needed in a work democratic system. But if they do, as with any other prolonged stasis, an understanding of systemic work energy processes and flow will be helpful for the consultant to see what must be done to relieve the stasis—and *in ways that fit the work democratic character* of the enterprise.

To return to our Disney Company example for a moment: A strike by Disney animators and supporting workers in 1941 culminated from mounting company labor problems, when the non-unionized cartoonists found little recourse to address disparities in wages, gender and creative-contribution recognition in the face of Walt's increasing intransigence. Externally, in the late Depression years and with America's entrance into World War II looming, the inflow of work slowed down as previously receptive international markets shrank. The organization thrashed about in the work slow-down, and Walt became restless and impatient. The company's difficulties were fanned too as it began to face sharp external media criticism for some of its aesthetic choices.

As certain latent labor issues festered and boiled over, it took Walt's brother Roy, keener in administration and finance and cooler in judgment than Walt, to see the import of the complaints and work to conciliate the dispute. Walt, who had grown autocratic in management style and strident in political ideology since the late '30s, had dug in and fought union organizing efforts at the studio fiercely. Roy, powerful as number two at the head of the company and no fan of union organizing himself, finally saw that Walt needed to be kept at bay in the struggle—and Roy asserted his own authority to see to it that he was. More than Roy simply giving in to the workers' demands, did he also sense what employees wanted was actually in keeping with the character of the Disney enterprise from its beginnings? Walt and others had famously worked very collaboratively and creatively together before, sometimes radically so, as he was even doing at the time of the strike in bringing the pathbreaking, feature-length *Fantasia* to life. Indeed, the work democratic thrust of the employee demands seemed inherent in the venture Walt from the start sought to cultivate, as even he voiced some recognition of during the labor crisis despite his strong antipathy to unions. My take is that the organization's underlying capability to self-correct saw the firm return to its truer character from which it had strayed.[15]

Sometimes if temporary blocking occurs, it may be apt to get the middle line remobilized, helping open up some number of sympathetic members to step back, take a breath and fresh look, and reach out more fully. The middle line's natural facilitative and integrative functions, up, down and across the enterprise, could help inspire and "oxygenate" the rest of the system just when it is needed. This may help the top see more clearly if it is temporarily stuck in a strategic issue compounding the troubles of a work slow-down; concurrent educational and coaching work with the top will help here too.

A Work Democratic Organization Case Example

The fullest example of a work democratic organization I have worked with is the Commonwealth of Pennsylvania. A state government made up of fifty-three independent boards, agencies and commissions, not each of which reported to the Governor, there was a federated feel and structure to the enterprise. Across its centralized and decentralized statewide agencies, 80,000 employees provided diverse services to citizens who had both common and individualized needs. Although a large state bureaucracy, led by elected officials at the very top, it did not generally reflect rigidity in its structure and functioning, or in its strategies and aims. On the contrary, it may be the healthiest organization I have ever seen, either in the commercial or public sector. There were clues early on in my extended consulting work there that the Commonwealth did not have a rigid organization character or heavy armor.

I had occasion to work closely with the state government on its two-year, visionary ImaginePA project. This was one of the largest efforts in the world whose aim was to implement an Enterprise Resource Package (ERP) system.[16] This information system implementation was coupled with significant organization process improvements for service delivery excellence. The project's aims and gains in the end touched every one of its divisions, members and constituents. The effort became widely known, and benchmarked by other state governments and commercial enterprises, as among the most successful ever of its kind, anywhere.[17]

The Commonwealth's work democratic character was evident to me in the way the state conceived the project; how its many, many employees dedicated to the project team engaged with the hundred person consulting compliment I was a part of; and by its conduct of the effort from beginning to end, including its very high achievements and genuine regard for people. There was stunning accomplishment with no real signs of exaggerated pushiness, as there are in organizations of a work aggressive character as we shall see.

Most of all, the work democratic quality was reflected in the lack of characteristic resistance generated by the project and in the fulfillment of the project's aims and its people, those who worked on the effort and the vast numbers served. The opposite signposts and effects—pronounced patterns of resistance and frustration—had the opportunity to show up at any turn in the project's course (at any moment really given the scale and scope of the effort). But they did not. In contrast, those pronounced problems usually do show up in most large-scale system and process improvement initiatives. Across organizations around the world, outright failure of ERP initiatives is common—abandoned projects after millions of dollars of time, labor and capital investment. Such initiatives are, in effect, interventions that have collapsed. My experience with dozens of ERP efforts, other projects and from the literature tells me such failure is almost always a function of the system's disordered organization character, inadequately attended to, if at all, in the design and conduct of the intervention.

The Commonwealth systemically displayed quite healthy features. This allowed the consulting team to proceed straightforwardly with technology, work process and human change activities in the conduct of the effort.

What follows are specific examples of the organization's free and effective movement that manifested in the project. Taken together, their qualities I believe add up to the undertaking of a work democratic enterprise.

- *The Commonwealth took the time to let the need for and nature of the project crystallize.* It had convened a team to learn lessons from its own earlier, troubled statewide data center implementations as well as study other large government and commercial ERP efforts. This included frank self-assessment and dialogue with principals of the other efforts; site visits too, to see how the systems worked in operation and to meet with their people and get their take. It is very evident the Commonwealth listened and learned from their own experiences and those of others.

- *Before project launch an executive steering committee was constituted whose first order of business was to more closely clarify the vision of the project. It did so in a series of fully attended, facilitated, group dialogues.* There was an easy and natural quality about the sessions. The group's early assembly and work together made for a hardiness in their subsequent functioning at the head of the effort. *The steering committee actually steered.* It neither overdirected nor functioned as a steering group in name only, there for lip service but little more, as is often the case. The Governor, Lieutenant Governor and cabinet leaders were well in the loop, engaged for visible contribution when needed. Agency heads were engaged as well too; early on they freed up large numbers of staff to dedicate as resources on the state's project team, which mirrored the functions and number from the consultancy to partner with day to day. In comparison, more chronically compromised organizations fight giving up resources to dedicate on even crucial projects.

- *Once the project launched, the nature and intended character of the project were clearly communicated to all management and staff, widely and with depth.* Such communications happened from the outset and at well-timed junctures throughout the life of the project, both planned and spontaneous communications. These included use of multi-media channels, live demos attended by hundreds, and thousands of structured and impromptu, highly interactive group and one-on-one meetings. Union management too was conferred with to assure their confidence that existing covered agreements would not be touched in the reconfiguration and compensation structure of new roles the system entailed. Vendors and customers were also communicated with early on and as the project moved towards go-live; some were met with in advance and all were briefed on what changes to expect and what would remain the same in their interactions with the state. Heavily armored organizations resist and, indeed, rarely or consistently do these things.

- *The project was not simply conceived as a "forcing function," often the case with technology implementations (that is, systems changes that force up other human and organizational changes, otherwise too difficult to directly face.) In its conception, there was serious regard for the human dimension from the get-go, individually and organizationally.* Compared to other efforts I had seen, very notable was the stature and number of Commonwealth players who were specifically dedicated to address *the human aspects of change*, along with the state's major investment in the project's sizable change-consulting team I led.

The state's careful selection of its consulting partner accorded the people side of change great weight from the outset. To choose its consulting partner, the state assembled a 40-person evaluation panel to meet with and compare consultant vendors to learn what they proposed and *how it felt to work with them.* Our team led its allotted day to present our proposal by engaging the panel in a real-time survey we'd specially constructed, an on-the-spot assessment and report out, followed by a large-group facilitated discussion *probing the change issues that they anticipated.* This allowed us to work with the data the panel members themselves spontaneously offered up—not ours—showing them what we had to offer and how we would work with them. Our credibility was rather immediate. While our aim was clear, ours was less a sales pitch; *they saw the value for themselves.* They were also clear in conveying their understanding that *continuity as well as change needed to be addressed.* This reflected a wider understanding we were dealing with flow in organizations—people and movement—and that we were not simply engineering structures and technologies, or only focused on mechanics.

- *The pace and tempo of the effort was natural. It did not feel forced or rushed, but neither was it slow.* This included little quality of a *constant* "emotional rush" (overexpansion) even when team members spoke about the project excitedly. Nor was a notable inability to express excitement about the project (overcontraction) evident. This too reflected natural flow.

- Quite generally throughout the project, *relationships between the paired client and consulting staffs went well, and our occasional conflicts were candidly faced and well worked through.* I saw this at close range a number of times. There was also little intra-team rivalry among the outside consultants; when this is otherwise conspicuous, it often signals countertransference of the conflicts inherent inside the client system.

I remember thinking the state's people were easy to work with, not pushovers but generally uncomplicated. I was struck by that in a drive up to Harrisburg one day for the project, as I looked at the state motto on its cars' license plates, "Pennsylvania—You've Got a Friend." And I saw a nuance in the ease of the working relationship: As we first got started, before they knew us well, I experienced client team leads as naturally cautious in their engagement with us. The reciprocal was also true with how we as consultants connected with them. But as we felt our way forward with each other, we each became ever-more trusting as partners; we were more relaxed, less distanced in our working ways together, and the initial, natural anxiety between the parties evaporated. Soon, there was little that could not be said with each other to address what was at hand, even when feelings ran high and the situation was difficult. The very expression of the feelings and acknowledgment of the difficulties sometimes made the issues that at first seemed so pressing less so, sometimes even moot. The character of the client-consultant relationship all looks quite different when working with systems that are chronically blocked. Unless the chronic character of the blocks is addressed, the client-consultant relationship will remain troubled. The quality of the relationship when the system is chronically compromised shows up in fits and starts.

- One notable anecdote in the way the top functioned: One C-suite officer who also served on the steering committee made no headway with the other executives when he proposed a change in standardized system design in the name of "reducing resistance." Despite his influence in the organization, the others could see his noble sounding rationale would undermine the initiative's very purpose. They therefore gave no weight to the suggestion. It drew no energy. The cross-cutting segment at the head of the endeavor functioned rationally.

- Another notable example: this one about how the top, middle line and operating core accorded with a work democratic manner of operating. *The Commonwealth easily understood the power of middle management's wide engagement in the initiative, including that of first line supervisors.* Not only was this deemed important for middles' own ideas and acceptance of the initiative, but for their crucial functional role to talk with their own people about what was really going on, both in small groups and privately. *Commonwealth members instinctively understood this was not merely functional technically, but critical emotionally for there to be trust.*[18]

In a series of cascading, interactive briefing sessions, all managers across the state were equipped with simple-to-convey, mass-customized materials to meet with their staffs to discuss individual job changes, to check for understanding, and to field questions and concerns—then transmit those for others' needed attention too. These materials were tailored for each manager's own immediate staff, including changes that each manager and supervisor would need to expect themselves in their own shifting administrative and leader roles. This understanding was not simply left to system training sessions to try to convey late in the game just before system go-live. That is commonly *too* late in most large-scale initiatives with all the needed technical information for those affected to assimilate, *let alone give them the advance time needed to emotionally process the coming, major change.*

Moreover, training sessions alone would have had no systemic, circulatory effect. In the approach we used here, employee feedback from the meetings went back up to the middles, then the top, to consider, process, and make final adjustments in technical and process features when warranted. And it was fed back to widen perception of how people were *humanly* responding to the system. *This approach to working across the board with the middles provided a path to join the entire organization together in the effort, socioemotionally and technically.* At the same time, it had the larger effect of building even fuller needed capacity for collaborative action up and down and across the enterprise. After all, that collaborative action is what the technology initiative had as a primary goal to begin with. *At the Commonwealth, the endeavor's very nature was fulfilled.*

Diagnostically significant was that the good sense of this approach was easily accepted in the organization. Typically, this extent of mid-manager and front-line staff engagement is fought by client management (and often thus not even proposed); the attitude commonly expressed is "there's no time for this, *they* must remain focused on their work" (a work-aggressive attitude). That character resistance didn't appear. Instead, *threading things all together as the approach did seemed natural to the organization because of its work democratic ways in the first place.*

THE WORK DRAMATIC ORGANIZATION CHARACTER[19]

The work dramatic organization gets its name because its general functioning is indeed just that: *dramatic.* It has certain characteristics of work democratic organizations—there is a spontaneity, participative and emotionally expressive quality in their bearing. The excitement of work, the value of relationships, and the aspiration of being a fully functioning organization are all present and expressed. But the similarities of the work democratic and work dramatic character types stop there. The work dramatic organization operates in a way that *dramatizes and acts out* its fuller aspirations but seems unable to live it in its behaviors and in its formal structures.

Gratifying work and achievement are present but sporadic, and a high level of habitual frustration is right at the surface, openly expressed but not full-throated. That is consistent with the lack of impact its members experience and frequently complain of. A plaintive, "done to" and "wronged" quality to the discontent characterizes what is offered up as not working—this its members offer up when unelicited and when questioned. A solidity seems missing in word and actual functioning. The focus of organization attention shifts frequently and sometimes surprisingly suddenly in those affected. In general, there is a *flighty and running away* character to the organization. Its members do not stop long enough to concentrate their energies nor, when necessary, fight for what they espouse and in fact seem to truly value. Their open fight for life is wanting.

In its origins, the type appears to have reached the work-democratic stage of development but with anxiety; the full work of the stage seems to have been insufficiently satisfied, so energy remains trapped inside the system as a whole. A significant work stasis results, the entire system now flooded with energy that is not effectively discharged. The trapped energy circulates—*runs around*—in the system. This gives the organization, manifested at each of its cross-cutting levels, the chief characteristics of restlessness, flightiness and expressed dissatisfaction with its achievements: The promise and potential of the organization, as its members keenly and constantly feel, has not been and is not fulfilled.

The type as I describe it below draws in part from Kets de Vries and Miller's "dramatic" type of organization.[20] But as they do not posit a work-democratic stage of socioemotional development, they emphasize leader-dependency hang-ups as part of the picture. Undoubtedly, those are present. Psychoanalytically, Kets de Vries and Miller rely on classic descriptions of a hysterical individual character on which they largely base their organizational type; I draw on this too, though with emphasis on the present-day energy stasis at work, which I believe is core to the type. Understanding the type's basic energy stasis and the manner in which it is expressed leads to a distinctive intervention strategy. My description of the character is largely based on the consulting case shared at the end of this section.

In my experience, the work dramatic character is not all that common on the organization scene, compared to the pervasiveness of systems that show the fight that's in them and are work-aggressive in bearing (as I will contrast in the next organization character type).

However, I have consulted with two young, network-based enter-prises that demonstrate quite a few of its features. These two are also drawn on in the description below and revisited in Chapter 8 on the special circumstances the network organization era presents. My ini-tial work with these two suggests that the work dramatic type may become more prominent as the network era further proceeds.

Characteristics and Symptoms

The central presenting characteristic of the work dramatic organi-zation is its flightiness. This shows up in manifold ways. Along with persistent issues in shifting focus, expressed discontent and lack of punch, the flightiness is evident in the hyper-agility of the type. This can be declared a virtue by its executives and staff, as I saw in the two network-based organizations conferred with. But in both cases there was a characteristic lack of attention on building organization-al capability and real muscle. Little value was placed on developing sufficiently stable and scalable internal operating structures. Reliable operating standards and protocols, top, middle and bottom, were thin; reactivity and impulsive action the norm. This was rational-ized in meetings and glossy literature as being "opportunistic" and showing commitment to "transformation." In fact, lack of energetic concentration was at core the issue.

There was a rushed, last-minute quality to much of the work as I was able to see it and hear it in both organizational cases. However, in actuality, a lot didn't get done as a function of inadequate concen-tration of collective effort. Few in the organization felt satisfied. I heard the CEO in one of the organizations complain bitterly—"do I have to do everything myself?"— so did executive vice presidents, senior middle managers and the tech professionals in the operating core. There was a good deal of openly expressed blame coming from all sides. In the name of "getting things done," the CEO moved in and out of areas on what seemed to others a whim; people reported willy-nilly in what little formal hierarchy there was; and divisional organization and people's roles and responsibilities were susceptible to being shuffled at any moment—in sudden reorganizations, acquisitions and sell offs that few saw coming. All this reflected lack of orchestrated, concentrated and combined effort. This left business unit leaders on little solid ground to bring *concerted* development efforts to fruition. As with the CEO, business unit leaders were reinforced in their already ingrained behaviors to go it alone with little consultation outside their silos. A good deal of political drama and jockeying for power were evident. In both consulting cases, structural rigidity, including *sufficient organizational armoring* at the top, middle and bottom segments, *was largely missing;* their extreme structural looseness, continually shifting organizational arrangements and relative formal shapelessness functioned as defenses against collective effort and thrust.

These systems' emphasis on agility paradoxically stifled movement. The frenetic character of each organization struck me as each of their major constraints. Their abundant energies had little place to go. They remained locked inside the system. I intend the irony when I say they are each examples of *work stasis across a system par excellence.* The challenges are very difficult to address with any method that does not effectively slow the organization down. It can be done, as we'll see in the fuller case below. But the frenetic quality of their movement militates against this.

The core of the issue is the runaway energy movement bottled up within the system; there is little effective concentration and discharge of the organization's combined energies in line with the nature of its work. This is why such organizations' efforts lack punch, which members at all levels indeed feel but can do little more than complain about or seek out one inadequate "solution" after another.

Sooner or later, the constant hunt for the shiny and new proves disappointing to the type. The list of remedies it seeks to handle its predicament seems endless. The sought solutions themselves are prone to be symptomatic reflections of the character. Organizational members seek to be heroes, surround themselves with heroes, and otherwise seek out other saviors and salvation—"game-changers" as they may call them: white knights to the rescue, silver bullet products and services, constant reorganizations and new acquisitions.

Its leadership and membership can get enamored by the latest management fads; it is *the flash* in the pan that stirs and excites them. This includes becoming enthralled with the latest OD fashions. This was exhibited in Chapter 1's example of the government agency smitten with dialogic OD and a consultancy which let them run on and on about the future; this, in spite of the issues that truly preoccupied its people and whose underlying character dynamics held the organization back. Dialogic OD was perfectly suited for the evasion; it explicitly rejects any diagnostic expertise that would have given the organization a better chance to confront and work through what would inevitably be deeply ingrained barriers to a more radical future. The susceptibility of this character type to trust fads is sincere in the moment; they are not just passing interests as they may be for some organizations seeking to try out new things. But for the work dramatic type, the solutions tried are often not well grounded, and therefore are routinely given up, switched out, followed by strong disappointment reactions.

Work dramatic organizations do not demonstrate the patience to build solidly for themselves. It's not that their dreams for something truly better are the issue. These are expressions I believe of latent health, of the desire for health. But, alone, they are just not enough. Had the type's executives and staffs the patience to ponder more deeply (an unfulfilled concentration effect in itself), they might have done better. Thoreau's words here are applicable:

> If you have built castles in the air, your work need not be lost; that is where they should be. Now put the foundations under them.[21]

Coupled with a slow-down strategy, as we will illustrate, helping the system come to grips with foundational issues, I have found, becomes key in intervention with an organization of this character. *Members of the work dramatic organization must come to see their constant mo-*

tion inhibits the force of their impulses for work to gel and be effective;
they must be helped to live into ways where they settle down enough
and able to structuralize their path to health.

Work dramatic types may be willing to engage a consultancy in this
way or not. Their relationships with consultants, certainly to start,
are predictably, markedly ambivalent. The characteristic flightiness
will manifest in *their movement both towards and away* from the
consultant sometimes instantaneously, and this back and forth will
happen over and over. They may have a history of having worked
with many different consultants, running from one to another. They
will project onto, challenge and test the strength of their consultants.
Do they stand for something? Can they be easily pushed around or
seduced? Inwardly, organizational members know they need to deal
with consultants who are open and accepting, but who will also say
what they really think, plainly and directly. I believe they inwardly
know they need a consultant, someone whose personal character is
characteristically different from theirs as an organization, someone
who will challenge *and* support them, someone they can count on
and come to trust.

Genesis

Based on the schema earlier offered up on socioemotional development stages, the work dramatic character has reached the work stage
of development. In the character's "pure" form as drawn here, the
organization has satisfied all earlier stages of development, including
having successfully satisfied the work-aggressive stage. The organization demonstrates the capacity to function in a manner that reflects
the completed work of the preceding stages—i.e., sufficiently effective vision, dependency and fusion capabilities, and the ability to
marshal its energies to get real work done. It is the work-democratic
stage, I hypothesize, where this type gets hung up. It has reached this
final stage of development but because of founder clamp down or
other major upsetting challenges at this juncture, the organization
does not fulfill the natural work of this last stage. It is able to perform

in some work democratic ways, as we discussed, but only partially so; its dammed-up energies have not sufficiently concentrated and thus are not fully available for robust discharge. In effect, the work dramatic organization is essentially a work democratic form but with extreme, chronic anxiety. This is reflected in its constant agitation, restlessness, flightiness and discontent.

By this logic, the system as a whole has no earlier developmental stage blocks to fall back on and anchor its energy around. Rather, *the energy becomes stuck it seems in endless circulation within the system—again, energy that is internally and appears to be eternally running around—without effective concentration or full discharge.* This accounts too for the type's *lack* of sharp internal organizational definition and muscular quality.

This seems to be a systemic, energetic phenomenon echoing what is seen in individual character development of the human organism. The hysterical character, in its pure form, has no pre-genital, psychosexual hang-ups to retreat to. The stasis and flooding effect within the organism as a whole are what present as the person's primary problem, not other localized symptoms in the body. Likewise, *the characteristics and symptoms of the work dramatic organization are reflected in how the system "runs" as a whole, they are not especially prominently anchored in the head, associated middle line, or operating core segment structures. The work energy stasis per se is the problem.* The other neurotic, armored organization types do show disproportionate, distorted effects localized in the cross-cutting segments, as we will discuss with each in the rest of the typology.

Sociotherapy

Two especially critical dimensions for the OD consultant to pay attention to are: first, building a highly trusted client-consulting relationship; and second, slowing the system down at every turn in the engagement so its members see how the running quality permeating the organization actually holds it back. These are both done in a number of ways.

While the first dimension, building high trust in the consulting relationship, is of course true in all effective consultation, with this character type it takes on a special valence. The work dramatic type's skittishness reflects a high level of caution and mistrust in receiving help. Indeed, the system will present this way, and the consultant should expect to see *flight towards and sudden flight away* from the consultant. The consultant may wonder about their level of interest, "Do they or don't they?" Being captivated then doubt, standoffishness and denigration can readily present. The consultant must patiently and effectively work through the attitudes with its lead senior clients, then others as he moves more fully into the system. Getting the client to talk openly about their doubts—resistances all—is essential in building trust. If consultants are preoccupied with keeping everything they hear from a client positive about their performance, they generally will not have the chops for this work. Reich, in his original, individual character analysis methods, and in his lead at the Vienna Polyclinic Technical Seminar, emphasized that eliciting the negative transference from patient to therapist must always be attended to before true positive transference can be established. In his classic text *Character Analysis*, Reich describes how he learned this the hard way himself.[22]

While being gentle enough on approach with the work dramatic type so as to be respectful and not frighten them away, the consultant must not walk on eggshells; he must be able to speak forthrightly and also show that he can hear out and respond to criticism fairly. All this is crucial with the work dramatic type. They will watch you closely and take your measure.

As the consultant works in establishing the relationship, there will be opportunity to start discussing the running-away quality. There is an art to this. This must be done at first generally with a light touch. But asking simple questions or making encouraging statements that deal with what is happening in the moment, without going prematurely deep, can begin to lift the veil. These might be statements like it's okay for them to press in on you with their questions, which they seem to want to ask but avoid (using excessive qualifiers, for example). This will create its own platform to probe more deeply—and for them to speak with more punch. Gently but firmly guiding the conversation and encouraging the client to talk freely about what's really of concern, right in the moment, is important. They will generally respect the consultant who handles this well, not letting them run on and on without getting to something weightier one senses they long to say.

These will all start to shape the way the second main point above is addressed: *Slowing the client-system down so its members can see what they are up against as an internal dynamic, then concentrate their energies for fuller impact.* There will come a time in the consultation, earlier than some might think, that you can begin to point out the quality of the character you are seeing—not as some intellectualized clinical entity, but descriptively, in terms of the real behavior at hand, using plain language. Such opportunities will likely, naturally emerge as you engage in action-oriented inquiry and development activities with them. Over time, the observations can deepen, as the client demonstrates readiness to engage that way with you and others. You as consultant must be patient and await the moment at hand. Your frustrations with the system will be a countertransference that can guide you in your reactions and timing. Because of the type's unpredictability, this is tricky and consulting mistakes can easily happen. The consultant with this type especially will be prone to do too much or too little, make specific interventions too fast or too slowly.

I want to emphasize it is generally *not* important or wise to go into unnecessary detail or the whys and wherefores of it all with the chief clients in general. There will be time enough for that when such intervention will have *emotional* impact. These are not intellectual exercises, and nothing is to be gained by rushing things. These matters are always ones of emotional acceptance for clients, including *their ability to tolerate seeing what is happening, keep their focus, and drive forward.* Underneath the general organizational character disorder, this capability is what the consultant is helping the client build. Consultants in fact face exactly the same challenge in the consulting task—and in the inner capabilities they must themselves develop to be effective practitioners. All of these considerations are magnified with the work dramatic organization character because of the very skittishness and at-large anxiety of the type.

As the engagement proceeds with this kind of system, the consultant can proceed with ever more action-research oriented roles, helping the clients find their own ways to projects with punch, both individual and joint projects they will find gratifying and whose results will impress both themselves and others important to them. They can be guided to understand that such a project be undertaken in a way which not only gets the work of the project done, but also builds muscle and structural cohesion in their capabilities going forward—both signs of energetic concentration. This way, they can go after the matters that count most to them. The consultant accomplishes this, as with the other character types, by working from the head of the organization down; first the top, then the middle line, then the operating core. At each level, the consultant goes back and re-loops the preceding level (and levels) back in as part of the intervention, so the learning and functioning starts to be unitary. Each level, I have found, will then grow more and more in synch in their joint work. As this therapeutic process evolves and takes effect—the moment-to-moment difficulties of transition also worked through—clients will experience the consultation as one of flow and find it very gratifying itself.

A Work Dramatic Organization Case Example

In Chapter 5, in the example of an operations division within Allied Bank, we focused on working with a number of the division's key players as an intervention into the middle line function of the whole enterprise to inspire systemic movement. In coming back now to this same group of players, I treat this division as a system unto itself with its own character and its own top, middle and bottom structure. Beyond the scope of the case, this has important conceptual and consulting practice implications. Ultimately, as consultants we must understand we are most always working with systems within systems. These subsystems can develop distinct organization characters themselves and as they operate with other subsystems within a larger system's character. We will return to these implications as part of Chapter 8.

The operations division in fact functioned more like an organizational network, rather than a fully elaborated hierarchical formal structure, though it still had evident primary cross-cutting segments within it. There were many peer-level and hierarchical dotted-line reporting relationships within and outside of it as a division. As its own system, it presented as work dramatic in character. Its principals began an internal self-development process that led to significant change in the organization's functioning and impact, with help sought from me for the kind of consulting support they knew I provided. As a result of our efforts together, I think it fair to say the division shifted from being work dramatic to work democratic in character.

The intent of the case discussion below is to give further color to the work dramatic organization character as a type and its sociotherapeutic consulting principles. The discussion focuses on three main aspects of the consultation:

- How the consulting relationship and character diagnosis were each first established. And what I sought to maintain as the goal and manner of the consulting relationship in order to deal with the presenting characterological constraints for the division's own success as a system.

- The introduction and turning point of the strategy that effectively slowed the organization down to face its issues and more completely focus its energies.

- The nature of the action-research projects the clients developed and took on. These were the concrete means by which the organization *enacted and structuralized* its new way of working—up, down, and beyond itself in its larger field, with both collateral internal Allied organizations and end-customers of the bank itself.

To refresh the reader's memory about the case as first presented last chapter: This was Allied's chief operations division whose senior group of managers occupied corporate-centered as well as field offices positions. The nature of their work was providing instrumental support for the main line lending and deposit activities of the bank.

I was approached by two of the most influential of the senior managers to see if I could help them and others in the organization have greater impact in their work. It felt to the two an opportune time to "maybe" try, especially given challenging conditions at the bank and where other renewal efforts had begun to take hold. But the division was lagging in impact they said, and there was much to be done if only they could get the footing to really dig in and make things happen. In this, they confessed they felt powerless, and they presented as restless and depressed. Their frustration and discontent were palpable. This was true of their peers in other regional offices, they said, as I had seen too in my other work at the bank and as I confirmed again when I soon met with them again too.

One of the two who approached me held a top regional position in the field, the other served corporately in a senior operations role. Both of them women, as were most in the division, they were formally schooled but largely came up through the ranks; the operations functions were mostly, though not exclusively, performed by women who had made their own careers this way. With the division largely operating as an outspread network in the wider company, the top regional manager served as a *de facto* leader of how the division's activities were carried out. Other senior managers at corporate and in the field took their cues from her. For example, her views were especially sought and carried weight in formulating and executing important new policies by the Senior Vice President/Cashier of the bank, with whom a dotted-line reporting relationship existed. She, the Cashier, and the other senior operating leader served, in effect, as the strategic apex or "head" of the division. I treated them that way, which is how they were also seen by bank executives in their dealings with the division. The two who first approached me were vocal about the need for doing something more. The Cashier hoped for that, but he was less active in pushing for it, less willing to go out on a limb to make it happen. Here too, practically speaking, he was taking his cues from the top regional player to be out in front and take the lead.

As I discussed earlier, a cynical shell presented as well. This showed up in initial conversations in what the two who had come to me said and how they said it, as I probed the possibility of working with them. The pattern was this: After first enthusiastically asserting the need for action, they would quickly follow with retreat to a "but what's the point in trying" attitude, as they complained about others holding them back. There was some hopelessness but also a bitter assertiveness about it. Still, they expressed excitement about what they saw as core to their work—the genuine value of working in behalf of customers and maintaining a well-run operation. Others outside the division with whom they worked saw them as effective and key players, despite the two's own dissatisfaction with their clout. In their mixed expressions going back and forth, and those of the Cashier's and their peers too, I was struck by what seemed like a more salient pattern: they struck me as *kind of all over the place*. Was this itself a clue to the character of their larger network as a system unto its own?

I saw their capacity to express their excitement about possibilities, and their reputations as serious organizational players, as something to build on—the health at work that was in them. I also came to see other ways they expressed themselves as deeply constraining. The signs of agitation, restlessness and the back-and-forth running away were hard to miss. These were consistent with my sense of their "being all over the place." The cynicism and depression were there, surely, but these seemed themselves to literally come and go too. For the division as a system unto itself, depression, though prominent, was not the dominant feature. *It was the running motion itself that seemed the constant, the core issue I thought.* I began to form a picture of the organization as that of a work dramatic type. As a theoretical aside, there is an art to diagnosing character: being able to see the relationship of symptoms that present, one to another, and see the most basic pattern they form, the underlying character they represent and the function they serve.[23] This is a principle in effectively diagnosing any type of organizational character.

I went back over in my mind what I had thus far seen. The running, flighty character was right there in how things presented, including how its principals discussed the prospect of working with me. First enthusiasm, then doubt. I was kindly invited and welcomed to discuss the possibilities, then criticized and subjected to suspicion. Was I an agent of the corporate powers, they asked, lumping me in with "the others holding us back?" This back-and-forth quality with me I felt was classic transference and also indicative of the character. The flightiness was reflected too *in the manner of expression* of the points they were making. Sometimes, when they were stirred, they would make a point of "drawing the line" of what they would put up with others they felt disrespected by, but these seemed reactive in timing, both brittle and, curiously, flimsy. More generally, they ran on and on, sometimes going in circles on topics that avoided getting to the point. There was a plaintive quality to what they said without a bottom line. They were finally able to get to the point, prompted by some gentle questioning by me, pausing things and asking what they were driving at. I saw this same manner of expression as I talked with others in the division.

I also found, by way of content, that one of the issues bothering them most, including the Cashier, was that they all got stuck in sprawling minutiae—voluminous policies and procedures they had to continually wrestle with. They saw themselves getting buried and busy in surface details. They recognized that the details were not unimportant. But they said so much of their time spent in the weeds reacting kept them bogged down from contributing something more, something that could substantially move the division forward. They weren't sure what it was they could do about it. *They recognized something was missing, they felt it, and they were willing to say it even though they didn't have an exact fix on things.* I found that expressed quality of not knowing to be encouraging in the prospect of working with them. I saw it as a sign of their seriousness and openness as leaders, and that there might be a real payoff in work achievement they would find gratifying.

I knew in working with them, the first order of business would be to solidify and slightly expand the leadership group. The sprawling network needed greater cohesion and representation for collective clout, and its top leadership team needed to be more fully formed. The original two pulled in a few others across the state—a total team of six senior leaders—who I would meet face to face every one or two weeks over several months to start. We would begin by more fully exploring the issues that had thus far surfaced, and, afterwards, zero in on what might be done.

All six knew, with barely a word from me, that the improvement process would need to engage the entire body of the division as participants. They also instinctively knew that the communications of their efforts needed to be real time and in person—not some glossy corporate, "change" initiative with "impressive" formal messaging. Their interests were not in being "impressive" (as one finds in work aggressive character types). They, instead, wanted to have effective, satisfying impact. Mid-managers subordinate to them across the division would also need to participate in policy and procedure review and change. Front-line workers would need to be engaged too with more than skills and behavioral training, though they recognized that might eventually be part of the picture. Changes in real work—its priorities and how it was performed, flowed, and organized—would have to be thoroughly addressed, with employees significantly engaged in work restructuring efforts. And compensation for employees would need to be looked at too. The six as a leadership team began to develop an ambitious and worthy scope for their change agenda.

I met with them facilitating their conversations on this, seeding ideas where helpful, and letting them really be the ones driving priorities and making things happen. Beyond our sessions, they did this in their conversations with each other; their other peers and staffs to let them know what they were up to and for real-time inputs; and in their meetings with other corporate stakeholders for needed support, politically and administratively, to back implementation of the new ideas. Some of the ideas for change were radical that entailed never-done-before practices at the bank and were in fact leading edge for the industry.

This series of meetings, facilitated or on their own, gave them time out of their restless day to day. Our own sessions especially slowed them down, which was my aim, given the agitated, running character I saw. As they slowed down, they had the time to concentrate their energies—and thoughts—to see the way forward.

This didn't happen all at once. At first as they slowed down, they would get restless again, "to get going," and I found it necessary to help them sit with their feelings that surfaced as we worked through the task material and what was emotionally unsettling. As a group in the sessions, they helped each other also see through the difficulties. They increasingly came to see they did not need to run from their feelings, neither their frustrations nor their passion for what they really thought was vital. Quite the opposite: This was the source they now saw of their power.

As these sessions continued, I took time out with them from the task focus to facilitate their own, shared reflections on what was shifting in their own manner of working, on their own "inner process" as a leadership team. A turning point came when the principal regional leader, the one who originally approached me to help, said to the group: "*Wow, we do, more than we think.*" The room fell quiet. The multiple meanings of her statement reverberated with all. Their roles were shifting from simply being busy doers, to ones who conceived new ways of working, then conceived how to make them happen. Their *thinking* together became important. That required letting go of the busy, the running, and instead starting to really concentrate. They were becoming truly strategic. They also came to value, as that statement revealed, that indeed there was real import in what they had been doing all along: More happened because of them than they had earlier credited. And not just more work, *but more work of value. That took real doing.* A new self-confidence had emerged.

Slowing them down to concentrate freed them up to see more clearly, and to dream up new projects to make their emerging ideas come to life. Their operations background in fact helped them be able to give sharp focus to the projects, in their conception and execution. These leaders got much better at asserting themselves on tasks they deemed strategic, and much of their earlier time spent complaining and blaming others simply went away. In absolute terms, as the reactive running diminished, they now had more, not less, time to complain if they had wished, *but they no longer had any energy for that. They had deeper satisfaction now than that.*

What I did in the consultation was mostly instinctive, in what I saw moment to moment. I followed the natural course of play. I did not use the character diagnosis heavy-handedly, but as referenced earlier as a kind of orienting map that stayed with me in the backdrop. Having the diagnostic background was particularly helpful when things got stuck or I got lost following the action. And it was helpful because I had a larger picture of what I was doing with them—*helping them be free enough from their typical frenetic motion to concentrate and think anew.*

As an intervention process, this was not about cooking up ideas or "managing change." Yes, from the get-go, new ideas about work that would work was in aim. But at their base was an emotional process: to help them finally stop the running and focus their work energies on what they could foresee would be significant achievements and deeply satisfying. The process itself and where it was headed was *felt* by them moment to moment as they worked together.

Using projects to enlist others in the change process and innovate new ways of working was key to the restructuring of the division. I mean "restructuring" in a double sense: instituting new formal structures in how the division operated (goals, roles, organizational arrangements, and comp) and in *the structure of its character* (from work dramatic to work democratic). Managers from the division's middle line and those in the operating core (including its hands-on, working managers) were widely and meaningfully engaged in work redesign, facilitation and communications across the network. In many ways, the organization as a whole became self-directing, with very high coordinating mechanisms and supporting norms to keep things on course and primed for further innovation. Several of the projects were:

- Review of the litany of policies and procedures and thematically grouping them for greater clarity and coherence; elimination of non-value-added activities; and policy innovations where there were gaps. These set new standards for operating performance—easier for all affected to understand and less likely to create busy-work. Their streamlining also helped strengthen the quality of operations because it was easier to get things right the first time.

- Major redesign of how regional office operations were staffed and organized. They were reorganized under flexible multi-skilled team structures rather than stovepipes. Jobs changed from many narrow, prescriptive ones to a much simpler design where a single job progressively widened in scope based on an incumbent's acquired capabilities. People would now be paid on the range of their knowledge and skills, not a particular job assignment ("pay-for-knowledge"). They would be mixed and matched with others in small teams of complementary skill sets at any point in time, as may be needed, and they would learn from each other. This made for more flexible, just-in-time use of staff, more responsive customer service, and it put a premium on learning, career development and team play. Operations actually got tighter, less sprawling, but there was greater discretion than ever before in decision making, at every level, as the moment called for. The division's non-headquarters leadership took the lead to work with HR to align the administrative dimensions of job grade, comp, and support reassignments into the new framework. This was not just "another" corporate-driven initiative being "done to" division members; they drove it.

- A wide quality of new curricula was introduced to support people's formal and on-the-job learning and knowledge transfer. This process too was conceived and self-administered from within the division, not by a corporate training and education department. This entailed wide participation to determine needed and wanted curricula, to negotiate with vendors, and to facilitate sessions by those who did the work itself. An extensive service quality training was introduced that complemented other concurrent customer focus efforts throughout the division and the wider bank.

- High participation in technology assessments and reviews occurred, including new requirements definitions, vendor selection, standardized report changes, and automations in work flow, which included document imaging and what at the time were other newly emerging electronic banking capabilities.

Regardless of the particular project, and others that continued to emerge over time, they all served as vehicles *to concretely enact the new ways of operating for the division. The series of self-directed projects provided means to structuralize the new ways*, so they were sufficiently coherent, dependable, repeatable and scalable. The added clarity and better-defined structure to the once diffuse network enabled its energies to be better focused for achievement—and which its people found much more enriched and satisfying than in the past.

THE WORK AGGRESSIVE ORGANIZATION CHARACTER[24]

The work aggressive character type seems to be the most dominant on the organization landscape. Its domineering quality is in fact its chief distinguishing feature. *It seeks to dominate*—its markets, its customers, its employees and all those in its orbit. That quality, as we will discuss, may be overt or subtle, but it is the basic dynamic whereby the organization functions. The work aggressive character is also dominant in the sense of it perhaps being the most pervasive among all the organization types. Most large corporate organizations around the world it seems function in various shades this way. The type is what many people think of when they think of a US corporation: very often male-dominated, competitive and macho in attitude.[25] But the type also describes how many entrepreneurial organizations basically work, as well as the way some large, modern network organizations like Facebook actually seem to operate, their different espoused values notwithstanding.

I have labeled this organization type as work aggressive because its dynamics seem to derive from the "unfinished business" of the work-aggressive stage of socioemotional development, the stage focused on the emerging organization's performance of its core work. This was introduced in Chapter 4, and the genesis of this type is discussed further below. This character type is similar to what Terrence Deal and Allan Kennedy originally labeled "tough-guy macho" and "work-hard, play-hard cultures."[26] These two variants seem subtypes of the main portrait drawn here; my hunch is that the second of the two variants is based on additional, earlier fusion-stage blocking incorporated into the developmental mix. Kets de Vries and Miller's "paranoid" culture type also seems a special variant of the work aggressive character, a function perhaps of earlier vision stage blocking not fully resolved. It is worth stating that all character types able to perform some amount of work in their markets, by definition, have reached the work-aggressive stage. But some it seems that also run into frustrations at earlier stages may partially regress to the earlier blocking and produce a mixed type. More on the developmental process of variants when we discuss the genesis of this type. In the end, the general sociotherapeutic goal is not to get caught up in every nuance of a particular character classification, but to understand the character's overall function well enough to help the client organization in its struggle to move more freely and work more fully.

Above all, the work aggressive type is focused on task and goal performance and on the strength of its performance. Pride in achievement is notable. Sometimes this is a genuine pride, and, under stress, when the organization's shortcomings are revealed, its expression will strike the listener as especially boastful. *Striking* too is a quality of the character. *The type's penchant is to hit hard and, even more, to be seen as hitting hard*—be they the points its leaders make or its impact on markets, customers and staff.

A heavy stress on numbers, performance measurement and dashboards to gauge performance seem to be very evident in this type. There usually is less emphasis on the human side of enterprise; when it is given some due, it is almost always itself especially subject to quantitative measurement. Its value is not expressed so much in its inherent human worth or qualitative, emotional dimensions. The human side is almost always spoken of in instrumental terms of "getting the work done." It is not treated as part of an integrated drive where human fulfillment is at one with product and service fulfillment. That contrasts significantly, I maintain, with what is seen in organizations that function in work democratic modes. Diagnostically, for the consultant, this is an important differential. Indeed, when push comes to shove, the work aggressive type may disparage people. Consultants I believe will see this emerge in transference with the type—always—if they work with them long enough.

In any case, insofar as people are regarded, they largely get reduced to "the human *factor*," and in recent years people are generally seen as a special form of "capital" or "talent to manage." People, in the last analysis through such a lens, are viewed as objects. This view today is widely normalized in the larger culture of work. The combined work of people is not seen as *the animating drive* behind the organization, naturally and spontaneously moving, seeking gratifying achievement. Despite the usual annual report rhetoric of "our people are our most important assets," this reduced view of people is institutionalized in accounting procedures that all public organizations must face: The human asset is simply treated on the *liability* side of the ledger, *not* as an asset. This given accounting schema, like the professional language of HR today, reflects wider social values. This certainly seems to have implications for which organization character types become prominent in the larger socio-economies in which they arise.

Behind the concentration on performance and numbers in this organization type, there is *an underlying emotional preoccupation with gaining and maintaining power. That is the work aggressive character's cardinal trait*, another facet of its search to dominate. The type's Achilles heel is that, *at certain limits, performance is sacrificed by those in the organization for the feeling of powerfulness.* This is readily seen in the attitudes of the top but also in those of the middle line and operating core. I have found that their recognition of deep and festering internal problems and their resolving them fully are typically defended against; this is done in ways consistent with the character dynamics—either by turning away or dealing with them hastily and superficially. Inwardly, the work aggressive type's members do not feel up to the task to really handle them. At some level, they feel inadequate, which is why the *display* of power and the *feeling* of powerfulness becomes more important than truly facing up to things and *being* strong. This is a clue to a primary sociotherapeutic path to help them, as we will discuss, assuming they truly seek help that would have a thoroughgoing effect. They typically do not. They do not like owning that they are in a vulnerable spot, let alone chronically vulnerable. If they do seek help, it seems the effort will likely be abandoned once immediate presenting issues are on the surface addressed. The attitude at that juncture, as I have seen it, will be: "We are getting work done now, what's the problem?"

Disclosed in interviews and in behavioral observation, its members almost always express latent fear of losing power, competitive footing and being rendered powerless. This is felt collectively at the enterprise level as a whole and individually. That is why the organization fears going too deeply into its challenges. It also accounts for why it is so often preemptively combative. The work aggressive type prepares itself for combat in its planning and go-to-market strategies. Whatever the current or anticipated reality of the competitive landscape, this bearing I believe is a clue to where it was frustrated developmentally in its past: how it got fixated work-aggressively and did not move on to the work-democratic stage of development. The organization is characterologically stuck. In a way, all it knows to do is to fight. This becomes pronounced when circumstances are difficult and stasis results. If dismissing the problems doesn't work, they try to fight their way out. This is not all bad, but full resolution will take fighting that goes further than the character form typically allows and fends off: *They will need to muster the courage to punch all the way through to the depths of the issues that hold it back.* Unresolved fear in the system holds them back. We will see this in the case study.

Characteristics and Symptoms

The organization with a work aggressive character likes to make a show of things. It proudly displays its goods and service wares in vaunted advertising and promotional campaigns. Being seen as impressive and "premier" in its markets, always striving to be "number one," is important to its leaders—and to many who join its ranks at all levels. That is part of the recruiting draw. When I visited the corporate offices of one famous fast-food restaurant chain, known for its very aggressive ways, I was struck by the breathtaking art displayed on its walls and hallways. Others of the work aggressive type present in precisely the opposite way: they *show off* their modesty.[27]

Consider BearingPoint and Deloitte. They *showcased modesty* at their corporate centers with the layout of their office space. Partner offices were smaller than a casual visitor might expect. This was not just a matter of limiting overhead expense, there to be sure. The firms also designed the space *to impress* visiting clients how frugal they were. I know. I attended insider meetings in which such rationales were top of mind. Nonetheless, status differentials—a telling feature of the character type—were present, and still showed up in an office's design features (for example, building floor location, privacy, and those with conference tables and windows). Relatively minor sounding or not, there were real feelings of worth attached around office space, also I think, at bottom, reflecting pent up frustration over the lack of heartfelt contribution in the work itself. The status differences also showed up in norms around just being in the office. For senior partners, office time was fine. But the bulk of the firms' members, including more junior partners, were expected to be out in the field, racking up client service hours or selling new work. Otherwise, you were disparagingly considered to be "on the beach"—not measurably pumping out money. Most of all, the differentials existed in steep disparities of compensation from top to bottom, including multiple partner layers.

In the type, internal competitiveness is openly welcomed, even if toned down by some in more recent years. Forced rankings of employee performance for comp and layoff lists have not historically been uncommon for the type. Exxon, which has historically displayed significant aggressive features despite I think ultimately being a different type, was famous for this. Diagnostically, the underlying stress on competitiveness is the tell. Again, it's not that competitive performance is unimportant in business; it is obviously important. It's the ubiquity and intensity of the emphasis these types of firms place here, compared to other critical dimensions. This is their universe. When pressed, its leaders will ask, "What else is there?" The heavy top line focus on sales, then margin, are the same. Human development programs and R&D investments are the first to go when cost containment is in the air. Some of these problems are self-propelled by the firm's character, like BearingPoint's; they are not simply functions of the market. Where there is chronic overreach, the firm is going to run into difficulties when circumstances get tough. Tough circumstances are often a constant in organizational life for any firm. It is the character at work that *exacerbates their effects* on the organization.

In all this, what is evident is the *push* of the work aggressive type. The push to do more and more, to ever expand in size, and for its people to work harder and harder, often with less and less when times are tough (less staff, promotions, raises and development time). Compare the obvious, constant pushing at BearingPoint with the evident lack of it at the high achieving Commonwealth of Pennsylvania in our earlier case examples. Operationally, BearingPoint's push for top line revenue meant quality standards suffered; they too got sacrificed in the face of the temptations of large, high revenue deals—ones with famous customers we could brag about. The work aggressive disorder proved fatal, as Chapter 3 described, as firm leadership and the middle line partners refused to focus on and address the depth of the internal problems that eventually proved overwhelming. The work energies in the system did not congeal to address them; the work aggressive character, it surely seems, in the end was in the way.

As people are pushed to do more and more, hours at work can become unrelenting, and employee burnout becomes prominent. Sometimes the hours are a result of senseless rework because internal structures and processes are not sufficiently developed or integrated to begin with. Again, often it seems the emphasis is on revenue generation and cash accumulation for its own sake, so investment may not readily go to needed internal process development. Some firms with this character recognize some of the issues when they start to lose employees in "the war on talent" (combat again). But these are often only dealt with symptomatically by building work environments for example that offer a constant stream of goodies (lunches, ping pong, rec centers—"impressive" features all). But as internal pressures mount for more and more performance and the concentration of effort does not get to the root of problems, the work environments at large remain dysfunctional. Some essentially become white-collar sweatshops. A recent podcast series from a former Microsoft and Facebook executive describes how relentless and deplorable work life can become for the "hives" of professionals at such contemporary work-aggressive behemoths.[28]

When the organization is on a winning streak and things are going well, each of the cross-cutting structural segments in the work aggressive type present as impressive in behavior and form. The top will appear focused, reality based, and balanced, if sometimes brusque in mood and action. They will have well-developed mechanisms to define priorities and goals, especially around sales, profits, productivity and cost controls. Executives will be well prepared in their reports to the board or in appearances before the media. The thrust of messaging will always be on performance of one sort or another, as reflected in the numbers. Planning capabilities for expansion and competitive strategy will be prominent. Operating style at the top—and throughout the organization—will generally come off as crisp, not fuzzy. While some executive-level work aggressive groups will concentrate their attention and internal investments into activities that are business development oriented, others may put some dollars into developing operating processes with sharp quality standards. This is both their rationality at work, but sometimes also an interest in being recognized an industry star for quality (an emotional draw to things of image again). This, for example, was a strong appeal to competitive US organizations in the '90s of the Malcolm Baldrige Awards—prestigious, highly quantitative, and a way to stand out in the field. Not at all bad necessarily, but it illustrates the extent of the character dynamic at work.

The push to be noticed, to draw attention to itself, is part of the work aggressive type's constant pull—*its constant push and pull*—to bring energy inside of itself. But the way it does so seems limited in actuality as its energies do not freely move "*all the way* in then out." This limitation, I believe, reflects the work aggressive's characterological distortion of the natural, rhythmic work cycles of expansion and contraction. *Energy neither concentrates fully in nor is it discharged fully. I think that is why there is a constant more-and-more quality to the type in its appetites and behaviors.*

As a whole, the work aggressive organization tends to function quite hierarchically. Power is apportioned from top to bottom to execute tasks; some in the organization will especially talk of the need for "seamless" execution. This is not just for task-related discharge, but to also project the character attitude of strength and toughness ("we have no problems here"). Mid-managers will look up the chain of command for direction but will in turn emulate the top in their direction of the operating core; this will show up in behaviors with their staffs. Sometimes managers in the middle will be puffed up with an inflated sense of importance. They are putting out their chests. Ambition among those in the middle for upward mobility is notable. The main of its members will hedge taking certain risks to avoid exposure and vulnerability of failing, but they will calculate certain of their moves to impress the top and get recognized as high potential players. The quality of the product and inner satisfaction realized is not as fully the focus. In general, the middle line will consist of distinct structures and roles, including a complex of specialized staff and technologies aimed at systemwide *coverage* (organization armor, I believe, when it functions like this).

Finally, in high functioning work aggressive types, the operating core will commonly be well-organized, and its members will be well-trained to produce goods and services and get them out the door rapidly and efficiently. Classic industrial organizations will be highly standardized and assembly-line-like in feel and fact, and software and other services enterprises will likely be attracted to innovations in work process and organization structures. Some big industrial organizations indeed were the first to turn to new kinds of organizing models to be more responsive—a worthy goal yet one also in keeping with the character.

At each of the major cross-cutting segments, a consultant should be on the lookout for overly hardened structures and work processes and character attitudes, if he is called in when difficulties arise for the firm. This too is indicative of organizational armoring.

These segment features will start to be distorted and sometimes look just the opposite of their well-functioning form when the system runs into trouble in its markets, economic or other destabilizing conditions. The top it seems will start to become increasingly imperious, then scrambled and immobilized; the middle line will not be puffed up but now look depressed and feel disempowered; and the operating core will start to feel victimized, ever more "screwed." This will show up in behavior and what each in the segments say. These are classic symptoms Oshry discusses in his general description of power dysfunctions in organizational life. In general, when life at the work aggressive organization gets bad, performance will have nose-dived and more or less broken down. The organization will now be less formidable in its pronouncements and actions, though at first at least still showing its characteristic signs of "covering things up" by making a show of strength. But it will still act and look less powerful. This is at odds with its character ideal (functionally equivalent to an individual's ego-ideal), which the organization will find disturbing. There may well be accompanying fear that they will crumble further, and customers, employees and shareholders may start to leave, sometimes in numbers.

It is only under such conditions that the top of the system will seek some kind of outside help. Even then, the type of help sought will often reflect the underlying work aggressive character. Two examples of this are sought for silver bullet technologies and the help of highly prestigious consulting firms to stop the immediate damage and get them back on their feet with striking, new ways of operating. These too may be maneuvers designed to impress boards, investors and the media—and make those in the system feel better and that they are "on top of things." Based on the character dynamics, a penetrating look at root problems and the emotional life of the organization will likely not be in the cards.

Genesis

The work aggressive character appears to arise from significant, only partially resolved challenges occurring during the work-aggressive stage of socioemotional development. The organization, in its primary early development moves through the early vision, dependency, and fusion stages but then stalls once it hits the work stage. Urgencies to get product out—either by founders, investors, or cash needs and competitive market conditions—may leave those in the organization anxious to get the work performed. They do so, but with push, and a kind of fixated anxiety—always hurrying and pushing. There will likely be frustration felt by some leadership and other team members that more time and preparation would have been valuable before getting going quite so fast. If the challenges are strong, this will be a more highly imprinted frustration, and the character dynamics will become more pronounced if they are not grown out of over time. The character itself will tend to militate against that. My speculation is that organizations with strong inherent, primary work drives may be able to push through this and experience movement to work democratic modes functioning at later occasions or life-cycle moments.

As it is, the work aggressive firm gets hung up at the work-aggressive stage, and never quite reaches the work-democratic stage. That would account for why the human dimension never moves past being instrumental in the "pure" aggressive type. Those that remain somewhat less stuck work-aggressively may be the ones that look favorably on devices such as "*balanced* scorecards." The work aggressive measurement and numeric fixation is there but more balanced in looking beyond financial metrics. In any case, the competitive landscape, aggravated by the explosion of data in the information age, will create an environment where stasis results, and armoring will mostly invariably result. This is why the push of the work aggressive will be harsh as it presents under new competitive threats, real or somewhat imagined. The built-up work energy will crash through the armor as it is discharged—the push of the original stage—leading to unsatisfied functioning in the performance of the work. The constant stress on performance in this sense is a ritualized acting out of trying to get the work energy fully discharged. This, however, I believe can only happen if there are qualitative shifts in socioemotional functioning. Few work aggressive organizations it seems will likely be up for this.

If there is leftover blocking at earlier pre-work stages of socioemotional development, subtypes of the character may result, exemplified as I suggested earlier in Deal and Kennedy's "work-hard, play-hard" culture and Kets de Vries Miller's "paranoid" type. In the first in-stance, some fusion stage frustration may linger; this would logically lead to both exaggerated work-hard, play-hard features. The organi-zation is bearing up in larger-than-life ways of working hard yet also finding ways to play together in activities of idealized "groupness" and amped up affections characteristic of the fusion state. These preoccupations get mixed in with the primary frustration at the work-aggressive stage. The paranoid style's constant suspicion and misperceiving dimensions would suggest residual inhibition mixed in from the vision stage, based on the development schema I have proposed. Both of these dynamics seem logically inferential to me but would need to be further researched and empirically confirmed to be understood more clearly.

Based on what we understand about individual psychosexual de-velopment, an organization reaching the work-aggressive stage of socioemotional development in general implies the type's fear of regressing to fusion modes of functioning. This is reflected in the bearing up of the organization, and its no-nonsense focus on num-bers. "None of this mushy people stuff," as it were, when the aggres-sive character expression is particularly exaggerated. The fear of this regression also seems reflected in the fear of crumbling and collapse when the organization is stressed—and thus it remains vigilant and on guard against at all times. These too are speculations at present, but I think they are tendencies practical to consider as consulting interventions with the type proceed.

Sociotherapy

The work aggressive type is an unlikely candidate for the kind of full-er sociotherapy this book proposes. They are reluctant to ask for help to begin with because it places them in a vulnerable state which is antithetical to the character. For some of this type, it will be anathe-ma. Regardless, help to them will always be received to a greater or lesser degree with antipathy, sometimes masked with showy forms of appreciation (a reaction formation again). This will be important for the consultant to probe and work through appropriately when help of any type is offered—superficial or help of deeper effect.

This conversation can start with questions by the consultant during exploratory first meetings about reservations and past experiences the client (or prospect) may have had in getting help. A bit of probing will likely reveal some dissatisfaction. That is important to let come out. A follow-up question to ask may be what reservations they have about working now with you. These should be asked as open-ended, not closed-ended questions to draw them out. The consultant should watch the reaction, including body language closely to see how the questioning is received. This will have diagnostic value. If in reacting, they stay engaged with the line of questioning, that is a positive sign in carrying on and in the client's potential. That engagement with them could lead to them turning things around and challenging you. Regardless, the point is they are engaged. Draw them out further and see what happens. If they show little interest in this line, it might be best to move on or proceed superficially in any next steps until there is a fuller picture of what is at play. In any case, it is generally wise not to overcommit time and attention. Going slow with this group level character type is not all bad, as long as you are not pokey. This lets them know you will be working a little differently than their typical brusquer ways, and you will be modeling some greater reflection and concentration of energy for them to get in the swim with.

When work aggressive clients or prospects present with difficulties, it will almost be cast in quantitative terms. Even if qualitative problems are presented, they will quickly be followed by their impact "on the numbers" or performance. The type will have a tendency to suggest or be attracted to "harder" rather than "softer" solutions, so leading with structurally oriented interventions—work design, organization structure, productivity or cost containment related measures, for example—may make most sense in meeting them where they are at. I think emotional issues will likely sooner or later surface, if they allow them to and the consultant is able to skillfully help draw them out when natural openings occur.

A strategy I have found useful in establishing the relationship with the type is to tell them that looking at problems head on is tough. They will see that as direct and hard hitting if you don't overdo it and say it respectfully. The client may well know this is the truth, especially those few that may be candidates for a deeper consultative process. This strategy, in effect, turns the tables on them. Implicitly, it sends the message that those who look at problems flat on are the realists, and those who wave them away (characteristic of the work aggressive type) are actually the "fuzzy dreamers." This is one more reason too to lead with harder-edged, structural interventions at first, so they don't peg you as soft. The effort here is to begin to crack open their presenting "no-nonsense" defense. This is an opening gambit of the consultant's in this battle of wits—which the consultation predictably will be with the type. You are playing chess. Hopefully, over time, they will come to see that it is strength to confront internal problems seriously, but this may take time because the character impulse is to throw that off and cover up any show of weakness.

Fortitude on the part of the consultant—*not* overreach, this type's own characteristic manner—can pay off. It helped me in the consulting case described below. *The primary therapeutic issue the character type will have is being able to attack their problems more deeply. The problem is not their aggression per se. Rather, it is that they do not sufficiently concentrate and direct their energies at their toughest internal difficulties or deploy it in behalf of fully gratifying achievement. Inwardly, its members characteristically settle for less which, again, is why they want more and more. The consultant will need to help them punch through to the depths of the problems they face, including tolerating the anxiety of not having instant answers or always needing to be seen as all-knowing or powerful. Once these task, attitudinal and emotional issues are faced and worked through, appropriate systemic solutions should be easier to jointly fashion with them, solutions that should help them stand safely and securely in their field. Their substitute "never enough" need to dominate should logically diminish.*

An issue with the type, as we've touched on, is that they may bear up against going deeper once their surface issues are resolved and presenting performance concerns are shored up. They will feel "normal" again and may well wish to stop the consulting effort. The consultant should not take this as his or her own failure. It is always the client system's choice about how far to go in the consultative process and *how far it can stand to go*. In this case, the consultant can just acknowledge the client's wish to stop or wind things down. If additional surface help is desired, characterological understanding can help the consultant support them in more modest change. However, it will generally be a mistake for the consultant to call such an alternative path "modest." They won't characterologically like that. Using harder language like "scale-down" or "more sharply define" should find more receptive ears with the type. Yet pursuing a more modest path should be better for both this kind of client and consultant than pursuing something that presents as bolder. The client can then proceed in the immediate effort with less overreach, and the consultant will better understand what may be possible for them to handle and that which may be harder; this should help the consultant better partner and guide. The consultant can act with less overreach too and be less likely to groundlessly stir them up and aggravate their situation. This more modest path may actually have a bigger, softening impact on the type's underlying character than something grander. The case below suggests this effect.

Work aggressive types whose leaders and people have the opportunity to experience more work democratic modes of functioning in the process may wish later to go down a fuller path. They may come to see this is the most secure path for them for the future, that with the least possibility of backsliding or to have to deal with the underlying fear of crumbling. Objectively their footing should be more secure, and they should be less likely to actually regress. They may come to see that "more and more" is not simply the answer. Those at the helm and those who work in their corporate variations may in the end realize, for all the income and accumulated wealth in the world, money, in effect, can't buy you love.

A Work Aggressive Organization Case Example[29]

Readers who go back to the beginning of Chapter 1 may remember the consulting case of the investment brokerage firm to which I was brought in to help reignite a stalled change initiative. Without discussing the organization character type by name in that chapter—a work aggressive character—much of the case was presented with how I made the diagnosis and framed the working approach with the CEO and internal working team. Now, I want to go back and consider the case in light of the explicit character terms discussed in this section of this chapter, including expanding on some of the case's other relevant details, my further work there as it unfolded, and the upshot of the effort.

I was called into the mid-cap company by the CEO, who had known me earlier from his prior executive role in the parent organization to which I had also consulted. The investment brokerage firm, originally founded by a very sales-driven entrepreneur, now the President reporting to the CEO, had recently broken away from the parent. The company was now standing on its own, including being listed in its own right on a public stock exchange. The CEO called me after another name consulting firm's efforts to help them clean up significant operating problems had stalled. The internal operations issues were causing performance numbers to start to fall, worrying the CEO and others in the company. This had prompted the work with the original consulting firm, though their help was sought somewhat begrudgingly. Now on its own, the company's penchant was to stand alone and not seek help. To some extent this was the CEO's view and certainly that of the President's.

The company had grown rapidly across the US. But the expansion had soon outstripped its internal capacity to accept and process placed transactions as securely as needed. This resulted in falling margins and rising write-offs, as some deals that would been sold to third-party institutional investors to service did not meet quality standards to be picked up. Thus, the backlog of deals in the brokerage firm's own portfolio started to pile up, with risky transactions to boot. The company's overexpansion first came to light when a suddenly contracting economy exposed its weaknesses, now in the public eye as never before. The CEO recognized the coming troubles more readily than the President.

The original consulting firm, in conjunction with an internal cross-functional team of mid-level working managers, studied the situation, then issued a report of findings recommending significant back office reengineering and new, enterprisewide information technologies. What was proposed was very ambitious. The consultancy also recommended they be retained to help with implementation. The idea to embark on the reengineering and technology implementation effort was accepted. It sounded bold and attractive. However, the CEO told the consulting firm no thanks with regard to their continuing help, "We'll handle things ourselves from here." Again, that was much the President's stance as well, who had resisted even the initial consultation.

After the consulting firm left, months passed and nothing happened. The cross-functional employee team now charged with implementation, floundered without guidance and with the sketchy plan the consultancy had left. The internal team I could see was well intentioned, led by a VP of Operations who was steady with good technical instincts and skills but poorly empowered in her daily operating and decision-making role. She scrambled in her day-to-day role trying to react to all the backlog landing on her desk, and she was also depressed, looking in vain for effective direction and support from above. She seemed to me resigned to the situation. The floundering of the mid-management cross-functional team reflected this too.

When the CEO finally called me to come in and take a look, I asked him why he hadn't called back the original consultancy. He said he wanted a fresh approach. I knew he had some trust in me from our past dealings, but he didn't say more, either about that or the other consulting firm. Additionally, the President who I had also worked with in the past, had run hot and cold in our earlier interactions. He could get excited at first about what we discussed, then shut the door when we got down to the tougher matters the discussions led to.

After the CEO first called, I met with him, touched base with the President, then had individual conversations with the VP, the team members, and met with the employee team together to get their take and see their collective expression about what was happening. I also spoke with the prior consultants (I knew one of its principals) to get their sense of what had occurred. The CEO was more sober in his view about the situation and in his business approach than the President; he feared the company's operating problems, including its comparatively weak internal structures and systems, could further deteriorate and seriously hurt performance and the enterprise. With time passing and no effective action, he could see the situation was now starting to get away from them. He and the employees, the President too, were growing increasingly frustrated, each for their own reasons. I sensed the CEO felt he was losing power and a sense of control. Regardless, even with the concerns he expressed, there was much pride in him about the firm, even a boastfulness about their accomplishments; the President expressed that of course, the employees too. But after brushing off the original consulting firm, I imagined the CEO felt quite alone and burdened. I reckoned it was not easy for him to call me for help, let alone call back the original consultancy and admit a kind of defeat.

I rather immediately saw the overreach the firm was caught up in. The change project was faltering because it was scoped too ambitiously and expansively to begin with, mirroring the very operating problems it sought to resolve in the first place. *In the way the project was originally scoped, the company had bitten off more than it could chew, reflecting its general pattern of operating.* This was reflected also immediately in the CEO's thinking the firm could go it alone in the project. The company had grown too fast and was now slipping, but all it had in hand to deal with it were the ambitious intentions of the project. And for all of the project's ambition, as initially conceived, it remained shallow. The consultancy was all too eager to only attend to formal structure; it went nowhere near the core dynamics of the system where emotions ran high but were dammed up. The differences between the CEO and President in business values and in the power and emotional conflicts they implied were unmentionable except in private sidebars—and in later, less guarded moments, eye-rolling. In ignoring this, the original consultancy had colluded with the company, intentionally or not.

The CEO told me he wanted to continue to stay focused on processes, systems and structures. At first, he left out his conflicts with the President. Dealing with it would have required more forceful assertion of his authority. The President too did all he could to keep quiet about that and his actual opposition to the project from the start. Their trying to skip over all this by only focusing on structure ("business only") was also overreach. It didn't work very effectively. The organization character issues leaked out far and wide.

I knew I needed to respect the resistances, understand their overall function and how they played out, but also handle things differently from what had thus far been characteristic. Without this, I understood there would be no real headway for them, or for me in helping.

As described, all these features that showed up are that of the work aggressive organization character: the overreach; the concern with performance and numbers; the emphasis on expansion and sales at the expense of sufficiently robust internal processes; the difficulty of admitting or confronting internal problems, especially those that are emotionally tough—skirting them with structural solutions and a "show" of being all about business. Add to this, leadership's sense of losing control of events and not being their master; the difficulty too in asking for help even when the facts warranted it.

Therapeutically, in arriving at a consulting strategy, I knew I needed to effectively slow the group in its overreach and get them focused on something harder hitting—that is, to get to what really was real. This would mean tightening up the scope of the reengineering and delaying the new technology. My interviews with employees and their own feedback to management confirmed that all the overreach of the project proved to be all-too-much to try at once. Being less expansive on the project right now would help the organization immediately get better focused operationally. At the same time, it would give me footing to begin to address some of their deeper issues at play.

As an aside, I want to distinguish that what presented in this case was distinct from the operations network division profiled earlier in this chapter as the work dramatic character type. That division presented as flighty and in retreat from the world. The chief presenting characteristic of the investment brokerage firm here was its overreach. Strategically, both organizations needed to be slowed down and better focused in the intervention approach but in behalf of dissolving different emotional, defensive functions each pursued. The consultant can only ascertain this by observing closely what is actually occurring in how the organization characteristically *moves.* Consulting tactics, different in kind and suitable to the needs of the case, will follow from there.

I told the CEO when I came back to him after the interviews and employee discussions, that the scoping-down, tightening up strategy was my sense of how to proceed on the project. He told me this sounded practical. They could go bigger later as they built the foundation for it, I said. I was direct, not wishy washy in my expression, as I knew that was what he and others in the organization would respect and was also the truth. The President went along with this, and a line was now drawn that made it harder for him to step over. If he did, he'd be more exposed than he wished, so the President was effectively held in check. The VP and team were buoyed to hear the new approach and, after being authorized to go the new way, went to work refocusing the effort with new enthusiasm and charge.

At the same time, this opened the door for me to begin describing the larger overreach I saw. I didn't call it "their character." I just described my impression of how the project had faltered because it went too big too fast, asking more of them than what they could get to. This was the problem of the scramble in operations to begin with, I said. They recognized the common sense of this. I didn't push them to do more; rather I prodded them to bite off less. The CEO was relieved to hear my take. And the President was not unhappy with the scaling down of the effort or its reasoning. I was working on getting them all on the same page operationally and *socioemotionally* through the vehicle of the project they had in vain earlier tried to make work.

I suggested to the CEO that he and I meet together with the President to discuss the more general proposition of operations' strategic value in complementing sales. I thought it important to get them talking with each other on this *without linking it too tightly on the project* at first. I thought this framing could keep things from going too deep emotionally too fast and not frighten them, but we at least could start to address it. The CEO said he would schedule the meeting with the President. Even at that, the CEO never did. I called him back a couple weeks later and asked him about the status of the meeting. At first he put me off with excuses of scheduling conflicts. I let it go a bit. I was reading this as his resistance; pushing him here wouldn't be wise, I thought. I knew I'd see him again, the President too, when I was out to work with the employee team as they launched their refocused efforts. I felt that some of the emotional issues' time would come. It did.

I scheduled a time to connect with the CEO when I was out there again. I didn't need to say much to him. Privately in his office, he brought up to me the issue with the President. Leaning back in his chair and turning his eyes to look up at the ceiling, he took a deep breath and sighed, "I just don't know what to do with him." Then with exasperation, rolling his head back and forth, he said, "He's just so over the top." At the same time he said, "He holds the key on some deals and staff. It's very hard for me to tell him no." His frustration at the bind he felt himself in was palpable. I sensed the CEO feared the President might quit on him or that he'd lose in an ugly fight. And that he would look "bad" to the original parent company, with which the CEO still had significant business dealings and relationships. But he was now admitting his doubts and fears underneath the bravado. There was little evidence the President would actually quit; in fact, quite the opposite, as the company had been the President's baby and he was still pushing on as was his way.

I stayed silent. I let the CEO sit with his anxiety, despair and mounting anger. I did not push him to try and skip over this. As I sat with him and remained quiet, I let him *feel* it. I suspected letting the feelings stir inside him, and his sharing them with me, would build his concentration to deal more firmly with the President. His fears in confronting the President had struck me as his own resistance from hitting hard, from marshaling his own aggression in facing up to the realities at hand. Now it was up to him to see this. He went on with me, "I don't want to get into an argument." When the moment felt right, I looked straight at him and matter-of-factly said, "Why argue with him? Why not just tell him?" He sat up, paid attention and, I saw, took this in. This again brought up some anxiety, and I just let the silence be for a few more moments. We had made some initial progress on the deeper problems at hand. This helped with emotional acceptance of what was at play and the CEO's readiness to deal with them.

Over the next few weeks, the CEO spontaneously began to assert his authority more seriously. He found the resolve to hire a new Chief Operating Officer to offset the President's power, the resolve as well to tell the President about the what and why of this in advance before doing anything else. The CEO was forceful but did not lose his cool, and the President did not turn tail and run. The President's impulses remained but they were now subdued, and he found his own way to begin to get on board. The President found a consultant he liked and could run with to help with "rapid-route-to-quality" training. Yes, it was the President's own independent way, but it played well with the general theme of the larger project.

Meanwhile, the new COO search was announced, and the VP of Operations, already feeling greater backing, began to make her and the team's own tracks in cleaning up and streamlining back-office operations. Their scramble and depression diminished. All of the actors were now moving more or less in concert in the effort, with positive effect outside the project too. *Ironically, it took them to cut back the overreach and face things as they actually were to forge ahead.* Their energies were better focused and deployed. The company remained, as I continued to work with them, essentially work aggressive in character, but their functioning in operations became more solid. Problems did not vanish between the CEO and President, but there was less energy behind them, and the two were at least no longer on completely different pages.

In thinking retrospectively about this as a case and its implications more generally for consulting, some concluding thoughts. In hindsight, the CEO's decision to have the original consultants only address the back-office structural problems, while a necessary ingredient for improvement, served as an evasion of an even more core issue of the company, which lay in the limiting aspects of its character, including how it manifested in his and others' leadership. In this sense, it is not surprising that the original change effort faltered. Its function at some level was to avoid the issues, not resolve them. Had the original consulting team grasped the character of the presenting resistances, they might have proceeded differently, though this certainly would have been no guarantee of success. As it was, they pushed an ambitious plan that overpowered the company's capacity to carry it out.

Clearly, it is not productive to blame the company or its CEO for not dealing with the more basic problems from the outset. Unfortunately, such blame has been the resort of many organizational thinkers and consultants over the years about clients who will not deal with important issues. Some, for example, have disparaged clients with "lethargy, convention, myopia, and elitism" for not following their advice or cooperating with their methods.[30] I heard this or its equivalent many times from colleagues in my consulting years, and sometimes I found myself going there and had to catch myself before going too far. But firms after all can only do what they can do at any point in time. *The reality of course is that organizations do not immediately deal with their core issues.* Consultants may wish them to, and they may build models and prescriptive approaches that assume this is how they will, or *should*, behave.

However, the fact remains that characterological issues are too deep and difficult to be dealt with completely at the start. Deeper issues more fully surface over time, and they very often do if the consultant is patient and able to see them as they latently present. By understanding resistances as they are characteristically expressed, a relatively orderly and methodical way for them to surface results. Consultants who follow such a path will soon find themselves confronted with two major requirements—one essentially technical, the other visceral.

Technically, the consultant must now be prepared to understand the character of resistances that present. This is not necessarily subtle. For the case here, the initial project's presenting lack of follow through reflected something obvious: Difficulties executing the plan reflected the fact that the company had bitten off more than it could chew. This in turn reflected the company's root emotional pattern of overreach whose function was to ward off dealing with its actual problems. This could be seen at almost every turn. The trouble was that reality broke through. The company's actual problems—both in its surface operations, and in the mainsprings of its emotional dynamics—would not go away. Once this was discerned, the consultation was able to address the client's immediate concerns and also get to some necessary deeper ground.

Emotionally, the consultant must have the will and stomach to stay the course. It may be easier to avoid what is an uncertain, difficult path, even if that is needed to address the problems the client wants or claims to want addressed. But then this is just the issue: discovering how much the client truly wants to achieve its aims. This commitment cannot usually be ascertained in advance. It must be discovered. Patience and resolve become especially important for the consultant, not the least of which because these are now needed from the client. The danger is less that the consultant will get ahead of the client, as is the risk when the consultant pushes or prescribes an agenda. Rather, the consultant must now contend with his or her own anxiety and that of their clients, who may expect results to happen more quickly than is practical. The work aggressive character, looking for rapid results and speed in all, epitomizes this. The consultant is at risk of acting on the countertransference from the type.

When this anxiety comes up for consultants, they must remind themselves the organization is basically moving as fast as it can and that, as a rule, meaningful change cannot be rushed. From time to time, they may need to tell their clients to slow down and affirm it's okay for them to have more realistic expectations of themselves—to scale things down, as was done here. This may not be easy, given the magical expectations sometimes invested in the role of the consultant. But, in the end, the consultant must master his own resistance to the consulting task.

CHAPTER 7

A Typology of Organization Character Forms (II)

O ur typology continues in this chapter with the remaining neu-rotic, armored organization character types. Unlike the first three types portrayed in Chapter 6, *the forms described here show regression in their functioning to blocks that have occurred prior to the work stage of socioemotional development. They reflect pre-work stage major inhibitions*, as first described in Chapter 4.

The three remaining types here are what I have termed the fusion blocked, the chronic dependent and the aggressive vision blocked organization characters. Each follows the manner of presentation as before: An introduction to the type, characteristics and symptoms, socioemotional genesis, sociotherapy and organization consulting case study. Major consulting intervention principles and some main techniques are likewise described. All the general considerations dis-cussed at the opening of Chapter 6 are also applicable here.

The Fusion Blocked Organization Character[1]

The fusion blocked organization character operates essentially as a machine. It grinds on in its well-worn ways, quite impervious to change, even when it is embraced. Highly structured, there is an obsessive, ruminating quality to its patterns of planning, thought and action. An outside observer gets a distinct sense the organization is running in place. When particularly stressed, as we will discuss, a premium is put on holding still and *control per se*, not movement and action. "Efficiency is their forte, not innovation," as Mintzberg has said of organizations operating like this, "machine bureaucracies," as he terms them.[2]

This classic type first emerged in the industrial era. It became pervasive in post-World II America for decades. Market environments were stable, and customer demand was strong. American car companies, for example, could churn out car after car with little competition yet from Europe and Japan, still recovering from the war. Their and other like companies' troubles began as markets became more turbulent and as watershed changes in information technology arose, demanding new organizational forms, products and services. Deal and Kennedy in their cultural schema refer to this type of organization as "a process culture."[3] Big banks, insurance firms, aerospace companies, and manufacturing conglomerates have historically typified them, although as we shall see in the case study, even smaller, social service agencies can exemplify them. Again, efficiency in internal process—*how* work is performed—is of prevalent concern, not market push. They more or less take their markets for granted. Frequently, those markets are highly regulated, demanding conformity in product, services and process. Highly dynamic environments prove difficult for the type, and they may seek consulting help to try and *restore* order. Diagnostically, this will contrast from a work aggressive type that may seek to establish solid order for the first time, given its impulsive ways.

Psychodynamically, Kets de Vries and Miller have termed this "the compulsive organization," where "every last detail of operation is planned out in advance and carried out in a routine and preprogrammed manner."[4] Everything about the organization seems methodical, compartmentalized and categorized. Everything is neat or, from the standpoint of the type, *should be neat*.

My portrait of the type here too is that of a chronic compulsive character, rendered in organizational terms similar to Reich's and Baker's description of the type for individuals. Doubt, caution and endless analysis are normative *precisely to hold movement itself at bay*. The *paralysis* in paralysis by analysis is precisely the point. This manifests especially as things go and *feel* bad for its people, individually and collectively. Energy devoted to eliminating variation and surprise leads to the character's love of precision, fine tuning and perfectionist ways. These organizations are very rule based from the board down to the operating core. Problem identification is fine, as long as it follows proscribed procedures, as in highly methodical quality protocols. The great emphasis on rigid, structured manners of operating makes the organization type *quintessentially armored. Spontaneity and its potential for disorderliness—messiness—are anathema and thus preempted or swiftly contained should they arise.*

Conformity is the rule, affect is characteristically flat, emotions not prevalently expressed. When they are, they frequently have a pleasant, cooperative tincture, to cover up the underlying frustration and "institutional blues," on occasion privately and guardedly expressed or grumbled about. Going along and getting along, not displaying great differences, is the canon—even when that might make a big difference in work and free human expression. These are the men, and women, in the grey flannel suits—or whatever the attire is of the day. Hourly workers tend to toe the line, and where there are unions, which used to be commonly the case with the type of meaningful size, elaborate labor-management contracts and arrangements are in place to ward off trouble, including "wildcat" strikes. Strikes are feared by corporate management and the wildcat variety vigorously fought by union officials. Emotion of course remains in the fusion blocked firm, but wide effort is made to keep it under wraps and keep things on an even keel.

One significant variation in the flatness of affect that may surface is something that at first looks quite its opposite: *an effusive expression of love for co-workers, the group or the organization's ideals.*

The affection expressed is characteristically exaggerated, if "sincere." Sometimes I have seen it literally come across as gushing, and I have come to take its characteristic appearance as a diagnostic clue to the type. I have usually found such a gushy display to be narrow and shallow. The group or organization does not seem quite able to go deep enough in the emotional realm to share negative, dark feelings when they arise —candid expression of frustrations, unhappiness or especially aggressive feelings at work about the group. These sentiments are kept at a distance. No-holds-bar excitement also seems to be missing in the expression; the ubiquitous gushy quality seems to deflect the more complete expression of affect.

More than in other character types, in the fusion blocked form, *the spontaneous expression of feelings of wide range is inaccessible or largely out of bounds*; some sentiments stay largely underground until what's expressed at the surface is probed. Even then, the system will tend to react by clamping down. This can result in the system's moralizing about what behaviors are acceptable to express or not, and the system starts to get prescriptive over what emotions are permissible to talk about, let alone show. This seems true in my experience whether the affect is characteristically flat or gushy. Both reflect the inner fusion block I believe the organization is hung up over: the unresolved and frustrated issues of group affection, togetherness and cohesion at the fusion stage of socioemotional development. From this, the name of the character type comes. In the section on this character's genesis, I will touch on how both variations of the character seem to originate and what is different about them in their development.

Characteristics and Symptoms

The chief characteristics of the fusion blocked character are its universal efforts at standardization and control. As an organization type it is preoccupied with internal operations and maintaining homeostasis. It seeks to avoid disturbances of any sort, internally among its multiple divisions and layers and externally in disruptions to its markets. The firms and the many professional associations they typically join (togetherness again), lobby for legislation to either prevent significant change in their environments or to improve conditions for the status quo.

Internally, maintaining work order and brushing off conflict are constants. This is evident, as we shall see, even in certain of its efforts to innovate. When the character is deeply entrenched, there is a single-minded focus with churning out work. Satisfaction comes from having performed work cleanly, little concern with fostering deep feelings of accomplishment. Product and methodical process are all. In fact, the mechanical quality of work is the ideal. Its people up and down the chain take precautions to avoid surprises and, at the bottom of it all, trouble. They are *moved* to take such precautions. *Their precaution is compelled.* Underneath that of course is worry—anxiety. There is great concern that things will fall apart, again, in Didion's phrase, "a center that will not hold." Feelings are always lurking in the background in the fusion blocked character, so sentiment is highly contained and mild in manner, or else noticeably exaggerated in the gushing variant. But the vigilance against the strong expression of feelings is wide. The vigilance is *automatic.*

The implication for consultants who seek to help such organizations is this: They must remember that the spontaneous, driving work energy that seeks fulfillment—objectively and humanly—is not absent in the system, nor is it ever truly far. That energy is ever-present, the natural root of all organizational life, as I've maintained since Chapter 1. What twists it here into its "all-and-only-work" sensibility, its staying busy, is the character of the organization. Largely speaking, the fusion blocked character I find is a defense against working more naturally.

Now, as I have argued, even chronically blocked organizations usually have some dimension of health in them because of the inherent nature of work animating them at their source. Most organizations are in reality admixtures of health and dysfunction. When the fusion blocked organization is relatively well functioning, its focus on work moderately reflects the natural drive for work. Regardless, whether well-functioning or troubled, the fusion blocked character that has arisen gets a hold of that drive and conditions it. This is what always gives the type's focus on work a mechanical quality. In the more severe instances, work will tend to be experienced as toil, servile in feel. *This reactive work quality is a major distinguishing feature of the fusion blocked type. Carrying out work as it is fully discharged in gratifying achievement has come to take a back seat to carrying on work for work's sake.* The natural ends and means of work are disordered in the fusion blocked character; they have become reversed. The organization's ends, in effect, become all about means—*process. The fruits of labor—work that is fulfilling and fulfilled—are not to be enjoyed.* Nor are they even the goal of work anymore.

All this creates tremendous internal tension inside the system, which builds and builds. As it peaks, this will sometimes symptomatically create exhaustion, members of the organization will present as fatigued, at moments expressing it. The bound-up work energy is only partially released in the reactive work it has as its major sanctioned outlet. The result is *massive stasis—the fusion blocked organization's deeply propelled quest for homeostasis and its formal structural mass.* The organization's fixation on group harmony and balance also shuts down expression of the frustration naturally arising from this state. Thus, mounting levels of human discontent turn inward and churn, further needing to be clamped down. The organization is trapped in a vicious circle. This is reflected normatively in its attitudes about work and ritualistic acting out to fend off spontaneous movement. Monotony and busyness become the order of the day. It is also reflected in the rigidity of the organization's formal structures.

Mintzberg's description of the machine bureaucracy's basic organization structure is quite complete. "A clear configuration of the design parameters has held up consistently in the research," he says.

> Highly specialized, routine operating tasks, very formalized procedures in the operating core, a proliferation of rules, regulations,

and formalized communication throughout the organization, large-sized units at the operating level, reliance on the functional basis for grouping tasks, relatively centralized power for decision making, and an elaborate administrative structure with a sharp distinction between line and staff.[5]

The major cross-cutting structural segments serve characterological functions in this type. Classically in the type, the operating core consists of narrowly defined jobs, vertically and horizontally, with highly defined workflows and little discretion in performing work. There is little room for individualism at work, the good of the whole is all. Intellectually, this goes all the way back to Frederick Taylor's manner of organizing work. While amended over many years, including contemporary approaches to work with appeals to "enterprise thinking" and "building community," *individual* emotional expression is commonly subordinated. Conformity in these contexts, too, seems to be the order of the day in the fusion blocked character.

The highly elaborated middle line is dominated by four groups:

- IT staff to automate and coordinate tasks and reduce the human element whenever possible;
- abundant planning staff to forecast work inflow and more completely regulate its energies;
- mid-managers to coordinate the output of the technocratic IT and planning specialists with the work of operating personnel; and
- administrative support staff to enforce policy and pump out programs and procedures to assure uniformity in operations.

Administratively, HR for example is often very concerned with standardizing and maintaining standards in job classification, comp and benefit packages, performance management and disciplinary counseling. When there are HR concerns about accommodating the human element in softer ways it will nearly always be about *standardizing behavior*; hence, the attraction to *mass forms* of training, coaching, outplacement, and *management* of change programs. This is not just an issue of scale. It is about *massifying* scale for purposes of guarding against spontaneous movement.

The strategic apex, or head of the organization, will be focused on fine-tuning performance and keeping the whole organization running in light of anticipated changes and strategic challenges. As Mintzberg puts it: "Just keeping the structure together in the face of its conflicts also consumes a good deal of energy of top management."[6] Strategic planning, less than strategic thinking, will occupy the way top management approaches the future, a distinction Mintzberg also has made.[7] This reflects the *analytic preoccupation* of the character. Where the top here has a whole-systems view it will tend to be mechanistic, as is the attraction for some to "*total* quality management" or the attraction to socio-technical design methods in how they've become engineering feats. Again, this is not to say that these methods in and of themselves are problematic. The problems lie in what the fusion blocked character makes of them. An engineering mindset at the top is evident, and many of these firms are in fact engineering in nature. The top, not readily seeing the forest for the trees, will tend to lose perspective in times of difficulties, and they will try to engineer their way out of them. I saw this extensively at work in a division at Motorola. Sometimes this mindset works favorably, sometimes not.

Lockheed Martin (LM) devised keen ways to see that innovation for crucial engineering projects were not snuffed out by the system. Cordoning off what became known as "skunk works" from the rest of the corporate bureaucracy, this has become a tradition within the company as well as other firms that have followed suit. At LM, these skunkworks have been high innovation teams whose missions are to imagine and cook up out-of-the-box designs for top-secret products, projects under exclusive customer contracts to satisfy exceptional demands (in LM's case, military customers' needs for radical, new kinds of fighter jets). *Each project begins as a small, specially tasked, highly autonomous team dedicated to breakthrough designs and speed to market; they have license to operate in "protected space," outside the strictures of the existing company bureaucracy.*

Historically, the first skunkworks were housed in separate buildings from headquarters or main plants, with whereabouts largely unknown. The teams are free to do their own thing within tight and often urgent constraints. Free give-and-take, highly talented individual contributors, strong collaboration, and strenuously expressed individual views are normal within these exceptional units. The projects themselves remain secret to protect them from intrusion—keeping at bay the characteristic doubt and "that will never work" mentality common in the fusion blocked firm. The aim is to create conditions so their players can think freely and go wherever they need to fulfill the mission swiftly—and, by the conventional standards of the firm, aggressively. Skunkworks it seems operate as bounded, mini-work democracies, jazz ensembles on a mission. They reflect the healthy energies operating in the system, both work aggressive enough and collaborative enough to get their innovation work performed.

Interestingly, for all their creativity and invention, these teams still reflect fusion blocked characteristics of the larger organization, but they are turned for positive effect: The teams are *highly defined* bubbles inside the firm, and *they avoid having to face conflicts in the system* that would otherwise inhibit their project from literally taking flight. Moreover, the approach reflects how much innovation in the first place in the fusion blocked character is fundamentally geared to *the way work is organized and performed. Once again attention is paid to internal process. But now the health in the system drives this interest in internal process differently: to get the typical impediments out of the way so that effective work and teamwork can spontaneously emerge, now in light of ends that are crystal clear.* Necessary conflict and surprise, both substantively and emotionally, comes out in the heat of design and as it works itself out in each group. Affect is not flattened out into pleasantry for the sake of maintaining group harmony. *The group is born to function synergistically with more fully gratifying achievement as the aim. The character of the corporate organization is turned on its head to tap into the natural work democratic energies inherent in the system.* It may well be in LM's case, the organization represents a mixed kind of character structure, with fusion blocking predominant among its other conditioned and natural strivings.

Engineering enterprises as whole systems can be very creative on much fuller scales than mini, counter-cultural project bubbles such as skunkworks are. Their engineering nature does not necessarily doom them to the risk-averse ways of the fusion blocked character. The Manhattan Project, more of a bounded network as noted in Chapter 3, essentially functioned as an enterprisewide skunkworks. NASA, constituted in 1961 from a variety of military and civilian agencies with a dedicated mission to land a man on the moon by the end of the decade, is legend for its original large-scale creativity and collaboration. This remains historical fact for the agency even if it slid in its post-glory years into operating more like a fusion blocked organization.

Large fusion blocked firms have also been among the first to embrace certain innovations in organization structure designs. Such firms were early adopters of matrix organization design to address increasing marketplace complexity, modifying straight-line-reporting hierarchies to become organizations with dual or triple reporting relationships (sometimes even more). These no doubt have some emotional appeal within the firm to try something new when deemed necessary, and I think a firm's push to do them reflects concurrent work aggressive strivings. But they also reflect the continuity of the fusion blocked character: Movement to a matrix design represents a mechanical, homeostatic adjustment to maintain the operations of the firm. They are fixated internally on integration and *mechanically* creating better cohesion. But they commonly yield up conflicts that prove difficult for the type: The ambiguity and conflicts of multiple reporting relationships create plenty of opportunity for conflict and dropped balls—anything but efficient. This was experienced at Exxon, whose business units sometimes thrashed about in their new, matrixed structures. These continue to be the appeal and problems of matrix designs as *massified efforts to create flexibility and cohesion*. In a certain sense, this is *the* chronic predicament of the fusion blocked firm.

Exxon too, was an earlier adopter of other organizational innovations. Awash in money in the late '60s and '70s, the oil giant was among the first major firms to experiment with OD.[8] T-group and team building programs, some of considerable size and scope, were established. The T-group program in particular surfaced and sought to address some difficult interpersonal dynamics in the firm, many never dealt with openly before. It was thought these programs would better help people open up and trust each other to better communicate, and thus be more candid on difficult-to-face business issues needing resolution. It was hoped the T-groups could help dissipate fear in the system.[9]

Exxon's T-group efforts at human change, however, in the end proved difficult and limited in reach. The method became "encapsulated" and failed to diffuse widely in the system. My sense was this happened given the larger characteristic fusion blocking that permeated the system. The company's interests in T-groups in the first place reflected the felt need to better deal with buried conflict and affective expression within the organization, symptoms quite aggravated in the fusion blocked type.

Exxon's push to deal with such problems through the T-group may have also reflected some aggressive strivings as well as impulses that were more work democratic. The program, planted in a large, mainstream hierarchy, was bold, adventurous, experimental and creative. And for systems such as Exxon's, dealing with the "fuzzy" side of organizational life must have been a welcome relief to the daily burdens of task, mechanistic process and unrelenting formal structures. Yet for all the program's innovation and human dimension, it seemed to reflect the firm's ongoing, predominant fusion block. Among participants, gushiness about the program and group idealization effects flooded the initiative. More widely, controversy and conflict over the program were stirred up in the organization; news about it circulated widely at the time throughout the system, much of it unsympathetic. In any case, the program, while technically well designed and offering value, turned out becoming an insular thing unto itself. It did not have the large-scale systemic effects its proponents sought from the start.

While fusion blocked organizations as a rule may favor interventions that are structural and mechanical in nature, it is not uncommon for some of them to want to address behavioral dimensions. Again, they tend to approach such efforts programmatically and with scale. Boeing and Ford were two companies where companywide community building conferences were used to bring people in the organization together to embrace product innovations. This bringing-people-together quality I believe is their draw—needed, yes, to perform the work, but reflective once again of the firm's character emotionally. It is a clue for practitioners looking for ways to support such companies. *The fusion blocked character is always one way or another trying to work out its issues of group togetherness—fusion.* It is not incidental I think that community building interventions when applied to organizations are typically quite structured to preempt much conflict arising among those convened; this can give the events a Pollyannaish tint that some fusion blocked organizations will find a draw. Socio-tech's tidy focus today on eliminating variance in work processes, together with its superficial checklists of collaborative behaviors, may also prove especially attractive to the type. That said, there may be firmer, healthier ground to build on in such instances: *work democratic strivings and the inner push to make them more fully come alive.* Consultants can tap into these strivings, if they structure socio-tech interventions in line with Trist's original conception or if they fashion future search conferences that emphasize building robust communities that face their conflicts squarely. Consultants can make a difference when they remain alert to whether the interventions they shape either reinforce blocked, characterological functions or serve more healthy drives still at work in the system.

Well-focused interventions can be valuable "ports of entry" in consulting to systems broadly of the fusion blocked type, ones still open to address their more basic challenges. I found this to be the case at Hewlett Packard discussed in Chapter 3. That business division, as it presented, was strongly fusion blocked: Its people's obsession with cultural self-analysis locked them up from moving more quickly in their product development cycle—and from *sheer movement* itself. *Yet they remained open for more fundamental, open help as they felt their own fatigue in going down the paralysis by analysis path. They felt relief and began to move when the character of what they were doing in the moment was confronted, giving them the chance to feel just how stuck they were.* In contrast, if they had been provided consulting that took them further down the analytical bunny hole, they would have continued to act out the very culture they sought to change. A shared emotional shift and broader understanding would likely have not emerged nor gathered steam.

Without some handle on the organization character dynamics as they operate, such consulting interventions left on their own can be self-sealing traps or arouse energies that will only stir them up, then go nowhere. The government agency described in Chapter 1 that was awash in dialogue, but steered away from its felt conflicts, epitomized these effects and never got off the dime. This agency seemed to have fusion blocked features, at least coloring its other characteristics and strivings. But, unlike the Hewlett Packard instance where help was accepted to face *felt* challenges, the agency remained trapped in an intellectualized approach; its inhibitions kept the upper hand.

Genesis

Significant frustrations at the primary fusion stage of socioemotional development appear to give rise to the character type in its pure form. Like all organizations that have developed to the point where they are able to function, the fusion blocked type by definition had originally moved on to the work-aggressive stage. But my conjecture is that encountering trouble there, much of their work energies get pulled back to try and resolve its strong, earlier fusion stage inhibition, with its own fears of collapse. There will be variable degrees of this in different organizations that reflect these overall fusion blocked characteristics. Nonetheless, the type at large is stuck in opposing forces between its work aggressive strivings and its deeply restraining fusion block that militates against their expression. With aggressive strivings always threatening to break out, the system is preemptively clamped down in tight internal structures. This seems to trigger two complementary surface reactions common in the type: *a sharp and narrow focus on task and a pleasant façade of niceness.*

Organization members complain little or kick about their condition ("I can't complain..."), but the impulse to do so is strong. It is covered up in its demands for conformity and group unity. This in turn expresses both unresolved needs for togetherness and rebellious individualism to break away from the group; the whole picture is one of avoidance of aggressive strivings. Once aggression is aroused it seems to kick the organization back into its fusion inhibitions, from which it is perpetually striving to escape. The motion of the forces back and forth are equal and opposite, hence the frozenness and running in place quality of the enterprise. Its energy is stuck. It must squeeze its work out through mechanical actions, efficient task demands, the suppression of emotional differences and, at bottom, the emotions themselves. Emotional *drive* is something that those in such systems sense they cannot control.

Logically, it is reasonable to assume the organization's inherent nature as it is moving through its primary developmental period will color the way inhibitions are received. If the emerging organization is an engineering firm or a bank—those whose very roots require mitigating risk—there will be a natural proclivity to push for caution and avoid risk. All things being equal, this would make the organizations especially sensitive as they reach the fusion stage.

This stage is the turning point for the organization to face and work through differences and conflicts as they erupt, intrinsic risks to group cohesion. The engineering organization's natural drive to design, to build, to fix—mechanical functions—may also make it harder to accept the softer feelings and affections of the fusion stage. Thus, in the face of sharp inhibitions encountered there, the system may strive to bypass working through their early conflicts and push its way to the work aggressive stage. This will only snap the organization back to the earlier fusion block, inhibiting it further.

This developmental pattern may reappear, if not appear for the first time, in the organization's later life (life cycle periods). As the organization grows in scale and settles into more routine operations, it can become less driven by novel, sometimes adventurous, entrepreneurial missions and become more conformist, cautious and concerned with holding ground already made. Many traits of the fusion blocked organization character may then start to appear. The history of NASA, another huge engineering enterprise, is suggestive here. In its early years, NASA appears to have functioned quite spontaneously; almost everything about it was invention, and there appeared to be a kind of natural order in the way the enterprise and its missions took shape. However, as its major missions were satisfied and subsequent flight scares and tragedies ensued, the organization grew more heavily bureaucratized and cautious. Internally, there was greater worry and fear. The agency pulled in. Their budgets didn't just shrink due to less demand for space flight, though this was certainly so. Externally, there was literally less excitement in the air. The character of the agency seemed to change, to revert to what looked like a more run-of-the-mill bureaucracy.

Thus, while it seems the nature of an organization won't predestine its character, certain potentialities or susceptibilities appear to exist as a function of its nature as the system encounters inhibitions at various developmental stages. This may be true for every organization character type. The case of a Central European graduate OD program I have come to know quite well (modeled on Pepperdine's MSOD design), almost universally reflects hang-ups in the fusion stage of group development, as I have seen in several of its cohorts over the years. This may be true as well for OD professional associations and OD as a "field" generally. I have almost always found that OD groups are hung up in the gushy idealism of the group as a romanticized object.

This tendency of the field to get hung up in togetherness also appears related to the nature of the work in OD—its emphasis on internal organization process and bringing people together to work as one. Indeed, the field is commonly criticized for being too preoccupied with "soft" internal processes—methods and means—not strategic ends. Understanding the field's susceptibility to operate in this gushy character mode also accounts for its reputation as dreamy-eyed and its easy embrace of fads, fashions and toolkits. Face-to-face conflict and substantive differences are frequently muted when OD people convene; I have witnessed many fear speaking out if it sets them apart. Phrasing of differences are rounded off with qualifiers, turned into questions of doubt, or sometimes simply withdrawn; there are often sudden silences in the air if a brave soul speaks up. There is general concern to be seen "as getting along."

In the Central European University OD program, cohort members rather consistently fall in love with the group, but they seem to just as commonly struggle in expressing individual differences. The cohorts get hung up to a greater or lesser extent when they hit the fusion stage in their collective development. Students have difficulties working through emerging conflicts in their work together. Then, insufficient group time is allotted to conceptually consider the nature of the conflict that emerged for wider (task-related) learning and practical application—for what this will mean for them as facilitative practitioners in group life. The task demands of the program's next scheduled learnings compel them to push on. Rather than milk the experience, the group, pressed by the faculty, drives on to consider other material. As I saw this, I always was struck that deeper learning from the fusion stage never quite got collectively processed for its *aha* moments. Looking at conflict squarely was siphoned off—and this in a program where practitioners need to be prepared to deal with intergroup conflict in their professional work! The learning (the work) of those in the university program in this way got sacrificed. I've seen this characteristic difficulty of facing conflicts endure in the program's post graduate conferences. I've also seen serious differences among the program's faculty go underground (not unusual in universities around the world), communications to others also falling off when there were difficulties to be faced and worked through. Substantively prominent in the curriculum is content such as collaboration, appreciative inquiry, dialogical OD and the attitude that "we are, after all, only dealing with *perspectives* in organizational life." The soft side of the field is emphasized, but methods that affirm and accept the expression of difficult feelings and aggressive strivings in organizational life are downplayed or devalued. And when such sentiments arise among participants in the program cohort itself, I've seen them frequently ducked, rationalized away or awkwardly handled. In this program, I have always found noteworthy *what wasn't obviously or sufficiently addressed, what was avoided.* (This I think is not a bad rule of thumb to keep in mind for diagnostic work generally.)

These traits *ward off* working through the inherent conflicts of the fusion stage and the more work aggressive strivings of the next. The field at large in parallel ways, I think it fair to say, including its most prominent professional association, The OD Network, remains rather like this, rather dreamy and soft. To counter this from within the Network, there have been recent efforts to introduce more academic rigor. These, however, are mechanical adjustments that do not touch the deeper, emotional blocking present. The fusion block creates difficulties for practitioners who seek more robust ways of working. That said, the emotional and task-related work needs of professionals do not go away. They remain, I think, in large degree unsatisfied, and the field gets in its own way of developing practitioners and methods to better help clients in need.

A final question to consider in looking at the genesis of the fusion blocked character is this: What makes for the difference in why a gushy version of the type appears in the first place versus the harder, more mechanical and straight-on affect blocked kind? Speculatively, the answer here may be related to *the severity and completeness of the block* occurring during the fusion stage. *When the block is quite complete, the very feeling and expression of affect may be troubled.* There may be a wish to avoid it altogether and push on (a work aggressive impulse). But the rousing of aggression, as we discussed, will stir the fear of affect, triggering regression to the earlier state and leave the group very inhibited and stuck. However, *when the original fusion frustration is less severe, partial satisfaction may result.* In that case, group members may be able to express (*and over-express*) the positive side of affect relative to each other and the group—that is, they may be able "to gush"—but they will have difficulties working through and integrating the rebellious work of the stage in their group life. I have seen some quit their groups at this point rather than try. Facing those conflicts head on would likely rouse more aggression, in affect and behavior, than they can tolerate. They too are stuck in the fusion inhibition.

This understanding of the completeness of the original block is inferred from a distinction used in Reich's individual clinical modality as Baker has clarified: *the extent to which the blocking of energy at the stage in question is repressed or is only partially so.* Applying this distinction to organizational life goes to how much satisfaction is experienced during a socioemotional stage; that is, how much are the natural work energies of the stage (described in Chapter 4) allowed free and fulfilling expression? The fusion blocked character with partial satisfaction may thus end up in exaggerated but restricted forms of expressed affection—its continual gushing of the energy. This represents an expansion of energy against the group's internalized block. In contrast, the classic variant that is more completely inhibited will manifest in harder and more affectively flat, structured ways—a contraction of energy against the original block.[10]

Sociotherapy

The basic socioemotional dilemma of the character type is its chronic inhibition of affect, its warding off of feelings of falling apart, on the one hand, and its aggressive strivings on the other. The organization thus exerts its energies on control and holding still, suppressing spontaneous movement. This points the way to the main sociotherapeutic strategy to handle the type—regardless whether a thoroughgoing restructuring of the character can be worked through. *The general consulting aim will be to help organization members tolerate as much spontaneous movement as they can, experiencing as much genuine work achievement and fulfillment as may be possible in the situation.* System members will let you know when they have had enough. The hope is that the system will at least better function and *some* symptoms remit.

The basic sociotherapeutic strategy will be to get the members to face what comes up for them, in what they *feel*, when the unworked conflicts of the stage which they will express as their presenting problems are most active. This will it seems, by turns, bring up softer yearnings and more aggressive strivings. When these feelings of discontent are permitted expression in the consulting encounter, members will yield to kicking about how they are stuck, wish to get going, to do something, *to move.* I've heard clients of this type, when they get in gear, move from dreamy feelings of group oneness to suddenly wanting to "kick ass" and force something to happen. This is their pent-up spontaneity and work aggression breaking through. Again, it is the emotional reality you are seeking them to see and to tolerate feeling. This should be done with some graduated effect, to not put them in a situation where they shut down completely or else are overpowered and they start to really fall apart or, at the other extreme, emotionally explode. It will be important for the consultant to remember the client system's underlying fears are real but expressed characterologically because of adaptive intolerance of *feeling* them. Slow them down enough to help them do this. This course of consulting action should help ready the organization members to then do something themselves appropriate in action. As they do, you will sometimes need to help the organization get going on a few first steps without going too far, then stop and further process with its members the affect that arises.

Tactically, you will need to choose when you use the word *feel*, when they seem ready to invite that in. With this type especially, it is generally helpful to work initially at more surface levels as they present, aware of the fact that deeper dynamics are present; then when there are signals of the client's readiness to address, move towards them more directly. Readiness will not always be a function of what a client declares. Fundamentally, we are dealing with emotional dynamics, habitual patterns at that, not matters of words. Members in fusion blocked organizations especially suffer highly habitual routines (compulsion), from either the suffocation or the gushiness of feelings. Stated or not, feelings about them are at least always lurking in the background, especially those who seek outside help of any kind. I have found that *problems for the partially satisfied type will present as soft issue complaints about group teaming, morale and trust. Those that are more completely suppressed may present with something as more structurally broken, roles and responsibilities needing to be better defined, for example, or help with designing the organization for better integration.* These are real issues that will need to be addressed, not swept away as "only presenting, but not the real issues" (sometimes an interpretive problem that consultants make). The presenting issues *are* usually real. But the socioemotional dynamics underneath them are the key to effective traction on them; they are also key to the amount of energy both consultant and client are willing to put into them. While working at the surface, the consultant must take care in not getting trapped in helping the client merely spin up new plans, projects, or action lists that never quite come alive. In my experience, this type of client will typically take you there if you let them.

Inwardly, some clients truly want help with the bind they are in. Some may feel it but may only have limited awareness of or not the words for. That's perfectly okay. The extent to which the character is at play will determine how much they can sense and see what the underlying issues may be. As you initially contract the situation, help them best understand where directionally you are going in your joint work. Don't lead them to think you are too unstructured, structured or gushy yourself; matter-of-factness in tone will make a difference. Contracting is important of course in any client situation, but with this type, extremely so. Their like of formal plans and planning—and below that, their deep need to manage the unexpected and avoid spontaneous movement—will make contracting and re-contracting critical. There, too, the consultant should take care to not get lost in formalisms, a risk with this type. I've seen some of these kinds of clients, for example, spend vast hours consumed with reworking project plans (and demanding that you do too), rather than attending to the work itself that's become problematic. The tail wags the dog. You can call them on this. When they start to loosen up about contracting issues over the course of a consulting project, I take that as a sign of progress. They are reflecting a capacity, if even only initially with you, in their ability to accept freer movement.

Regardless of the type's particular stony or gushy coloration, they will convey a sense *that something is broken and must be fixed.* They will ask you, "Can you help?" Using language that does not preclude working with the emotional dynamics is important to help ready them, but it can be a mistake to talk about "exploring emotions." They will almost only talk of behaviors, not feelings. And the use of the word "exploring," while it may sound like you will not push them, may leave them in too suspended a state, a state of uncertainty. Certainty, predictability, clockwork is what this type wants. They have walls and boundaries to defend. Fusion blocked character members may even say, if pushed, that feelings cannot be measured, so therefore they are not useful to deal with. This type *loves* measurement. This is exemplified in the phrase often heard in business, "If you can't measure something, it is not real." Nonetheless, you can bet this client will sense that feelings are there and pressing in on them—they *worry* about them. At some level, this is what they are asking you to help with: *to avoid feelings*. This is their character speaking. None-theless, feelings will find their way into the consulting equation if you let them come up naturally. Watch *the way* the clients express the presenting problem, not just to what they say. In contracting, it is fine to say you will be working with them on root causes in addition to helping them with the immediate issues. Everything will of course be dependent on how the client presents. Clients will be cueing you throughout about language and how direct you can at first be.

It is important for consultants to stay in touch with their own feel-ings moment to moment. This of course is a universal principle in ef-fective consulting with any kind of client. But with this organization type, it will take on special importance. The consultant should be attuned when he starts to go dead himself in listening to the client. This type can talk and analyze things endlessly, so you will naturally start to tune out. This is a signal of the client's own tuning out and, depending on the when and where of it, a signal that the underlying emotions are pressing in on them. The deadness serves the function to contain the emotions and the spontaneity. In this vein, this client may try to drag you into endless questions and analysis—all symp-toms of the type. This will also include listening to you endlessly. Sometimes they will speak the perfect organizational language of the day, if they've read some current books on the topic. They can look like the model client. Don't be fooled. This too is the organi-zation character at work. With endless questions and analysis from its members, listen and respond kindly, but be brief (not curt) about it and firm enough to switch the track and get down to work with them. These are qualities you will be modeling and teaching them. This helps get them out of their characteristic rut and to respond in the moment.

I want to stress that it is not plans and tracks which are the prob-lems in and of themselves. For some organization character types, as we will see with Allied Bank, plans and tracks are essential to help them beef up. The problem is that the fusion blocked type *loves* plans and tracks; this love of them is part of their defensive structure that preempts resolution of their troubles. Thus, sociotherapeutically, it will be constructive if at some right moment you can do the following: get them to see *that* they love plans and tracks and measurement (this love, another form of gushing); then probe what else they worry about, sense or fear will happen without them. Their learning to better tolerate feeling and seeing what is difficult is essential. If you've created a safe and trusting environment for them to be with you, this approach will give them some relief. Their expression of it with you represents energetic discharge, hence some relaxation for them should happen in its wake. You are loosening up *their character structure.* The sociotherapeutic principle is to do this with ever greater intensity throughout the consultation in all your interventions, whatever their surface content, and of course as the situation calls. If the fusion blocked client wants to talk about or process what's happened with you right afterwards, use simple language. Don't go into elaborate conceptual explanations. That likely is their character defense creeping back in and trying to pull you in.

My presumption with this type is often conservative about how far it will go and how fast I can work. In this sense, Tom Peters' old prescription of "thriving on chaos" to reanimate sluggish bureaucracies I always found *precisely the thing not to do.* Such systems may only best be able to get cleaned up. Shaking them up too much too fast will aggravate their condition. Again, in contracting, using the language at first of helping them to "clean things up" may be effective. This will have the value of not pushing them *too* hard at first (which will scare them) and at least provide the option of "clean-up of matters" as a minimum outcome. (The language of "clean-up" will likely appeal to this character type because it fears the messiness of organization life.) *Their pushing you to do something more than the minimum is a good sign.* It signals some of their buried aggressive impulses and desire for movement. As one variation on the use of the language here, you can tell them you will help them work *to* develop *capability to better spontaneously clean up issues*, beyond the immediate ones. This will likely be paradoxical to them, but possibly intriguing. It may help establish the basis for a longer-term play engaging deeper issues.

Paradoxical use of questions and humor can be important, too, especially with this type. Paradoxical questions will evoke some spontaneity as they are difficult to respond to in a rote, pre-programmed manner. They thus can be effective to use, as character resistances appear. For example, when their caution or doubt in a situation strikes you as exaggerated, you might ask something like, "What do you think would happen if you put your doubts aside?" You are getting them to doubt the doubt. Behind characterological doubt is fear. When they suspend their doubt, you are implicitly getting them to talk about what they fear and to also be more spontaneous in the here and now with you. You are taking them off their knee-jerk track of doubt and helping them get to what is more central in their situation.

As with paradoxical questions, humor can have effect because it has *affect*. For instance, when I sense a client is *almost ready* to see the folly of their endless, superficial planning, I sometimes tell them of a saying attributed to Peter Drucker: "Show me a project plan that was executed as planned, and I'll show you one that was filled out after the project." Or I will ask them if they've heard the Yiddish proverb, "Man plans, and God laughs." I will nudge them with statements that are unexpected and whose content stress the value of letting go and of spontaneity. Of course, such statements should not be made in the midst of serious, dead-on planning. Help them understand the difference. This is seeing the forest for the trees, the ability to make distinctions another characteristic difficulty of theirs. Not only is affect flattened out in the type, but essential distinctions are often flattened out too, homogenized. (Cognitive behavior theorists call this reflexive tendency "generalizing.")

In the fusion blocked firm, the elaborate middle line will be a special area of focus for systemic change, but, depending on the port of entry, one must always try to find work ways to make contact (and contract) with the head early on. Making good, human contact at every level of the system is cardinal with this client. Those are vital interventions here unto themselves. The chronic affect block inhibits good contact, so learning that it's okay to connect with you in a different way helps them develop capability to do this more fully with each other on their own. You are helping make contact-at-work move into their experience. Work across segments at first and create vertical linkages between them in your interventions as you go. The principle is to gradually involve people from up and down the system together to better enable system flow. Factor this into your intervention design as you work with the system over the course of your efforts. This should help create better emotional contact across *and* up-and-down the organization, thus better unitary movement. Large-scale, internal community building interventions may be effective for just these reasons apart from their substantive outputs.

A Fusion Blocked Organization Case Example

The consulting case here differs in kind from those used to illustrate the other organization character types. This case is one where I did clinical supervision of a developing OD practitioner in his internal consulting role to an organization. The organization had strong, fusion blocked organization characteristics. For purposes of the case, I will call the practitioner I worked with Alan.

The case will be instructive for the reader I hope on two major counts: first, because it shows how I came to recognize the character structure of this firm itself; and secondly, because it shows how I guided my supervisee to understand the character and what to consider in his role intervening with it. More broadly, the organization will be of interest here I think because it is an example not of a corporate bureaucracy, neither engineering nor financial in nature (as this character type can often be), but that of a 200-person, social service enterprise, exhibiting all the features of a fusion blocked system. In this way, the case illustrates that the type is not confined to massive sized organizations, and that a character type can aptly describe an organization of any sort and scale. The diagnostic concerns and intervention strategies and tactics will generally be the same, with the particulars of course varying depending on the circumstances and facts of the case. Finally, practitioners may find the case useful because it helped Alan advance his understanding and positioning as a change agent within the system and as a consultant to other organizations prospectively too. As he and I worked together, his own development and capacity deepened as he helped the client. His deepened capacity was one of the aims he told me about when he first called; how we would work to do this in the context of looking at the case as it unfolded is what I told him.

To begin: The organization was a well-established agency in the Midwest. Its mission was to serve as middleman between the state government and other organizations that provide social services to at-risk adolescents and their families. Their own services were to help the state award contracts and funnel monies to public and private welfare agencies to serve the clientele and their local communities. In doing so, they provided project management oversight and technical advisory support to the welfare agencies and the state. It had both concentrated power as an organization unto itself, but its control of all its activities was inherently slippery because it had no direct authority over allocation decisions (that was the state's) or the performance of the work to the teenagers served (that belonged to the public and private agencies). Just so, the organization had to operate within strong statutory law and internal policy directives, and the work performed was subject to media attention. In all this, we see the inherent constraints and risks natural to the organization that it must contend with. These in particular represent fertile ground for a fusion blocked organization character to emerge. The nature of the organization's work and end-constituency, social services support to adolescents and their families, makes it ripe for tension to arise between its softer, humanitarian and community values and its harder, compliance-related risk, fiscal and project management demands.

When Alan first called me to work with him, he presented with a good sense of these challenges. I had known him from earlier developmental work we did together in a different, mixed group of OD professionals. He was smart and, while still early in his career, adept and well-experienced, having served a good number of years with the organization and having recently completed an advanced OD degree. Our consultation ran eight months.

When we first talked, he described his position, positioning, and the situation of the firm. He was officially in an outward-facing project management role, but he provided a good deal of *ad hoc* facilitation support for internal company meetings and for change initiatives he was active in. The facilitation support he provided usually came from requests to him by executive, divisional and other managers and always from his own interests in helping the organization make more of its potential. Even though he was formally tasked in a bounded-scope project role, he had positioned himself to work across the organization and "between the lines," and he was seen as competent in doing so. He had good access with top management, where there had also been recent changes. He was growing restless, and with his new degree in hand, wanted to do more.

We began our every-third-week sessions. He told me he had gotten wind of a new, potentially interesting job opportunity brewing in the firm. He expected to be approached by a recently promoted top-manager heading up "strategy and transformation"—a manager he had known there earlier, Louisa—to formally apply for, then step into the role reporting to her. The role was still on the drawing board, but as he understood it, it was being defined more narrowly in a way that might actually lessen his ability to work across organization lines than he had. He would meet with her to discuss the opportunity before it went much further he said, but he waited and held back from talking with her. He wasn't quite sure how to approach things in the moment.

He told me If he were to take a new role in the company, he wanted one that would better leverage his capabilities and where he could make a fuller contribution to the enterprise, one that would better help it fulfill its important mission. He saw a need to better sew the organization together to get its important work done. In the various groups he had facilitated, he said, people very usually got bogged down in never-ending considerations about process details, not getting on with the critical tasks at hand. I could see and he told me too that as an organization member himself dedicated to its mission that aggravated him. He also told me he recognized that he sometimes got caught up in acting that way himself. Alan described a paralysis by analysis at work, adding he was "fatigued." He knew others were too in what they often told him privately.

He and I talked to clarify what he wanted most in a job. He was able to quickly describe it as one that could focus on the essence of issues that presented and that cut across the enterprise. He was weary of just working around the edges. He wanted to fashion a dedicated, full-time OD role for himself, one that was formally recognized. As he described it, the formal positioning of a new role was important to him. That made sense to me in that he was tired too of only working in an off-the-cuff way, appreciated by many, but not formally recognized. He wanted to work with explicit sanction and clearer value. But I wondered to myself did that also reflect his own desire for acceptance within the firm, to be "official," because there was something going on inside himself at work he didn't quite accept. Initially, I kept that thought to myself, and stayed with what presented at the surface. He hoped he could shape the new role on the table. He certainly seemed to have the creative chops to do so.

But there was a rub in going for the new job. He had serious reservations about working with Louisa, yet he hadn't really talked with her about their differences. Louisa it turned out wasn't sharing her preliminary thinking about the job with Alan either, presumably because of her sensed but unstated differences between them. Alan told me she had a reputation for micromanaging people and process, and he foresaw working under her would be tough. She always seemed to manage having things done her way, by methods she would insist on. He had seen this in her before when they had engaged and how she had worked with others. To make matters worse, she used the language of "empowering others" and behavioral science, in which she was trained. Her language was the opposite of how she actually behaved.

Alan didn't work like that. In fact, he had earned his reputation at the firm for his flexibility and "organic style," helping groups steer through difficult conversations and end up with good results. He was not formulaic. Achievement quite generally meant a lot to him, but he worked in a way that was freer in flow with high regard for others and more in fact spontaneous. Others at the company considered him a breath of fresh air. From his description, Louisa sometimes regarded him that way too, occasionally seeking out his inputs like other leaders in the organization did. At other times, however, she would cut him off. He was concerned that the new job as she was formally shaping and defining on her own would put him in a box, especially concerning in a role where he would officially report to her. Alan feared he would be too strictly told what to work on and how to work on it, when just the opposite, creativity and a freer hand in a change-related role, were needed. The cross currents left him stuck in approaching Louisa to simply have a conversation about it. He was even concerned that things would go bad if he met with her to discuss the role; she'd perceive it as a challenge he feared and make things worse between them. So, he simply went on hold. There was a kind of temporary paralysis in moving forward. Louisa was moving slowly too.

Alan's expression told me quite plainly he didn't want to work under Louisa. He liked that she could be firm, when others in the company weren't. But he was put off by how single-minded and compliance-oriented she was. I imagined she must have been very frustrated herself and tried to bury that in work—her dictums to "just follow procedures." However, *I was less focused on her "style," than what her actions said she must be inwardly feeling.* As Alan described it, I saw Louisa's attitude was one that would quickly turn to "kicking butt," making others angry and scared. Alan had some of that reaction himself to Louisa. People learned to conform to her ways, but not without ricocheted discontent, and he did not want to put himself in that situation. Taking the job would mean a steady diet of that he thought. He analyzed and worried about the possibilities, torn because he also did not want what might be at core a good opportunity to slip away.

From what I began to understand about the organization character, I read this impulse of Louisa's as bigger than simply a management flaw (though the way she expressed it certainly was). I inferred she did not like the dithering around in the organization, the constant back and forth of so many in considering policy and program options and change—the not getting-on-with-things. The organization was extremely analytical in habit, and people, many with advanced degrees, talked and talked. Alan had flagged this pattern in the firm early on in our sessions and was himself bothered by it. So, I surmised that Louisa feared if she did not make things happen—in effect, force things—the organization's work performance would suffer. Demanding others comply with her ways became her means. This led to a sharp, reactive focus on work, even harsh. But it came at the expense of people not drawing close to each other, with little trust to differ then come together for greater results. In fact, they turned away from each other, they could never quite come together as one.

To pause our narrative for a moment. There are very fusion-inhibition-like characteristics at work between Alan and Louisa: the frequent reservations, frustrations and underlying fears, including that differences would turn into conflict; Louisa's controlling behavior and fixation on task, side-by-side her use of soft language; Alan's worry that the formal role being fashioned would squeeze him into a box (conformity); the loss of natural spontaneity—prospectively in the job and more immediately in not just approaching each other from the start to think together in exploratory conversation. Rationally had they been able to do that, it might have led to fuller, faster design of the job and saved needless time and worry. Were these indeed signs of a larger fusion blocked organizational character at play that was in the way? Were these signs that Alan might need to better understand to work through the immediate situation and get better positioned to help the organization more widely? Might I need to better understand the character at work if I were to help Alan the best I could?

I first got a glimpse of the fusion blocked character of the firm when Alan, very early on, had me read the company's five-year strategic plan. The document used flashy graphics and big, bold fonts to outline an elaborate plan, but I soon got lost trying to follow all its details—its layers and layers of details and subplans. The report was extremely analytical and measurement oriented (including its stated justification that "what you can't measure isn't real"). There was obviously effort put into emphasizing priorities, values and commitments to action, all laid out in a hierarchy of logic. Yet instead of providing defining clarity, these ended up reading like one chockful list after another, where it was hard to grasp the main points and see the overall picture. I found my attention drifting as I read the report and, after a while, just gave up trying. I found it hard to imagine how a public or private agency, government regulator, or individual citizen could follow it much better. However, *how* the report presented was telling, an early clue to the organization's character.

Here was a complex organization *trying to be efficient* in what it said about itself, using checkboxes, grids, and lockstep logic. The organization worked very hard trying to convey that. Pulling all the exhaustive detail and analysis together must have consumed countless hours from many; the planning and the plan represented a massive internal project in itself. But as I read the final report, the company in its details only became more and more opaque. It became harder for me to distinguish one of its activities from another. There was sweeping language about mission, service to communities and the need for collaborative alignment—in its own way, gushing language that seemed intended to inspire. And there was effort to convey the human face of the organization; there was a small picture of all the firm's people standing together in front of the headquarters building, dressed casually, smiling for the shot. Yet for all of this, my experience reading the report was to be bored and to tune out, not drawn in and excited. I wondered if this somehow resembled people's inner experience working there. Finally, the plan also suggested to me that the firm's internal structure was highly articulated, with many senior managers and what seemed like a thick formal hierarchy for a relatively small organization. Large sized headshots of a dozen leaders, each with complex, fancy titles, were featured.

In all, this early read of the strategic plan led me to think here was a fusion blocked organization character. My conversations with Alan confirmed this impression.

The character and normative attitudes of the type kept appearing in Alan's description of the firm: its busyness; how meetings became rituals of process; the penchant for analysis and second guessing; the love of procedure, method and measurement; people's worry about being liked, using all the right words and not to be seen as complainers; the little conflict that was openly addressed and withdrawal from substantive differences, not their working through; the continual pressures to perform and conform; the underground frustrations that had no place to go.

Alan also described the firm's organization structure as I had glimpsed it in the strategic plan: It was complex, designed to fit multiple priorities, offerings, geographies and its many kinds of stakeholders; there were "organizational boxes for almost everything." Extensive apparatus was in place for governance, mid-level management, communications and reporting. Sophisticated information systems existed, and there was complex internal wiring to connect the organization's myriad programs, projects and units. All this formal structure fit an understanding of the company as a fusion blocked type too, cast in modern form. Using the language of empowerment, alignment, collaboration and networks, all the structure represented bureaucracy *par excellence*: organizational armoring to hold the organization together. Indeed, *holding together*, in the double sense of the phrase, seemed the aim.

Alan's natural pull to work more spontaneously was counter-cultural for the firm. Yet his striking success there over the years suggested the way he worked was attractive to many. His structuring and facilitation of meetings stirred a sense of freedom and openness in them that they had otherwise grown used to having to leave at the door. He made it easier for people to say what was on their minds, know where each other stood, and thus better come together—*the unsatisfied fusion drive*. This must have been the same quality Louisa was drawn to in Alan for no little reason because it actually worked. But she also drew away from it. Alan's impulse ran the risk for her of being *too* loose. Indeed, this epitomized the difference between them and where things threatened to break down.

The role in question was one Alan could have easily gotten had he wanted. The affinity between Louisa and him to begin with was their shared frustration that important work in the firm did not get done. They had previously talked with each other about the shortage of outcomes. But there was a world of difference in what they sought to do about it. To get the firm's mission accomplished, Alan saw people's need for more fluid ways of interacting, for *a free-give-and-take where essential matters could be faced*. In contrast, Louisa strove to cut through the distractions of the firm by dictating procedures about how to proceed. She predetermined outcomes and did not want them to more organically grow. Her impulse was to mow down whatever got in the way. This I took as a sign of her own frustrated aggression held in suspension by the fusion block. Louisa was tapping into the frustrated energy spontaneously arising in herself. But she expressed it by micromanaging and superimposing structure to force others to move. That actually often slowed matters down, as it did on the job's design, and always drove further discontent underground. Alan's way was fundamentally sounder—*to loosen up structure, so that the heart of matters could come out and so there would be no need for endless processing and process to avoid it.*

But Alan had trepidation loosening up himself as he thought about talking with Louisa about the job. He balked on approaching her because of her reputation. This was not all irrational of Alan of course. He had good reason to pause. Yet he *ruminated* on it. He had sat on his own aggressive strivings to push and just talk with her. He feared she would shoot his proposition down, be seen as out of line, not a team player, not compliant. Underneath, I sensed he feared forcefully speaking his mind to her. His worry weighed him down. I saw this as his own inhibition, not just Louisa's. *Both their attitudes were characteristic of the firm, features of the fusion inhibition.* She likely worried about approaching him too. This contributed to her not talking to Alan openly about the role from the get-go. Conflicts would have to come out or otherwise be fully borne, and true to the character, they were avoided.

The situation dragged on, unresolved. Alan and I kept coming back to the situation, as it was the heart of the consultation about his professional future and his desire to better use and deepen his abilities.

I let go of my first temptation to push Alan to talk with Louisa and just find out more. His worry was too much in play. I wanted to help him get underneath his worry—to his fears about what would happen and his frustration over being stuck—"do I even talk with her or not?" The time felt ripe to ask him what he felt about being immobilized. I could see as we talked he feared he might get sucked into taking the job, which he didn't want and would in fact hate. I paused to further concentrate the moment. His manner said he hated being stuck. In fact, he said so. As he came to this, *he was able to feel his frustration to more fully bear it. His very getting in touch with what he felt, not just doing something about it, is what enabled him to move on.* Talk with Louisa or not, he could again feel his energies want to move, to spontaneously get to work.

We explored whether there were others at the firm he could talk with about the new kind of role he wanted. He had relationships with other senior executives, who had admired his work in the past and might be sympathetic to his aim. I asked him might they be open to a conversation about helping shape and sanction the role he had in mind? He approached one of those C-suite leaders. But he soon discovered that executive had folded in the face of Louisa's competitive drive. That leader's drive to push back was held in suspension too.

Alan had of course considered leaving the firm. But he knew he would be leaving a lot on the table in terms of relationships he had built over the years; he'd also be leaving the more spontaneous way of working he had created for himself and others, which he valued and realized wasn't all that common in organization life. He didn't want to just jump. Was there another way of building on that, accepting his observations about Louisa at face value, letting go of the hope that their conflict was somehow reconcilable? Inwardly, he still hoped that would change. So, for the time being, he just continued in his current job, yet found a few other internal clients he could help in his more natural way. That satisfaction, ironically, gave him courage finally to face Louisa and talk about the job, once she formally finally composed its description after several months and posted it.

The two of them met. Louisa could see Alan was not chomping at the bit about the job. As they talked, he described the way he was "half-hearted" (his words to her) about the job because of the way it was focused (programmatically on behavioral training); he directly stated his concerns he wouldn't have a free enough hand; and he offered an alternative view of what a role could look like. There was a bit of back and forth on this, but she ended up not offering him the job. Alan saw directly and clearly that their differences would not be mutually resolved. *Instead, he left their conversation inwardly resolved to accept that as fact, including now having to accept his fuller, felt disappointment which he had previously hoped to avoid.*

Feeling that disappointment, in fact, let Alan more fully let go. He started operating more fully building on how he had worked all along. He gave his spontaneous way of working freer reign, more sanction from himself. The need for formal sanction from and fusion with others substantially lessened. The formalisms of work for Alan dissolved in favor of a factual build-up and build-out of his own work democratic impulses. He no longer considered his work too ad hoc; he now saw it as the essence of what he did. The work won out, work that was not one more form of busy work, but where he could help teams carve out their own space to work more freely. He found increasing satisfaction and achievement in that. So did the teams.

After our consultation ended, we talked six months later as follow up. He described his inner resolution of what had been inhibiting and how it led to his fuller way of working. He saw now that he was creating an informal network of teams within the firm that would work in alternate, freer ways in fulfillment of the mission. I told him this was essentially what Lockheed Martin had done with its skunk-works—but that he was actually working in less boxy ways and with greater inter-connection across the teams he helped. Like LM, he was turning the culture on its head. He was in effect, "lighting many fires" throughout the system to help facilitate change, one of the wonderful aphorisms of OD great Herb Shepard.[11]

When we talked, I reinforced he was now more fully tapping into the health inside him and that which was latent in the organization, doing what he could within the constraints of the system's character. Earlier in our months together, I had begun to give him some educational guidance on the notions of a fusion block and organization character, because it was apropos to deepen his capacity as a consulting professional, part of his original aim. His continuing work at the firm would not likely lead to radical change. But it would help some there who found Alan (and who Alan found himself) work in ways where the fusion inhibition lessened and where more natural, gratifying and productive ways of work could grow.

Ironically, Alan told me that Louisa, in the end, did not fill the position. She had grown increasingly frustrated and came to share with him some difficulties she experienced trying to make wider change happen. Alan was able to listen more fully now to her with no other agenda. He was free of the compulsion, both outer and inner, *to have* to work with her. But he could see that if Louisa's frustration bubbled up enough—in the face of enough practical difficulties carrying out her own job—she might yet be open to work with him. But he could now let her be the one to push for that. *He had broken the stalemate between his own fusion needs and his own, more work aggressive strivings; his own push was now deployed in the deeper pleasures he found in his work.* Were he ever to help her in the future, he could make league with her based on his own experience, armed with new OD practice knowledge. He could help her accept that her aggressive strivings were healthy but misdirected and actually bottled up by the fusion block operating within her and the firm at large. That would not be easy or simply done by feeding her models. He would need to help her *work through* and face the conflicts and frustrations as he did in himself. Should favorable circumstances yet prevail, he now had a path to help her better function in a way she felt more fulfilling and saw better results with, without sacrificing all he had gained.

A postscript: Alan's resolution was a good one. It was not a grand one that led to a restructuring of the firm's character. But he went further, along with those he touched, in effecting change than in other fusion blocked firms. In general, I have found fusion blocked organizations to be the most difficult of the types to help change. They literally *stand against free movement and operate under internalized compulsion.* I have found them difficult to work with as a consultant, easy for me to get lost in mechanics, analysis and lose my way; hard to *feel* my way through. They are human systems that have become machines. Thus, with this type, Bob Tannenbaum's original "this path has a heart" general teaching is especially apt. The most important thing consultants can do is to draw back, stay in touch with their own native humanity and help clients see theirs, not deny them, however difficult that may sometimes be, situationally and emotionally.

THE CHRONIC DEPENDENT ORGANIZATION CHARACTER[12]

What I have termed the chronic dependent organization is a system dedicated to its mission towards which it steadily drives, if unhurriedly with little gusto or expressed satisfaction. Its members drive themselves hard to meet the goals of the organization, as they typi-cally feel they cannot depend on leadership above them for direction and support. Indeed, they often feel let down by leadership. This will even be the reaction of top internal leadership who will feel let down by the board of directors above them. The ideals up and down the organization are high, as are sometimes its people's hopes, but disap-pointment and sometimes a hopeless quality are in evidence, while the work is still dutifully and independently carried out.

The chronic dependent type differs substantially from the fusion blocked character in that its felt disappointment is closer to the sur-face in its members' work lives, and although they can be reticent to say much about it, they more frequently do. This may commonly come out as cynicism, with attitudes when support isn't forthcoming of "what did you expect?" and "what's the point in trying to do some-thing different?" Although these systems are very hardworking and frequently achieve significant operational task results, work by and large is *not* experienced as toil, as it is in the fusion blocked organi-zation. Nor is work for them a proud display of prowess, as it is in the work aggressive character.

The whole system in its inspiration, mood and tempo can present as depressed. The type as I have described has some similarities to Kets de Vries and Miller's "depressive style" of organization in its outward manifestations.[13] Nonetheless, the regularity and sustained drive with which this system typically operates sets it apart from the more sluggish, bureaucratic characterization of the form as they stress. My portrait draws substantially from Reich's and Baker's unique elucida-tion of the chronic depressive individual character type—specifically in the way its functionally equivalent etiology and energy dynamics play out in the organization system's realm. While this kind of system may indeed have a certain level of low energy *vibrancy* and a quiet-ness about it, the organizational type as I've seen it hardly as a rule is sluggish. On the contrary, the organization seems to have a good deal of rational and determined fight in it, as the two cases described in this chapter illustrate. This organization type is tenacious and dependable. The organization character as represented here draws its name from the sharp inhibitions encountered with its founders during the dependency stage of socioemotional development—and in its ongoing relationship dynamics with its later leaders.

My first experience working with such a system was with a technical support department of a savings and loan association years ago, which I say more on in the general discussion below.[14] The fuller case study at the end of this section is that of a two-year, enterprisewide consultation I completed much more recently with a multi-municipal district transit authority.

Characteristics and Symptoms

The chronic dependent organization is internally efficient and comparatively stable. While its energy is deployed in its dedicated work, much of it also concentrates internally in order to drive its work to completion. In this way, it *conserves* its energy; it does not excessively display its energy or make a show of things, as does the work aggressive type. There is a low-key quality about the character here. The organization's internal leadership and supervisory ranks are focused on the primacy of task-related demands, rather than seeing to the softer support and nourishment of their members. There is not quite enough available energy for that. Most all in the system thus learn to operate quite independently. At every level, there seems to be a strong work ethic and steadfast concentration on the mission. Sincere faith in and loyalty to the mission makes up for what is not forthcoming from leadership above; the focus on the mission gives members some independence too from their want of personal support from leaders. Members' own high standards and demands on themselves will sometimes lead them to underestimate how effective they have indeed been in their work, especially as they've had to operate relatively alone. *They are characteristically hard on themselves.*

The system runs smoothly as long as its immediate surrounding field is stable and there are no major changes its members must make or innovations to proactively originate. However, when the system is stressed with unexpected changes in its environment, it can begin to flounder as staff looks in vain for more vigorous direction and support from above to help give them the needed boost to meet the new challenges. As this occurs, the organization's steady forward motion will be slowed, and its members will look particularly uninspired. Existing operating work will likely continue to get done, but at the limit will look like the organization is merely hanging on, merely surviving, not thriving. Zest will be missing, and little felt joy at work will be evident. There will be insufficient energy and steam in the system to be very vigorous, let alone original.

Complaints about lack of leadership and needed support to cope with the changes will start to surface. The complaints themselves are symptoms. As tension piles up inside the system with less outlet to meet the new circumstances surrounding its mission, expressed cynicism, demoralization and hopelessness will more fully appear; I have seen these expressions break through in private and sometimes peer-to-peer conversations. *The signature independence exhibited by the system will start to look increasingly dependent, members will look and be increasingly needy.* Yet this too will tend to be prohibited from outright expression, discounted or covered up by the members themselves. The chronic dependent type's members are not accustomed to letting their wants and feelings be known to leaders above them, let alone make their own demands on them. They will tend to meet their collective condition with sharp inner repression, first tying up the energy in the system more completely, then re-doubling their efforts on task. This is how they seem to perpetually drive themselves.

Organization members will often think that they *should make no* demands, that *they have no right* to make such demands, and that they should learn to operate ever-more independently. They will believe the fault is theirs, again. Unfortunately, exposure to modern schooling in ideas of "empowerment" may sometimes aggravate this belief. Members *not* speaking about what they truly need becomes a moralistic matter for them, rather than seeing that speaking up is a vital requirement that will now (or soon) be critically needed to serve the mission. The characteristic suppression here I believe is a defense against natural, spontaneous work and the inherent support needed from above (and then with each other) integral to it. Thus, their work itself gets characterologically compromised. Its members retreat and contract from what is actually needed for the work. Their dutiful functioning on the current tasks thus exaggerates and masks their chronically unmet dependency needs for leadership direction and support. *The dynamics and inwardly felt tearing between dependence and independence becomes the central emotional hurdle of the system, manifested most prominently in the weakened relations and satisfaction between leaders and the rest of the organization. The effects will show up prominently in the middle line, which will become disheartened.*

Specifically, I have found what causes less energy to be available to the middle line is a pronounced block in the COO functions (or its equivalent, including that of a group serving that purpose); the COO function does not openly feed enough information, resources or other felt support to the middle. For any variety of reasons particular to its circumstances, this COO function becomes congested, constricted inwardly and limited in its ability to discharge the full scope of its functions. The middle line roles and structures therefore never quite get enough intake of energy to fully breathe, feel inspired, or indeed *co-inspire in* how they work together. This then affects the mid-line's interactions up, across and down the rest of organization. Middle line functions in the type thus tend to fend for themselves to keep going, which makes for their own conservation of resources and the focus on just getting things done, where they drive the operating core to focus heavily on its tasks. Not being able to rely on the leadership above, members then pull inward to drive themselves and others below to simply do the work. However, the lack of inspiration will mean there is little joy, satisfaction or other human sentiment pumped out and expressed throughout the system. This results in the general picture of ever-dutiful tasks being performed.

At the very top vision segment of the organization, there appears to be little excessive holding or blocking of energy. While effective, the CEO function does not present as particularly powerful in the chronic dependent character. The case discussions reflect this. The CEO function may lack a highly inspired coloration. Yet its dedication too to the work of the mission seems to provide the basis for the very top to perceive the environment clearly; executive decision making proceeds rationally and practically. In the instances of the type I've seen, executive functions have been measured in judgment and open to learning. What is constrained at the top is the ability to hold lofty hopes and more radical aspirations, then work to operationalize them. The organization, conservative in the way its energies move, appear to do better at maintaining, adapting and extending the status quo than innovating. This should prove adequate as long as bolder action is not required. The top may indeed see the radical import of events as they occur, but they will have difficulty translating the new requirements into action. This may lead the organization to seek outside help.

I saw this at work, along with other dynamics of the character, in a consult I did with a technical support department for a savings and loan association, early in my OD career. At the top of the department was Dan, who served as its executive leader, and Sarah, who effectively served as its COO. Dan and Sarah reached out to me to help them move through new corporate demands being thrust on the department, demands that would be disruptive to business as usual. Historically, the unit was quite efficient in processing its large volume of work. It was not flashy at all, in fact it was quite low key, yet steadily drove on. The department had earned a reputation for its real dependability within the wider association.

Sarah and Dan told me that the new changes coming called for fundamental consolidation of certain operating roles in the field and for the department to reconfigure its own way of doing business; this would require the department to quickly plan then establish new formal operating arrangements and technical processes. But the two leaders also saw the coming changes meant the staff would need to be humanly supported in new ways as never before, beyond their mastering the new technical work. The staff, some fifty in all, included existing direct reports as well new members who would now need to transition into the unit from the field. The biggest challenge Sarah and Dan said would be that all this had to be done when the staff was already discouraged and overwhelmed with the volume of work they were handling. As we shall see, despite the unit's people being able to get a lot done, they typically had reflected an air of quiet desperation and "driving on in spite of it all."

As I first spoke with Dan and Sarah they saw the technical and human challenges ahead clearly. But they felt surmounting the challenges, even with the great drive of the department, would be a stretch for each of them and for their people. Dan was already consumed with many technical responsibilities outside the unit. He would need to continue to concentrate there as well as on major aspects of the coming structural changes, including offering more support to those affected in the field. As importantly, Dan saw he'd need to find time and energy to talk with and support Sarah in her efforts.

Sarah was well-regarded technically as a general matter. But she had almost always been aloof in dealing with the staff's human concerns and frustrations over work. Dan recognized he needed to encourage Sarah to better open up communications, to encourage real listening and "real talk." He also recognized he needed to step up his own game that way and to better shield the department from various corporate obstacles. Sarah was quite personable one-on-one, even warm, but *in managing* she focused her available energy on seeing that the unit's large volume of work steadily got out the door. But it was at a price and pace where the staff felt driven and depleted. The staff was already worn out, and now much larger change and new levels of work were coming.

Sarah knew she needed to better manage *humanly*. She recognized she needed help in thinking through the more radical nature of the work redesign. She was able to see that it afforded her the opportunity to bring staff together to *technically* plan the work. But Sarah was feeling overwhelmed too, much like the staff, and was disheartened. She said to me what difference would it make anyway? More work was coming and that was that. And how on earth, she wondered, could she deal with all the frustration, hers and the staff's? They seemed to be locked in their cynicism and hopelessness. That dispirited her further because she wanted to drive on and make headway.

Sarah brightened a bit when I suggested to her that that the technical planning offered all of them more than a technical opportunity: it gave them a basis to join together to open up and work through their frustrations, while also planning their future work to better, continuously satisfy human concerns. If we set up a series of meetings in the right way, I suggested, each could have a chance to express what they were feeling at work, to hear and support each other, and gather strength. I asked her would she be willing to give it a try? Would her team members immediately below? To move in this direction, Sarah saw she needed to significantly step up her own leadership game and truly be supportive of the staff. There was an immediate opportunity to do that, I told her, in how she approached them to discuss such meetings' prospects. We sketched a plan for how she might do that in a first conversation with staff, including hearing their thoughts about it, and my own follow through with a first round of confidential, one-on-one conversations to hear them out and help shape group sessions if they thought them viable. Their consent of course was crucial.

I held the interviews with her half-dozen second lieutenants and a few other key staff. It was evident that Sarah was liked personally, but she was considered rather unapproachable, and her support in "the human stuff" was scant. This situation had festered a long while. Everyone interviewed expressed their dedication to the business, but also some real unhappiness at work—as much as I've ever seen in my career, even all these years later. The members had long held in upset, disappointment and sadness. Some teared, some blamed themselves for failing. Over and over in the interviews, I heard how hopeless just keeping up with the daily workload had become in light of Sarah's and their own exacting work standards. They were devoted to getting what they saw as their important mission done and done well. They didn't want to let others down. In actuality, the performance of the unit was much better than they gave themselves credit for. But those in the group now feared the new circumstances would overwhelm them, making the way they had customarily hunkered down impossible. Most expressed despair.

All the players were relieved to talk with me. The mid-managers had generally felt they were in a box not being able to talk. Indeed, Sarah herself felt constrained; she had previously assumed there would be no appetite above her at corporate for whole new ways of working that would require field unit changes, changes all outside of her scope or even able to influence. When I asked, she acknowledged she had never before really questioned those above her about it. She had felt that was pointless, defeated from the start. She felt there was little else she could do than simply keep driving on in the unit's day-to-day work. Even Dan too felt his hands had been tied corporately. Neither of the two had mustered the energy to push back on leaders above them, even though their own stock was relatively high. Instead of being proactive, they dutifully performed their work. I believe the chronic dependent character preempted a more proactive response from Dan and Sarah. The opening to do things differently only came when the wider savings and loan situation demanded it. The human issues present, and that they feared would only further come, were the biggest hurdles. The kind of emotional resignation that Sarah and Dan exhibited is not all that unusual in corporate life of course. But that, I think, only underscores the powerful, unmet dependency needs operating in so many firms.

Through our private discussions, the staff, like the two leaders did see the new changing corporate situation might offer a break in the old ways. But their cynicism persisted over whether they could get things together enough to make it happen. I heard some ask, "Was there enough trust and support to do that together?" Sarah was will-ing to give it a real go, and the others truly wished for something better too. *This would mean working through some history togeth-er and their feelings about it, not just getting to the task side of the challenge as was their customary way. Too many feelings were right at the surface for that now.* Such a path would not be easy, given their long-suffering ways of working together. In facilitated group ses-sions, they would have to marshal all the push they could to express their frustrations and disappointments with each other and those above them before they could let go; and they would have to do more than simply blame themselves. However, in the end, their ability to actually move through this together would be what made the differ-ence. It freed them up to do the needed work of the change: to plan the reconfiguration, transition staff and function differently. I saw that the pressure and the pent-up emotions inside them needed to be relieved before substantial progress could be made. The *stasis* of their emotional energies had to be handled.

Prior to getting to work together on this change, a significant prob-lem for the leaders and the rest of the staff of course had been their assumption that its existing organization model could not be ques-tioned or creatively challenged. While there was no doubt some po-litical reality to just how far the model could be altered, this assump-tion and their lack of trying to do anything about it were in keeping with the character of the system. The externally driven technical changes afoot destabilized the character, making a new, more human game now possible.

Sarah and I met frequently one-on-one throughout the process. In coaching sessions, we worked through her own frustrations and dis-appointments with those above her and with her staff; this helped her better come to understand how and when she typically withdrew then marched on in spite of it all. Because I could see she was open to it, I pressed firmly in on calling out these reactive traits. I called her attention to when she did this with me, pointing out also how I had observed her do this with team members in staff meetings. As

Sarah's ability to tolerate seeing this dawned, she began stepping into a leadership role that shrank less from dealing with the emotional experience at work and that embraced her more human sympathies to support team members.

Sarah and I began to convene weekly working sessions with this group of staff, where they began to open up and breathe together—*to move together, with the mission of the redesign now as their north star.* To get there, we spent the first number of group sessions after-hours working through their difficult feelings with each other and the problems they saw coming out of it. I helped them first to just keep talking about their feelings at work, rather than problem-solve. The sessions were not easy, but all of them together hung in there and so did I. As we worked together over the several months of the consulting effort, we were able to shift focus more and more from the debilitating emotional issues to the work of the technical redesign. I believe this is what allowed the design task to become a much more full-throated and full-hearted affair than it otherwise would have been. Their emotions had come to the surface in all the private prework to the group sessions, and they were much more ready to speak about them openly with each other. The group's need to turn away from the emotional difficulties at work and shrink inward lessened substantially. Their cynicism and feelings of dejection began to abate. Sarah's continued to do the same. The whole unit saw its work redesign task through with the high quality that had always distinguished its operating work, but that the members now experienced some greater satisfaction in.

Overall, the unit's spirits lifted, its pace quickened, and the results proved strong under the new operating arrangements. Indeed, the drive for work, so characteristic of the department from when we began, was now even more clearly powered. People up and down the unit now operated in a way that was more *empowered.* What made the difference, given the dependency issues at hand, was *they now were—and felt—supported.* The dependency inhibition that had long hung them up had been sufficiently resolved. More than simply "reinforcing behaviors" or having to be "constantly conscious" of new thoughts or ideals, as many other OD interventions would have had it, their continuing work together *structuralized* the way their energies now moved together. The department was more outwardly heralded than ever, and its members seemed more internally relaxed than any time before in their work together as a unit.

Genesis

The chronic dependent organization character has reached the work aggressive stage of socioemotional development, but because of earlier unresolved blocking at the dependency stage seems dragged back into those dynamics, coloring the way its work energies drive in the world.

Founders and other early leaders of an emerging organization who do not provide nourishment and support to team members will effectively force a sense of early separation and independence before their dependency needs are fulfilled. Founders and others anxious to get on with things may not invest enough energy into preparing and developing new members to be ready to perform. Or compelling work tasks may come upon the system too fast for its players to work through the dependency needs.

When the dependency stage is fulfilled, both members and leaders come to be able to trust the presence of others and count on each other for support. *They develop confidence in the support of others at work.* However, with sharp inhibition at the stage, members will tend to be quiet in their reactions, turn their energies inward to compensate for what is missing, then, left on their own, drive themselves on, heads down with dedicated loyalty to the mission. But they will move on with unmet needs still lingering, their longing for support still in force. They will enact this dynamic over and over to try to fulfill the empty feelings inside—and to avoid the disappointment and other feelings that have resulted. Sometimes, these sentiments will be covered up with cynicism, and when their continued striving for felt support declines, they may give up hope it ever will come.

Members of an organization who are *partially* able to fulfill the stage may gain enough satisfaction to be more openly rebellious to authority. But they will still evince signs of the dependency block as the organization grows. Members of such outfits will make a greater show of their independence, sometimes being brash about it, "standing alone, needing no one," as if a character in an Ayn Rand novel. But this attitude will mask expression of their *need to need* and want of others for support, particularly of the softer kind. A chronic anti-authority attitude is different than true standing alone. I believe true independence is rooted in true leadership support and enough early nurturing of members inner vitality. The consultant will need to be observant of the qualities of the independence and the feelings it conveys to tell the difference between that which is compensatory and that which is more genuine. Hardiness and heartiness are indicators of the more fulfilled kind of independence: paying dividends even when the circumstances are tough.

Present day blocking in the system seems to manifest primarily at the COO level, or its equivalent. The inhibition may present in a variety of ways. If it is a group serving the COO function, it may mean its members are tied up in continuing internal conflict and bickering and less able to provide adequate support to those below, most immediately the middle line. With little inspiration and other intake of support coming from above, the middle line will themselves have trouble functioning in concert, and they will often appear dejected and depressed. Middles will have trouble expressing their sentiments about frustrations at work, especially to those in leadership above. They will expect of course others in the operating core to work hard like themselves, but their greatest demands will be upon themselves. At a deep level, I believe they feel abandoned in their roles. We will see this in the transit authority case study below.

I believe essentially with the type, people's dependency needs are frustrated and turned inward against themselves—so much so, that they may first come to blame themselves for the troubles experienced before they blame others. This is the dark side of the type looking and behaving so responsibly. This can muffle a more aggressive expression of energy outwards in the task work, even as the system plows on. The system may in effect be leaning on its work aggressive energies to pull away from the dependency block. This I think accounts for why the system is persistent but does not especially look forceful (like a pure work aggressive type), as the chronic dependent organization's energies remain tied up contending with the unmet needs of the earlier block. The system will bear a lot but will falter when the sheer weight of accumulated frustration or big, new demands makes members' continued swallowing of their own feelings no longer viable.

Sociotherapy

Because the energy of the organization is basically turned inward on itself, the intervention strategy for reversing this will be just its opposite: *to help turn the system's energy outward so felt wants and needs for support are expressed.* The consultant will need to press in on this and work through their expression until the affected groups' energy invested in the dependency hang-ups dissipates—ether through direct fulfillment of the need or through their ability to emotionally face its absence through expression of their feelings of loss, then find an effective alternative and move on.

Blocking at the COO level will need to be addressed. Sometimes simple, good emotional contact with the incumbent may go a long way, as it did with Sarah. She personally remained open to learning and experienced the aloof role that she first felt had to play as foreign to her instincts. Other times deeper ways of relieving the pressure on the COO will be needed. The CEO functions above can certainly help lighten the load by their direct engagement and encouragement of the COO, and so can support from senior administrative support to the COO directly situated below. The consultant can work with both those parties in coaching sessions to help mobilize their support of the COO. When the COO functions are collectively represented by an executive group, the consultant will need to facilitate sessions with the group as a team. This will include separate contact with its members who are most open to help bring their peers along or else render their resistance less consequential.

Regardless of whether the COO situation is that of an individual or a group, the consultant will need to always work on relieving the congestion at that level with this type by facilitating expression of the choked back feelings of the COO, the held back cries for support. In private counsel, the consultant should generally let those occupying the COO function name and express their own unmet wants, frustrations and disappointments as fully as they can muster. This will take repeated attention throughout the consultation, especially as you move up and down the organization, where freeing up the turned back energy and emotion in the other segments will tend to at first reignite the COO block.

I want to underline two consulting intervention principles here to make such attention effective. First, the consultant must approach dealing with clients' wants and feelings in a way that is natural to the work at hand—and that the client sees as natural to the work. *Dealing with clients' feelings, as a rule, should always be tied to their feelings about their work. This is a matter of what is evoked in them in and how they address it in the working situation; the focus is not on their individual psychologies.* The latter is not your domain in this work. Generally, if your work together feels to the client too much like psychotherapy, you will as consultant have missed something.

Secondly, the supportive, open nature of the relationship the consultant establishes from the start with the system will be essential, whether performed one-on-one or in groups. For this character type especially, given the unsatisfied hunger for leadership support, an empathic and encouraging relationship with executives at the top and senior-level middles will be crucial. You will have to help them tolerate opening up and not shut down in their leadership work. This may not be easy and for some not part of their prior experience at work. This may be the first chance some will ever have had to make good contact and trust the presence of another where they felt truly supported as leaders and organization members. The aim is to help those in the chronic dependent system see that grounds for some genuine hope may actually exist.

Lots of consulting attention to the middle line overall will be important with this type. First work with some of its most vital players to open up, express their views, and to discharge their sentiments, helping them individually and together as a group. You will of course need to have established enough trust and safe conditions to do this. This will help get the system to breathe. It will force some expansion and intake of energy in the middle and at the top, then prompt *release of energy too throughout and out of the body of the system*. This will create an inner push on the blocks that you can then address. Getting those from COO related functions to join with middles in sessions as early as is realistic will help them move in a unitary way. It will be particularly helpful if you facilitate such sessions at first. The trick of course is not to join the top and middle too quickly, that is, before enough trust is established there too in working with each other or with you altogether. When group meetings are held, it is common of course for middles to more or less shut down in the presence of leaders who they do not know well. You will need to work with the top especially beforehand to prepare them to come to such meetings in open, supportive ways. All of this provides grist for the mill for your immediate follow-up processing with the tops and middles, individually and together. This is the sociotherapy in action.

Depending on the nature of the support desired, you will need to pay attention to whether structural design or more behavioral interventions are apt. I have often found some kind of design suggestions are helpful to give them at the outset regardless, as these carry less valence at first than does a behavioral focus, much less an emotional one. Formal design work will also have a certain face value to it. Nonetheless, as trust is established in the consulting relationship, I have found members in the chronic dependent system will rather quickly lead you to the emotions they wish to open up about, then to what has kept them bottled up. Help guide the discussion so it stays with the feelings expressed and the members do not seek immediate refuge in heady analysis.

When character resistances appear that interfere with expression of feelings, pointing them out can be helpful. With this type, I often point out the way the actual facts of the situation facing the organization's members contradict their more cynical bearing. I sometimes call this out with them quite emphatically. Because the type is relatively stable and self-sufficient, the people in the system can generally bear a lot, and your directness can register with them positively once you start working together and they come to know what to expect in your work together. They are not especially skittish. You don't have to be as measured, comparatively, as you do with those in a work dramatic type. That is a more fragile system, more easily provoked, and thus subject to more easily shut down. With chronic dependent organizations, describing the way their character attitudes function in the moment can also be effective because their people tend to see quite clearly. It is with mobilizing their assertive (and, yes, aggressive) energies that they will need help, including supportive reminders that it is often the better course to step towards expressing them, not just hold them all inside.

By unmasking the character, you are helping to redirect their strong drive to work—and as they literally turn it on themselves. You will be helping them drive on expressing their unmet wants and sentiments—in this type, their quieted needs for support. In working with them in private counsel, I have found the expressions of these wants will move back and forth from those of today to those that were more deeply frustrated in the past, then back again to the present. It is the sentiment underneath the chronic attitudes that you are getting them to help better tolerate and express. These are layered and require work. Underneath their cynicism frequently lies disappointment, then hopelessness, then sadness. Anxiety, frustration and anger may be interlaced there too. If the issues run that deep, the members will lead you there when they are ready and when you are patient, assuming the ground has been laid.

As you work consistently with the top and middle segments, they will tend on their own to bring the operating core along in the process as a matter of course. I have not found much intervention necessary from me with the operating ranks with this kind of character. Working with a few key staff members along with the middle at selective moments can be useful.

A Chronic Dependent Organization Case Example

Several years ago, I completed a two-year consult with a multi-municipal district transit authority where I rather quickly saw chronic dependent characteristics at play. The system exhibited many of the features and dynamics described above, and the consulting stance and intervention course I took helped move it through a challenging, enterprisewide change initiative: the implementation of a whole new set of workforce-related IT applications, organizational and business process changes that affected its entire 12,000-person population. A radical change in the organization character did not result from the consulting effort. But the initiative succeeded where other comparable efforts in the firm in the past conspicuously failed; those had left a legacy revealing of the character which needed to be overcome. The case provides particular value I think because it allows us to see at close range the constitutional and socioemotional genesis of the chronic dependent character, and because of the way the consulting work proceeded with a group-based COO function and an enterprisewide middle line.

The enterprise built and maintained the physical infrastructure for, and continuously operated, all rail and bus transit services connecting multiple metropolitan centers over a tri-state area. It also continuously operated the vehicles around the clock every day of the year. The fifty-year old enterprise moved nearly a million passengers to and from work each day; its reliability and constant service were thus crucial for the lives of its riders, for commerce, and for the municipal governments and other kinds of interests served. Just as there was physical transit infrastructure to upgrade and extend, its internal organizational information systems and business processes now needed to be modernized. Aging track, train and bus vehicles required serious attention, but so did organizational and systems arrangements to meet demographic changes in the workforce and to harness the capabilities of new information technologies.

I led a handful of dedicated change resources as part of the wider consulting project. That project included heavy program management and many business systems specialists stitched together from many firms. I was invited originally to be part of the effort because organization change management (OCM) was an important company concern. It had had two recent failed efforts to swap out portions of the same technology and unsatisfactorily remedy them after-the-fact. These failures were expensive and widely in view across the organization.

After meeting with the senior sponsoring executives and program leaders to contract my approach, I immediately began what I called a risk and readiness assessment to help the client system see what it was up against in making the initiative a success. I used Lewin's force field analysis framework to do the assessment. My aim was to discover and help bring to light what organizational forces existed that would drive towards successful implementation, and what forces existed that would restrain it. The former largely represented the positive, spontaneous energies and practices that could be supported to make the effort go; the latter represented reflections of the character constraints needing to be surfaced and mitigated. The forces were described in the very practical terms that the people in the system used. My job was to hear people talk about what was at hand, then articulate them as thematic patterns of thought and action in the organization that would have serious effect.

The assessment was jointly undertaken with those in the client system. I engaged the system widely. In addition to interviewing some two-dozen senior middle line managers and others below, this gave me immediate access to interview and work with the entire Executive Steering Group (ESG) made up of top executives from across the firm. Above this executive team was a General Manager (GM), an Assistant GM, and a Tri-State Governing Commission. These very top functions did not exert great day-to-day power, and there was no officially designated COO. The ESG served the COO function for the firm and for the project. Overall project team representation from the client system was designed to mirror the full structure of the firm. This created opportunity for me for systemic reach with all the major cross-cutting structural segments —including, as it became central for the character, the COO-related and upper middle line functions. Over the course of the effort, I worked extensively with each, as they operated within themselves and together, to address their prominent and persistent blocking.

The qualitative readiness assessment interviews, also backed up by a broader, simple quantitative survey, revealed many aspects of the chronic dependent character. Based on these, and corroborated in my many further individual and group interactions with the ESG and middle line, I came to understand the following patterns were at work:

- Great concern existed that the crush of 24/7 year-round operations would outstrip any effort at internal organization modernization. The organization drove itself relentlessly to make sure its mission-critical functions were scrupulously met. These were considered sacrosanct. There was anxiety all around about the big change initiative: Either the effort would be a distraction from vital operations or else it would be the excuse given why the effort had little chance for success, thus creating a self-fulfilling prophecy. The anxiety itself could be immobilizing if it were not adequately and *humanly* dealt with.

- Wide cynicism and expressed despair presented in the organization's ability to execute such an internal initiative, requiring co-operation from the top of the organization and across its siloed functions. Collective hopes invested in important efforts like this in the past had been dashed multiple times. People were jaded.

- People by and large had reacted by losing faith in the top to provide the needed wherewithal for the effort to actually be successful. Even members of the top believed this. Although the initiative was comparatively well-funded and top-level pronouncements of support were very public, the Associate GM, ESG members and upper middle line remained skeptical about just how much needed action they would really be able to drive. They wondered aloud how much support they could really give for anything other than getting the trains and buses out on time. Some at various levels did register some hope that this time might be different, while others were grim about the prospects. The lesson many had learned from the way the organization customarily managed was to keep their heads down and just plow ahead with day-to-day organizational life on their own, noble sounding corporate initiatives be dammed.

- A deep fissure existed between the rail operations executive on the one hand, and the HR and IT executives sponsoring this workforce modernization initiative on the other. Rail, from a revenue and overhead standpoint, was the big dog among all the mission functions. The rail executive was particularly known for marching to his own music irrespective of the interests of others on the executive team. Many on the ESG had confidence issues in IT and HR, but the aggressive ways of the rail leader especially stuck out. There was a lot of swirl and workarounds in the way the executive team functioned to wrestle with this, resulting in stalls in communications and decision-flows down to the middle. Participation on the internal project team from the rail organization silo was numerically less and less consistent than those from other units.

- Very good clarity was evident, top to bottom, about the change situation as a whole and its challenging dynamics, but converting that to needed, collective action was seen as dim.

- Numerous shadow systems and informal working relationships, completely outside formal channels and sanctions, operated to get internal processes to work.

- Great faith remained in the mission of the enterprise among the long-tenured professional and blue collar, unionized workforce.

- Pride in the work accomplishment and safety record of the enterprise was high, and its operating performance record, while not flashy, was steady and strong.

- This time, to address the serious concerns about program execution, the firm doubled down on its project management help from the outset. A strong program management team and system integrator were contracted with and depended upon, with very detailed project management, reporting and monitoring plans (including that of OCM, as originally conceived by the client). The consulting contingent was matched with dedicated company resources. On top of this, a separate outside project manager was hired to keep the organization and the consultancy on course, *to push them, to drive them.*

- Nonetheless, there was significant concern that too narrow a hewing to the project plan would preempt seriously needed engagement of those in the organization to own the effort. There was concern the organization could get *too* driven marching to the plan and not allow enough time for emergent technical, business and human concerns to really be attended to. Relying on only mechanical program change requests to amend the plan were likely to be unwieldly for a project of this scope and the organization's history. The organization would need to be able to respond creatively and quickly in the moment to make a go of the project. *Spontaneity would need to occur and be allowed.* Outsourcing the auxiliary program manager role reflected the tension in this, just as that role's demanding, driving quality reflected the chronic dependent character at work. From the start, I identified as a major risk factor to success the tension between the organization's tendency to relentlessly drive itself on tasks and its simultaneous need for more generous human attention.

It is precisely in this last way, in fact, that I began to expose the organization's character attitudes—making use of my observations and the very data those in the organization provided in their work with me in what they said and how they acted and reacted. This was pure characteranalytic consultation in how I engaged and intervened. This approach provided reliable means to surface the underlying anxieties and sense of hopelessness, and behind that, people's frustrated needs for support. The top and middle's capacity for clarity in what they saw happening in the organization turned out to be an important factor in the initiative's favor. So did their capacity to feel and access their frustrations. I used many of the pre-contracted deliverables—assessments, plans, workshops, group and leadership action planning—as vehicles to help them see and make contact with the central emotional dynamics at hand. The original assessment, once publicly discussed and sanctioned, helped marshal support for the kind of change effort that was actually required. I made use of the vaunted program structure to serve the freer operating needs of the enterprise, needs its people begged for but felt in their hearts they'd have trouble satisfying.

A broad range of design, community building, and many individual and small group sessions were employed in my effort. Wherever I could, I joined many different types of activities and intervention tactics *to bring people together where they could support each other, where they could feel and express their concerns, so they could see that forward action could actually be enhanced, not "derailed," by mutual support.*

I pressed relatively hard on the IT and HR executives to reach out to others in operations and the ESG to broaden the sponsorship and understanding that this was an *enterprise* workforce initiative, affecting everything, not a siloed HR or IT project. They began to forcefully advocate the need for people to hang together and support each other for enterprise success. The HR and IT executives stopped taking it on the chin as they had in the past, internalized from the way they had previously been blamed by others. In the process they made their own departments function more effectively too. I also worked with the Assistant GM, an astute player and observer of the scene, to help focus more of his energy and support for the effort. The more vigorous efforts of these executives helped others on the ESG come around. I worked with the ESG in special leadership workshops and in regular progress report sessions it joined with the many mid-level project managers.

These sessions were not all smooth going, but they proceeded and provided means to collectively work through many task issues and shared frustrations experienced over the course of the effort, issues and frustrations that had also been held over from the past. Interestingly, in the midst of it all, the rail executive who had caused such consternation left the firm; it was understood he increasingly felt closed in on by others on the ESG, and that appeared to factor into his decision to leave.

As I saw it, all these top-level activities in their combined effect *helped clear the COO-block that had choked back collective engagement and hope to make the project be a success.*

With much less contention within the ESG, energies gradually turned outward to support the project. Driving the project forward came to be seen as needed to remain *dedicated to the mission of the enterprise.* Other effects included: the top and middle segments were less hard on themselves, less pitted against each other or from within. It was no longer much the case that isolated individuals had to cooperate in the shadows through subterranean networks. More *public* real talk was evident. Now more unified, the top and middle started to relax the relentless march against project plans, drawing on their other inherent strengths in seeing things through. More than privately engineered workarounds, they began to tap their spontaneous, creative forces more fully together, more publicly and more flexibly. The plans of course remained important, and so did the impulse to drive, but now the top and middle increasingly let the plans serve them and the larger mission of the project and the enterprise.

Once the newer, clearer path forward had gained its footing, I was able to taper back my consulting role. The firm's top and middle, with the dedicated help of others on the consulting team, were able to pull in the great mass of operating core members to complete the project. The new technology deployed successfully without major glitches, and when the few downstream technical difficulties arose, they were well handled. By project-end, a lot of the grimness and cynicism I first saw had passed. Things with respect to this project no longer felt hopeless, and the company now had a significant internal project success under its belt. The company, in the process, realized new technical and human capabilities it could build on in the future.

Diagnostically, I want to note that in understanding the chronic dependent character, as with any character type, *change consultants must do more than simply look at behaviors; they must look at what functions the behaviors serve.* Sometimes different character types will exhibit similar presenting behaviors. For example, this type, like the fusion blocked character, can habitually exhibit skepticism. However, close observation of the moment right after you make an intervention will reveal that the skepticism of the fusion blocked serves the function of control and holding still, of stopping movement *per se.* In comparison, a chronic dependent type will evince its skepticism (and its more extreme form of cynicism) as protecting members from feeling their despair, their hopelessness of ever getting emotional support. The *objective function* of the skepticism will be different. These are quite distinct phenomena. The consultant must be patient enough to see the distinctions, not lump behaviors together categorically. This is the value of operating in an action-research mode and with an understanding of character functions.

Understanding the socioemotional genesis of the types can help the consultant see these distinctions—of what the common presenting behaviors are warding off. Identifying the formal structures that are most obstructing in how the system functions (like the ESG was in this case) will help to further clarify the picture. In the case of the chronic dependent character, an obstructed COO function points to the system's key, historically unfulfilled dependency needs.

In this consulting case, the tri-state governing commission and GM functions relied on the force of the enterprise mission to do much of their top-level work, leaving the COO function essentially in charge. This is where the organization's actual operating power was. This is not surprising given the firm's constitutional make up: Its core function centered around operations and continuous service, and its tri-state origins also meant it likely that a *coalition* of executives would make up the COO function. *Yet with little active mediation from above, the COO coalition was left susceptible to overconcentrate its power—and in silos.* That could work as long as operational activities and projects to be executed were relatively stable and siloed (like getting the trains out on time, or engineering projects laying down new tracks). But it would easily be vulnerable to obstructive functioning once new inter-operating requirements and mutual support were needed, especially where human concerns were at stake. This was exactly what threatened the internal modernization initiative as it began.

The character of the firm's lumbering on, its driving on in the face of chronic internal obstructions, was how it had always sought to deal with its condition. But, as I see it, that characteristic response had historically entrapped the organization at the same time. Its plowing on in spite of the COO obstructions continued to build up tension in the system; this led to a work energy stasis, anchored at the COO level, perpetually fueling the unresolved chronic dependency needs. Proper attention to and remediation of this finally became critical if the current needs of the business and the success of the workforce modernization effort were to be met.

A final word: In dealing with this character type, I had to take special pains to establish myself as trustworthy to organization team members. That people saw me as independent, though a part of the rest of the consulting team, allowed me to carve out a special role to work through the emotional dynamics with them. Establishing that supportive independence took time and was itself not a simple matter. There were a lot of needles to thread to make it work. However, it was important that I be received not simply as one more figure marching to a plan or driving them to march. On the surface and at the start of the effort, that driving role for OCM presented by the system as something of a want. Yet that too surely seems to have been a symptom of the organization's chronic dependency structure. More deeply, they needed someone to talk with and lean on for *human* support—and who people knew I was talking with and hearing from all the rest in that way too, individually and collectively. The role that I developed, I think it fair to say, helped bring the organization together so those needs could be better felt and faced, expressed and resolved.

THE AGGRESSIVE VISION BLOCKED ORGANIZATION CHARACTER[15]

This last of the organization character types presented is what I first described years ago as the aggressive vision blocked character.[16] That is a long name, but it precisely describes the major blocked way its character plays out: *its routine tendencies of blind action and hyper-reactivity*. Its major blocks occur at the work aggressive stage of development and, even more fundamentally, earlier at the first socioemotional stage, the vision stage (as was introduced in Chapter 4 and as we'll discuss in the type's genesis section below).

Kets de Vries and Miller have described two types of organizations— the "paranoid" and "schizoid" organization styles—that are incorporated in the single type rendered here.[17] My sources for the type are two-fold. Intellectually, it derives from Reich's and Baker's still distinctive description of a paranoid schizophrenic individual type, whose features and energy dynamics this kind of organization resembles, both in character attitudes and how they are embodied in the armoring of the system. The chronic attitudes are embodied in the organization's cross-cutting structural segments that are functionally equivalent to those of the human body.[18]

Perhaps more significantly, however, this organization type was derived from the first large-scale case I ever worked as a consultant—the Allied Bank case profiled fully in this chapter. While I was first studying Reich's clinical modality as part of my master's work, I was immersed in the case, an enterprisewide OD effort that provided the experiential and inductive grounds for the formulation of the type—and beyond that, for the general theory and method described in this book.

I chose to call this type, an aggressive vision blocked character, not "paranoid" or "schizoid," because I did not wish to use a name that was simply synonymous with that from the individual, psychiatric domain. Despite functional equivalencies, I wanted here, as in the naming conventions in the rest of the typology, to emphasize distinctions between the organizational and individual realms, and to not mix socioemotional development stages with the psychosexual. *In both realms, we are dealing with the same root bioenergy. But they each function in distinct, as well as common ways, because they represent different kinds of natural energy systems.* Knowledge from Reich's work lets us fundamentally understand the basis for the similarities and unique aspects of each domain, including their intervention possibilities, although a tremendous amount of course remains to be understood and worked out for addressing the dynamics of organizations. My main point here is that we have it in hand to do better than simply spill more ink on the question of "metaphors" in organizational life, as the literature in the field routinely states. In both individual and organizational worlds, we are dealing with the flow of a tangible natural energy, whose chronic blocking has painful human consequences.

Characteristics and Symptoms

Blind belligerence is perhaps the most defining characteristic of this type. This trait may not be immediately obvious, since when things are fine in its environment, the quality is largely masked in its face to the world, its *façade*. But when the system is stressed and under fire, this trait becomes pronounced. This is a principle that can be seen in the way the other character types also start to display their own chief distinguishing features, behind what can be their presenting façades.[19]

"Vision," as is commonly understood in business and OD, is highly distorted in these firms at the top, as in their clear formulation and actual expression of coherent strategic direction. Confusion is prominent; the organization's sudden, unexpected shifting priorities and focus are common. Indeed, that is what the firm's own employees have essentially come to expect from it, so there is a breathlessness among staff always waiting for the other shoe to drop. When there is surprise among employees, it is more often because the firm unexpectedly does *not* operate that way.

More pointedly, lack of clear perception of the internal basis of its difficulties is quite notable at the top. *The organization's "split" is between the felt, inner excitement of its members' combined work drives and their collective perception of them.* When the system's drives are frustrated in the here and now, the source of the difficulties is commonly perceived as *merely* coming from outside, not because of the collective inability to tolerate the force and feelings of inner excitation and sensations at work. The system's problems are characteristically "disowned" at its head. This is functionally equivalent to the nature of the schizophrenic split in the distinctive way Reich and Baker have described in individuals.

Organizations of any character, as we noted earlier, will be compromised in their visioning capabilities because of the drag of early blocks, which will limit what they will be able to fully look at and see. However, *the aggressive vision blocked type is characterologically incapacitated in its visioning functions due, I believe, to the deep, historic mark of its vision stage inhibition.* When combined with its work-aggressive stage block, the strong tendency of its top executive team (the CEO-related functions) to project and rationalize its sentiments onto others—the attitude of *"anyone but us"*—is conspicuous, certainly to those who are targets of the projections, internal or external to the system. Others in the organization, managers and staff, but also those outside—competitors, regulators, and customers—are routinely held to be the culprits. In this kind of organization, although not a simple matter for most corporations, the executive suite's inability to come to grips with its own impulses and performance is wide. Citing directly from my original write up in *The Journal of Orgonomy* of this organization character type:

> *A highly reactive stance* is taken *vis-à-vis* the external and internal environments, a stance from which the organization's confused formal direction and vacillating strategies directly issue. Poorly defined goals, incompletely delineated target markets, inadequate articulation of policy, and poorly integrated organizational arrangements—all inevitably follow. Throughout the system, fantasy and factionalism abound.
>
> As with the firm's top managers, its middle managers and employees are reactive and disown problems that are theirs: Problems are always seen as someone else's fault, some other division's responsibility, the blame of top management or "the culture," and so on. At every level of the system is found fear, suspicion, and persecutory (victim) sentiment. There is a super-sensitive and "touchy" quality to the members—anything external might set off their aggression....
>
> Because the aggressive vision blocked system lacks the capacity to [make good contact with others], to grow and truly develop its internal resources, the organization scatters its attention forever outward in search of new opportunities to ameliorate its condition. This, in turn, creates a perpetual cycle of failed start-ups and aborted expansionary activity, be it at the departmental, divisional, subsidiary or field unit level. In general, the aggressive vision blocked firm has an expansive "field," with ill-defined boundaries, in which its activities occur and managerial decisions are made.[20]

At the level of the basic cross-cutting structural segments, describing what I saw from my consulting experience at the time, I found:

> The upper [CEO-level functions] of the head to be highly compacted and isolated from the rest of the organization. The top, where the armor was most heavily concentrated, rarely made contact with other levels of the system. The administrative staff roles surrounding the uppermost segment rigidly guarded and screened any communications into and out of the function. Armoring in the segment was also evidenced by the highly disproportionate power and decision-making trapped at this level, by the fearful deference to the very top [by the rest] of the organization, and by the presence of other narrowly defined information channels to scan the external and internal environments. . . . *The top was quite disoriented in terms of its strategic direction, as well as unapproachable on issues of its disorientation.*
>
> The lower, COO level of the head segment was also severely blocked and served to insulate the chief strategy-making complex from feedback and the rest of the system. Organization-level improvement strategies suggested to [the COO] level of the system were typically choked off. The visioning apparatus of the system was thus effectively isolated and rendered immobile.[21] In the character type at large, the head is functionally "split" from the body of the organization, which itself is comparatively formless and *lacking* in structure (confusion again); there is a power vacuum in the middle line and the operating core because of the tremendous amount of energy trapped within the head. This lack of structural definition in the body of the organization leads units within the middle line to vie for power with each other but to do so within the overall limits of holding still and seeing how top management reacts next to each of their moves. This serves to keep the system as a whole on hold.[22]

Although there is a fissure between the head and middle line of the organization, it is different in kind than what I described as it exists in the chronic dependent organization character. In the chronic dependent, the very top remains quite focused through its consistent concentration on the mission—it does not vacillate in its strategic direction—and it does not overly hold on to its power. The chronic dependent type's top keeps good contact with others in the system, it does not routinely blame others, and it remains realistic in how it gauges its internal and external environments. In contrast, the aggressive vision blocked organization's very top sucks up power from the middle line and renders it characteristically immobile, keeping the entire system on hold and making it hard for it to simply drive on. In the aggressive vision blocked system, the greatest armoring is anchored in the heavily marred CEO vision segment, and only secondarily at the COO level which serves the function to insulate those above it.

The residual health in the aggressive vision blocked system is that its comparative lack of structure in its body, and the body's isolation from the head, allows for some expression of spontaneous movement; members and units that have kept contact with their inherent natural work drives can find some ways to still creatively move. Even the strategic CEO functions have retained some fragment of this, by virtue of their ability to vacillate and their impulse to react to changing circumstances. The problem of course resides in the way the top *reactively acts-out* this spontaneity and misperceives its damaging "forces" as always coming from outside itself. In contrast, the chronic dependent organization is, if anything, overly responsible and self-blaming; the aggressive vision blocked type attributes its problems to others and is impetuous in action.

Genesis

The blocks that have proven historically damaging to the aggressive vision blocked character are those occurring at the primary vision stage of socioemotional development and again later at the work-aggressive stage. Because of sharp frustrations occurring at each, the system I believe is pulled back to its first developmental blockage in its visioning functioning, and this imbues all its later ways of operating. Given the basic blocking there, the energy of the system is also pulled back through fusion and especially dependency needs, so residual frustrations incurred there will also be reactivated. This secondary blocking at the dependency related structures—the COO related subsegment of the head—I found to be particularly strong.

The choked off functioning of the COO is its own deference to the top leaders; this reflects the COO's own dependency needs in this type and suggests it is grounded in fear. This current-day disability of this lower head function also serves to energetically shield the very top of the system: Contact and interchange between the COO and CEO levels remains inhibited. Consequently, the energy that remains trapped at the very top continues to build and be walled in, with little outlet other than in its distorted, *aggressive visioning discharge*. Its discharge is aggressive because it has been dammed up then pushes through its armor, propelled too by its frustrated work aggressive impulses. The composite picture is one of a system engaged in *blind action*. The old joke here is "Ready, Fire, Aim." *Without being able to look and see clearly, the top is left in a state of being overly imaginative and rushing to action that is not grounded*: Fantasy and imagined threats and slights get activated. Poor decision making and its fallout can easily occur.

How does such a striking visioning inhibition happen in the first place? It seems likely to occur especially because founders, as leaders in the earliest life of the organization, become anxious for mission related task results, and push the organization to "just go there" before it has sufficiently satisfied the natural work of the visioning stage. The work of the stage never gets adequately attended to, so the organization becomes destined to act it out, again and again, in an effort to complete the discharge of its unmet visioning needs. This forceful push from the founders and leaders early on may also be basic in creating the type's work-aggressive stage block—fixating the organization there too because the natural work of that stage—*learning to confront its own limitations*—also was not met. The hasty ways of the organization here will only reinforce and further lock in the dynamics to keep it from truly moving forward with clarity. We will see this in the Allied Bank case.

There is one other dimension to the genesis of the type. This may be a constitutional factor as first discussed in Chapter 4. If the nature of the organization is unclear—or mixed—at its conception and incubation, its original purposes mixed or confused, this would seem to necessarily mark the organization once it hits the fuller visioning stage after it is up and running. The confusion never seems to have gotten through or resolved itself during the "organizing period" just before the organization's birth. We will see this too at Allied. One of its two founders focused on a lofty, dreamy vision of the enterprise, while the other, more nuts and bolts, focused on "getting out there" to operate and "make money." I believe this set the enterprise up from the get-go for a mixed mission. This manifested in the very top's split between what excited it and how it perceived itself, a split emblematic of the character type. Constitutionally, this would seem ripe for exacerbation during the new organization's following socioemotional development period, as it reaches the visioning stage.

Such constitutional considerations during the organization's embryonic life are also suggested by what Reich surmised from the cases he had seen in the onset of schizophrenia for individuals: There were bioenergetic disturbances in the womb before birth or in just days immediately afterwards, before the onset of primary psychosexual development.[23] Applying this to the organizational world implies that some preemptive opportunities may exist for support in the earliest incubating period of a company. Measures to do this would include helping the emerging leaders see the value of not rushing the organization through its early development period to only get-to-market.

Sociotherapy

This is a system the OD consultant must approach and work with carefully. Because of the fear and mistrust in the system, caution is needed to not frighten its members away, which can show up in this type as a sweeping, aggressive brush off. They will hardly engage you to begin with if your help looks too soft, or else when they engage you, it will basically only be on their terms. As a rule, the help they seek will only be instrumental and transactional—not strategic. A relationship you establish may be stable as long as you fit within the mold, but if you step outside of it to challenge business as usual, you may become an object of ridicule or contempt. This is their transference at work. Whatever the merits of the objective situation in the triggers, their reaction to you seems grounded in their rejection of their own inner challenges and the way they discharge their energies in projection.

They are slow to admit problems that require serious collaborative inquiry and partnered resolution. The system will not readily see it needs help or be open to receiving, even if it senses it might. A good deal of groundwork will need to be laid in preparing the organization to work with you. When they do seek help, despite what may be brash talk, the major blocks will need to be worked towards gradually, rarely head on. Work backwards from what presents at the surface to eventually deeper levels of feeling and expression, as the system members can tolerate it. This is especially true with the individuals and groups in *the most constricted segments, the depressed middle, the occluded COO level, and the heavily armored very top.* It is generally not possible, for example, to simply go into the organization by taking the top team off site on strategic retreats to work on its "vision." *The problem of vision won't even be seen*; they are *aggressively* vision blocked in their collective emotional structure. If you succeed early in convincing them to take the time to go there, there will likely be little emotional charge that appears because of the deep blocking. My experience with the several organizations of this type I have worked with has been that such retreats remain superficial exercises—and are largely seen by the executive team as a waste of time. Better to focus with them on the immediate problems as they present them, where there *is* some energy surfacing, facilitate their experience of working on them collectively, then work down more deeply from there. Here, it is good to heed the advice that my teacher and supervisor, Dr. Peter Crist gave me early on in my training: *There is nothing deeper than working with what's right at the surface.* In how you engage and intervene, you must fashion *avenues of approach that themselves will mobilize the organization to look and see as it presents in the moment;* the actual work of the organization will present *real-time* opportunities to set clearer and steadier priorities, and to better harness its imagination. That *is* working on its vision, especially as you start. Again, the Allied case ahead will show how this was done.

As consultant, you will need to gradually earn the trust to work at ever increasing higher levels with increasing depth. You will need to prove your value at first through simple contracting and follow through. But as they see your competence and open the door for you to work with them more fully, you will need to revisit patterned behaviors with them over and over as they surface in different situations during the course of the consultation. Each segment will need repeated attention, especially looping back and mobilizing the CEO and COO functions, because the vision block and its secondary dependency pullback will keep reappearing as the middle line and operating core segments become freer. This is to say, in the aggressive vision blocked system, the organization's characteristic *reactivity and reaction will return*, and not much progress will look like it has been made, even after much work. Some in the organization, and more than a few at the top especially, will question your worth and value all over again.

You will need to find ways to keep punching your ticket and earning your way into continued work with them. This can be done, and they can come to trust you quite deeply. This is not a simple matter of a workshop or two, launching a program here and there, or teaching them models, which will be more or less rejected out of hand. In fact, the organization will logically mistrust you if that is the way you operate. Trust will be earned if they see you consistently at the table, chipping away but working more deeply and creatively as you go, and, above all else, treating them with real respect for their inner sentiments and wishes as they start to disclose them. The ones in the system dedicated to helping the organization get truly better will.

Many of the people in the aggressive vision blocked system remain close to their feelings about work, including those at the top; it is the organizational character that has them discount or go out of contact with them quite radically, *so they don't quite literally know what their work—or work to be done—is.* But to the extent some still have a *feel* for their work and you've established a basis for trust, their spontaneity will start to break through and, as I have found, they will come to be more relaxed in their expressions of their inner thoughts and sentiments with you. Securing trust throughout the engagement will be important as you continue to work with them ever more fully in their real-time work. Their impulse to be in the moment, if they are feeling safe, can serve them well in this regard. This doesn't mean they will no longer strike out at you, sometimes from out of the blue; they will. But my experience with this was to see this lessen, be less charged, and in one prominent case to largely evaporate.

This type does not suffer from being overly armored as a rule, except quite prominently in the head. But, even there, those at the very top do not like rules and convention. In fact, they are inwardly tired of all the weight they carry. That is the basis for their indiscriminate discharge of all the energy trapped there at any disturbing target that passes. So, *it is essential you intervene in ways that gives them a chance to "get this out of their system," but rationally and constructively.* You can process this with them in real time to see the difference—the difference between rational and constructive action on the one hand, and that which on the other hand is not, that which serves other knee-jerk functions not warranted in the moment. *Here, too, you are working with them to see.* When they turn their guns on you, if you can honestly remain light about it, this may prompt them to see how hollow that is and is propelled by something inside them more important that can then be worked with. I have found ways to do this.

You will need to be creative in how you help them see such distinctions and not overly worry about being too prescriptive. Unfortunately, the intuition to sometimes be prescriptive is often *trained out* of OD consultants. The aggressive vision blocked organization is hampered by its confusion, so some prescription will be appreciated by them—and is in fact needed. Endless questioning of them will likely heighten their confusion and make them want to understandably and impatiently turn away. But you can be somewhat prescriptive and still be curious and work with them collaboratively in fashioning the interventions that uniquely fit their wants and needs. More than a few at the head of the organization and down the line will come to respect you for this and resonate with it. They will give you more and more openings to work with them, and, interestingly enough, this is a path they will help them start to take the lead for greater ownership and inner directedness. Yes, it is true they likely will not lay everything out strategically and planfully, as a more academic orientation might wish would happen and teach as the thing to make happen right away. And yes, they may lean on you more prescriptively than certain process consultative or dialogic approaches would suggest. But my experience is they will increasingly invite you in in ways that suit their groups' wants and the organization's emerging needs as a whole. They will increasingly open up and, without even quite realizing it, become more intentional. This happens because their congested energy is relieved, so they can operate more naturally, not because you have "taught" them about "intentionality," "modified behaviors," or let them spin endlessly in their own confusion. They are coming to more freely discharge their own energies naturally and constructively.

Getting them to tolerate their inner sentiments, to feel and look at them with you in your work together is key. This should also start spontaneously to happen in their work with others in the system. You can do this as you intervene structurally with the segments, separately and in ways you facilitate their joining together, natural to the tasks at hand. As progress is made, the organization's sheer reactivity will gradually start to recede. It will be less of a factor in how they present and work with you and each other.

I found, generally, that interventions that focus on structural ways of getting to their pressing business concerns are most helpful. These will need to be highly tailored, not canned methodologies. But this customization plays into employee engagement at all levels, tops, middles and bottoms, because the success of the intervention seems to especially require this in this type. Keep talking with them about what they are trying to accomplish, through your own thoughtful observations and comments. This is clarifying from a visioning standpoint in and of itself. You can do little better in a world of "ready, fire, aim" than help them see outcomes and objectives embedded in what they are doing. This will help them see the value of their not just reacting impulsively, darting from one concern to the next. *You are helping them tolerate being able to focus,* helping them make their implicit outcomes—work-related outcomes that have remained fuzzy and confused—clear and explicit. When they *see* their confusion that is itself a positive sign. By working in this way, you are addressing the chronic visioning problem in an action-oriented and *actual* way: You are *restructuralizing* their capacity to slow down and see things with more perspective.

Sequentially, I have found working with the middle line important as a place to start with this system. First, because you can go a little deeper with them than the top at first. The middles will often present as depressed, looking for help. In contrast, the top, both COO- and CEO-related functions, will likely shut down if you work with them too quickly or too intensely at first. They won't be able to withstand or tolerate it energetically. And early success that you have with the middle will count with the top. Some will see the middle start to "get out there more," and they will thus have less to "blame" for inaction. By starting with the middle, you also won't be seen as so isolated from others, leaving yourself more vulnerable to attack by the top were you to have only begun working with them.

As you mobilize the most central groups in the middle segment, helping them to better work together and co-inspire, more will then start to happen. This work with the middles located centrally in the system can be concurrent with your support of the middles in the field, helping them better coordinate with each other and making their actions less scattered. Such work with the interior and those closer to the perimeter of the organization will give greater definition to what has been more structurally formless. This effectively creates "containers" to better hold, concentrate and discharge their energies, also building some credibility and trust within the system as you go.

This work with the middle line will have two systemic, mobilizing effects: *It will start to draw energy down from the highly occluded top and simultaneously create openings for freer interchange between the top and the middle.* You will need to be observant here, and time the way you encourage and help link the top and middle segments together. Of course, some of this will start to spontaneously happen on its own, without you setting up the play. *The top and middle will start to link together on common concerns because they will see that is natural to the immediate task work that needs doing.*

Fuller openings will also start to naturally appear for you to work directly with the top, establishing relationships and vehicles to connect them on strategic concerns. Just making good human contact with them will be the most important first thing to do. It will be important to be natural and matter of fact here, not overly deferential or fawning (fear again) as many sometimes are in their presence. I myself, early on in working with Allied's COO, took him out to a little, hole-in-the-wall burger joint for lunch, with an ice-cold milk, near the corporate offices, to talk over an upcoming event of his. He loved it and was relaxed. Helping mobilize the COO functions will also have the same effect on the CEO level that your work with the middle line did with the COO: It will draw energy down from the top and help to loosen it up; this in turn will let more air in to work with the very top. When the situation permits, getting the CEO and COO functions to work together on immediate matters of mutual concern will help mobilize them to better collectively see and rationally discharge their executive responsibilities.

Extensive work with each alone and jointly is needed once you are seen as trusted with the top. These are the deeply anchored blocks in the system's functioning that you have now worked your way up to address. Their tendency to withdraw into their own worlds and armor up will be recurrent. Sociotherapeutically, you are moving from the middle, then clearing the blocking in the COO related functions, and finally working your way up to tackle the most entrenched holding in the system—that at the very top. By definition with this type, your work there will need to be persistent.

As all this happens, there will also be simultaneous openings for the middle to work directly with those below in the operating core, who they both direct and serve. Because of the scale this implies, you can assist here too through vehicles that may be a bit more programmatic for wider reach. All this, too, will give needed structure and definition to tasks that have tended before to be more random and hit-and-miss. *You are beginning to help the system concentrate and more fully discharge its energy as a whole.*

As you do this, a key to thinking about intervention activity is how various activities and programs, in their thematic thrusts and common parties' concerns, can be interwoven for composite effect. You are *interlacing* interventions. These are not one-offs or the "cascading" of canned programs. The interlacing should happen, up, down and across the segments in ways that follow the natural work of the system as it unfolds. This literally ties the organization as a whole together, softening up the armor where it has been most compacted *and* firming up structure where it has been insufficient. The inner drives of the system can now better be discharged with less need to pass through the character. As the hold of the character diminishes, it starts to lose its energetic function and more natural work democratic impulses can come to the fore.

The Allied Bank case below demonstrates how many of the principles just discussed work in practice. As we move on to discuss the
case, I especially want to note that my moment-to-moment interventions did not come from "applying" my idea of the character type,
but by concentrating on what worked and self-correcting on the fly
what didn't. I was immersed in trying to help the organization as
best as I could. Retrospectively, seeing how the activities mapped out
gave me a sense of the larger character type at work and the general intervention strategy needed with this kind of organization. My
concurrent study of Reich's individual equivalent character modality
and the specific type as it resonated here gave me a touchstone for
this mapping.

An Aggressive Vision Blocked Organization Case Example[24]

At the time of this case, Allied Commercial Bank was a thirty-year
old, public company based in California. At its height, it had thirty
branch offices in communities throughout the state. The firm catered
to domestic and retail and commercial businesses, with a special capability in the import-export industry. Its headcount totaled 3,000
throughout its banking and subsidiary operations. Its assets were
over seven billion dollars. Allied was founded by two import-expert
merchants, who, beyond their other common interests, just emotionally "clicked." Excited at the prospect, they co-conceived the new
enterprise because, in their own words, they "felt there was a need
for a bank that was able to look at the customer through the businessman's eyes." In their earlier dealings with other banks in their
import-export business, they felt all too often that point of view was
overlooked, and that who they banked with in the past were not attuned to the businessman's vision. So right away, at the organization's
conception, we have a preoccupation with the vision of the organization, with what and how collectively it "sees."

Temperamentally, Allied's founders disliked the regulatory and internal bureaucracies that were typically constraining the services of
banks. From the start of the enterprise, their intent was to aggres-

sively finance the dreams of California businessmen and women like themselves. Its organizational motto was "TNT—Today Not Tomorrow." Intended positively, this was intended to convey the spirit of, "We will not tie you up in bureaucracy like other banks do, we are here to help you make things happen." However, we shall also see how the TNT slogan signaled its *explosive, reactive* dark side. This motto was part of its façade at work.

Soon after opening its doors, Allied gained the reputation among its peers and among the rest of the business community as a pretty easy lender to go get money from. Allied would consider financial transactions that other lenders would turn down fairly automatically as too risky. Over the course of its first twenty years, this led to rapid and progressive expansion of facilities, capital assets and employee size, all in spite of regulatory and industry traditions that cautioned against such aggressive growth. At the same time, deregulation of the financial services industries at the time had created a marketplace that was increasingly blurry in its boundaries, as well as sharply competitive. *The organization thus expanded, at its beginnings and through its teens, in a way that was aggressive and at the same time, in the blur of the action in the market, disoriented.* Allied met with some success in its first years because of the sheer talent of its players, its more adroit scale, and as its markets were not destabilized enough to derail it. Over the years, the firm had experienced some occasional financial difficulties and organizational setbacks, but generally speaking, the firm managed to grow, pushing past its problems, if rather incompletely addressing them.

Ten years in, the founders had begun to let go, *partially*, hiring additional senior level executives and professional officer staff to expand the company further. The founders retained their roles as Chairman and Vice Chairman of the parent holding company, AlliedBancorp. The bank itself was far and away the principal entity within the holding company. The founders thus continued to play roles inside and outside the company. But decision making at the top was left fragmented and confused as to where clear authority lay.

Profits soared, employees reported that the firm was an exciting, fast-paced place to work, if, they admitted anecdotally, "sometimes crazy and frustrating." Turnover and employee burnout were high. Indeed, internally Allied remained disorganized in a swirl of confusion in its goals, policies and operating processes as it sought to aggressively go after new business. But management asserted that a structurally fluid state was necessary to remain reactive to its customers and to its now more changing markets. This claim was no doubt true, but it was also part of the firm's façade. A rationale was in play not to create coherent structure when it was increasingly needed to effectively scale and operate. Without the adequate structure to operate, what had originally seemed a grand business vision began to be grandiose.

Then suddenly in the early '80s, as the economy began to slide, the bubble burst. Bad loans started mounting in record numbers, and the portfolio was heavily lopsided to the import business. In fact, the import-export trade had always been the bank's first love, despite its expressions of being a domestic, commercial and retail-focused institution. Operational overhead and non-performing loans had steadily spread without adequate structure and controls. The situation grew worse and worse.

This got to a point that the company was no longer only dealing with profitability problems; it began to fight for its life. The government regulators finally stepped in, slapped heavy remedial demands upon the company, including having the founders further step aside and insert a new executive level over the bank. Generally the firm responded to the demands and the situation by clamping down on the organizational structure, and seemingly letting go of their grand vision altogether. They were no longer *pushing* it. Growth was shut off, and the firm contracted sharply, including closing a number of its branch offices. The expansionary dreams that the firm began with, were replaced with a mood that was tense, and fear was pervasive. One particularly palliative response by the founders was to appoint a well-trusted retired executive of theirs in the new role of chairman of the bank that the Feds had forced between them and the COO. He was a very good-hearted, low-key, smart man who had mentored the COO earlier in his career. He came to provide some temperance to the fear at the top and over time helped modulate some of its confusion and aggression. Remaining mostly behind the scene, he had the ear of the founder-executives and the COO when he chose to exercise his power. It was against this historical backdrop that my OD work with Allied began.

As part of the human resources division, though operating with a good deal of discretion, I approached management to develop a plan to help in their effort to downsize the bank. I had devised a way to do this using its existing patterns of turnover, while tightening up and reconfiguring some of its organizational structure. I was able to propose this, because I had leveraged a past role in recruitment and staff planning into a newly fashioned internal OD role with the support of a few senior operating executives. Some confidence in me had developed because of some creativity demonstrated in handling my narrower prior transactional role, working with them and supporting their middle line and operating units. When I had floated the idea of the new support plan, the COO himself was intrigued that there might be a way to help further downsize the bank without causing more of a stir, making use of the patterns of attrition as I had studied it. I pitched that project in conjunction with a larger OD role, while I readied myself for grad school in the field. I thought at some point in the future, beyond the immediate downsizing project, I could introduce some needed communications, training and other development support to help the company be a better place to work. I didn't quite know how much I would learn in OD and come to think about its theory and practice! There was a latent spirit—and resolve—inside the firm I thought I might tap into, although with the great, immediate troubles the firm faced, an OD role focused on getting at the "human stuff" may have seemed quixotic to take hold. It did I know to some, as it even did to me at times. But I had some license to proceed and did not give that reservation however too much attention. I pressed on.

Before going on to briefly survey these organizational interventions themselves, I want to further detail some of the presenting characteristics of the firm at the time my OD work began, because it's here that clarity around a type of organizational character emerged, as it was reminiscent of one of the types of individual character dynamics I would soon came to study in Reich's clinical modality.

One of the distinctive normative attitudes of the firm I saw appearing during this period was its blind belligerence. Hostility directed by organizational members at each other, across functions and outsiders needing cooperative action could suddenly erupt. When Allied was doing well, this attitude seemed to be masked by a presenting front that simply looked aggressive. But when the wider deterioration of the business came, along with a weakening economy, the high level of attribution in it also became obvious. For example, the top executive group would routinely project its own inner sentiments onto others. Many of the problems that were being faced at the time were wholly attributed to the economy, competitors, regulators, customers, employees, and not infrequently to each other. It never quite seemed to be a matter of their coming to terms with their own performance.

The same phenomenon existed among the mid-management ranks, and among frontline employees too (loan officers and operations personnel). They were frequently reactive, "touchy." Their first reaction as a rule was to disown problems that were theirs and go on the offensive. Fear, suspicion, a victim-mentality, and even attack was prominent when people were stressed. In my own early intervention efforts, I experienced transference. For example, it was said that I was the one who was bringing up problems, wasting people's time, and the like—even though I was generally cautious and attentive in my approach. This, from the middle line, and the executive suite as I came to work with them more fully. One of the founders later sarcastically ridiculed me to my face for getting "a mighty fancy sounding degree" on completion of my graduate coursework—even after he had been appreciative of my other efforts to help.

Another basic characteristic of Allied that became evident with time was the inherent split between the vision and inner emotional charge of the organization. As noted earlier, import-export oriented transactions are what truly seemed to turn on the organization's management and the staff, yet somehow they couldn't readily admit this in official announcements. There was a need to proclaim that the focus of the organization was primarily that of a general merchant bank. This stance I should add was by no means cosmetic. Members appeared to be quite sincere in their beliefs. It's just that the espoused beliefs and actions were at odds, and no one quite seemed aware of it, or at least prepared to openly talk about or address the imbalance. This lack of integrity of the firm's vision, I believe, originated at the point of organizational conception. Remember when the bank was conceived, its founders' identification with banking was equivocal. In fact, they had a certain disregard, even contempt, for the financial services industry, while at the same time sensing its deeper potential. This deeper sense was the spirit of the enterprise I myself had a kept a feel for, and I knew others there did too.

Finally, the way this vision block played out in the organization seemed anchored in the current-day functioning of the top management segment, the head of the organization. Both the founder-CEO level and COO related management functions consistently failed to formulate strategic direction, articulate sharply defined goals, or commit to target markets, failing also to develop coordinated policy and open feedback mechanisms, internally and externally. All of these of course are natural functions of a top leadership team, part of its *raison d'etre*. But at Allied the top segment had not functioned this way. The head, in effect, was isolated and cut off from the body of the organization—and from the outside, despite some grand wining and dining of high-end customers. This left the rest of the system confused, comparatively unstructured and relatively diffuse. In fact, one C-level executive had privately joked with me offline, in his own words describing the firm as "a headless horseman." All the power remained in the head but was not effectively discharged. The energy was structurally entrapped at the top of the organization, paradoxically rendering it immobile. The top didn't and evidently *couldn't* guide. Allied remained essentially blind as it galloped. A characteristic lack of defined processes existed in the middle management ranks; insufficient controls were in place, and middle managers at wide reported a feeling of powerlessness and despair; all more so, as the situation worsened.

The firm, in other words, was mainly armored in its head. Power and decision making were essentially sucked up by the head of the organization, keeping middle management on hold and mushy, leaving little energy in the rest of the system to concentrate on orchestrated tasks. Confused action, motion and commotion—*not movement*—were common. For example, there was recurring frustration, as some expressed, for example, over the "frequent rework that led nowhere." This description seemed to me to characterize the way the three major segments of the organization (top, middle and bottom) functioned. It was at Allied that I first came to see how each of these layers were *subsystems in the way each of their collective energies functioned and merged.* I took note of the quality of relationships established within each and the extent to which they operated in service of movement towards each of their natural function or how they tended to draw away from them.

In any case, it dawned on me that Allied's characteristic modes of acting and reacting were anchored in these three major cross-cutting subsystems. The shape of Allied's overall organization structure struck me as mirroring the distinctive way the body of one of the individual character types I was studying presented: a tightly compacted top segment; a disempowered, immobile, "uninspiring" middle; and an operating core whose units were diffuse, not sharply demarcated, yet stuck with mechanically pushing out work and product. More generally, this structural anchoring of an organization's character dysfunction, was suggested by Reich's understanding of how the soma of the human organism housed functionally identical psychic phenomenon. Under adverse conditions, the character dammed up the flow of energy, which then spilled out symptomatically after it continued to build, causing further difficulties.

My intervention strategy for Allied was basically emergent. It came from the case itself, not from a formal plan. In fact, when I began my work there, I had no clearly formulated sense of organizational character, let alone a way to assess or approach it. As I looked back, I could see an overall logic behind it, a logic, again, that turned out to be much the same as the treatment strategy found in the equivalent individual type: It was essential to get with the top to help unblock how it actually functioned, at first seeming impossible because the block by the top wasn't even seen. Problems mind you were *felt* by the top, but *the perception of them* was distorted, routinely projected onto others.

This meant I couldn't simply go in, urge and then perform vision exercises, popular prescriptions in business. (To wit: "Let's go off-site, talk and write mission statements, and clarify our strategic priorities.") The top, as a group, would see such a suggestion itself as misguided: "Why would we do that? We don't have that problem." Indeed, in another private, candid moment, the C-level executive I referenced earlier confessed to me: "Don't be ridiculous, we could never do that." In fact, they might tend to regard the suggestion, true to the character type, as an attack. I could sense fear even in suggesting it. This was not just my fear but the C-exec's own fear—his fear of public ridicule from his peers—helping keep the top segment locked up. In this way, my sensed fear was also countertransference.[25]

It's not just that Allied top management did poor strategic planning or that it blamed its problems on others. Many experienced OD consultants see that the top of many organizations routinely, if counterproductively, do this. It's that Allied essentially had almost *no* strategic management apparatus, and in fact had contempt for such planning and, virtually, planning itself. Instead, blind action, as noted, was its defining characteristic disability. This is just the opposite of the character of the banks Allied went in business to compete against—banks which top to bottom were consumed with bureaucratic detail, process and planning, all in an effort to avoid risk seemingly at all cost. That is the equivalent to a compulsive character dysfunction—the fusion blocked organization character—requiring a different set of interventions, as earlier discussed, when such help is sought because the risks of the character's corrosive effects are too high to not address.

At the top of Allied, a different kind of approach was required, something that would still have the practical effect of helping unlock the top, without worsening the situation by overreaching or creating power vacuums that would heighten tensions. Because of my past tenure working with the middle line, I did have some credibility going into the new role with them. I had worked with them, for example, on productivity studies that helped some better advocate for themselves; the studies gave them quantitative ways of calibrating their needs, when they felt short of needed resources. They were able to do this in ways that both the top and peers could collectively see. The studies thus effectively induced the executive operating group to clarify and commit to target goals that before had been left fuzzy. That intervention alone had some clarifying and empowering effects for individual middle line units, those located in the corporate center and in the field. After this and some other initial work engaging the middle line, my work with the top began with the downsizing efforts.

With the support and inputs of the COO and each of the EVPs in charge of business units (the firm's Management Committee), I operationalized the downsizing project. It was based on the premise that we could further shrink the organization using the firm's already existing high level of attrition. Based on a trend and distribution analysis, it was relatively predictable what, when and how many staff from different employee groups would leave; that made forecasting staff operating expense for the executive operating group more transparent, and thus more manageable. At the same time of the downsizing project, I also supported committee members' efforts to shore up certain work structures as people left their units. These efforts also helped management immediately see and address some of the confusion present, while reducing employee fear and suspicion, because layoffs were avoided. That was the immediate panic running through the system: "My God, we're contracting the organization, I'm going to lose my job." That fear was lessened. People in the organization saw the new way decreased the need for layoffs.

The way I devised my bi-weekly committee report out on the process had two functional benefits. First, it served as a kind of gentle, forcing function for this COO level group to cooperate on a clear, whole organizational goal, requiring the joint attention and action of every executive to make it work. Secondly, it shared their collective effort's results, with immediate financial impact *which together they could see*. This was a repetitive, reinforcing process for the duration of the project, which also gave me a lane to make continued, regular contact with them. This helped get them moving more effectively as a unit, very different from their customary bickering over turf. This process then let me turn my own attention to further mobilize the middle of the organization to operate more vigorously, in line with what they had always wished. Their common fear had been if they stepped out too boldly with an executive team that sucked up power, they would be slapped down, and so they commonly went on hold. For this further middle line work to occur, the energy at the top had to be loosened to preempt some of that reactivity and the fear it induced. This was the larger function of the turnover-based downsizing project I introduced. In addition to working with COO and Management Committee, the project also helped open the door for me to work at the founder-CEO level because their own energies were more available; with the Management Committee now functioning more vigorously, the founders (even from their official roles now aside) did not push them so hard. Finally, the project also opened the door for me to make contact with the inserted bank chairman who had come back from retirement and was largely operating behind the scenes.

I reengaged the middle line units in several ways and worked with a range of them simultaneously for maximum reach and impact. One effort, responding to some emergent demand, was to facilitate the convening of a cross-cutting mid-management task force to assess the current state of the bank; a few senior mid-managers had begun to discuss the idea among themselves and with two or three of their executive bosses and with me. They asked, could we form a special task force of managers to put together a strong series of strategic, bank-wide recommendations for all of top management to consider? One of the braver members of the Management Committee now found the chops to step out of the fold to get the effort sanctioned by his executive peers and to have each nominate a key player for the task force; he also offered himself as general sponsor for the effort.

The feedback that came from the task force was really the first of its kind that the top had ever engaged in such a formal, open way. The channel from the middle to the COO level, and even the CEO functions, was now opening. Even though not all of the task force's recommendations were immediately implemented, some of them were, and the process linked up the top and the middle. The task force served as a first entry into foreign territory for both, bettering communications, information exchange and real back and forth flow of concerns. The upshot of the process helped open the eyes across the CEO and top team-levels to the scope of Allied's problems as perceived by respected, key middle line personnel. And the Management Committee considered these issues out in the open without choking the effort off. As with the earlier downsizing initiative, the task force had the effect of helping top management *together better see*, including their own better use of power of what they were now willing cooperatively to back.

I soon began publishing and editing the company's first serious effort in executive and employee communications, disseminating systemwide information up and down the organization. The intent was to promote a renewed sense of vision, values and open discussion of new ideas. It sought to capture and rekindle the original spirit of the enterprise. The inaugural edition was enthusiastically received from the Board on down, prominently featuring an interview with the founders, and commentary by executives, mid-managers, and employees. From reactions all around, it was evident the quarterly did not feel like rhetoric, people felt it as open, a "free press" as one senior mid-manager put it.

Over its many editions, I continually worked with the CEO-founders level, the COO, and other executives to help them articulate their ideas and messages to the rest of the enterprise. It even gave me a platform to bring the contributions of the bank chairman out from behind the shadows with more public history of the bank's inner growth being recounted. Meeting with them all this way gave them time to think and react less impulsively, reflecting individually and together. It also provided me a means to cement a working alliance with several of them that went quite deep, our conversations helping spur them at times to take organizational action they saw as needed. In the spirit of colleagueship, Allied executives on their own increasingly supported one another in the dilemmas they each wrestled with. And quite apart from support activity I was engaged in, Allied executives drove efforts to tighten up structures throughout the system, particularly middle level staff control groups. They installed various goal setting, coordinating processes and monitoring mechanisms in the credit and accounting areas. Collectively, these activities came together to help clean up the organization and create better coherence and clarity in the organization. The structural activity in particular helped create needed armor in the system below the level of the head. Allied needed —and its people top to bottom sought— better structure and consistency, where it had previously been mushy and sprawling.

This firming up of structure also provided a basis for the company to next address some of key operating issues. I continued to work across the middle line to further solidify these managers' own sense of empowerment. With the imposition of the new structure and controls, as much as line and staff unit managers saw its need, some of them also began to fear getting somewhat suffocated; they had been used to seeing so little governance from above, or its opposite, reactive clamp down. These mid-managers were now blinking their eyes at the progress that they saw. Thus, it was necessary for me to continue to work with the middle to help get them moving more fully again, if their emerging way of functioning and impact were to last. Where there had been previously expressed interest, advanced technical training, personal development and team building efforts were all introduced. I provided counsel and facilitation support to key mid-line managers in their launch, development and own leadership of each of these efforts. Combined, they created a notable muscular effect among many in the middle and in the operating core who were affected.

My aim in the way middles were convened with the operating core was not only to sharpen individual skills and competencies, but to give them an opportunity to feel a fuller sense of their own power, connection and tangible contribution. It was literally a matter of building up the inspiration of the organization's mid-level people who led the charge. Mid-managers began to breathe more freely, no longer as a group holding their breath wondering what would come next. The efforts helped "charge them up" on the natural facilitative roles they had longed to play—creating operating protocols, developing and conducting training, and better directing, coaching and hearing from their own people.

The strategic intent of working to open up the breathing of the middle was to help pull energy down from the top of the system, creating an inner push on the blocks; this would in turn manifest the deeper nature of the vision block at the top, with less risk of having the top shut down. This emphasis at this turn in the engagement was roughly equivalent to what would be done therapeutically with the similar type in individual therapy in such a moment: helping the chest to open up, through inspiration and expiration, drawing energy packed up in the head, down. The organism comes to better tolerate this movement without shutting off in the eyes. Clinically, this supports clearer vision and contact, from which deepening progress can be made.

Good contact with those in the system helped me gauge the right touch needed, not to try and do too much or do too little. The continued work with the middle gave me openings to reengage the top in key moments when their strategic play was essential. I worked with top leaders to help prepare them to recognize and act in such moments, planned or on the spot. I also encouraged those opening up the quickest to seize opportunities as they presented, initiating important conversations and visibly leading company forums where they spoke their minds. This helped preempt a reactive backslide into their own old ways of clamping down, as the middle began standing tall. I was working to soften the characteristic reactions real-time. The Management Committee members had longed to be supportive but previously had been afraid to speak up too publicly. Projects I worked heavily with the middle to facilitate now included a systemwide program to better synchronize loan quality and marketing objectives, and another in boosting the recognition and value of the operations management function. Each helped address historical dichotomies in vision at Allied in vital work areas.

A range of methods—survey feedback, problem solving forums, and large-scale internal community building interventions—were drawn on to connect top leaders, middle managers, and senior operating personnel. The methods used addressed work issues widely seen as timely and important. Significant numbers participated, and key mid-line players were prominent in shaping the design of the methods used. Some spontaneously fashioned new operating roles they stepped into and developed new formal structures that could make a meaningful difference. Many up and down the organization were now working in a more empowered, self-directing, and synched-up way.

The organization, with clearer vision and voices at the top, began to declare its niche markets and positioning within the state's commercial mid-market more definitively. Its original love of providing financial support for import-export transactions found a dedicated home in a newly designated business unit, as a special niche. Allied also began to focus on ways its internal organizational arrangements "wrapped around" the niche markets, as it built out infrastructure—policies, processes and systems—to support a better, clearer working presence in those markets.

The founders too came to be less at war with each other. Some of their continued infighting with each other—where once they had said they "fight like brothers" about who had the upper hand—lessened. The more visionary of the two, Ralph, began to be more grounded, and the hard-driving nuts and bolts of the two, Stan, increasingly yielded to the other, seeing the need to foster a wider vision that hearkened back to the original dream of the bank to do more than simply make money. I worked with Stan on a speech he took on as his own, delivered many times, and committed to with Ralph in widely publicized print media. Following its good reception, they kept coming back to me to talk about where the organization was going. Ralph and I developed an especially close relationship, where he openly shared his frustrations and disappointments in others he had expected more of. But he was opening up, including sharing what he thought he needed to more fully own himself, including just being clearer.

In one of our conversations together Ralph commented about the COO (we'll call him Bill), who seemed beholden to the ever-driving Stan, always busy in action and reaction. Looking at me, Ralph shook his head from side-to-side and sighed, "How do we get Bill to just put his feet up on the desk sometimes—*and just think*?" This remained, I thought, a masked expression, one-step removed, of his thoughts about his partner Stan's incessant action, but he was starting to go near the conflict. My reply to him was simple: "We don't. Bill's got a lot of virtues, but he's not a guy to ponder here like that." That struck Ralph. But what he did from there struck me too. In the wake of the newly published corporate magazine that introduced what was to be a regular column by Bill, he wrote a memo to Bill commenting on the continued importance of his strategic communications to the organization, closing it with "I'll look forward to seeing it each issue." In the memo, Ralph copied Stan and every member of the Board of Directors and Management Committee, as well as me. Ralph was making league with my efforts to help him and the organization: to help open up the COO so critical thinking might better flow, while being more focused himself and opening up the eyes of the very top. *Ralph himself was in that moment being more guiding.* This helped secure the footing for regular top-level communications to the organization from the COO, relieving some of the historic block.

With this, Ralph and Stan together asked me to help draft another statement of the bank's newly emerging strategic positioning. I offered them several drafts—each one, which they ardently rejected because they couldn't agree what needed to be said. In helping prepare it, I had struggled in several private meetings to pull out of them a common articulation of the vision, even after all the progress that had been made. Finally, acknowledging my own frustration, I told them, I was simply going to write something *I felt* most deeply described it. I was an employee after all too, I told them. It was a strong, visionary statement. But when the three of us met together to discuss it, Ralph, again the more visionary of the two, told me: "Well, you finally got Stan and me to agree. We... we... *hated* it! It was so... so *esoteric.*" *He was simultaneously expressing his unadorned emotional reaction—both of theirs, in fact—and his own increasing appreciation for a statement about the enterprise's future that needed to be grounded.* As soon as he said it, the three of us all had a good laugh. A final, new statement came out of it from there, which he and Stan heartily endorsed—one that was not far off from what I had in fact proposed. It had after all reflected an unexpressed spirit about Allied's future direction, grounded in their deeper, founding aspirations.

As the enterprise got on its feet, this did not mean everything was smooth sailing. The core of the founders' deeper fissures continued, and throughout the organization, emotions and conflicts continued to be triggered because the work issues themselves were charged. Strong feelings began to be publicly expressed within the organization. But members could now better tolerate their expression, and I was able to help a good many work through the issues as they surfaced. Members now had a platform and reason to work through them. I want to note that throughout this entire period, I ran into characteristic resistances and fear. It was not easy for management and staff to face their own anxieties, their own and others' suspicions and frustrations, and at the same time still move forward. But they did, and they showed courage in the process.

In my role, I helped people move through these, as they increasingly called to work with me, individually and in group settings. In the meantime, the organization seemed to improve meaningfully. Over time, Allied developed renewed financial strength, improved earnings and employee morale, and a restored sense of self-confidence. With external regulatory controls now lifted, and the economy brightening, the organization began to rekindle its original spirit and energy. Slowly, the firm began to expand and grow once again. The intervention and recovery process I've described took five years. It was a very self-propelled collective effort.

Although after all of this the firm had not fully come to grips with the source of its chronic vision block, it did have a renewed capacity and seriousness to begin to address it. Through the work together, Allied came to accept and institutionalize clearer goals, sharper operating controls, organized feedback, group problem-solving, and employee involvement strategies. Moreover, much fear abated, people at all levels more readily spoke up, and the general mood was one of happiness.

One last thing to stress: In my work with Allied, I simply served as one catalyst for change. All the major thrust came from within the firm itself. As an internal consultant, I did situate myself organizationally in such a way to be able to help foster and sew together different intervention efforts for combined effect—those I helped spur and facilitate with the many actions that spontaneously occurred on their own up and down the organization. At the time, I thought of myself as a foot soldier in the recovery effort, and I am sure others regarded me as that. But in retrospect, I think respect for my efforts was wider than that —to be sure, but one voice among many, but a voice that others heard and had effect. I was seen as someone who would listen and was trusted to make good use of what was shared if fit. The sheer numbers and quality of help sought by top, middle and bottom from me—and the sensitive issues and sentiments they shared knowing I was widely engaged—suggest this was the case.

I continuously needed to contract and re-contract my way forward with each of my efforts, especially at the beginning of the process. I did this matter-of-factly, not timidly. Greater trust in me from all levels in working with the system gradually grew. This manner of approach is common best practice among experienced OD consultants. Contracting is not a one-shot affair but intimately tied up with the process over time. Resistance, in some degree, continually resurfaces as the force of the defensive character remains and is gradually dissolved.

In the final analysis, many forces worked together in the organization to help bring the health of the organization forward. Most notable was the intense will of so many critical players in the firm, including its top leaders, who really wanted to see the company survive—and more than that, to flourish. Despite its aggressive vision block, the firm kept contact with a vital core, with its deeper yearnings and what excited the firm from the very start. These were to make genuine contact with its customers and capitalize on their dreams in a way that did not tie them up in bureaucracy. The trick throughout, and as the efforts continued, was to try to accomplish this in a way that was sound, emotionally satisfying and roundly productive.

PART III:
IMPLICATIONS

CHAPTER 8

SPECIAL ISSUES
IN THE NETWORK
ORGANIZATION ERA

I n the third and final section of this book, we turn our attention to the social implications of the workplace trap. This chapter looks at how the changing nature of organizations, given watershed shifts in the socioeconomic and global, interconnected technologies, offers us the potentiality of new kinds of collaborative enterprise. But also, given the continued suppression of vital work energies in the workplace, how these organizations present both old and new types of characterological problems for people at work. In some ways, this chapter presents the view that "the more things change, the more they stay the same"—and how, in the face of tenacious holding, they can even get worse.

Yet my interest is in offering more than a critique. My hope is that clarifying the dynamics of flatter, more network-based organizations in our still evolving information age gives us greater understanding of contemporary dilemmas of the workplace. This understanding I believe points the way out of the trap to fulfill the promise of what a better organization may be—a work democratic organization for our times. I write this for organizational change thinkers and practitioners to help them make a difference in their own work. I also write this for all of us who live and work in these new kinds of organizations, both today and as they are still emerging.

The next, final chapter after this moves us out of the dynamics of organizational systems into the realm of how wider social systems function. We will move from the micro-organizational world to the implications for the macro social order itself. Reich's searing discoveries about human energy at work and natural energy systems, gives us new ways to think about social change in general and to understand the levers for broader, aggregate institutional reform. The aim is nothing short of understanding how we may better rehumanize the life of society to better support workplace life.

THE EMERGENCE OF THE NETWORK ENTERPRISE

Beginning in the 1980s, futurists and organizational thinkers, from Alvin Toffler to Peter Drucker, envisioned the "coming of a new organization," the network-based enterprise to meet the challenges and opportunities of a new socioeconomic and technological global order.[1] Traditional organizational forms—both steep hierarchies and more simple based entrepreneurial ones—lacked the ability to combine speed and adaptability to keep pace with the ever-proliferating demands of complex information requirements, as Harvard's Richard Nolan was among the first to describe.[2]

The advent of wireless network technologies created the reality for whole new thresholds of connectedness and collaboration spanning time and place. Just as innovations in electric light, steam and gas-powered technologies enabled the nineteenth century's Industrial Revolution, the wireless information technologies emerging in the late twentieth century ushered in a post-industrial information age. Historically, where factories had once replaced craft shops no bigger than what a waterwheel could power, they themselves were now being technologically eclipsed by ever-sprawling enterprises no longer geographically confined. They started to operate ever-more virtually. Nor would business concerns any longer be confined to what supervisors could simply oversee—literally, what was within their line of sight. Spans of control would open up—*and had to*. The demands of an economy increasingly dominated by knowledge and services organizations, over and above previously dominant manufacturing concerns, required entirely new organizational forms. Such a shift represented what Toffler called civilization's "Third Wave" and Drucker, the "Knowledge Society."

A strategic IT thinker such as Nolan built an important consulting firm helping a worldwide following of organizations think about and start to move to the IT enabled network form—flatter, more collaborative enterprises, highly adaptive to rapidly and ever-changing markets. The new organization would increasingly be held together by the power of a guiding vision, ubiquitous technological networks, well-focused and synchronized infrastructures, and by interdisciplinary project teams assembled on demand. These were its principal features.[3] Such organizations would need to have new kinds of operating models to string these features together. These operating architectures would need to be more tangible than general ideas about agility or techniques mechanically applied from agile software methodologies, as we often hear today. *They would need to reflect quite specific governing and operating organizational functions suited to the information age.*

Nolan himself delineated such functions in his distinction of information age versus industrial age management principles.[4] While Nolan didn't spell it out as such, these new organizational functions would necessarily be carried out by each of an enterprise's major cross-cutting structural segments: a head that guides, a middle line that facilitates, and an operating core that discharges the organization's basic work in fulfilling, productive ways. It's not in Nolan's conception that the basic organizing segments didn't persist, but that they could take on radically different forms than those of the industrial hierarchies of the past. These functions would now be part of the very fabric of the new enterprise, part of, as I have put it, its *constitutional nature, natural to its work.*

An organization's inner and outer boundaries would fundamentally be less constrained than in the old systems. More fully interdependent ways of working would lower the walls between divisions and departments within a firm, sometimes getting rid of them altogether. And wider ecologies of organizations—including partnerships, alliances, and trans-organizational systems—would more fully come into play. A large system's viability, its success or failure, increasingly depended on interconnectedness. All of this would inherently require clear, empowering organizational leadership and cultures to help such systems thrive and grow.

This would put a new premium on the fulfillment of work democratic strivings, as defined in Chapter 3. More specifically, a premium is put on the type of culture I have described as a "work democratic character," following Reich's prescient description years before such technology was ever developed. I believe assisting organizations develop such a structure—and develop the conditions for such a character to emerge to support it—will largely be the doorway for productive socio-technical and *sociotherapeutic* intervention in the coming years. We will return to this at the end of this chapter.[5]

It is not surprising that many of the first of these organizations were IT-oriented in their product and service lines. As I have previously written:

> Apple, Microsoft, Google, Facebook, and Wikipedia are examples. But so are non-IT firms in their markets like Amazon and Uber. Common hallmarks are their capacity for speed, adaptability, and innovation, and their ability to scale and make alliances in complex, information rich environments.[6]

Sometimes in their transactional capabilities, these organizations must have exquisitely designed, finely tuned supply chains and customer service capabilities to reliably deliver on their promise. Amazon is a vivid example. However, even at that, I see that *the new breed of organization is fundamentally playing jazz, no longer strictly following tight scripts* in the service of pre-articulated goals and given realities. As a *company*, it has to be able *to spontaneously move*. This is to say the new organizations are playing jazz *when they function well*. Not all of them, as we will discuss shortly, do. Some modern organizations, unfortunately, are notoriously bad at it.

Nonetheless, *given their nature, enterprises of this new breed must continuously tap into their immanent, creative energies, supported by responsive organizational arrangements*. This is what makes "batch of one" delivery or, even more obviously, enterprises continuously pouring out unique services and customized outcomes rely heavily on interdependent project teams—teams operating up, down and across the system extending deeply into its field. Some of these project teams, when transactional, will be standing teams. But all of them to a greater or lesser degree will be subject to be variably deployed, reconstituted and redeployed on a moment's notice. Collectively, they form an *ensemble of teams* orchestrated by the power of the venture's central vision and supporting organization infrastructure processes, networks and channels.

The inherent, looser boundaries of such enterprises—to allow for their fluidity, resilience and expression of their work energies—is their strength. But it is also their Achilles Heel. *Fuzzy boundary conditions can make for blurred vision when sharp observation and distinctions are needed, and they can lead to a penchant for expansiveness without due concentration of effort*. In the face of unsatisfied work aggressive drives too this expansiveness will start to look imperialistic in its markets. Facebook as a company looks like this to me. The enterprise can develop an intolerance of taking the time needed to cultivate more organic development of their people, goods and markets—in other words, of *all* its relationships. *The network enterprise's composite work energies may fail to sufficiently develop and pulse*. Moreover, the enterprise can be vulnerable to *not even seeing the need for concentrated development and rhythmic movement*.

This can lead the new organization in the opposite direction of its very potential: making human relationships less, not more important; haste, not concerted action, can become dominant. When organizations are founded under adverse conditions, I believe, such a nature can short-circuit their socioemotional development, rendering them susceptible to fixed blocks that give rise to rigid, chronic character disorders.

In the new, network-based enterprise, this can sometimes be more insidious than ways more conventional organizations have historically manifested their blocks and collective neuroses. To ward off seeing clearly when things go amiss, leaders of the new breed may herald its "boundarylessness" as a sign of its responsiveness, agility and power to connect in today's, high-speed world. Its illness will be seen as health. This rationale I think is rhetoric, nonsensical and even dangerous. It is not unlike what we saw in Allied's extreme rationalization of its "flexibility." It is part of the organization's façade, further obscuring and hobbling it. When severely blocked in its ability to concentrate, the networked organization is loosed upon the world, often with little definition or focus.[7] Incapacitated in its ability to develop others or itself more dimensionally, this can leave its people and processes from meaningfully coming into their own. Their members will start to look and sound the same to monotonous effect—not accomplished, diverse instrumentalists making a sonorous whole. Definition and distinction, and thus a fully charged unity in all its richness, are lost. When this happens, the door to severe organizational character disorder and outright pathology is opened. The organization as a workplace becomes toxic.

Before turning to these characterological implications, it is worth noting that the risks of loosely coupled enterprises are not new to organization theorists or change practitioners. Classical General Systems Theory has long recognized that fuzzy boundary conditions tend to create problems in organizational coherence and identity.[8] Rising ambiguity and sudden power shifts can swell, reflected in problems of managerial authority and task, role and relationship anxiety. Larry Hirschhorn and Tom Gilmore as early as 1992, contemplating the increasing breakdown of rigid, *formal* boundaries in what they called "the boundaryless organization," wrote:

> Indeed, once traditional boundaries of hierarchy, function, and geography disappear, a new set of boundaries becomes important. These new boundaries are more psychological than organizational. They aren't drawn on a company's organizational chart but in the minds of its managers and employees. And instead of being reflected in a company's structure, they must be "enacted" over and over again in a manager's relationships with bosses, subordinates and peers.[9]

An understanding of the energetic basis of work and group life allows us to understand the root dynamics at play are more than psychosocial; they imply more than mental maps to be newly drawn or new behaviors to enact, though these needs surely surface. They are powered I maintain by the way the spontaneous movement of work energy, primary from the outset in the life of an organization, is chronically blocked. The organization's natural ability to charge, concentrate, flow and discharge energy becomes disturbed. It learns from its earliest days such concentration and expression of energy are intolerable. More natural rhythms in the organization are replaced by substitute forms of operating that are doomed in their ability to be humanly fulfilling.

CHARACTEROLOGICAL RISKS

The work energy dynamics of any organization, healthy or chronically blocked, always surface phenomenally as one's feelings at work and how they are collectively experienced. But when our vital work energies are especially suppressed, the entire situation becomes *emotionally loaded*. I saw this in a very brief consult and facilitation with a new breed of software services firm.

I worked with a group of thirty senior directors of a product innovation division in a young, mid-cap organization. The division was the biggest business unit of the firm. I was approached by the division's OD manager who put me in touch with its EVP leader to prepare and facilitate a three-day offsite. They wanted to consider strategic and operating difficulties among the top of the division in hopes of getting the group to better focus on the issues and to *better see itself as a group* in its joint endeavors. In my preparatory conversations and interviews, and later when I saw them in action, I observed a high level of frustration and interoperating conflict. Turnover had already been significant among the directors and more was brewing.

The firm was loosely structured organizationally in the name of remaining responsive and opportunistic to rapidly changing market conditions. This carried over into the looseness of the division's structure. Despite being public, the firm's founder and CEO continued to operate entrepreneurially, and he intervened materially in the division's operations. He continued to have faith in the division's EVP but was out of touch with the consequences of his own actions. The CEO flooded the division with one new operating responsibility after another before allowing the dust to settle organizationally. Prior changes were never quite digested before new ones came. And the CEO indulged and even sanctioned end-runs around the EVP, second-guessing operating decisions. This drove the EVP bonkers, and it stirred up random behaviors, power conflicts and upset among the director ranks. There was little notable satisfaction in their work.

The division's thirty directors were highly paid, many of them high-tech engineers, lured to the firm with the expectation they would operate with substantial charter and discretion. *In my first interviews with them, many of them said their hearts were afire when they joined, excited about the firm's drive and prospects of freedom offered to be inventive. Yet, once down to work, they experienced their own sense of control as very limited; decisions made all around them were unanticipated, reactive and impulsive; decisions within the organization they said, "went all over the place."* The division's functions were splintered, and they became factions in how they wrestled for power. Business results and member retention suffered. The link between operating process and results was largely sensed by the directors, but it was not well understood, even though the dynamics stared them in the face. Frustration ran high and wide; it had a grip on them.

The organization was "boundaryless," in the traditions of hierarchy, in the other ways Hirschhorn and Gilmore warned, and in *the ever-spreading ways its energy moved: The ground never stabilized enough for the players to develop informed, trusted working relations or a shared identity*. Indeed, just as the CEO modeled the opposite in his actions, the directors throughout the division continuously enacted dysfunctional ways of engaging each other.

Under such conditions, a great deal of anxiety and unhappiness was provoked. This left the leaders, groups and organization susceptible to extreme forms of "uncertainty reduction," or in the terms that cognitive and behavioral theorists describe, to simplification and attribution, black and white thinking, and habitually dysfunctional norms. I saw these were all ways of how the system played out suppressing and turning back the original excitement of its members at work. Their natural and conditioned anxiety was, too. Confusion and bickering proliferated, and this further fueled executive suite reaction. The division EVP's tendency was to pull in and withdraw (he some months later in fact quit the firm), and the CEO become ever-more reactive to assert control; he sought refuge in concrete, spur-of-the-moment action in hopes of immediate results. The CEO told me he sought to avoid "fuzzy strategies with far-away outcomes." A downward spiral followed.

I did my best in the short time I was there to help the players step back and see the dynamics. However, I never got the footing to help them get a handle on the whirling motion they were caught up in that kept them locked up. In the way the organization moved, there was no time for that—and little interest. People continued to whirl, some like the EVP later spinning off to do their own thing altogether.

This system reflected work aggressive characteristics, those of a vision blocked and even fusion blocked character too. But for our present purposes I want to bring out how the organization exhibited the serious risks that organizations of the network age run.

- *Energy is widely and thinly dispersed, ever moving outwards.* There are few boundaries to contain, concentrate and structure its full discharge. This leads to pockets of hyper-reactive efforts to hold onto, then suddenly wield, power. Instead of the tendency for a group's work to naturally merge and flow together, there are bumps and grinds. One does not see patient development in the growth of individuals at work or the assembly of a group. In fact, *there is very little assembly.* It is "every man for himself." Relationships are minimized and activities become highly transactional.

- *As energy does not smoothly build and discharge, power tends to back up, then pool up at the top.* The organization, far from being distributed in its power, starts to become especially hierarchical, with just a few at the top holding systemwide clout. With founders still in charge, this will start to look like the early days of an entrepreneurship that never matured. This mode of managing remains, despite the ever-outward push of the firm and its continued expansion in size. Again, I think one sees this acutely at Facebook in how it is managed; only a few at the top hold *controlling* power. In this sense, the firm remains primitive. It has never really developed or matured. Its founders act like parents who never quite let go.

- *Constitutionally, the organization is at risk of becoming systemically incapacitated to develop structural definition and draw on individual strengths.* People start to act and react very much the same. There is little variation in the system as individuals remain stunted in their growth. Indeed, there is no time for that unfolding differentiation. This is not a matter of "accepting ambiguity," as some may suggest. *People, rather, are drowning in ambiguity and revert to an undifferentiated mass.* They are forever in a scramble and widely experience exhaustion. Systemically, the organization expands but with indistinct structures, processes or a membership that actually is diverse. The proliferation of this state constitutes the expansion. As a mini-social system, the firm, as Dr. Charles Konia has contended in another context, starts to func-

tion like an organism with cancer: It is beset by the rapid proliferation of undifferentiated, immature cells. *The system depleted
in its energy, has little left to concentrate for healthy development.
Instead, the energy remaining moves ever prematurely outward to
replicate itself until the system becomes a hardened mass and finally itself gives out.*[10]

- *Socioemotionally, the firm is ripe for blowing through its developmental stages, taking on an impulsive character.* These boundaryless organizations resemble borderline characters as they have
been described individually in their development and functioning. *No* primary developmental stage has been fulfilled, every
stage has been frustrated. Even partial containment of the frustration (as we see in more traditional firms) is difficult when little
stable structure has been established at all.

- *Visceral contact between people is highly displaced by virtual contact,* which is deemed perfectly fine. The speed of the network
organization makes online channels of communication, not
those face-to-face, the rule. Zoom and other multi-media technologies have helped, but even there, faces seen on screens remain two-dimensional; we are not encountering people visceral-
ly present in the room. *The nonverbal realm—long understood to
be ninety percent of communications—is seriously compromised.*
Dialogue alone, while a start, is not enough to counter this trend
either. This too will place an emphasis on words and behaviors,
not feelings, as the sentient world is eclipsed. This is Dialogical
OD's great emphasis on mindset shifts and intention. But nonverbal expression and that which is simply felt and spontaneously
swells up in people will be less. *Vital information in the information age is thus lost.* Human meeting and encounter, when all is
said and done as Buber recognized, is grounded not in words or
the endless possibilities of the mind—but in "the one taut string
of spirit." The ever-interchangeable world of I-It leaves one swirling around in a vortex.[11]

- *Burnout and resignation* are high. The information saturated,
loose formal structures unleash real and emotionally charged responses often inadequately addressed: information overload, job

transition and loss, and competence about using the new tech-nologies.[12] Extraordinary rates of turnover, people not sticking with an organization through its ups and downs, and the like—all this has been termed "the great resignation." It has been at-tributed to numerous factors, including post-COVID workplace changes, new generation workforce values, and simply poor management. However, nearly every time I've seen unusual rates of organizational turnover, unless the work opportunity people are leaving for is exceptional or it's just time for something fresh, I have found this to be true: *Emotional resignation always pre-cedes formal resignation from the organization.* Wilhelm Reich understood long ago how emotional resignation always preceded the somatic illnesses of certain functional disease states in the in-dividual—the organism literally shrank in its energy functioning which he called a *biopathic* disturbance (the spread of the dis-ease state he recognized as the contorted energy still striving to move). In organizational systems, all this must be more than the effects of psychological "stress," though this is certainly involved. *This is a giving up of the heart from work.* The organization is sapped of the vital energies it needs in which to live and grow. Traditional dimensions of loyalty and courage when things get tough—these are literally out the door. Burnout and high turn-over are not unique to the network enterprise, but it seems ex-acerbated there with the relentless pace and long hours many of them expect. It is a matter of what is felt—deep frustration—or sometimes not felt at all: lack of emotional contact in a virtual world, not a world of flesh and blood. Workplace life becomes robotic, with no anchors of meaning, an information-age version of Chaplin's *Modern Times.* Anonymity and lack of emotional contact, emblematic of the network age, comes home to roost. Serious sociotherapeutic methods, while no cure-all, I believe are among the best means to address it.

As a consultant, I came to appreciate how a proposed interven-tion could put an organization network at greater risk, if it was not grounded in an appreciation of the form's downside possibilities and what a network actually needed to do to be successful. This was the case of the US government intel agency, discussed in Chapter 5, which we return now below to consider.

Two consulting firms, mine and another, had been simultaneously engaged to help the agency become better equipped organizationally to thrive in the fiercely competitive US intel community. Many of these three-lettered agencies were at each other's throats competing for the same federal clients and funding. Moreover, in the wake of the Cold War's end, the entire intel community was now besieged with radically new asymmetric threats from hostile players around the world. The tandem consulting group my team worked with at the agency had rightly helped guide the agency's leadership to think of itself more fully as a network. But then, in a flight of fancy, told them all their staff should become "generalists" to help integrate the work of other agencies for the clients—to, in effect, serve as "renaissance men" synthesizing all the information that was coming to the clients from the other agencies. This had a certain ring and "cool" to it and a surface appeal. The consultancy told them this would give them the strategic upper hand with the clients. In fact, had the agency's executives followed the advice, they would have likely led the organization to the bottom, putting the agency at risk of folding.

The major flaw in the advice was that its proponents were urging that all the agency's people become generalists and provide no specifically defined value, no specifically derived and heavily analyzed intel of their own. They would operate in a more fully boundaryless way, its people all becoming functionally the same. *They would become more undifferentiated, not less, already a problem to begin with*, in answering the question, "What *unique*, compelling value do we provide?" Furthermore, the competitive and chaotic landscape provided no basis for the agency's people to get any footing to serve as integrative specialists or those who convened others to facilitate integrative analysis.

The proposition it surely seems would have put the agency in permanent competitive disadvantage with the other agencies with their customers. The other agencies would be the only ones providing content-rich knowledge, knowledge which the customers craved to carefully and jointly analyze with those who provided it. Indeed, because of the data's first-hand technical nature, those providing it could be the only ones equipped to join the customers in such analysis. Thus, had the proposition been adopted, the need for the original agency could readily vanish. The real world of fierce competition, the hunger for concrete knowledge, and scarce funding might assure that outcome. I worked with the agency's leadership and the co-consulting group to look closely at and reconsider the proposition.

In our conversations, I took the client and the consultancy back in time to the Manhattan Project from the 1940s to consider how it functioned as a robust, knowledge-creation enterprise. (The intel agency was essentially a knowledge enterprise.) The Manhattan Project operated as an organizational network with two major centers across the country, a project with mission critical deadlines and of the highest government importance; it also operated without other like-competitive programs vying for DC's attention to undercut it.

Fortunately, I had a card up my sleeve for research about the Manhattan program. My aging father had served as a young chemist at Oak Ridge on the project, and I phoned him to ask him of his experience. I inquired, how many people on the project were generalists? He told me, "One, the barber. He cut everyone's hair the same." The rest, he said, all had to be deep specialists in their fields and know how to operate at the interface with those in the other disciplines for joint effect.

There was no pretense that they were all renaissance men. Robert Oppenheimer, the project's technical director had of course deep knowledge of theoretical physics and of the unique nature of the technical problems at hand. So even Oppy, a true renaissance man himself, functioned as a specialist on the project; it entirely informed how he helped shape and in the moment move-in-and-out of the diverse project teams to help steer the effort. Even General Groves at the very top of the effort at the Pentagon was more than a generalist. He was no scientist, but he was expert enough in administration to garner ongoing political support and run interference with DC. There were enormous egos, passions and splintering of ideas to manage on the project. Oppenheimer performed unswervingly in helping manage the technical conditions for success, with General Groves' administrative leadership support for cover. *Those conditions and the true specialization of all were such that the many small teams operating within the project themselves solved the technical problems and those of their workable integration. They did so in ways that were largely spontaneous and self-managing, there was no group of outside "generalists" convening people or intervening.* In essence, such generalist roles were what the proposal urged to the intel agency in how its people should function.

The moral of the story: When working on efforts that are truly technical, specialists deep in their fields are required, including best knowing what is specifically required from their end for their work together to flow. Generalists are going to get fooled (unless it is the barber cutting hair). They are too removed from the actual work situation. It is those who create the "stuff" in the first place, under the right conditions, who can yield the composite effect. To return to what we said earlier: Accomplished jazz ensembles require virtuosos on their instruments, specialists who know how to play at the interface with others for entire effect. This is what makes work-democratic functioning networks, jazz ensembles or Manhattan projects, possible.

I told this story in a meeting with the agency's leadership team, with the other consultancy present, and even they joined together and agreed. Everyone laughed about the barber and we all began to assess other ways of proceeding at the agency with what the workforce must become. The proposition was withdrawn, and an alternative strategy, built on teams of more bedrock specialists, was fashioned so the agency could better flourish as a network.

The agency, already something of a functioning network, avoided a regression in its manner of operating into a proliferate mass of undifferentiated roles. Its character seemed to operate as a work aggressive organization with some level of vision blocking, as manifested in some of the confusion of its core purpose or drive. It still retained some primary work democratic impulses in how it functioned by virtue of the capacity it retained to spontaneously self-organize. Its basic health was also reflected in its recognized need for due structure in the first place—its need for a new operating model in general, and, in particular, its ability to anticipate what would occur if it blindly followed the "renaissance man" prescription. In this respect, it was not thoroughly vision blocked. It retained capacity to see ahead and *to reason and feel its way* to a greater sense of mission fulfillment. Another modern network organization I was familiar with was not so fortunate. It continued to be swamped, operating with a different character: a work dramatic type.

A high profile, rapidly expanding, global software services firm remained in the grip of its entrepreneurial founder, running from offering to offering, never quite able to stabilize its structure. Its market mission seemed clear to its founder, still closely leading the organization as CEO, and to its high-paid professional staff. They were excited and genuinely enthusiastic about its drive to provide services that bettered relationships for its customers and their customers. This excitement and even clarity about the mission existed, even while many seemed obsessed with dramatic financial gains and staff fear of the charismatic founder existed side-by-side with their excitement. There seemed little real human contact underneath the declared day-to-day roles. People just ran on.

The especially *dramatic* quality of the interest in making money was itself a clue to its character, as were the drama the CEO provoked and the shook-up excitement of the mid-management and staff. The organization as a whole had a wild frenzy about it. There was a great deal of motion and running around by all to grow things; it got to the point where panic would set in. The founder kept on the run: What do we need to do next, and next, and next? And people themselves wondered: What would ever satisfy the founder? The firm grew and grew in size, but it seemed like it never got out of its infancy. The enterprise never developed container structures for more rhythmic decision making and performance that could solidly scale. It shook as it performed like a rocket, thrilling but scary for those inside who never felt strapped in. Even the CEO felt this way, he just kept pushing on the pedal. There was no quest for building a better operating model. The higher and faster atmospherically the enterprise went, the scarier it got. Such an organization could burn itself out. It *lacked* armor where firmness was needed. There was high turnover, including that eventually of the founder, who himself left under a highly publicized misconduct scandal.

With both the intel agency and software enterprise examples of organizational networks, we can see that the network form is susceptible to different forms of character disorders. Their socioemotional blocking seems variable depending on its players and developmental circumstances. Moreover, they seem vulnerable to characterological blocking in special ways: *The very nature of network enterprises renders them susceptible to constitutional problems of structural incapacity.* It will tend to jettison or throw off efforts at differentiated structure; these will be considered what gets in the organization's way, rather than a deep symptom of its distress. When those in the system start to rationalize this in a way that is not open to contravening facts, it may be indicative they are beyond help and the organization is on the path to self-destruction. Every case will be different, but it is a sign perhaps that the pathogenic process has taken over. It may be a cancer that cannot be stopped.

These constitutional vulnerabilities seem native to the network enterprise, if the character that develops does not sufficiently cultivate their work democratic strivings. *Such organizations can become permanently disabled in their constitutional form to hold and discharge their energies. It may be less the type of character disorder that is the problem than the extent of its disorder in the face of the organization's inherent charge. A deeply anchored character disorder in the face of a strong drive will likely be stirred up and reinforced in its hold. This seems to be the central risk and dilemma of the network organization form.*

PREVENTION AND INTERVENTION

As we discussed in Chapter 4, an organization can become very sick, or develop the propensity for sickness, even before it experiences sharp inhibition in its primary socioemotional development stages. Its earliest constitutional phases before that, as the firm is conceived and organized, seem to be even more foundational to its later state of functioning. In the case of those collectively in the network enterprise, their core excitement may never be far, but the excitation will become distorted if the organization impulsively blows through its developmental stages where little satisfaction accrues. It will establish a basic instability in character.

There are two ways of going about helping such organizations. One is prevention, the other intervention. Prevention will be the most important, because such organizations are still emerging on the landscape. Helping these organizations develop sound constitutional and supporting character structures to begin with may be the best assurance for their success. Remediating organizations that are already broken, especially if the pathogenic process has taken hold, will be much harder.

Remediation will largely need to focus on the character as it has come to exist and presents. In the case of a work aggressive or work dramatic type, appropriate support will need to help slow down the system's constant activity, which is driven by anxiety. Consultative support will need to help those in the system step back and look more broadly at what is going on. With a vision blocked type, you will have to especially work with the leadership and those below in the system to not get trapped in overconcentrating power at the top. Relieving the pressure stuck at the top will be important, as will developing structural, muscular definition in the middle line and operating core. Regardless of the character type, the sociotherapeutic goal will always be to pull the organization in from its tendency to ever-expand its boundaries and help it better tolerate, concentrate and discharge its energy. Helping such organizations think about, then develop, well-honed mechanisms and organizational processes to do this will help build binding infrastructures. So will help enacting norms that support such concentration of effort. This will entail helping those in the system to see through the illusion that such concentration will be "limiting to their freedom." That, in a way is the point. You are helping them to become very good at *focusing charge*, not spraying their efforts all over the place or elsewise covering it up. As you work with them, it will also be essential to help them identify with their core work democratic strivings—to help those in the system *feel* them—seeing and differentiating their urge for genuine creativity from something that is just impulsive. The major way out of the workplace trap must always better enable an organization's people, individually and collectively, to work from the heart: what gives its people real fulfillment in the work process and in the fulfillment of its goods and services.

In the case of prevention, the effort will not be to fix or redesign broken systems, but to support the design of an organizational network that leads to genuine fulfillment, objectively and humanly. This will require substantial work with a founding or newly minted leadership group to design an operating model that accords with the healthy dimensions of an organization network: the power of a clear central vision, supported by robust *and* flexible infrastructures that give both needed definition *and* elasticity to remain adroit and inventive. Helping the leadership understand how self-regulating teams must be formed and connected as an ensemble will also be part of this operating model development effort. The connectivity of the teams, up down, across and outside the nascent cross-cutting segments, will require sufficient scorecards, channels and networks.

This can be done in work design efforts, highly collaborative with the leadership team, joined by others, that are socio-technical in effect in the sense Trist first identified. The prevention effort must allow time to work through and fulfill the natural work of each of the socioemotional stages as the young organization passes through them. *This will help the firm literally firm up.* It will help keep it from becoming atomized—the great risk inherent in the network form. *I anticipate such efforts at prevention will be what largely makes OD's contributions in the future substantial*:

> This is the pivotal contribution practitioners in the field [of OD] can now make: The development of network enterprises—their overall architectures, infrastructures, cultures and leaderships— is the core work of a re-birthed OD. Due to the network organization's very complexity and collaborative nature, this work must be carried out in a collaborative design process, a full partnership between consultant and client system, one that considers the enterprise as a whole open system in its socio-technical dimensions.[13]

Helping organizations *not* overreach in the beginning, to do what they must while coming to *emotionally tolerate needed development* will be critical for the consultant. You will need to help them understand the self-defeating efforts of premature expansion.

As an example: It sure seems that many help desks of service-oriented firms operating today directly reflect the *lack* of governing understanding what the network age requires—effective access to on-line, 24/7 support. To say some of these service support functions today—and the executive groups that fund and sanction them—are not-ready-for-prime-time is, I think, a generous way to put it. The firm's *prematurity* in getting such support functions out there for the first time—without sufficient hiring practices, empowered roles, training and their own supporting systems—is the source of the difficulty to be faced. Labeling them "customer care centers" will only prove disingenuous. Few of the firm's customers or its own people will be fooled. Efforts at prevention can help preempt costly intervention later—which sometimes will frankly just be too late. Unwanted turnover in customers and employees will be in high gear.

ONE MORE DARK SIDE TO OBVIATE

Network enterprises have one more dark side for practitioners to help obviate, a side that when it goes bad can represent out-and-out pathology.

> One aspect of this future work will be for practitioners to help organizations better understand and move through the "dark side" of networks. It is a commonsense observation that network connections between people can be superficial, and because of their transparency lead to anxiety and issues of trust. [Some social media sites] among users are an example. Technology is not a magic bullet. It can be used in limiting, self-defeating ways and as we've seen in cyber-security breaches an instrument for corrupt ends. Just because organizations are functioning networks is no guarantee of them creating deeper patterns of human connection and authenticity.[14]

When the security breaches of an organization are continuous and beyond its structured means to address, this will likely mark the point of no return for the enterprise, even when it is joined by others. Short of a transnational global framework for action, no amount of help will be enough to address the data and human network breaches that bad actors in social media use for nefarious ends, political and otherwise, across the globe.

Whether addressing the characterological limitations or their more warped pathologies, the need will always be for practitioners to help others zero in on the essential. Consultants will need to understand that any wishes of their own to evade issues and avoid hitting things directly on the head will do little good in their work with a system dedicated to addressing its difficulties. Tact and timing for readiness are of course one thing; running away from the issues quite another. Effective consultants must help such an organization's people and the organization as a whole come to see what they are good at as well as how they are ineffective. Practitioners are at their best when they help people in systems not be afraid of their potential for greatness—or to come to grips with their own shortcomings that threaten their viability and greatness, not papering them over or using means that have no real chance of success.

As Reich said in his famous talk to "the Little Man" in us all: "A doctor, a shoemaker, mechanic or educator has to know his shortcomings if he is to do his work and earn his living."[15] Fundamental issues in whatever one's work is call out to be faced. The great man or great woman in each of us knows this. A hundred years earlier, Thoreau put it this way:

> I would not be one of those who will foolishly drive a nail into mere lath and plastering, such a deed would keep me awake nights. Give me a hammer and let me feel for the furrowing. Do not depend on the putty. Drive a nail home and clinch it so faithfully that you can wake up in the night and think of your work with satisfaction—a work which you would not be ashamed to invoke the Muse.[16]

This is of course no different in any age, network era or not. The larger laws of work and life apply.

CHAPTER 9

SOCIAL IMPLICATIONS, TODAY AND TOMORROW

O rganizations, in the end, represent a special case of a social system. They are mini- or *micro social systems*, but with defining features that make them more specialized in their development and functioning than wider, *macro social phenomena*. Our final chapter explores what an energic understanding of organizations implies for understanding the larger social world.

Reich made the great leap forward in understanding social phenomena in these terms, beginning with his *Mass Psychology* and as he opened it up much more fundamentally in his discovery of orgone energy and subsequent investigations. The present chapter builds on his work only as further rudimentary exploration and from what I have learned about the nature of organizational systems. Because this chapter on social implications is exploratory, though grounded I believe on a sound basis, much of what follows is inferential and represents my own reflections. But the implications I think have significance for understanding the life of society in new ways—for understanding pivotal dynamics in social movements, change and institutional reform. And the implications build more widely on the main interests of this book: thinking about rehumanizing the workplace, today and in the future.

WHAT IS SOCIETY?

So, what is society? The human animal is a biosocial, energetic creature by nature, as we have contended from the beginning of this book. Human "society" does not stand outside our existence as creatures. From conception through birth, our sociality is part and parcel of what has made us and makes us who we are. Our biological energies stream together and constitute a world over and above us and, at the same time, are the very ground from which we emerge as social creatures in the first place.

Reich understood this energy as the life force per se that permeates all living things and whose purely physical source imbues all of nature itself, including nonliving natural systems, such as weather systems. Experimentally, he found this energy pervades the atmosphere, making the idea of a physical vacuum essentially a special case of a distilled movement of the ubiquitous energy he termed orgone.

In human affairs, it is commonplace to say, "We do not live in a vacuum." We are surrounded by a social field of energy in which we move. Lewin was among the first social scientists to make this explicit. Reich's understanding, because it was rooted in a tangible understanding of the energy's natural properties, makes this understanding of the "social field" literally come alive. A larger social unit begins to form the moment two or more people come together to live, work and play—often in pursuit of shared or common ends. This is the beginning of any collective human social form, including that of the family, a community or a commonwealth. Our energies *associate*. Under positive conditions, these social forms represent inherent, spontaneous movements of energy, mutually pursued. And when supported, they can lead to ends that are fulfilled and are experienced as fulfilling, exciting in fact, and after a period of buildup, concentration and discharge are followed by a feeling of ease and relaxation.

These shared ends or functions can be tightly or loosely bound. Organizations represent a form that is relatively loosely coupled compared to a biological system. Families, too, by virtue of divorce or death, are definitionally more loosely bound than a biological system. Living systems are bound by a skin, a membrane. Social systems of all kinds have no physical membrane—though, as they grow, they come to have customs and, for very many, religious rites and rituals to bind and perpetuate them based on our more inherent longings to be together. Religious rites also provide an anthropological channel to be at one with—and feel at home in—the cosmos.

As organizations are peopled, they consist of intermeshing living systems that join together temporarily and intervally (of shorter or longer durations) for a larger unitary aim or set of aims. *When we speak of society more generally as the field in which individual life and organizations arise, we are addressing a phenomenon that is even more loosely coupled.* Its functioning is naturally less bounded than an organization and certainly less so than that of the individual human animals who live within it. *The coming together that represents a social order serves the function of creating the context in which even more distinct forms of life are born and are borne.* This is true I think whether that social order is that of a family, another small group, association or an organization.

As I have argued throughout this book, organizations develop character structures that serve as boundary defining, mediating functions between inner and outer energetic demands. Their character structures arise and operate within the organization itself. They help distinguish the organization from the rest of the world and set the terms with which it largely engages in it. The language that has been used in business and in social science more generally to describe this character is that of "organization culture." This gives the organization identity and its stamp of life. For our purposes, organization character is more specific than the concept of organization culture, as it specifically refers to the energetic function of culture: mediating inner and outer worlds in the way energies within the system stream, buildup and concentrate, and discharge for joint effect. Or how they can otherwise get inhibited in compromised functioning. Additionally, character mediates what and how much energy is allowed to enter the system from the outer world after it is up and running.

Culture, as the term was originally used in anthropology, also of course has an external meaning. An organization, in addition to having its own internal culture or character, also resides in a wider culture that lies outside of it, and, in its own way, *mediates the field's interactions* with the systems within it. This use of the word culture is consistent with what we mean when we say a microscopic form of biological life is "cultured" in a laboratory. Culture in this sense is the surrounding external medium that nourishes and helps give the organism sustenance to grow—or, if it is a toxic medium, can kill the organism by sucking its energy out to serve its own functions. The wider culture conditions the life of the organism. This is just so as families condition the developing life of the child within them, positively or negatively. Families do not necessarily determine the course of the child's life after birth, because the child has his own vitality, his own life, his own resilience. Under favorable conditions, families can help children thrive and flourish. However, under bad conditions, families, as well as other social conditions, can impair and quell the life in their children; the parents can soak up their energy for their own purposes, while the children develop neurotic defense mechanisms—character structures and chronic armor—that sooner or later prove dysfunctional.

In the same way, though generally more loosely bounded, societies, it surely seems, condition the organizations that operate within them. The organization by virtue of its peopled life and natural, core functions has its own energy and ways it wants to move. In this sense, after the organization's conception and birth, it is innately free; it is not "caused" by the larger social order. But its continuing life is certainly affected by its surrounding conditions. Those conditions can support and nourish the organization's vitality and life, or, under adverse circumstances, they can prove damaging. Under the poorest conditions, the effects can be toxic. The toxic outer state may then give rise to a toxic, inner organizational state. The system builds its own defensive organization character and armor to protect itself. But eventually the organization's character and armor can prove hobbling. When this is the case, founders and the wider social and economic culture in which an organization is born can produce toxic internal cultures. In this way, the bigger "life of society" is almost always a factor in considering the health and pathology of any given organization—and, as a wider matter, the workplace at large. The prevalence today of what I have called the workplace trap indicates the toxic effects of the wider social order in which organizations today operate. For example, if the animating drive for organizations routinely gets turned into *only* making money (capital accumulation for its own sake divorced from systems' natural work functions), the workplace will be compromised. Work will by and large suffer in society and people will be widely unfulfilled at work. The biosocial energies of people will go haywire *en masse*.

When this happens, many other problems ensue. Overall, the society may turn its own energies inward in ways that are especially distorted, constraining and walled in. *Social armoring* may thus develop. In their own integral and core spontaneous movement, individuals and smaller social units within the larger social order may eventually come crashing through its armored walls in a fury. In fact, all hell may break loose, as Freud originally feared, but ascribed to a metaphysical defect in man. Reich helps us to appreciate this as Freud intended in his description without discounting it at all. But Reich's work also allows us to see this distorting phenomenon more deeply without resorting to metaphysical explanations—and, if we are up to it, to find a fuller way out.

SOCIAL MOVEMENTS, CHANGE AND INSTITUTIONAL REFORM

Some propositions, followed by discussion and examples:

- Social movements are the spontaneous movement of human energy that has at least started to concentrate for an emergent end; the movement of human energy begins to *amass*.

- The pulsing of human biosocial energy for buildup, charge, discharge and relief is *always* at the core of social movements. These are reflected in people's coming together for unitary movement and discharge of their energies.

- *Emotionally*, people coming together in social movements (or social process) of any kind or scale reflects their longing for support, to belong, and for achievement. This is neither good nor bad in itself. *It is.*

- These longings are *natural, human needs* that seek fulfillment; when not, they are frustrated, reflected in their poor concentration and expression socially.

- Social movements run the gamut from being those that are generally *healthy*—that is, that move in the direction of freedom and further support of spontaneous, creative movement—to those that are more *pathological*, where the twisting and chronic constriction of the energy's more natural movement is such that it produces destructive, sometimes very violent effects, inwardly and outwardly.

- The direction—or *aim*—of a social movement is not always known in advance but its course—*or coursing*—becomes clearer as it is enacted and gains force.

- There *is an excited and whirling quality* to the movement as it gathers steam. It also to a greater or lesser extent creates a *stir*, positive or negative, in the wider field within which it occurs and has emerged.

- Social movements are themselves *conditioned by their wider fields*, affecting them in operating freely and constructively or in highly reactive, constricted ways that can then be abruptly loosed and destructive.

- Social movements *may or may not be tightly bound*. The closer they function with associations and even organizations at their helm, the tighter they will tend to draw *boundaries* around themselves. They will develop a regularity about them, customary ways of doing things—say, *customs* and *traditions*. As they move to more highly concentrated, organized states, they will develop *rules and laws.*

- Social movements, depending on the state of their development and organization, develop a *character* about them, qualities that describe *their state of movement, including their vibrancy (or charge) or their stagnation (stasis).*

- They also generally *induce the rise of leaders* to help bring the movement to *a head.* In the movement, they too may be healthy or more pathologic in effect. This will always be a function of *the nature and character of the social movement* as it works upon their individual character structures.

- As they develop, all human social movements also appear to give rise to *ideologies*—cognitive and emotionally rooted expressions of their aims and interests—that *attract or repel* people from participation in them.

- Depending on the nature and development of the social movement, and the extent of its constructiveness or destructiveness, *the ideology can function either rationally or as "rationalization"* (in the sense that it serves as an excuse for the movement that is destructive). The rationalization may claim the effort is in the service of freedom when it is destructive of free movement; the words alone used do not reflect the movement's actual course.

- Social movements *naturally constitute networks and channels* for interaction and communication among their participants and those in its field. These can be rudimentary or more sophisticated in form, depending on the level of organization that has developed and technology available.

- Constructive, *organized* efforts to bring change to a social movement, will succeed or fail to the extent they take account of these dynamics.

These propositions are variously illustrated throughout history and in today's world. They bode significance I believe for the future of our social world.

As leisure time became more available during the Industrial Revolution, organized play and team sports such as baseball in America first developed and spread. Such a social movement was relatively benign, bringing pleasure to many. But it was not without its inner constrictions and armored social walls. Play in the leagues that had formed was off-limits to ball players of color. This eventually gave rise to the self-organizing of the first Negro Leagues in the late nineteenth century. Social movements in art and music have largely been benign, direct expressions of creative energy, and in watered-down fashion, "popular culture."

But some social movements whose purposes concentrate around positive social aims face incredible risk for holding those aims: counterforces that are engendered to stop them. The nineteenth century's Underground Railroad—literally a human network that extended from the Southeast, Midwest and Northeastern United States and Canada—served entirely positive social aims, helping slaves gain freedom. *Free movement* was its ends and means—*and of those born by nature to be free, not what social convention deemed*. But the movement and its emergent leaders like Harriet Tubman did so at great threat, confrontation and human cost. Slave patrols arose, organized from families, neighborhoods and state legislatures to hunt down fugitive slaves, inspiring terror, beatings and death. These patrols were predecessors to the Ku Klux Klan that shot up at the close of the Civil War to violently fight slavery's end and aftermath. The Klan reflected a purely malignant, metastasizing social movement built on grotesquely whipped-up socioemotional drives. Lynching became its peak, perverse, *unitizing* thrill: ritualized, collective strangulation, cutting off the breathing and life of another. While the Klan long continued as an underground movement (literally veiled), continued custom and administration of the law remained on its side, and race ideology was completely part of its fabric.

At base, the Klan's continued spread and aims functioned to suck out the life of others and feed off them—to feed off what had originated from *the forced labor, the usurped work energy*, of others. And the

Klan has been but one, if highly concentrated, expression of the pathology. *This was the social cancer that was left unresolved at the time of America's conception as a country, a pathological state of character I believe antithetical to the Union's nature.*[1] *This deep, energetic contradiction is what continues to give "racecraft" its great force in America to this day.*[2] Despite huge gains in freedom, at huge human costs, the cancer is still with us. The Civil War and over 150 years of political, legislative and educational reform since, still have not been able to fully do the job. The energetic dimensions are still not clearly seen. That *may* render nearly impossible fuller mobilization to bring it to an end. It has been ingrained, strictly speaking, in the *character* of the nation.

The inner energetic propulsion of all social movements, positive or negative, tends to have them push onward and outward—to expand in their wider field—after their initial gathering of energy. Depending on the nature of its function (both as conceived and as it emerges), such expansion can be constructive or destructive—or an admixture of the two. Another example from the nineteenth century is America's westward expansion; the spontaneous draw of people to the West opened up possibilities for further peopled movement and settlement from the East, including the building of the first transcontinental railroad joining the country as one. But the push to drive west also portended destruction of indigenous peoples, herds of animals like the buffalo, and land. Like consequences seem inherent in all imperial forms of expansion.

I want to make note that, depending on its nature, some social armoring in and of itself may be quite positive: The destruction of wildlife and the land in the US in the nineteenth century gave rise to a natural social movement to build healthy walls—healthy armor as it were—to defend against this. The National Park movement arose to set aside nature preserves that people could perpetually enjoy without fear of the wilderness areas' destruction. Even members of the cavalry were dispatched to watch over the areas and protect them against harm.

Compared to Western peoples, indigenous societies' rites and rituals were quite affirming of life in the wild and as people spaciously roamed; they did not try to tightly domesticate and "bound" life and the land. Yet they also had elaborate oral traditions, and some indigenous nations like the Cherokee developed sophisticated constitutions. Indigenous peoples could be armored certainly in their own way, they could have both extemporaneous and organized bursts of butchery and violence. But as cultures they remained animistic about nature, not primarily mechanistic and mystical as in Occidental and Oriental civilizations that had more elaborated forms of armor, despite the positives that also accompanied their social dynamics.[3]

These are all examples of *animating* social energy at work. The whipping up of the energy as it moves—the *circling* of the wagons—its concentration and turning inward, but then *getting stuck in the face of threats,* is what gives rise to its chronic character and armor and the bursts of energy to push past them. *For good or ill.* The threats come from without, from the wider, moving and encircling social field. They can also come to arise from within the social unit itself; as the energy concentrates inside, it can get stuck with threats then gelling there. Crime within a society (or subgroup of society) is an example. Piracy on the high seas reflects both external field threats and internal development gone haywire. Great emotional energy, terror and fear, accompany these movements.

We see a kind of piracy operating today on the economic landscape. Many corporatized, capital enterprises "appropriate," as Marx would say, the labor-power of free men and women, where they no longer have a direct relationship to the products of their work. This is a deeply anchored social phenomenon with accompanying ideological rationalizations. This sets the stage, I have come to see, for the emergence and perpetuation of the modern workplace trap, where human unhappiness—and lack of fulfillment—at work are so common. People's natural, spontaneous work energies become encased in organization character structures and armor. Whatever else Marx may not have gotten right, he seems to be analytically correct in his understanding of the labor theory of value and labor's appropriation for ends which are not inherent to the nature of the work performed.

The amelioration of this at a wider social level does not essentially lie in politically organized, social engineering, which at times can make the situation quite worse. Those may be partial fixes and sometimes necessary, and even then, they will carry a cost. Generally, more organic, freer work-democratic means, as Reich described, it seems will prove vital to turn the tide. I will return to this below in this chapter's section on Rehumanizing the Workplace, including the limitations that are imposed on organization reformation, while not rendering change, even of a significant sort, impossible.

Social armor can exist in clustered communities and at wider social unit levels. Professional milieus of all types can and do develop armor, drawing explicit and implicit boundaries in what is acceptable and unacceptable in how people act and what they think. University departments are certainly like that, as reflected in the old saw "publish or perish" and in other conventions, too; such convention can at times support and at other times prejudice free inquiry. On a macro scale, social armoring can be a regional, national or global phenomenon, reflecting cultures in the anthropological sense, each with their own variations. Social mobilization, such as occurred in World Wars I and II and amidst the fear of WW III, represented literal armed, social movements of global scale. Today, the alarm, reactions and non-reactions to global warming represent worldwide social movements tied to industrial civilization, replete with political ideologies, right and left. (That doesn't mean all opinions on the subject have equal merit. There is an objective truth—Nature—that in the end will have the last word.) While certainly driven by the individual structures of bad actors, nefarious social media hacks and abuse represent *systemic* social movements. They have gathered steam in our times. Social armoring is acute in the actions and reactions of people *en masse*.

Challenges to social armor as it has come to pass may be rational, as in the case of the Underground Railroad, or it may be irrational (that is to say, destructive). The way the movement for *Liberté, Egalité, Fraternité* of the French Revolution turned into the bloodbaths of Robespierre, giving impetus to a new reaction in the rise of "emperor" Napoleon, is an example of such a destructive turning of a social movement. The overthrow of the Russian Czar to Stalin's forced famine of millions is another. The burning of the *Reichstag* for its failings that signaled Hitler's rise and the German Nazi party—its march to the unspeakable—is yet another. In each case, the distorted leadership that arose both reflected the groundswell mass social movement underneath it and helped wind it tighter, ever more crushing to anything in its path. Reich's descriptions of this in *The Mass Psychology of Fascism* and in *Listen, Little Man!* are masterful.[4] Reich understood *the energetic, emotional movement of what quite specifically gathered, got twisted, then violently burst forth.* These cannot simply be "political" movements, I believe, of which one holds varying "opinions." Surely they encompass that. But more largely they represent emotional, energetically driven phenomena that can be seen if the observer is sufficiently open. *These are actual socioemotional phenomena.*

Reich's special name for a socially destructive energetic movement was "The Emotional Plague." Like the bubonic plague of the Middle Ages, Reich understood that the whipped-up fury the emotional plague betokened was that of a contagion, destructive in both ends and means, a biosocial pestilence. His hope was that honest men and women would be able to clearly spot it; find effective means to combat or quarantine it; and for the rise of something he envisioned as a growing, constructive movement of "social psychiatry," understood in bioenergetic terms. Here too his emphasis was on protection of life and on prevention, more than intervention. Intervention at this level he came to see might well be too late, run the risk of getting caught up in the maelstrom, and make things worse.

Social movements are wave-like phenomena, so treating them as mechanical matters to be engineered, reengineered, or simply behaviorized out of existence do not measure up from the outset. This of course has implications for what might be thoughtful public policy and education. But even these in and of themselves, it seems, will often not be enough. Clearer resolution I think will largely require fashioning ways to *surf* the waves, steering through them, and getting out of the way so that the spontaneous movement of energy struggling for expression—especially that which is profoundly healthy—can concentrate and come forth; not denying healthy movement, pretending it does not exist, or otherwise holding it back. Sometimes this will need to be done gradually, if a mass of frustrated energy has accumulated so its expression does not end up in a crash. Even so, it seems inescapable that good judgment and feel for what the situation is at hand will need to be applied for best effect by those who seek to do good.

Mass movements, as Eric Hoffer long ago recognized, are not all healthy. He had a real feel for their pathology. But he tended to treat *all* modern social movements as pathology. He did not see the spontaneous movement of creative energy, freely moving to join with others as healthy, constructive at their source. Sometimes, were I able to say it to Hoffer today, charity *is* charity. Sometimes creative joint effort on a large scale is just what any good doctor would order. Hoffer did not give adequate attention to this, tending to see participation in social movements as only the mark of a "true believer." Were those who fought Hitler in World War II simply "true believers?" Or did something deeper, more objectively grounded animate them? "True believers," as Hoffer characterizes, exist surely, as I hoped I have illustrated here, including in tidal-size destructive movements today. Mass confusion is hardly a thing of the past. But Hoffer himself it seems turned his view into something of a true belief.[5]

Human social movement of all kinds needs a deep look in terms of understanding functions of natural energy systems. There are movements and there are movements. Distinctions are important between authoritarianisms of all kinds, on the one hand, and genuinely more self-regulating, work-democratic forms of social life, on the other. Not all unbridled social movement will lead to the anarchy, the wild unleashing of the *id*, that Freud feared. Yes, we see some of this in effect on the social scene today, much more I think than many people are prepared to look at flat on. Thus, due attention is best given to that which is actually pent up; or which may be difficult to live all at once; or before people feel fully ready to do so. Human caring in social undertakings, in their formation or reformation and in the nature of their aims, is decisive.

Healthy movements, spontaneously organized—like the Underground Railroad or the well-functioning jazz ensemble—will find ways to order themselves on their own accord and in very human terms along the work democratic lines that Reich envisioned. These are rooted in one's natural care for one's work and for people. Rigid formal hierarchies, heavily armored, are not necessarily inevitable. Healthy and unhealthy social units, families or organizations, can and do exist. People who seek to move forward will need to discover which are which generally by themselves—and as they work with others they are close to and have real affection for and common aims with. Constructive movement forward cannot generally be imposed or superimposed from above. It must grow from within, conditioned by hospitable environments. Part of this, but only part, is encouragement by those who arise as leaders who call forth our best. We all carry the burden and possibility of life inside us and with those on our journeys, together and alone.

We are all leaders. Followers too. The question, as Reich asked, is *will we have the courage to follow our inner voice, to do life's bidding, to not turn away as do hard and timid souls, who only do it because life has passed them by?*[6] Reich, I was impressed when I first read him, despite his deep appreciation of the difficulties, remained open to the idea that life, in the end, will find a way. That is because he saw what is at root in life is not an idea but, in the first instance, a natural fact.

REHUMANIZING THE WORKPLACE

Today's toxic workplace is a macro social phenomenon. Our organizations are micro social reflections of a range of predominant characterological disorders, as I have contended throughout these pages. In organizations, work energy congeals at manageable levels of collective action and for the system's renewal. *I would generally argue, more than political and legislative and educational action, our work institutions—organization by organization, and vital work, activity by activity—are the most central nexus for effective social action.* This is where people make their living and live so much of their lives in close proximity and concert with others.

Color prejudice in America, for example, was given one of its greatest social blows *via voluntary action in the workplace* in the brave and creative partnership that emerged between the Dodgers' Jackie Robinson and Branch Rickey—and in the social mobilization that occurred in its run up. It did *not* come from immediate political or legislative action. As Rickey told Robinson at the outset in their joint gamble, "You will need to beat them on the *field*." Despite all the pointed threats and hostility, Robinson did that decisively in his creative, spontaneous and brilliant play. Many ballplayers and fans alike came for the first time to see the hollowness of the old racial animus. They *owned* the observation. Together, they came to love the game more than ever and a significant dent was made in longstanding, destructive social armor, not just in baseball but in the wider social field.[7]

Organizations, large and small, are certainly affected by the wider social dynamics that surround them. The dynamics of capital economies pose conditions under which companies are founded, develop and in which the mass of people who work are employed and earn their livelihoods. These conditions, unfortunately, include clouding the purposes of the work to be performed. Accumulating capital as an end in itself can begin to take precedence over the goods and services produced and their contribution to life. This is to be distinguished from the buildup of capital essential to the life and continuity of the business; that serves a primary work function of the organization. But accumulation of capital, *when it takes on a life of its own,* is another matter. That can be quite evident in many mid- to large-size enterprises, though small businesses too are not exempt. Unfortunately, intermediating tasks, structures and processes can develop inside the firm, serving principal functions of capital acquisition for its own sake divorced from the larger natural function of the enterprise; energy will be drawn away from the integrity of product, process and the human relationships needed in their creation and fulfillment. Under these conditions, people's energies that seek gratification in work and achievement will inevitably get compromised. The individual workplace becomes a trap. When this happens in organization after organization, we can clearly see a wider social process is in play.

The way such distorted intermediating functions distance people from their own labor power is not limited to capital enterprises. When power concentrates in the hands of managerial elites in formally not-for-profit enterprise, the same effects seem to accrue. People become more or less alienated from the products and processes of their own labors; the intervening administrative or managerial layers draw up and direct their energies of spontaneous functioning, frequently to debilitating effect. When too much energy pools up at the middle and the top of such systems, the entity becomes congested or fails to fully function. Firms become less and less self-regulating. They become "run," *their people feel run.* The worst form of these, as Reich came to identify in his *Mass Psychology,* are the totalitarian-run states, right or left, that concentrate the means of production in the hands of a ruling elite—*state-run capital enterprise.*[8] Oligopolies and monopolies are the result. Free movement on the field is inhibited, sometimes altogether blocked. There is little "market movement," sometimes in the short run at least.[9] The names and faces of the players and big dogs may change, but the *character of the work* is the same.

Hand-in-hand with ever widening activity in service of capital accumulation in the trap becomes conspicuous consumption. *This accumulation and consumption for their own sake become significant products of the trap,* sometimes what stand out most as their products and effects. Sadly, I think, organizations' functions in finance, marketing and sales, executives and staff, too often help assure this is so, beyond their more natural, healthy functions to be performed. On the Hill in the US, and in like ways in other countries, lobbying seeks to assure this too as external drives into the field. People's *needs* when this is the situation get sacrificed, subordinated in service of distorted aims. Think, for example, of the cost of life-saving pharmaceuticals in the US. Whose interests—and what functions—are served? I conclude this is the character of the organizations and the character of the wider social dynamics profoundly in play.

Furthermore, needs get turned ever more into cravings and wants—by those seeking to accumulate and by those seeking to consume more and more. *Natural functions get twisted and proliferate in their twistedness.* The chase after imagery and *symbols* of happiness—not the gratification of a job well done—becomes the brass ring. These are not just the excesses of what Galbraith called "The Affluent Society"; I believe they reflect Debord's much more characterologically perceptive, *"La Société Du Spectacle."*[10] These wider conditions set the terms for organizations to get stuck in work aggressive or other compromised strivings. They set the terms for their people, as well as those touched at home and beyond, to get stuck in breathless or quiet desperation, a treadmill that people will frequently experience as impossible to get off. I have heard many people in my work and others more generally speak of this with anguish.

Often, all this feverish chase is rationalized as "the way it is." This is often the holding of proponents *and* opponents of the prevailing order. But need it be so? Are the manifold forms of the chase what are at root of the troubles? Or are they too symptoms, indicative of something else literally at work? *I believe understanding this "something else" at a social level of analysis points the way out of the work-*

place trap, at individual organizational levels and, in aggregate, on the wider social scene.

There are exceptions to those firms that principally go into business, and continue to do business, to "make money." The Disney Company, as I argued in Chapter 4, has kept the center of its founding function front and center—to offer pleasure through entertainment media for the enduring child in us all. For over a century, the primary purpose of its world of companies has *not* been that of wealth creation; those remained by-products and subordinate to its primary *work* aims. The problem of making capital-formation primary, and not keeping it instrumental, is that it will always distort the nature of an enterprise; it will distort the organization's nature *constitutionally* and bleed through all its later development and functioning. Its *work function* will definitionally get subordinated, not devoted to mutually fulfilling ends within and in the field. Gratifying achievement at all levels, individually and corporately, will be compromised.

In some ways, Disney is the exception that proves the rule: Organizations, I have argued, are founded in the first instance through free movement that congeals around a core function. It surely takes fortitude for a firm to stay focused on the principal animating aims of its work, especially in a socioeconomic world pressing in with other conventions. However, such exceptions will always be with us just because work energy is at the biosocial root of human existence, as Reich elucidated. Society doesn't forever stand over and above the individual. Our social formations and forms are reflections of something that is *innately* human—and therefore they are malleable in line with genuine human needs, should people remain open and up to it. This makes possible the end, as Reich put it, "to harmonize the conditions and forms of work with the need to work and the pleasure of work."[11]

The ingenuity to start a business—or begin any human endeavor that engages another in any way—represents the spontaneous movement of this primal energy itself. Human social movements and social forms, even when they are tightly bound, are not monoliths. More-over, while made up of human creatures, social forms are not animals in and of themselves; thus, *by nature*, they do not have tightly bound life spans as long as their *natural* functions in their field remain vi-able. Social units and systems at root are fundamentally in motion. However, those that have become chronically armored (their natural movement persistently blocked) remain frozen—until they sooner or later die.

When founded on compromised functions, all social systems—be they families, movements, organizations or nation states—buildup, divide and block energy in a way that forms the ground for them to especially run their course. Families may suddenly split. Movements may peter out. Imperial expansion will come to an end—and then collapse. Empires throughout history, not just Rome, have risen and fallen. In contrast, social systems that keep more of their vital spark alive—*their natural energies freely moving, building and discharg-ing*—stand a better chance of weathering changing social conditions for longer times. Even when the changing conditions are not neces-sarily hospitable, the systems that are able to handle themselves this way will tend to be more resilient.

So, what does all this mean for the workplace writ large? How do we better tap into this root biosocial energy on a wide scale for greater fulfillment at work? What must we do as communities and people? And once begun, how do we keep it going?

Here too, Reich is instructive. His answer, in a way, is simple. *We do what has always been done, nothing more; what is there lying in wait and if we do what is in our inmost hearts to do.* Again, in his talk to the "little man" in each of us seeking a better way (and he does not exempt himself), Reich says:

> [You ask,] "What then must I do to be the mainstay of society?" Nothing new or unusual. Just go on doing what you're already doing: Till your field, wield your hammer, examine your patient, take your children out playing or to school, write articles about

the events of the day, investigate the secrets of nature. You're already doing all these things, but you think they're unimportant and that only what Marshall Medalchest or Prince Blowhard says or does is important. . . .

If once you knew that you *do* count for something, that you *do* have a sound opinion of your own, that your field and factory are meant to provide for *life* and not for death, then little man, you yourself would be able to answer the question you just asked. . . .

Just go on doing what you've been doing and wanting to do all along, work, let your children grow up happy, love your mate at night. . . . It is all in your hands.[12]

This, Reich encourages us to know, is within our grasp. *It is the living energy in life that we each must accord its due.*

To do this, it is incumbent on us to understand how we habitually come to undercut this in our lives—in our typical actions and reactions at work and at home—whenever we are divorced from our basic feeling for life, when we cut ourselves off from the stream of life inside us and inside others. Reich, unlike so many others who watered this down, was unstinting in clarifying how cutting oneself off from the living and feeling of life *always* adversely shows up in the provinces of love, work and knowledge—the twisting of our sexual and work energies and in our ability to see and think clearly. We set ourselves up for getting lost this way time and again—and in an infinite variety of ways—when we make too much of our adopted conventions; when we confuse what is secondary with that which is fundamental; and when we stray from what is primal in life because of our great fear of being alive.

That we have gotten off course, Reich tells us, is not originally our fault, conditions being what they are. But, he says, it is our responsibility to take care of it in each of our lives. This cannot be delegated to "diplomats or power politicians," he says, whether in our workplaces or on the larger social stage. We have to begin to make the move, deep within ourselves and joined by others of like heart and mind, if we want something truly better in our lives and world. We need to take the world into our own hands, not blindly but with open eyes.

Yes, there is individual therapy, important for each to make use of as may be helpful personally and in our families. But because the energy is ubiquitous in our wider social lives, and the social world is so dominant, Reich gave precedence in that realm to focusing on what he called *"vital, necessary work."* That, as he saw it, along with prevention of destructive conditions for children and adolescents, was the essential ground for wider social betterment, human achievement and fulfillment.

Reich understood vital, necessary work to be all work whose performance is *"vital to the existence of society."* This includes, in addition to that performed by industrial and corporate workers, "the physician, teacher, technician, laboratory worker, writer, social administrator, farmer, scientific worker, etc." Reich is driving at all work that is inherently rational in its aims and goods. The definition Reich gives us allows us to better see that the emergence and actions of power-politicians, because they feed off what is primary in the life of society, are always secondary and frequently irrational. They are *not* primary work functions. In healthy organizations, the rise of such secondary ways of functioning is rendered substantially moot. In such a healthy case, as Reich describes, "the self-administration of the firm" is carried out by those responsible for performing the vital, necessary work. Formal, politically charged bureaucracies—those I have identified with organizational-level character disorders—are *not* effectively self-managed. Their inherent self-regulating capabilities are sharply limited because their free movement is sharply constrained. What have come to be obstructive, internal, systemic functions usurp a great deal of their energies.

The work democratic character is qualitatively different in how it functions. It is expressly self-regulating in line with more natural ways of working—i.e., the way the work energy naturally moves when conditions are favorable. As I have argued from the beginning pages of this book, that energy is inherent in all organizational life to begin with as it forms and evolves; it is not something grafted onto the system or engineered into existence. This energy is able to flourish in organizations whose characters directly function work democratically. This kind of organization develops organically from its early years on as long as it is able to move through new challenging conditions it may encounter. Its character supports and optimally reflects the nature of its work democratic energies without stymying their flow, so its health tends to be self-regenerating.

Reich's precise use of the term work democracy is unparalleled. It is not so much that it is a structural reality with behavioral dimensions, as others who have used very similar terms, such as Emery and Thorsud, have discussed.[13] It does come to have such features, yes. But its essence lay elsewhere: *Reich alone saw the biosocial energy at root in work democratic modes of functioning. Just so, work democratic processes are present from the beginning of an enterprise—and they exist whether the system is functioning in a healthy way or in a chronically inhibited state that feeds off its energy's dynamics.* This represents an entirely new basis for understanding in the social sciences. Expressed in its broad terms as Reich originally defined:

> Work democracy is the natural process of love, work, and knowledge that governed, governs, and will continue to govern economy and man's social and cultural life as long as there has been, is, and will be a society. Work democracy is the sum total of all functions of life governed by the rational interpersonal relations that have come into being, grown, and developed in a natural and organic way.

> Work democracy is not an ideological system. Nor is it a "political" system which could be imposed upon human society by the propaganda of a party, individual politicians, or any group sharing a common ideology. There is no single, formal political measure by means of which work democracy could be "introduced." Work democracy cannot be introduced in the same way as a republic or totalitarian dictator is introduced. There is a very sim-

ple reason for this: *Natural work democracy is always present and is always functioning, whether this or that political party or ideological group know of its existence or not.* The process of natural work democracy can be in diametrical opposition to social institutions or it can be more or less in accord with them. Wherever it functions, however, this work democratic process demands that the social ideologies and institutions be brought into line with natural needs and interpersonal relations, in the same way it is clearly expressed in natural love, vitally necessary work, and natural science. These vital social functions can be thwarted or they can be encouraged; working men and women can be conscious or unconscious of them. But *they can never be destroyed.* Hence they form the solid basis of every rational social process. . . .

For the first time in the history of sociology, a *possible* future regulation of human society is derived not from ideologies or conditions that must be created, but from natural processes that have been present and have been developing from the very beginning.[14]

Applying Reich's understanding here to better organization functioning means the fundamental path for renewal does not lie in "creating" or reengineering the system's dynamics. What needs attention are the conditions under which the organization's inherent dynamics get twisted or supported in the first place. When the system is persistently troubled, the organizational character must be addressed to come into alignment with the inherent work energy which it contains. This will always be the responsibility for those in the system as they want and are able to move towards, assisted from time to time by interventionists they seek who are armed with the know-how, the skills and the genuine care to focus here. Attending to such changes will be a gradual process for any organization, its pace based on its own emotional capabilities to tolerate and absorb them and the quality of the help they receive.

I have sought to outline the theory and method for such an approach in this book. What I have described as the basis for help reflects long held values in OD of self-renewal and self-regulation of an organization system that gives full weight to its human dimension. This applies to the aggregate workplace more widely in society. Still, even at a macro social level, I see this begins with those individual systems which seek to move more freely and robustly. That wider effect has been part of OD's longstanding dream too. *Sought-for-intervention into systems that are ready represents intervention into the workplace trap in its broader, macro social sense.* Organization intervention seems a very good locus for the pursuit of meaningful social action; the sheer number of people in the workplace yet the get-your-arms quality of organizations underscore this. Prospectively, through helping organizations in this way, many lives can be touched at a deep core of their functioning, the effects of which can then ramify out more broadly in the social universe.

Those in the change consulting field who assist in this endeavor will need to operate robustly themselves and with care, as they use the method as guide but in the end attend to the actual problems and opportunities of the business and people at hand. Platitudes and pipedreams will not do. Knowledge and effective emotional contact will be essential. Working with established individual organizations that seek remediation from their difficulties or with emerging ones that seek to preempt typical problems can be a powerful potential role for consulting practitioners. I expect this need will become ever more urgent—and vital—in the coming years.

Much remains to learn and build on the approach described in these pages. But I believe some important ground has been made. The extent of readiness for clients, communities and consultants to pursue the approach further will be a matter yet to see.

PREFACE

1 This view of the history of OD is in a paper of mine, "The Rise and Fall of OD—and Two Paths Forward," *Organization Development Review*, vol. 50, no. 2 (2019): 14–20.

2 The language of "fractionated technique" is Edgar Schein's, from a February 3, 1988 lecture at Pepperdine University, MSOD/Nu Class, Shadow Mountain Resort, Palm Desert, CA.

3 *Man In The Trap* is the title of Baker's book outlining the full clinical modality (New York, Macmillan, 1967). See especially the inscription on p. viii, which draws from Reich's original use of the phrase in *The Murder of Christ* (1953; reis. New York: Farrar, Straus and Giroux, 1971), 1–5.

4 The fuller passage from Bennis is: "One of the best ways of diagnosing cultural readiness has to do with the way the client system reacts to and establishes a relationship with the change agent. The quality and vicissitudes of this encounter—insofar as it is a miniature replica of the intended change program—provide an important clue regarding the fate of the OD program... the problems that inhere in the relationship are probably symptomatic of the problems to be encountered." *Organization Development: Its Nature, Origins, and Prospects* (Reading: Addison Wesley, 1967), 46–47. James Krantz and Thomas Gilmore have an excellent chapter on this, "Understanding the Dynamics Between Consulting Teams and Client Systems," in Manfred Kets de Vries, *Organizations on the Couch: Clinical Perspectives in Organizational Behavior and Change* (San Francisco: Jossey Bass, 1991), 307–330.

5 The main chapters of the master's thesis were serialized in *The Journal of Orgonomy*, vol. 23, no. 1 (1989): 27–46; vol. 23, no. 2 (1989): 190–209; vol. 24, no. 1 (1990): 81- 98; vol. 24, no. 2 (1990): 219–232; and vol. 25, no. 1 (1991): 93 – 97. The *Journal* is the main publishing arm of the American College of Orgonomy where I trained.

PROLEGOMENON

1   Freud's use of language in just this regard could be particularly biting. From his opening paragraph of the 1923 lecture, "The Dissection of the Psychical Personality": "Ladies and Gentlemen—I know you are aware in regard to your own relations, whether with people or things, of the importance of your starting point. This was also the case with psychoanalysis. It has not been a matter of indifference for the course of its development or for the reception it met with that it began its work on what is, of all the contents of the mind, most foreign to the ego—on symptoms. Symptoms are derived from the repressed, they are, as it were, its representatives before the ego; but the repressed is foreign territory to the ego—internal foreign territory—just as reality (if you will forgive the unusual expression) is external foreign territory. The path led from symptoms to the unconscious, to the life of the instincts, to sexuality; and it was then that psychoanalysis was met by the brilliant objection that human beings are not merely sexual creatures but have nobler and higher impulses as well. It might have been added that, exalted by their consciousness of these higher impulses, they often assume the right to think nonsense and to neglect facts. You know better." *New Introductory Lectures on Psychoanalysis* (1933; reis. James Strachey, ed., New York: W.W. Norton & Co., 1965), 51.

2   Edgar Schein, *Organization Culture and Leadership: A Dynamic View* (San Francisco: Jossey Bass, 1985), 312.

3   Wilhelm Reich, *Character Analysis,* 3rd ed. (1948; reis. New York: Simon and Schuster, 1972). The first edition of the book was published in 1933.

4   In addition to the wave-like motion of the readouts, other observations made Reich question whether bioelectricity was the basis of the emotional energy. See Dr. Richard Blasband, "Orgone Energy as a Motor Force," retrieved on line from *Humanity Development Library 2.0.* This article succinctly describes a number of Reich's laboratory findings in biology and physics with their unexpected properties.

5   This account can be found in Myron Sharaf's definitive biography of Reich, *Fury on Earth* (New York: St. Martin's Press/Marek, 1983), 466.

6   Sharaf's moving reference to how Reich "died of heartbreak" is in *Fury* on p. 477. The full title of the first of Reich's republished work is *Wilhelm Reich, Selected Writings: An Introduction to Orgonomy* (New York: Farrar, Straus and Giroux, 1960).

7   EMDR, or Eye Movement Desensitization and Reprocessing therapy, made popular in Dr. Bessel van der Kolk's *The Body Keeps the Score: Brain, Mind and Body in the Healing of Trauma* (New York: Penguin, 2015), seems most effective in less complex, less layered, less early childhood-rooted cases of trauma. It largely bypasses the re-experience of traumatic moments while it concentrates on a grounding in eye movements; these appear to mobilize the self-regenerative properties of the energy in the body to make synaptic connections and

out-process certain painful memories. Reich's therapy and understanding of the streaming of orgone energy in the body—how it naturally moves, gets disturbed and is then held organismically—gives clarity to the conditions under which EMDR as a technique appears to work and when a deeper, more comprehensive avenue of approach is required. After all, early childhood-rooted disturbances giving rise to the biopsychic character types are the rule in our culture. Baker's work especially has demonstrated that mobilizing the eye segment is essential, along with other interventions affecting the autonomic nervous system, *precisely to liberate buried expressions of emotional energy* streaming and conditionally held throughout the body and whose stasis fuels the trouble. The wish to bypass difficult emotions in the healing process is certainly understandable. But sometimes, as Reich elsewhere noted, it is "a wish for roses without thorns." Nowhere in van der Kolk's book is Reich credited for his pioneering work or for the depth of the problems and root energy phenomenon it addresses.

8   "Reich had a pervasive influence on twentieth century culture: in psychiatry (Anna Freud, Otto Fenichel, Erich Fromm, Erik Erikson, Melanie Klein and others), body-psychotherapy (Fritz Perls, Arthur Janov, Alexander Lowen, Moshe Feldenkrais, Ida Rolf and others), literature (J. D. Salinger, Arthur Koestler, George Orwell, Saul Bellow, Aldous Huxley, William S. Burroughs, Allen Ginsberg, Jack Kerouac, Norman Mailer, Sigurd Hoel and others), music (Kate Bush, Patti Smith, Lennie Tristano, Gil Evans, Bill Crow, Jeanne Walsh Singer and others), philosophy (T. W. Adorno, Max Horkheimer, Michel Foucault and others). At various times, other figures in the arts have expressed more than a passing interest in Reich (Jack Nicholson, Sean Connery, Orson Bean, William Steig, Kenneth Noland, Jo Jenks, Mike Kelley, Elaine de Kooning, Dan Graham, Carolee Schneeman, Jeanne Fitzgerald and others)." Retrieved from the Home page of the Wilhelm Reich Museum and Trust, https://wilhelm Reichmuseum. org/, 2022.

9   New work on the dynamics of scale in the universe are raising questions that could "wreak havoc" with particulate physics and ideas of "mass" as fundamental units in nature. Natalie Wolchover, "A Multiverse Impasse, a New Theory of Scale," *Quanta Magazine*, August 18, 2014. Even quanta turn out to be particulate— packets of energy, where something more primordial is at work. Compare with Reich's work in his farseeing essay "Survey on Man's Roots in Nature" in *Ether, God and Devil/Cosmic Superimposition* (1951; reis. New York: Farrar Straus and Giroux, 1973), 173–180. In distinction, Reich came to understand the phenomenon he named orgone, from multiple lines of experimental evidence, *as a mass-free energy, that has inherent transformational properties—generative of form in the first place, including microscopic, transitional forms of life*. His first laboratory work here, when he was in Oslo between 1936 and 1937, is recorded in *The Bion Experiments: On the Origin of Life* (1938; reis. New York: Farrar, Straus and Giroux, 1978). Years after Reich, diverse findings at the frontiers of classical science— detection of very low mass, electrically neutral, highly charged

neutrinos in our solar system and beyond; detection of endogenous, biophoton emissions; and discovery of profuse, primitive microscopic forms of life that develop in "extreme," inhospitable earthly environments and their biosignature possibilities in "empty," anoxic space —all point to how far Reich was ahead of his time in what his orgone energy research was on to. These are not proofs in themselves of course of Reich's work. But at the very least, they contradict distinct "explanations" that were given at the time Reich worked to dismiss his findings. See Dr. James DeMeo's comments on these phenomena and Reich's research that predated them, retrieved in https://www.biologicalmedicineinstitute.com/wilhelm- Reich, 2022.

CHAPTER 1

1   A version of this case was first presented in my paper, "Characteranalytic Organization Consultation: Its Distinction from other Business Consulting Approaches," *The Journal of Orgonomy*, vol. 27, no, 2 (1993): 227–231.

2   *Reich Speaks of Freud* (New York: Farrar, Straus and Giroux, 1967), 23. This is an original interview of Reich by Kurt Eissler, MD, of the Sigmund Freud Archives, recorded in 1952.

3   It never occurred to Freud that a person's instinctive life was not shaped by society, notwithstanding that some of his critics contend he failed to take into account "social factors." Here is Freud on the subject: "The contrast between individual psychology and social or group psychology, which at first glance may seem to be full of significance, loses a great deal of its sharpness when it is examined more closely. It is true that individual psychology is concerned with the individual man and explores the paths by which he seeks to find satisfaction for his instincts; but only rarely and under certain exceptional conditions is individual psychology in a position to disregard the relations of this individual to others. In the individual's mental life someone else is invariably involved, as a model, as an object, a helper, as an opponent, and so from the very first, individual psychology is at the same time social psychology as well... in this extended but entirely justifiable sense of the words." Sigmund Freud, *Group Psychology and the Analysis of the Ego* (London: Hogarth Press, 1922), 1–2.

4   Wilhelm Reich, *The Function of the Orgasm*, (1942; reis. New York: Farrar, Straus and Giroux, 1973. This is a scientific autobiography and not to be confused with the original 1927 work with the same title). In these terms, it was clear to Reich that full, loving orgastic discharge between the sexes was not a common experience in our culture; it was substantially compromised in people on average—even truer today it seems than in Reich's time. Also, as Reich increasingly saw the organism as an energy system operating "in a sea of energy," he came to understand that the function of the orgasm was not primarily procreative, but an essential way the organism regulated its energy. A pulsating organism would continue to pile up energy if there were not a functional outlet for its release, over and above what is used up in growth and normal day-to-

day living. Indeed, all sexual activity is not procreative. Procreation to Reich seemed itself a special case of the larger, ubiquitous process in nature he called superimposition, whether or not separate life forms emerged.

5   Wilhelm Reich, *The Cancer Biopathy* (1948; reis. New York: Farrar, Straus and Giroux, 1973).

6   Reich, *People in Trouble* (1953; reis. New York: Farrar, Straus and Giroux, 1976), 48–76.

7   Kurt Lewin *Field Theory in Social Science: Selected Theoretical Papers* (New York: Harper and Row, 1951).

8   Reich, *Cancer Biopathy,* 15–150.

9   Bronislaw Malinowski, *Sex and Repression in Savage Society* (1927; reis., Oxfordshire: Routledge, 2001). Reich pays tribute to Malinowski's field research and findings with the Trobriand Islanders in *The Invasion of Compulsory Sex Morality*, 3rd ed. (New York: Farrar, Straus and Giroux, 1971). This is a revision of the original work published in 1931.

10 E. O. Wilson, *Sociobiology* (Boston: Harvard University Press, 1974). Unlike Reich, Wilson does not recognize the existence of a driving primal energy at work. He essentially looks at the *mechanisms* of biosocial life.

11 In this way, we can see that reality is not so much "socially constructed," but *biosocially emergent.* Compare the standard work here by Peter Berger and Thomas Luckman, *The Social Construction of Reality: A Treatise in the Sociology of Knowledge* (New York: Anchor Books, 1967) with Reich's writings. See especially Reich's "The Biological Miscalculation in the Human Struggle for Freedom," for the practical consequences of this distinction, a chapter in *The Mass Psychology of Fascism*, 3rd ed. (1942; reis. New York: Farrar Straus and Giroux, 1970), 316 -359.

12 Beyond Wilson's research as an animal behaviorist, there have been efforts to bridge the divide between biological and social anthropology in its own tradition, including Tim Ingold and Gisli Palsson's *Biosocial Becomings: Integrating Social and Biological Anthropology* (Cambridge: Cambridge University Press, 2013). In Reich's own time, A. Irving Hallowell, in a brilliant Presidential address to the American Anthropological Association in 1949, goes to the significance of the relationship of the two domains: "It is paradoxical I think, that whereas opponents of human evolution in the nineteenth century were those who naturally stressed evidence that implied discontinuity between man and his primate precursors, anthropologists of the twentieth century, while giving lip service to organic evolution have, by the special emphasis laid upon culture as the prime human differential, once again implied an unbridged gap between ourselves and our animal forebearers. Yet continuity as well as differentiation is of the essence of any evolutionary process. So, where may we ask, do the roots of culture lie at the pre-human level? Even the concept of human nature in the minds of some has become relativistic—relativistic, that is, to the particular cultural form through which it is empirically manifest. But if this is so, what is the emergence of a

cultural mode of adaptation a function of?" Reprinted as "Personality Structure and the Evolution of Man," in *Culture and the Evolution of Man*, ed. M.F. Ashley Montagu (New York: Oxford University Press, 1972), 245–258.

13 Gilmore Crosby, phone conversation with author, January 11, 2021. For more on Lewin and the birth and continued relevance of the T-Group method, see Crosby's *Planned Change* (Oxfordshire: Routledge, 2021).

14 Karl Weick, *The Social Psychology of Organizing*, 2nd ed. (Reading: Addison Wesley, 1979).

15 This clarifying distinction I believe satisfactorily resolves a long-debated question in the organizational literature, as in M. Keeley, "Organizational Analogy: A Comparison of Organismic and Social Contract Models," *Administrative Science Quarterly*, vol. 25 (1980): 337–362; also, Gareth Morgan, *Images of Organization* (Thousand Oaks: Sage, 2006), 33–66. Reich's experimental discoveries about the energetic properties of both living and natural nonliving systems take us well beyond metaphor. This said, my formulation here only represents a beginning at understanding human organizational systems as a unique, natural energetic form. My sense also is there is much to be better understood about other natural functioning systems, both living and nonliving, perhaps with important implications, by further studying the special *intermediate class* of energy system that organizations represent.

16 Reich, *Character Analysis*.

17 Philip Selznick, *Leadership in Administration: A Sociological Interpretation* (Evanston: Row Peterson and Co., 1957), 39.

18 Schein, *Organization Culture*, 312. Emphasis added.

19 Manfred F.R. Kets de Vries and Danny Miller, *The Neurotic Organization: Diagnosing and Changing Counterproductive Styles of Management* (San Francisco: Jossey Bass, 1984).

20 Peter Block, *The Empowered Manager: Positive Political Skills at Work* (San Francisco: Jossey Bass, 1987), 28–32.

21 Emerging groups appear to go through a set of socioemotional stages in ways not unlike how individuals in their early childhood years go through common psychosexual stages of development, conditioned by their upbringing, A number of organizational scholars have noted this functional equivalence. This is discussed more fully in Chapter 4.

22 Reich was not alone to use this phrase, although meanings of it likely varied. Around the time Reich was in Oslo, the phrase "workplace democracy" was in use, including innovative efforts at plants in Scandinavia and elsewhere around the world to operate on a wide, worker self-management basis. See, for example, J. Andersen and J. Hoff, "Workplace Democracy in Scandinavia," *Democracy and Citizenship in Scandinavia* (London: Palgrave Macmillan, 2001). The possible tie

in with Reich's use of this language, given his immersion in social activism of the day, is another story worth inquiry.

23 At the organizational level, the work democratic character is functionally equivalent to what Reich called the genital character operating within individuals. See Reich, *Character Analysis*, 169–193.

24 Barry Oshry, *Seeing Systems: Unlocking the Mysteries of Organizational Life* (San Francisco: Berrett Koehler, 1995). Oshry clearly understands systemic interplay of the three segments.

25 Henry Mintzberg, *The Structuring of Organizations* (Englewood Cliffs: Prentice-Hall, 1979.)

26 Edgar Schein, *Process Consultation Revisited: Building the Helping Relationship* (Reading: Addison Wesley, 1999), 11–17.

27 The contrast here and language draws from Floyd W. Matson's synoptic historical interpretation of twentieth century science, social science, and philosophy—their synchronous development as the fields tried to break free from the legacy of Descartes' and Newton's view of man and the universe as a vast, complex machine. *The Broken Image: Man, Science and Society* (New York: George Braziller, 1964), 254–255.

General note: *Much of Chapter 1 is based on a January 2021 talk I gave, "Wilhelm Reich on the Biosocial Nature of the Human Animal," sponsored by the Wilhelm Reich Museum and Trust, and draws from an article of the same title in the* Annals of The Institute for Orgonomic Science, *vol. 17, no. 1 (2021). Some of this chapter also draws from a talk, "Work Energy and the Character of Organizations: An Overview and Case Study," given at a conference of the American College of Orgonomy, Annual Scientific Meeting, Princeton, NJ, October 15, 1989. Used with permission.*

CHAPTER 2

1 Donald Schon, *The Reflective Practitioner: How Professionals Think in Action* (New York: Basic Books, 1984).

2 The quotation is from Richard Beckhard, perhaps the first to use the term "organization development" in reference to the field. Retrieved from *Pepperdine's MSOD Founders Video*, 1998, https://vimeo.com/27865074.

3 Schein, Pepperdine MOSD/Nu Class lecture previously cited.

4 The only exception to this that I know of is my own work, based on the original graduate thesis I did published in *The Journal of Orgonomy*. "Work Energy and the Character of Organizations," 1989–1991.

5 A fine survey of the field is the most recent version of the standard work by Warner Burke, here with Debra Noumair, *Organization Development: A Process of Learning and Change*, 3rd edition (New York: Pearson, 2015). An interesting history of OD can be found in Art Kleiner's *The Age of Heretics: A History of the Radical Thinkers Who Reinvented Corporate Management* (San Francisco:

Jossey Bass, 2008). Finally, Marvin Weisbord offers a unique perspective on the development of the field as he came to terms with it in his own development and the method and practice of "Future Search," in *Productive Workplaces: Dignity, Meaning and Community in the 21st Century*, 25th Anniversary/ 3rd ed. (San Francisco: Jossey Bass, 2012).

6   Crosby, personal communication, 2021.

7   Lewin, *Field Theory*.

8   Alfred Marrow, T*he Practical Theorist: The Life and Work of Kurt Lewin* (New York: Basic Books, 1969).

9   An aspect of driving forces that Lewin remained less clear about is the extent to which such forces can "pull" an organization in its movement rather than "push" it. Classical physics of course recognizes the pulling action of an object in a gravitational field between two objects, leading to the objects' movements and their orbits. This takes on a special resonance in Reich's understanding of a dynamic energetic continuum operating in all space, especially as it applies to human behavior. A human object can be pulled to another in powerful ways—as in sexual attraction between two bodies—ways that are not often understood in terms other than the psychological or psychosocial. In human affairs, the mutual pull of attraction is not customarily understood in biophysical, energetic terms.

10 For a history and summary of a range of large scale, "community" building methods, see Barbara Bunker and Billie Alban, *The Handbook of Large Group Methods: Creating Systemic Change in Organizations and Communities* (San Francisco: Jossey Bass, 2006). These methods have dated back for more than sixty years.

11 The story of this intervention and its dynamics is recounted in an article of mine at the time, "Hidden Within the Spirit," *OD Practitioner*, vol. 21, no.2 (1989): 5–8.

12 Lewin, *Field Theory,* 1–29.

13 Eric Trist and Kenneth Bamforth, "Some Social and Psychological Consequences of the Longwall Method of Coal Getting," *Human Relations*, vol. 4 (1951): 3–38.

14 Wilfred Bion, Exp*eriences in Groups* (New York: Basic Books, 1959), 93.

15 Eric Trist, "The Evolution of Socio-Technical Systems: A Conceptual Framework and Action Research Program," *Issues in the Quality of Working Life,* vol. 2 (Toronto: Ontario Ministry of Government Services, 1981).

16 William Passmore, "Overcoming Roadblocks in Work Restructuring Efforts," *Organization Dynamics*, vol. 10, no. 4 (1982): 54–67.

17 I have characterized Schein's understanding of this in "In Celebration of Ed Schein: His Lasting Importance to the Field," *Organization Development Review*, vol. 53, no. 4 (September 2021): 46.

18 Schein, *Process Consultation Revisited.*

19 Goldberg, *"In Celebration of Ed Schein,"* 47.

20 D. G. Bowers, *Perspectives in Organization Development* (Ann Arbor: Institute for Social Research, University of Michigan, 1970), 16. Reprinted in Newton Margulies and Anthony Raia, *Conceptual Foundations of Organizational Development* (New York: McGraw Hill, 1978), 111–112.

21 Karl Weick, *The Social Psychology of Organizing*, 1st edition (Reading, MA: Addison Wesley, 1969). The book's second edition was published in 1979.

22 Weick, *Social Psychology of Organizing*, 91–92.

23 Henry Mintzberg, *The Rise and Fall of Strategic Planning* (New York: The Free Press, 1994), 321.

24 Henry Mintzberg, *The Structuring of Organizations* (Englewood Cliffs: Prentice Hall, 1979), 5. See especially pages 17–34 for a description of what Mintzberg deems an organization's inherent structural components.

25 Like Trist, Mintzberg also sees a corollary administrative system—a "support staff" function—operating in complex organizations. That, along with another subsystem function, the "technostructure"—represent specializations of the middle line, facilitating the flow of work between the organization's strategic apex and its operating core. I describe these subsystems substantially in Chapter 5.

26 Oshry, *Seeing Systems*. Oshry also importantly includes a fourth subsystem, the customer, in the dynamic exchange and dance because of the interoperative nature of the organization in its field of play.

27 I see Oshry's overall emphasis on "power and systems" as an analogue to the coupling of energy and character. The difference is that in the former the two components are general and non-specific: "Power" is not seen as a tangible energy that moves, concentrates and functions in ways requiring systemic discharge; nor is "system" seen in its special case form as character, an enveloping structure that gates the movement and expression of the energy in specific, systemic patterns. While Oshry's formulation as it is works, its generality I think yet limits its consulting application *practically, in the way real world cases more concretely present.*

28 Daniel Katz and Robert Kahn, *The Social Psychology of Organizations* (New York: John Wiley and Sons, 1966).

29 Katz and Kahn, *Social Psychology of Organizations*, 16–17.

30 Kets de Vries, *Organizations on the Couch.*

31 Kets de Vries and Miller, *Neurotic Organization.*

32 Ian Mitroff, *Stakeholders of the Organizational Mind: Toward a New View of Organizational Policy Making* (San Francisco: Jossey Bass, 1983).

33 Larry Hirschhorn, *The Workplace Within: Psychodynamics of Organizational Life* (Cambridge: MIT Press, 1988), 10.

34 Manfred Kets de Vries, "Our Addiction to Charismatic Leaders Needs to Stop," May 26, 2021. Retrieved from INSEAD blog, https://knowledge.insead.edu/

blog/insead-blog/our-addiction-to-charismatic-leaders-needs-to-stop-16676.
Kets de Vries sees the remedy as *instilling the right education*: "A good and just
society is one populated by citizens who are concerned about the dignity of others
and the good of the whole. *Getting there will necessitate a robust programme of
values-based education – nothing short of an educational paradigm shift – to instill
a degree of moral and intellectual sophistication.*" Emphasis added. It is interesting
I think in his blog that Kets de Vries also references Weber, the father of modern
sociology who originated the concept of "charisma," as leading us astray in his
description of it as a force of "exceptional power" that could be so seductive.
Weber, a contemporary of Freud's who grew up 300 miles away in the Austrian
Hungarian Empire, saw the emotional attraction of charisma to a mass of people
as a kind of relief valve from the "iron cage" of institutional bureaucracy, another
seminal idea he developed. The draw of charisma, as Reich underscored in his
Mass Psychology, is essentially sexual longing. For me, Kets de Vries' critique of
Weber reflects the larger post-Freudian uneasiness with sexuality as a driving
social force; this results in the later psychoanalytic rejection of the primacy of the
libido and, in any case, as something that must be tamed. For further background,
see Arthur Mitzman's socio-psychoanalytic treatment, *The Iron Cage: An Historical
Interpretation of Max Weber (*New York: Grosset and Dunlap, 1971).

35 Larry Hirschhorn, "Extending the Tavistock Model: Bringing Desire, Danger,
    Dread and Excitement into a Theory of Organisational Process," *Organisational
    & Social Dynamics*, vol. 21, no. 1 (2021): 114. Emphasis added. The reference to
    Csikszentmihalyi's concept of "work as flow" that is "*intrinsically* satisfying and
    motivating" is on p. 120, emphasis added.

36 Margaret Wheatley, *Leadership and the New Science: Discovering Order in a
    Chaotic World* (1992; reis. San Francisco: Berrett Koehler, 2006).

37 L. Douglas Kiel and Euel Elliott, eds., *Chaos Theory in the Social Sciences:
    Foundations and Applications* (Ann Arbor, University of Michigan Press, 1997).

38 Patricia Shaw, *Changing Conversations in Organizations: A Complexity Approach
    to Change* (New York: Routledge, 2002).

39 Jacqueline Kelm, *Appreciative Living: The Principles of Appreciative Inquiry in
    Personal Life* (Wake Forest: Venet Publishers, 2005).

40 David Cooperrider and Audrey Selian, eds., *The Business of Building A Better
    World: The Leadership Revolution That Is Changing Everything* (San Francisco:
    Berrett Koehler, 2021).

41 Jerry Harvey, "The Abilene Paradox: The Management of Agreement," *The Abilene
    Paradox and Other Meditations on Management* (San Francisco: Jossey Bass,
    1988), 13–36. As an article, this writing was originally published in the journal
    Organizational Dynamics, Summer 1974.

42 I followed a hierarchical distribution in this case on purpose—to take the
    system literally as it presents for maximum acceptance, then address blocks to
    each of its layer's functioning. I approached the group in the workshop largely

layer by layer, with others from the unit always also engaged, for purposes of whole system acceptance, integration and flow. This general way of working, and its sequential variations by organization character type, is more fully described as a sociotherapeutic principle in Chapters 6 and 7. Such an approach takes cognizance of the importance of how to best sequence working with the organization's cross-cutting segments in any particular case, freeing up energy in a way so the system as a whole does not break down and can tolerate and express its integrated movement.

43 Children in my experience often are able to move through difficulties more easily than adults, because children are generally less personally armored and closer to their feelings. The quality of contact that parents, teachers and others who work with children makes a difference in the interpersonal trust that children are able to feel.

44 Max DePree, *Leadership is an Art* (New York: Bantam Doubleday Dell, 1989), 109–112.

45 See the discussion of "the new paradigm" in Jane Watkins, Bernard Mohr, and Ralph Kelly's *Appreciative Inquiry: Change at the Speed of Imagination,* 2nd edition (San Francisco: Pfeiffer, 2011), 1–19. The rendering of the bulleted items here is mine.

46 Gervase Bushe and Robert Marshak, "The Dialogic Organization Development Approach to Transformation and Change," in W. Rothwell, J. Stravros, and R. Sullivan, eds. *Practicing Organization Development*, 4th ed. (San Francisco: Wiley, 2016), 407–418.

47 "Ground" is a concept used in Gestalt theory. There is "figure" and "ground," sometimes shifting, even dizzying in how they may be perceived. I am saying that in post-modern conceptions, there is essentially no ground, only figures—a myriad of "images," as it were. That idea was emphasized many years earlier by Kenneth Boulding, cited in Chaos applications in social science, in *The Image: Knowledge in Life and Society* (Ann Arbor: University of Michigan Press, 1956). However, the idea that life can be reduced to images and imagery is the basis for a devastating neo-Marxist critique of post-industrial, consumerist society— all consumption, very little real production. See Guy Debord's *Society of the Spectacle* (1967; reis. Detroit: Black & Red, 2016). This is the dark side of life "at the speed of *imag*ination," which Watkins, et. al., effusively endorse. In this sense, post-modernism can be seen less as a set of ideas than ideology, a movement charismatic in appeal.

48 Akomolafe Akinola Mohammed, "A Critique of Descartes' Mind-Body Dualism," *Kritike*, vol. 6, no. 1 (June 2012): 95–112. Actually, Descartes' famed "I think therefore I am" dictum was his rationale for why an external world existed—that he was a thinking being he himself could not doubt. Certainty was the aim, so was the proof of an external world outside the mind. So, Descartes ends up being a radical proponent of the mind and a mechanistic brand of empiricist all at once.

In this, Descartes' dualism reflects the "mechano-mystical split" Reich identified as a deeply ingrained ideology of many civilizations, prominently the West, since ancient times. See Reich's chapter on "Animism, Mysticism, and Mechanistics," in *Ether, God and Devil/Cosmic Superimpostion* (1973), 77–120.

49　Charles Darwin, *The Expression of the Emotions in Man and Animals* (1872; reis. London: Penguin, 2009). There is a good deal of very contemporary research in developmental psychology and other disciplines on the primacy of the emotions in body-mind functioning. An overview of the classical and contemporary literature is in the chapter by Lisa Barrett and Kristen Lindquist, "The Embodiment of Emotion," in G. R. Semin and Eliot R. Smith, eds., *Embodied Grounding: Social, Cognitive, Affective and Neuroscientific Approaches* (Cambridge: Cambridge University Press, 2008).

50　Max Scheler, *Man's Place in Nature* (1928; reis. New York: The Noonday Press, 1971).

51　Max Scheler, *Ressentiment*, Lewis Coser, ed. (1912; reis. Milwaukee: Marquette University Press, 1994). Scheler's views here anticipated those of Fritz Perls in his development of Gestalt therapy and its central notion of "unfinished business." Perls himself it should be noted was supervised by Reich in his early psychoanalytic training days. Reich's understanding is the most grounded, as he sees the fully embodied nature of the process: The bitterness that always accompanies resentment reflects the sour turn of the energy inward in the organism, its walled-up buildup, then its harsh discharge as it forcefully pushes its way through the armor, twisting again as it is projected blindly onto any irritating object in front of it; the objects stimulate the original frustrated energy and trigger the unfulfilling energetic discharge.

52　Philip Blosser, "Scheler's Ordo Amoris: Insights and Oversights," *Denken des Ursprungs/Ursprungs des Denkens: Schelers Philosophie und ihre Anfänge,* in Christian Bermes, et al., eds. (Jena: Kritisches Jahrbuch der Philosophie 3 Würzburg: Königshausen & Neumann, 1998): 160–171. Originally presented as a paper at the Third International Symposium of the Max Scheler Gesellschaft, in Jena, May 22–24, 1997.

53　"Goethean Science IX: Goethe's Epistemology," retrieved from *Rudolf Steiner Online Library,* https://rsarchive.org/Books/GA001/English/MP1988/GA001_c09.html, February 2021.

54　"Edmund Husserl: Phenomenology of Embodiment," retrieved from *Internet Encyclopedia of Philosophy: A Peer-Reviewed Academic Resource,* https://iep.utm.edu/husspemb/, 2021.

55　Ludwig Wittgenstein, *The Blue and Brown Books* (New York: Harper & Row, 1958), 6.

56　The quotation is from the foreword by the renowned Heideggerian philosophy professor Hubert Dreyfus. David Sudnow, *Ways of the Hand: A Rewritten Account*

(Cambridge: MIT Press, 2001), xi -xii. Emphasis added. The original account, with the subtitle *The Organization of Improvised Conduct*, was published in 1978.

57 Chaim Potok, *The Chosen* (New York: Simon and Schuster, 1967).

58 Stuart Chase, *The Tyranny of Words* (1938; reis. New York: Harvest/HBJ, 1959). To this very point: In the history of psychoanalysis, as far back as 1893, Breuer and Freud recognized that consciousness alone, even memory of traumatic events, did not dispel symptoms; only a strong emotional reaction accompanying the memory—an *abreaction*—would have that effect; see their joint first chapter in *Studies in Hysteria* (1895; reis. Boston: Beacon Hill Press, 1950), 1–13. However, as Reich later put it: Psychoanalysis wound up dead-ended in *words, only psychology*; as the approach moved increasingly towards ego-psychology, away from soliciting the expression of the involuntary emotions. Psychoanalysis as a whole could not penetrate to the level that Breuer and the young Freud had observed was needed for therapeutic effect. See the interview of Reich in *Reich Speaks of Freud*.

59 Thomas Kuhn, *The Structure of Scientific Revolutions,* 4th ed. (1962; reis. Chicago: University of Chicago Press, 2012).

60 See Pat Williams' introductory comments in addition to Tannenbaum's on why the feeling dimension must remain central if change practitioners are to be effective; *Pepperdine's MSOD Founders Video*. Says Williams: "If your heart's not in it—something's wrong, you're wrong, your power's wrong. There has to be a connection between mind and heart." Tannenbaum goes on to urge commitment to a lifelong quest of "learning more about yourself in greater depth and breadth." He urges practitioners to do "continuing personal work" to ever-more deeply face their own feelings and know thyself. Paraphrasing him closely: "Without this self-understanding, *blocks get in the way that foul up both seeing and actually helping*, helping not in a narrow, self-interested way but in true service."

CHAPTER 3

1 Robert Blake and Jane Mouton, *Building a Dynamic Corporation through Grid Organization Development* (Reading: Addison Wesley, 1969).

2 Don Hellriegel and John Slocum, "Organizational design: A contingency approach," *Business Horizons*, vol. 16., no. 2 (February 1973): 59–68. A discussion of contingency models as they relate to leadership style can be found in chapter seven of James Bodwith, et. al., *A Primer on Organizational Behavior*, 7th ed. (New York: John Wiley, 2008), 221–228.

3 Barry Johnson, *Polarity Management: Identifying and Managing Unsolvable Problems* (1992; reis. Amherst: HRD Press, 2014).

4 Reich, *Function of the Orgasm*, 250–298. These pages are the source of my discussion that follows.

5 Wilhelm Reich, *The Bioelectrical Investigation of Sexuality and Anxiety* (1942; reis. New York: Farrar Straus and Giroux, 1982).

6   This cyclic series of events is evident in any natural bodily function, as can be recognized quite immediately. Just so, it operates this way in sexuality too, culminating in natural orgastic discharge, in adolescence and adulthood, in its fullness. Reich simply described its specific features and function, including that which is voluntary and that which is involuntary. The trouble, as Reich saw and foresaw, is that our culture for millennia has made recognizing and living this taboo, and continues to do so today, even in the wake of the sexual revolution, confusing all manner of phenomena perpetuating its suppression.

7   The constitutional capacity of the organism to tolerate inner and outer movement it seemed was also in play. We will see how an equivalent constitutional capacity becomes important in an organization's life in Chapter 4.

8   This soon led Reich to a new way of looking at and investigating a range of functional or chronic disease states, including cancer, which he called *biopathies*. (Reich, *Cancer Biopathy*). These states Reich saw in his laboratory science work operating at a cellular level of the organism's continuing organization—cells disordered in their motility and capacity for differentiation, affecting their normal process of division and rate of proliferation, with the potential for eventual conversion into lumps of tissue. Reich understood chronic, pathogenic disease states as primarily systemic in origin, specific disturbances of natural pulsation.

9   Malinowski, *Sex and Repression*. Also, Wilhelm Reich, *The Invasion of Compulsory Sex-Morality*, 3rd ed. (1951; reis. New York: Farrar, Straus and Giroux 1971), 38–93. The first edition of the book was published in 1931.

10   Reich, *People in Trouble*, 53–76.

11   Mintzberg, *Structuring of Organizations*.

12   Fred Emery and Elnar Thorsrud, *Democracy at Work* (New York: Springer, 1976).

13   Ken Burns, et. al., *A History of Jazz, Episode 10*, "Masterpiece by Midnight," Washington DC: PBS, 2001. Retrieved from https://www.yidio.com/show/ ken-burns-jazz/season-1/episode-10/links.html.

14   Even with the grimmest of products, the scientists who worked so interdependently and collaboratively—their individual egos and vanities aside— were excited by the pioneering nature of their work in splitting the atom and its prospective host of peacetime applications. Very many, as did its technical director J. Robert Oppenheimer, saw its World War II mission as urgent in the world— even though they later protested any further use and production of the A-bomb and more terrifying weapons. See Richard Rhodes, *The Making of the Atomic Bomb* (New York: Simon and Schuster, 1986).

15   The discussion and citations below draw from Burns, *History of Jazz*, Episode 8, "Risk".

16   A wonderful, penetrating book on the history and sociology here is the sisters Karen and Barbara Fields' *Racecraft: The Soul of Inequality in American Life* (New York: Verso, 2014).

17 Parker was diagnosed at the end of his life as schizophrenic. His profile, as described here, fits Reich's energetic understanding of schizophrenia and the way it biophysically presents with heavy armoring in the brain and the defining split between perception and bodily excitation. *Character Analysis*, 399–503.

18 Reich, *Mass Psychology of Fascism*. It is a furious excitement that, as it breaks through the armor, *circulates viciously*. Convertible too, as Reich noted, to the racial blood purity theories of the Nazis, a mass effort "to get away from that dirty sexuality." Reich, in his early efforts integrating concepts of Freud and Marx, saw these sex-negative, worshipful father figure and race attitudes passed on to children through the authoritarian family, itself serving the conscripted labor needs of the capital economy; i.e., the more or less forced alienation of people from their own labor, *where they no longer literally owned their livelihoods*. This whole set of circumstances was a loosed chain of destruction Reich later came to see as an energetic, social maelstrom.

19 Oshry, *Seeing Systems*. Also see Oshry's *The Possibilities of Organization* (1992) and *In the Middle* (1994), both published through his firm Power & Systems, Inc., Boston.

20 For more here, see my paper, "The Relationship of Individual Character and Work Group Character," *The Journal of Orgonomy*, vol. 27, no. 1 (1993): 94–104.

21 The following network organization design intervention and its rationale are further described in my article from the *Organization Development Review*, "*Rise and Fall of OD*," 18–19. Dick Nolan's landmark discussion of these organization architectural requirements, given the imperatives of information complexity and scale, was first described in Richard Nolan, et. al., "Creating the 21st Century Organization," *Stage by Stage*, vol. 8, no. 4 (1988): 1–11.

22 A description of BearingPoint's downfall including its CEO departures, can be found in a series of *Washington Post* business section articles; two are Ellen McCarthy's "BearingPoint CEO Blames Former Management," February 2, 2006; and Zachary Goldfarb's "BearingPoint CEO Steps Down," December 3, 2007. A subsequent *Post* article in 2009 cited a fourth, brief custodial CEO's recognition of the need for the business to finally concentrate on its real work. The terms of the sale of the firm after its filing Chapter 11 are summarized in "BearingPoint to Sell Business Units to Deloitte, PwC," *Washington Business Journal*, March 24, 2009. A very brief treatment on the organization failures that led to the firm's demise, and that cannot accurately be ascribed to the economy, is Scott Baker's "BearingPoint Breaking Up," *Redmond Channel Partner*, March 26, 2009. Baker also notes with sadness some of the immediate messy aftermath of the firm's breakup, including what amounts to plundering by a dozen of its former executives and board members, a reflection of how extensive the pathology had become.

23 Price Pritchett, *After the Merger: Managing the Shockwaves*, 3rd ed. (1985; reis. Dallas: Price Pritchett & Associates, Inc., 2014), 101–107.

24 Goldberg, *Journal of Orgonomy*, vol. 24, no. 1, 84.

CHAPTER 4

1   Bruce Tuckman, "Developmental Sequence in Small Groups," *Psychological Bulletin*, vol. 63, no.6 (1963): 384–399. Also, see Tuckman and Mary Ann Jensen, "Stages of Small Group Development Revisited' (1977), reprinted in Walter Natemeyer and Paul Hersey, eds., *Classics of Organizational Behavior*, 4th ed. (Long Grove: Waveland Press, 2011), 280–287.

2   A very recent review of published articles about group development dynamics reveals these studies are very weighted to individual therapy groups rather than a broader array of general work groups. Indeed, the article appeared in a journal sponsored by the American Psychological Association (APA), *Group Dynamics: Theory, Research, Practice*, the only journal dedicated to bringing theory and practice across the sociodynamic field together. See Yun Lu, et. al., "Are the Ambitions for *Group Dynamics: Theory, Research and Practice* Being Fulfilled? A Social Network Analysis of Citations of Journals Publishing Group Research," vol. 21, no. 3 (2017): 178 –185

3   Schein, *Organizational Culture and Leadership,* 63–84.

4   Erik Erikson, *Childhood and Society* (New York: W.W. Norton & Co., 1950).

5   Whatever its value, the penchant for drug intervention today with sick individuals almost never takes this biosystemic context into account. Reich's pioneering work in medicine points in a new direction, one that does not leave out pharmaceutical use but encompasses it in a way that, strictly speaking, is far more consistent with the rudiments of natural science.

6   Perhaps this helps account for why some children prove more resilient than others in moving through toxic childhood conditions.

7   This seems so even when a young person's life may end through desperate, self-destructive acts or accidentally through wild abandon. Indeed, I believe that Reich's understanding of natural energy dynamics, given very adverse biosocial conditions, largely explains the high rates of teen suicide today. Reich provides clarity on how natural, intense sexual feelings, ignited in adolescence, can get dammed up and create overwhelming pressure in a teen's life. In today's chaotic and highly moralistic world, few emotionally safe outlets exist for teenagers' full, gratified expression of love and their most basic feelings of life. Under the saddest circumstances, as the dammed-up energies for teens mount and mount with nowhere to go, some may come to feel desperate and "trapped" themselves with no way out. If there is no emotionally equipped adult available to guide them, the worst may then happen. The condition is set up for it, depending on whatever immediately may trigger it.

8   At a wider social level, the origin of the American republic is referred to as its *constitutional period*. A convening of founders occurred—*a constitutional convention*—having begun with some basic conception of the nation to be created, grounded in the Declaration of Independence. The elemental form of a new *union*

was shaped at this time, in fact emerging out of an earlier time of trial and error. A prior "Articles of Confederation" of autonomous states proved too loose for viable nationhood. Thus, a new *federated* government was constituted, one with greater cohesion to serve a common purpose and common constituency—what over seventy years later at Gettysburg Lincoln articulated as "government of the people, by the people and for the people." In this respect, the American republic had a primary *internal* constituency to serve certainly at the time of its founding.

9   The discussion of the Disney companies as organizational and social phenomena can be found in Neil Gabler's *Walt Disney: The Triumph of the American Imagination* (New York: Vintage Books, 2007).

10 Even a T-group at conception is naturally bound.

11 The degree of facilitator intervention and use of periodic "teaching" moments can vary in practice, but the manner of working I describe, of letting the group members learn through their own experience, is the classic nature of T-groups.

12 The exceptions here in classical T-groups are when researchers are present who may observe or later review the results of the proceedings. Real-time observation was done originally using two-way mirrors with research-observers hidden out of view. To this extent, observers are situated in the group's field and represent a kind of external constituency. Those outside looking in of course may still have some latent effect on the T-group operations, as members will have been told up front they are being observed. I participated as a research-observer recently in a virtually conducted T-group, using the technology's ability to view the group from a separate "online room" out of view. The participants were of course told of my role.

13 See especially the table in Schein, *Organizational Culture and Leadership*, 70. The whole chapter it is in is devoted to the discussion of the stages, pages 63–84.

14 For Freud's own description of the stages, see especially the chapter on "The Development of the Sexual Function," in Sigmund Freud, *An Outline of Psycho-Analysis*, James Strachey, ed. (New York: W.W. Norton & Co., 1949), 9–13. Freud's first essays on childhood sexuality were published in 1905.

15 The Freudian psychosexual stages are definitionally associated with bodily erogenous zones, oral, anal, phallic and genital stages. Freud, *Outline of Psycho-Analysis*. This is consistent with a biopsychic view of the developing organism that Reich formulated and how he came to understand the emergence of a genital character structure, the function of the orgasm, and a later fully grounded somatic clinical modality. Indeed, Freud's psychosexual stage-erogenous zone conceptualization is the seed for Reich's further, plainer, biologic comprehension.

16 Warren Bennis, "Toward a Genetic Theory of Group Development, *Journal of Group Psychoanalysis and Process*, vol. 1 (1968): 23–35. Also see Ray Lacoursiere, *The Life Cycle of Groups: Group Developmental Stage Theory* (New York: Human Sciences Press, 1980).

17 Baker, *Man in the Trap*, 18–20.

18 The phenomenon is not something readily seen or conceptualized about in group stage theory to date, whose basis has largely been that of T-groups; turnover in those laboratory groups, through people quitting or getting terminated, occurs less in the midst of its work than in the real world. This natural understanding of this stage of group work helps us see how *waste*—as a regular phenomenon of that which is unretained in the system—is subject to conditioning that can make its flow, processing and discharge easy, excessive or constrained.

19 This is treated as roughly equivalent in function to the ocular stage of psychosexual development, unique to Reich's clinical modality. See Baker, *Man in the Trap*, 18–20. My original treatment of the organizational vision stage, as well as all the organization stages that follow in this section of the chapter, are in *The Journal of Orgonomy*, vol. 23, no. 2, 190–209.

20 This is my best understanding, not having been present at the founding or at its earliest years of development. However, the following account is based on substantial interviews of mine with the founders about Allied's earliest years; hours reviewing documentary material; and what I observed working back from later contemporary issues that I attended to in a supporting OD role.

21 Roughly equivalent to the oral stage of development in the individual realm. Baker, *Man in the Trap*, 20–21.

22 This can happen a lot in entrepreneurial organizations that have not matured and when the charge of the founder-leader overly concentrates.

23 Roughly equivalent to the anal stage of development in the individual realm. Baker, *Man in the Trap*, 21–23.

24 Harvey, *Abilene Paradox*, 13–36.

25 Roughly equivalent to the phallic stage of development in the individual realm. Baker, *Man in the Trap*, 23–24.

26 Roughly equivalent to the genital stage of development in the individual realm. Baker, *Man in the Trap*, 24–25. Reich's emphasis on genitality set him apart from all the rest in the psychoanalytic movement, including Freud, because he saw its actual manifestation in the full, physical loving release in the function of the orgasm. This serves a metabolic function in the organism, grounded in what he later found to be the pulsatory movement of a ubiquitous, tangible energy and as it operates in the human animal. Most all other forms of psychotherapy and psychiatry to this day remain focused on mentalized states, and in this sense, remain intellectualized and, in one manner or another, mechanistic.

27 See, for example, John Kimberly, Robert Miles, et.al., *Organizational Life Cycle* (San Francisco: Jossey Bass, 1980), 1–14. However, even here, the lack of knowledge of *natural, nonliving energy systems* leads to references to "biological metaphors" as ways of understanding social systems. An actual, primordial energy

with the properties as Reich described in both living and natural nonliving systems is not recognized.

28 Richard Nolan throughout his academic and consulting career made innovative use of S-curves in thinking about IT and organizational related maturity capability. One application of it is in the book with David Croson, *Creative Destruction: A Six-Stage Process for Transforming the Organization* (Boston: Harvard Business School Press, 1995).

29 Understanding the phenomena energetically adds dynamic dimension to what has been classically recognized in OD. See Roger Harrison, "Choosing the Depth of Organizational Intervention," *The Journal of Applied Behavioral Science*, vol. 6, no. 2 (1970): 182–202. By "depth," Harrison is referring to the level of "individual emotional involvement in the change process."

CHAPTER 5

1 This classical view of organizations as information processing complexes, for example, can be found in Jay Galbraith, *Designing Complex Organizations* (Reading: Addison Wesley, 1973), 4–29. Organizations do of course process information, but this is only one aspect of their energetic functioning. The idea that information processing is the centerpiece of organizational functioning, sets up the premise that *the reduction of information uncertainty* is the organization's principal function in service of its main purpose. This is Galbraith's claim. This is equivalent to the psychoanalytic view that anxiety reduction is the central force in individual human life. An underlying driving energy is not recognized, nor as a consequence adequately addressed.

2 Even crowds, however, demonstrate exceptions in the development of emerging, persistent and formal structures. A simple example is the way a makeshift musical band of fans seated in the bleachers at the Brooklyn Dodgers' Ebbets Field came to form—its so-called "Sym-Phony" orchestra. Originally, the band spontaneously emerged but then these fans came back game after game, and year after year, to joyously blare out their music. In a terrifying other example, *de facto* leadership can emerge in a mob, a whirlwind of activity where human energy is whipped up by those outside of it and within to take destructive action. Donald Trump's real-time fomenting of the riot at the US Capitol in January 2021 stirred up self-appointed and other organizers of the attack. The mob, top to bottom, took on a form. Both examples illustrate that a continuum of biosocial group and organizational effects—including emergent roles and structure—develop and exist. The implications of this for wider social movement and institutional reform, understood as fundamentally energetic phenomena, are addressed in Chapter 9.

3 Mintzberg, *Structuring of Organizations;* Oshry, *Seeing Systems* and *In the Middle.*

4 My first application of Reich's work with regard to organization structure can be found in *The Journal of Orgonomy*, vol. 23, no. 2 (1989): 201–209. Its treatment in this chapter goes a good deal further.

5   Roughly equivalent to the ocular and oral segments in the human body, as Reich defined them, and also some functional features of the internal organs within them. Some equivalent aspects of the cervical segment may also be localized here in an organization. For more on Reich's understanding of these human body segments, three of the seven total identified, see Baker, *Man in the Trap*. 48–55. Interestingly, on a more general note, all seven human body segments (pages 42–43), completely independently arrived at by Reich and Baker in their observations of and work with patients, approximately accord with the seven *chakras* of the human body, where *prana* is thought to concentrate, identified in non-Western traditions.

6   Baker, *Man in the Trap*, xiv. The rest of the citation about the clinical modality is also relevant for OD: "I believe the concept is sound; what is necessary is more knowledge of how to use it. Theoretically, it should be possible to help everyone, but we do not yet know enough. Character structures are usually mixtures of classical types and often quite complex; some cases cannot be helped at all. At best, [individual] therapy is only a personal solution, the final solution lies in *prevention* of neurosis, not in its cure. Here, too, Reich showed the way."

7   Roughly equivalent to the thoracic and diaphragmatic segments in the human body, as Reich defined them, and also some functional features of the internal organs within them. Baker, *Man in the Trap*, 55–59.

8   This appears to be the same as the middle somatic segments of the human organism—the thoracic and diaphragmatic segments—as both are only *indirectly* affected by the psychosexual blocks. Within these somatic segments, lie more exclusively inwardly processing organs; *thus, constitutionally as organs, they may energetically be predisposed* to ricochet off of psychosexual blocking in different ways. This is worth further study, I believe, in the individual realm and for its organizational functional application too. In any case, disordered effects of character (itself an energetic subsystem) will affect the functioning of middle segment structures—both in organizations and in the human organism.

9   Oshry, *Possibilities of Organizations*.

10 Roughly equivalent to the abdominal and pelvic segments in the human body, as Reich defined them, and also some functional features of the internal organs within them. Baker, *Man in the Trap*, 60–61.

11 This is evident even when organizations make use of customer satisfaction surveys, with Likert scales for recording feedback. Often these become bureaucratized inputs and channels themselves, not used for identifying and addressing genuine problems in work process, but to mechanically reward or discipline individual service delivery performance. I have seen such surveys generate anxiety and fear among those being rated, and frustration among customers when they do not see process issues fixed that are recurrently reported. Customers can experience such surveys as adding insult to injury, if not simply a nuisance. This is similar to how employees frequently react to general employee

attitude surveys, where too often little ends up being done corporately to respond to process problems repeatedly identified year after year.

12 This intolerance, should it occur, will it seems be largely a function of the character structure of the organization or that of the consultancy. Their money-making impulses and entrenched anxiety to do something now may get in the way of going more slowly, even when objectively required.

13 Clinically, Reich elucidated how emotional "contactlessness" is literally a result of a person's perceptions being cut off from excitation, momentarily or chronically. See Baker, *Man in the Trap*, 67–73. At the extreme, this is the basis for the biopsychic "split" in schizophrenia. The schizophrenic may indeed sense things deeply, but his perception of it will be characterologically distorted. We saw this in the personal example of Charlie Parker in Chapter 3. Those with paranoid variations of the character type will typically feel deep internal stirrings, but because of the split, will reflexively project and misperceive them as coming from outside themselves, as external, persecutory threats. There may indeed be real, external triggering events at work, but, when certain armoring is present, these will be habitually seen and responded to in distorted ways. Reich, *Character Analysis*, 310–328. This happens even to the average person "when they lose it." It is a *biopsychic process*, not simply a clinical "entity." More generally, lack of contact and emptying out feelings from perception—rather than seeking to restore their natural connection—is quite common in our times. This itself has deep roots it seems in a cultural order that suppresses genuine contact made with heart and makes a prejudice of "Mind."

CHAPTER 6

1 Reich, *Character Analysis*, 153–281.

2 Baker, *Man in the Trap*, 99–152. The presentation of the organization character types below is modeled on Baker's manner of presenting the individual types. I want to note that Dr. Baker, one of the preeminent students and colleagues of Reich's during his last American period, was asked by Reich just before his death to help assure the continuity of his landmark work into the future. In addition to the publication of *Man in the Trap*, Baker saw to the founding of the American College of Orgonomy and *The Journal of Orgonomy*, active since 1968, and to the training of scores of physicians and others beginning even earlier.

3 Goldberg, *Journal of Orgonomy*, vol. 24, no. 1, 81–98; and vol. 24, no. 2, 219–232. The title of my originally published version, "Some Circumscribed Forms of Organizational Character," is a tribute to Reich's titling of the section in *Character Analysis* describing the individual character types.

4 Kets de Vries and Miller, *Neurotic Organization*.

5 Resembles the genital character at an organization, social systems level. See Baker's description of the individual character type, *Man in the Trap*, 101–104.

6 Goldberg, *Journal of Orgonomy*, vol. 24, no. 1, 83.

7   Block, *Empowered Manager*, 7–98.

8   Kets de Vries and Miller, *Neurotic Organization*; Hirschhorn, "Extending the Tavistock Model."

9   The literature here is extensive. Some titles to compare with Reich's use of the term are: Emery and Thorsrud, *Democracy at Work*; Emery, Thorsrud with Eric Trist, *Form and Content in Industrial Democracy: Some Experiences From Norway and Other European Countries* (London: Tavistock Social Science Publications, 1974); Paul Bernstein, *Workplace Democratization: Its Internal Dynamics* (Kent: Kent State University Press, 1976); Max Elden, "Democratizing Organizations: A Challenge in Organization Development," Robert Tannenbaum, et. al., eds., *Human Systems Development* (San Francisco: Jossey Bass, 1985).

10 Reich, *The Mass Psychology of Fascism,* 286–288. Earlier in the inscription, Reich uses the phrase "changing the *nature* of work" for work democratic forms to emerge; actually I think Reich is not quite accurate here. Strictly speaking, it is the *character* of the work (not its nature) that inhibits the system's inherent energies from coming to the fore. Therefore, it is the character of the system that must be the target of change.

11 The arrival of the network organization era, including its wider socioeconomic and cultural context, was foreseen and popularized over forty years ago by Alvin Toffler in *The Third Wave* (New York: William Morrow, 1980). Richard Nolan forecasted in some detail the network organization form, in Nolan, "Creating the 21st Organization, "), 1–11. Also see Nolan's continuing clarification of this in his book with David Croson, *Creative Destruction* (Boston: Harvard Business School Press, 1995), 1- 67. Finally, another early seer on the organization network form and the historical, social context in which it would take shape was the renowned management thinker Peter Drucker. See Drucker's "The Coming of the New Organization," *Harvard Business Review*, vol. 66, no.1 (1988) 45–53; also, his *Post-Capitalist Society* (New York: HarperCollins, 1993).

12 There are numerous problems with the distorted state of executive compensation. As Karen Dillon in *Harvard Business Review* has written: "Defining what's wrong with C-suite pay isn't easy, because there are so many things to throw into the mix. Peter Drucker famously decreed that CEOs should not earn more than twenty times the average salary in a company. Many top execs earn far more than that now—some studies suggest as much as 300 times the average salary. The most common criticism, however, is that smart executives, boards, and their key advisers have been able to game the system so that comp packages skirt tax penalties and mechanisms that peg pay to performance—virtually guaranteeing that executives have little incentive to mitigate risk taking or to focus on long-term performance." This increasingly invites governmental regulation of executive comp, as Dillon, emphasizes, with significant social and political implications for the future of capital enterprise: *It seems without effective internal self-regulation, external regulation invariably arises.* "The Coming Battle Over Executive Pay," vol. 87, no. 9 (2009), 96–104.

13 Oshry, *In the Middle*, 88–98.

14 Nolan and Croson, *Creative Destruction*, 51–67.

15 For a discussion of the background to the strike and its fallout, see Gabler, *Walt Disney*, 374–379. The interpretation of events in light of organization character dynamics is mine.

16 ERPs are essentially common relational databases that replace an organization's completely separate batch processed systems, usually patchworks of systems that organizations outgrow once they are of scale. Firms come to require quick access to high quality, integrated data for enterprisewide information, reporting and decision making. ERP vendors represent a huge industry in and of itself. The software is pre-configured based on "best practice" standards by industry type and is sold in suites of applications (or "packages"). Their great promise is to sew together an organization in its information infrastructure (its central IT processing and channels). However, despite their allure and popularity, ERPs very frequently fail during implementation. I think this is primarily because the organization's character dynamics warp their execution. The dynamics are not adequately accounted for in project approaches, even when supplemented by conventional change management methods and culture models. The way cultures constrain energy movement in chronically dysfunctional ways is not specifically understood. This is the relevance of the OD theory and method here based on Reich's work. ERPs are also troubled during implementation because their baked-in "best practices" prove too rigid for the spontaneous movement still needed in the organization.

17 William Wagner and Yvonne Antonucci, "An Analysis of the ImaginePA Public Sector Project," *Proceedings of the 37th Annual Hawaii International Conference on System Sciences* (January 2004): 1–8.

18 This emotional root of trust is something quite different from the usual "buy-in" sought behaviorally by many organizations managing change. On the Commonwealth of Pennsylvania project, the approach used to engage the workforce was not a matter of selling anything to "buy," but rather creating the ground of trust for people to find their own ways as a matter of course.

19 Resembles the hysterical character at an organization, social systems level. See Baker's description of the individual character type, *Man in the Trap*, 104–110.

20 Kets de Vries and Miller, *Neurotic Organization*, 31–34.

21 Thoreau, *Walden; or, Life in the Woods* (1854; reis. New York: Dover, 1995), 209. Thoreau adds yet: "It affords me no satisfaction to commence to spring an arch before I have got a solid foundation. Let us not play at kittlybenders. There is a solid bottom everywhere. We read that the traveler asked the boy if the swamp before him had a hard bottom. The boy replied that it had. But presently the traveler's horse sank up to the girths, and he observed to the boy, 'I thought you said that this bog had a hard bottom.' 'So it has, ' answered the latter, 'but you have

not got half way to it yet.' So it is with the bogs and quick sands of society; but he is an old boy that knows it" (page 213).

22 Reich, *Character Analysis*, 21–25. Reich writes that "in a case of classic hysteria," by inadequately recognizing the negative transference at work, while focusing on the positive one, "I allowed myself to be lured into a chaos by [the patient's] recollections, a chaos from which I was not able to find my way out. . . . It was not until another patient told me, some months after the termination of an unsuccessful analysis, that he never trusted me, that I learned to appreciate the danger of the negative transference that remains latent. That patient [earlier in the analysis] recalled beautifully for a year and a half in a good positive transference. This experience prompted me successfully to seek a means of drawing the negative transference out of its concealment in order to avoid such a thing ever happening again, and so to fulfill my therapeutic duties in a wiser way. Most of our meetings at the Vienna seminar, were [then] also concerned with the negative transference. In short, we see that this was not the blind spot of one analyst. Failure to recognize the negative transference appears to be a general occurrence. Undoubtedly, this can be traced back to our narcissism, which make us highly receptive to compliments but quite blind to all negative tendencies in the patient unless they are crudely expressed. Psychoanalytic literature is conspicuous for its references to the transference in its positive sense." Despite the differences between the individual and organizational realms, Reich's words seem like they could be applied today to how many in OD skirt dealing with the negative feelings that come up in the client-consultant relationship. Practitioners are largely preoccupied with receiving "positive feedback." The foundational trust is not built with clients for them to share what they find hard to face in organizational life, including the felt difficulties they encounter with the practitioner. This affects the entire course of the joint consulting endeavor. The souped-up "positive" aspirations of post-modern approaches in OD, as discussed in Chapter 2, seem to only reinforce this basic problem.

23 The value of character analysis, as Reich found in his clinical work, was that the therapist did not get stuck in chasing a scattered array of symptoms. The analyst could now focus on and better ascertain the underlying characteristic pattern the symptoms formed and see their function. This became cardinal in diagnosis and treatment, something unfortunately that modern day psychology and psychiatry have largely forgotten; today, the psychotherapeutic field seems lost in symptoms and syndromes much as they are, without understanding their functional bases. This has vital implications for OD in its organization-wide work. We will come back to this in Chapter 7, as a principal technique in carrying out the theory and method in this book. But for now, hear Reich on this: "Diagnosis should not be made according to the symptoms but according to the neurotic character which lies at the basis of the symptoms." Reich, *Character Analysis*, 192. The trick is to see what predominantly presents and, even more to the point, *the manner* of its presentation and the functions it serves.

24 Resembles the phallic narcissistic character at an organization, social systems level. See Baker's description of the individual character type, *Man in the Trap*, 111–116.

25 The gender of those leading organizations in the mix today have somewhat begun to change, with more women-led firms and women otherwise in executive-level corporate roles having increasingly risen. There still is a long way to go in this regard. But a question I think interesting to ask is what is the correlation between women-led firms and the character of the organizations they lead? Women have had to fight hard for top roles, roles with line impact, and roles where they can continue to compete. This might set them up to lead enterprises that, at least in the moment, are rather work aggressive in character. For a statistical, global look at the corporate shift in gender, without considering organization character dynamics, see https://www.catalyst.org/research/women-in-management/, March 1, 2022.

26 Terrence Deal and Allan Kennedy, *Corporate Cultures: The Rites and Rituals of Corporate Life* (1982; reis. Cambridge: Basic Books, 2000), 109–116.

27 Psychodynamically with individuals, this is classically considered a reaction formation. Baker describes the energetic basis of this, *Man in the Trap*, 62.

28 Retrieved from Philip Su, *Peak Salvation*, https://peaksalvation.com/, 2022. The series also explores the implications for the larger social order and the future of work.

29 This section, as in Chapter 1, continues to draw from material of mine originally part of "Characteranalytic Organizational Consultation," 227–230.

30 Gary Hamel and C.K. Prahalad, *Competing for the Future* (Boston: Harvard Business School Press, 1994). They do realize work reengineering initiatives are not enough, but then go on to push prescriptive global strategies that do not reckon with the character dynamics that limit the organization's capacity for change. The understanding in these authors' assertions, I submit, does not go deep enough.

CHAPTER 7

1 Resembles the compulsive character at an organization, social systems level. See Baker's description of the individual character type, *Man in the Trap*, 124–127.

2 Mintzberg, *Structuring of Organizations*, 346. Full discussion of the machine bureaucracy is on pages 314–347. Mintzberg does not focus on the psychodynamic aspects of the organization, but his description of its formal structural features and the basic way it works fits easily with my description of it characterologically.

3 Deal and Kennedy, *Corporate Cultures*, 119–127.

4 Kets de Vries and Miller, *Neurotic Organization*, 28–31.

5 Mintzberg, *Structuring of Organizations*, 315.

6   Mintzberg, *Structuring of Organizations*, 321.

7   Mintzberg, *Structuring of Organizations*, 311.

8   Harvey Hornstein, phone conversation with author, October 27, 2016. Hornstein sees the "flush with cash" circumstances then of major corporate players such as Exxon (Esso at the time), not as determinative, but as *a necessary precondition* for large company investment in OD in the '60s.

9   How damaging, unspoken conflicts in particular triggered early OD efforts at Exxon is told by Tony Petrella, young at the time as an internal consultant; see my article "Tony Petrella and Me," *OD Practitioner*, vol. 50, no. 3, (2018): 65–67.

10   Baker, *Man in the Trap*, 17. Here is the distinction as Baker has put it for individuals during their psychosexual development stages. "Emotional trauma may produce one of two results at any stage: (1) repression or (2) lasting unsatisfaction. In the former the individual never develops pleasurable functioning at that stage, largely through deprivation; and in the latter he constantly tries to obtain a once-known satisfaction. In either repression or unsatisfaction cases, armoring occurs and we say the individual has a hook or block. The circumstances surrounding the development at each stage determine the character formation. Each stage overlaps the subsequent one and there is frequently no sharp line between them."

11   Herb Shepard, "Rules of Thumb for Change Agents," *The OD Practitioner* (November 1975): 1–5.

12   Resembles the chronic depressive at an organization, social systems level. See Baker's description of the individual character type, *Man in the Trap*, 138–140.

13   Kets de Vries and Miller, *Neurotic Organization*, 34–38.

14   This savings and loan case, originally drawn from my master's thesis, was published in *Journal of Orgonomy*, vol. 24, no. 2, 219–223. I originally called this organization type "The Chronic Depressive Character." I have now changed the name of the type to more closely follow the socioemotional development stage from which I see it springs.

15   Resembles the paranoid schizophrenic at an organization, social systems level. See Baker's description of the individual character type, *Man in the Trap*, 141–147. Reich's original description is in the third edition of *Character Analysis,* 399–503; this includes Reich's still unique understanding of the bioenergetic basis for "the schizophrenic split."

16   Goldberg, *Journal of Orgonomy*, vol. 24, no. 2, 226–231.

17   Kets de Vries and Miller, *Neurotic Organization*, 23–28, 38–40.

18   The individual type's features include characteristic confusion, a reactive sort of blind aggression, a deep split between what is felt (excitation) and what is seen (perception), undue sensitivity, and extensive projection. Somatically, the type presents as highly armored in the head (especially the eyes) and blocking in the throat, often lightly elsewhere in the body (poor definition in the musculature).

Breathing is typically shallow. Depending on the severity of the case, the type can still be a candidate for serious clinical therapy in Reich's modality, with psychotropic drugs as adjunctive, because the organism is seen as a bioenergetic unity in developmental arrest, though deeply "split" in its functioning. Types can range where these features can be more modest (with the person able to function fair to pretty well) to those where disorder is highly pronounced (from being barely able to function to essentially totally "gone"). When the surrounding conditions deteriorate and social support is missing, the schizophrenic characters especially go into distress and, at their worst, get completely debilitated.

19 Reich was the first to make use of the word *façade* to conceptually differentiate what presents as a person's "social face," from that of the storehouse of distorted, wild impulses (the Freudian *id*) that it covers up, and which in turn sits atop the most primary, life functioning energy of the human animal (before it is developmentally arrested in childhood). See Reich, *The Mass Psychology of Fascism*, xi-xii. In a like way, it is evident that organizations develop façades of their own—official pronouncements, mottos and, for example, expressions in annual reports too that present their face to the world. Such an organizational façade both masks and reveals the system's underlying character disorder and its still more deeply driving, creative and spontaneous energies. The Allied Bank case to follow shows a vivid example of this.

20 Goldberg, *Journal of Orgonomy*, vol. 24, no. 2, 228–229.

21 In my original article that this passage is cited from, a footnote appears that points out the functionally equivalent somatic blocking in an individual schizophrenic: "Not only is the ocular segment blocked, but there is a severe constriction in the throat which, from an energetic point of view, serves as a second line of defense to insulate the ocular segment." *Journal of Orgonomy*, vol. 24, no. 2, 229–230. Reich's somatic understanding of the individual type helped me make functional energetic sense of the block very obvious to many at Allied Bank's COO level, literally in over his head, *habitually* doing the CEO's bidding. Again, see the case study below.

22 Goldberg, *Journal of Orgonomy*, vol. 24, no. 2, 229–230. Emphasis added.

23 See Baker's discussion of this, *Man in the Trap*, 141–143.

24 This case discussion is based on my talk at a conference sponsored by the American College of Orgonomy, "Work Energy and the Character of Organizations: An Overview and Case Study," Annual Scientific Meeting, Princeton, October 15, 1989.

25 It seems that transference and countertransference operate in the energetic field between the client system and consultant. This is what gives them power. I believe an understanding of how natural, human systems interoperate in a field that itself is energetic helps illuminate transference and countertransference as phenomena.

CHAPTER 8

1   Toffler, *Third Wave*; Drucker, "The Coming of the New Organization."

2   Nolan, et. al., "Creating the 21st Century Organization."

3   Nolan and Croson, *Creative Destruction.*

4   Nolan and Croson, *Creative Destruction*, 9 -17. Nolan and Croson compare and contrast *principles of organizational functioning* between "industrial and information age economies." The specificity and clarity of their description is still striking. So is their identification of the kind of internal infrastructures needed to support an ensemble of self-designing teams and bring the network organization to scale (pages 35–37). It should also be noted that Nolan indicates his past collaboration with Alvin Toffler from which his thinking emerged (page 21).

5   Describing the new kind of organization as a network may not be sufficiently defining. Crediting my colleague Claudy Jules for the idea, I earlier noted: "Some change scholar-practitioners contend that the idea of a network is even too narrow to capture their essence, that enterprises with such permeable, 'fuzzy' boundaries are better described as 'platforms.' YouTube and LinkedIn are instances here, where their vast 'external' networks of stakeholders are simultaneously consumers and creators of content, but also customers when they buy enhanced services." Goldberg, "Rise and Fall of OD," 18.

6   Goldberg, "Rise and Fall of OD," 18.

7   I must confess when I first heard a motto used in the OD Network— "Beyond Our Boundaries"—I was struck by the absurdity of it. Here was a field trying to get traction and have a greater impact. Yet here was an appeal in the face of its amorphousness heralding the need to step outside of its ill-defined boundaries. This was tantamount to saying the field had no distinct value to offer. What else, however, is a value proposition for? Again, we see the façade at work in a venture's expressed motto. The association failed to develop—in fact, its membership notably waned—and instead of playing a more robust role in a world of high-speed change, the field came it seems within reach of disappearing.

8   Katz and Kahn, *Social Psychology of Organizations*. W. Aghina, et. al., "Rethinking the Boundaries of Your Organizational (Eco) System," *McKinsey Organization Blog*, December 16, 2019.

9   Larry Hirschhorn and Thomas Gilmore, "The New Boundaries of the 'Boundaryless' Company," *Harvard Business Review,* vol. 70, no. 3 (1992): 105.

10 Charles Konia, "Cancer and Communism," *The Journal of Orgonomy*; Part II, vol. 20, no. 2 (1986): 195–213.

11 Martin Buber, *Good and Evil* (New York, NY: Charles Scribner's Sons, 1952), 126–127.

12 Some of the ideas expressed here are drawn from an unpublished paper of mine with Stephen Pile, "Meditations on Strategic Change Consulting in the Age of The Digital Enterprise," 2021.

13 Goldberg, "Rise of Fall of OD," 19.

14 Goldberg, "Rise of Fall of OD," 19.

15 The whole passage is this: "A doctor, a shoemaker, mechanic or educator has to know his shortcomings if he is to do his work and earn his living. For several decades now you have been taking over throughout the world. The future of the human race will depend on your thoughts and actions. But your teachers and masters don't tell you how you really think and what you really are; no one dares to confront you with the truth that might make you the unswerving master of your fate. You are 'free' in only one respect: free from the self-criticism that might help you to govern your own life." Wilhelm Reich, *Listen, Little Man!* (1946; reis. New York: Farrar, Straus and Giroux, 1974), 5.

16 Thoreau, *Walden*, 213- 214.

CHAPTER 9

1 This nature I believe is represented in the Declaration of Independence, on which the Second Continental Congress' assembled signatories "mutually pledged to each other our lives, our fortunes, and our sacred honor." Interestingly, the contradiction between the nature and character of the country was reflected in the insuperable conflict over slavery even in the drafting of the Declaration. A passage condemning it was excised in an earlier draft, a "compromise" deemed needed at the nation's earliest conception. The repercussions were lasting. See https://www.history.com/news/declaration-of-independenc e-deleted-anti-slavery-clause-jefferson#:~:text=What%20isn't%20widely%20 known, cut%20from%20the%20final%20wording, June 29, 2020.

2 "Racecraft" is the word Barbara and Karen Fields coined to describe in social anthropological terms the belief system that racist thought and acts reflect, *Racecraft*.

3 Reich, "Animism, Mysticism, and Mechanistics," 77–120.

4 Reich, *Mass Psychology of Fascism*; and *Listen, Little Man!*

5 Eric Hoffer, *The True Believer* (New York: Harper and Row), 1951.

6 This is a paraphrase of Reich from *Listen, Little Man!*, 127.

7 Today's efforts to *compel appreciation* for workplace diversity through forced re-education and legislation seem far less effective. While some of the activities may indeed be needed, they also seem to foster spiraling reaction and the rearmament of bad actors in our schools and on the street—at real human cost. However, that such bad actors continue to be allowed to laxly purchase firearms seems an obvious distortion of freedom—what Reich today might call "a hideous distortion" of freedom. This I think surely does call for the need for healthy social

armor, legislative lockout, appropriate incarceration or other judicial punishment, as fits a crime commissioned in firearms' manufacture, sale, purchase or use.

8 The following passage gives Reich's own early sense of what happens to work energy and the structural devolution as bureaucracy in organizations. Writing about the historical degeneration of the Soviet Union's approach to work in its industrial organizations, he says: "The *triumviral directorship* and the *self-administration of firms* were abolished when a *single* manager became the *director* of a firm, assumed individual responsibility, and advanced to an independent position of leadership. True enough, this 'director' still stemmed from the workers, i.e., from the body of workers of the individual firm, but this *autonomous* manager of the firm was soon forced to develop all the characteristics of an overseer, bureaucrat, or ruler who was no longer a part of the mass of working people. Indeed, it is here we find the roots of the Soviet Union's 'ruling class.' But this does not refute the fact that every work process is by nature and of necessity a *work democratic process.*" Reich, *Mass Psychology of Fascism*, 290.

9 This calls up John Maynard Keynes' famous retort to classical economists about how the short term in human affairs, not just the long term, matters much too: "In the long run, we are all dead." *A Tract on Monetary Reform*, (London: The Royal Economic Society, 1923), 80–82.

10 John Kenneth Galbraith, *The Affluent Society*, New York: Houghton Mifflin, 1958); Guy Debord, *Society of the Spectacle.*

11 Reich, *Mass Psychology of Fascism*, 288.

12 Reich, *Listen, Little Man!*, 116–121. Emphasis is added in the last sentence.

13 Emery and Thorsrud, *Democracy at Work.*

14 Reich, *Mass Psychology of Fascism*, 311–314.

T hose who wish to know more about Wilhelm Reich and his work are directed to the following primary and secondary sources.

Reich's own writings consist of clinical, sociological, natural scientific and more essay-like works. *Character Analysis*, first published in 1933 and added to substantially in its third edition in 1948, brilliantly describes his early methodological efforts to understand and treat emotional difficulties, both neurotic and more seriously pathologic conditions, as well as specifically defines the basis and characteristics of emotional health. The first edition was long considered a classic in the psychoanalytic literature; the third edition, because it incorporated his increasing emphasis on the body and what emerged as his understanding of orgone energy streaming in the organism, based on his subsequent laboratory work, took his original insights and character typology further. It is noteworthy that in medical schools' teaching of the text, psychiatrists in training were told to stop reading it before they got to the new section on orgone biophysics. Aspiring doctors who wished to seriously study Reich's work had to go through medical school without referencing their interest or else risk expulsion. This silencing of expressed interest within the medical and scientific communities at large remains basically true to this day.

From a historical perspective, Reich's 1946 scientific autobiography, *The Function of the Orgasm*, describes the fuller development of his work and thought as it applies to his clinical breakthroughs and discoveries in biology and physics. His original clinical research work in 1927 with the same title was republished as *Genitality* in 1972. The series of 1952 interviews of Reich conducted by the Sigmund Freud Archives appear in the volume *Reich Speaks of Freud*. The interviews are well worth the read to get a deep sense of Reich's voice, his enduring respect for Freud, and an understanding of how Reich's ongoing work built on Freud's original findings and hopes for a grounded, biological understanding of human energy dynamics, conditioned of course by unreceptive social realities as they affect infants, children, adolescents and adults.

The biological and physics work is quite deeply explored in its basic science and applied medical contexts *in The Cancer Biopathy*, first published in 1946. This remains a radical challenge to medical orthodoxy today. Reich's primary understanding of endogenous disease states seems key to gaining fuller comprehension of what today are called "diseases of unknown origin," while incorporating modern, classical medicine's understanding and essential value in theory and treatment.

Reich's earliest experimental studies during the years 1934 to 1938 can be found in *The Bioelectrical Investigation of Sexuality and Anxiety* (1945, later reprinted in 1982). *The Bion Experiments: On the Origin of Life* (1938, republished in 1978) recounts his subsequent work in biogenesis. Both volumes describe his experimental set ups, observations, and developing implications for theory. *Ether, God and Devil/Cosmic Superimposition* (1973, first published separately in 1949 and 1951) is a combined version of two shorter works that defined his conception of research and implications for astrophysics and cosmology. Two qualitative essays from it that I always found especially striking are "Stage and Meadow" and "Survey of Man's Roots in Nature."

Reich's sociological masterpiece is *The Mass Psychology of Fascism*, again, in its enlarged, third edition published in 1946. It particularly stresses humanity's innate longing for freedom, and the fatal consequences when greeted by acculturative conditions that lead to the biophysical incapacity to accept it—to run from nature, inside and around us. Reich's 1953 book, *People in Trouble*, republished in 1976, builds on the development of his thought on the vital expression of work energy for individual and social health. His 1946 *Listen, Little Man!* is a personal, not scientific, statement about his life's work, and his 1952 *The Murder of Christ* is a powerful essay about the devastating social consequences of humanity's remaining "sitting in the trap." Neither are for the faint of heart.

Turning to the secondary sources, Elsworth Baker's *Man in the Trap* is a lucid outline and explanation of Reich's clinical modality. It was originally published in 1967 and again in 2000. In particular, I find its Preface still perhaps the clearest, most compact exposition of his work. Ola Raknes' *Wilhelm Reich and Orgonomy* (1970) also remains a clear and straightforward introduction to the far-reaching ramifications of his work.

As biographical entries, Myron Sharaf's 1983 *Fury on Earth* is the fullest account to date. And Reich's son Peter, in his 1973 *A Book of Dreams*, gives a poignant, literary rendering of his father and what it was like to grow up with him. A recent entry from a serious historian of science is James Strick's *Wilhelm Reich: Biologist* (2015). Drawing from Reich's recently unsealed laboratory notebooks housed at Harvard and from other historical material, Strick details the intellectual and scientific milieu in which Reich's natural scientific investigations took off.

Finally, the reader is encouraged to look at current and back issues of *The Journal of Orgonomy*. Published by the American College of Orgonomy, the *Journal's* articles have appeared bi-annually every year since 1968. In depth clinical case studies, updated and extended scientific investigations, and social analyses can be found by those who carefully followed Reich's work since his death. The first, full-length, factual documentary about Reich and his work, *Love, Work and Knowledge: The Life and Trials of Wilhelm Reich*, was directed by

Kevin Hinchey and Glenn Orkin, and produced in 2017 in affiliation with the Wilhelm Reich Museum.

All the primary sources above by Wilhelm Reich are published by Farrar, Straus and Giroux. The listed secondary sources can be found in various formats through an internet search.

ABOUT THE AUTHOR

**MARTIN GOLDBERG** has been in the Organization Development (OD) field for over thirty-five years. For many years he served as a partner and practice leader in change solutions for a major global consulting firm, and he has been in private practice since 2010. He has written and published widely on OD theory and practice, and he serves on the editorial board for the *Organization Development Review*. Side-by-side his graduate studies in Pepperdine University's pioneering MSOD program, he trained as a social scientist in Reich's clinical modality with its college of psychiatrists in Princeton, The American College of Orgonomy, to apply it to the organizational world. Today, he focuses on research and writing, practitioner development, and teaching in organizational dynamics, leading a yearly Organization Behavior seminar at Pepperdine. He did his undergraduate work at UCLA and Reed College. He lives in Easton, Maryland near the Chesapeake Bay and is the father of three. He can be reached at mdgdistantdrummer@gmail.com.

INDEX

Page numbers in **bold** indicate tables.
Page numbers followed by n denote notes.